BEYOND THE SOUNDTRACK

The publisher gratefully acknowledges the generous contribution to this book provided by the Ahmanson Foundation Humanities Endowment Fund of the University of California Press Foundation.

Beyond the Soundtrack

Representing Music in Cinema

Edited by

DANIEL GOLDMARK
LAWRENCE KRAMER
RICHARD LEPPERT

UNIVERSITY OF CALIFORNIA PRESS

Berkeley   Los Angeles   London

University of California Press, one of the most distinguished university presses in the United States, enriches lives around the world by advancing scholarship in the humanities, social sciences, and natural sciences. Its activities are supported by the UC Press Foundation and by philanthropic contributions from individuals and institutions. For more information, visit www.ucpress.edu.

University of California Press
Berkeley and Los Angeles, California

University of California Press, Ltd.
London, England

Chapter 8 is a version of the essay by Philip Brophy, "How Sound Floats on Land—The Suppression and Release of Folk and Indigenous Musics in the Cinematic Terrain," in *Cinesonic: Film and the Sound of Music,* edited by Philip Brophy (Sydney: AFTRS Publishing, 2000). Chapter 15 is a revised version of the essay by Krin Gabbard, "Miles from Home: Miles Davis and the Movies," *The Source* (University of Leeds)1 (2004): 27–41.

Library of Congress Cataloging-in-Publication Data

Beyond the soundtrack : representing music in cinema / edited by Daniel Goldmark, Lawrence Kramer, Richard Leppert.
    p.   cm.
  Includes bibliographical references (p.), filmography (p.), and index.
  ISBN 978-0-520-25069-7 (cloth : alk. paper)
  ISBN 978-0-520-25070-3 (pbk. : alk. paper)
  1. Motion picture music—History and criticism.   I. Goldmark, Daniel. II. Kramer, Lawrence, 1946–   III. Leppert, Richard D.

ML2075.B475   2007
781.5'42—dc22   2006025494

Manufactured in the United States of America

15 14 13 12 11 10 09 08 07
10 9 8 7 6 5 4 3 2 1

This book is printed on New Leaf EcoBook 50, a 100% recycled fiber of which 50% is de-inked post-consumer waste, processed chlorine-free. EcoBook 50 is acid-free and meets the minimum requirements of ANSI/ASTM D5634–01 (*Permanence of Paper*).

Contents

Illustrations

TABLES

Phonoplay

Recasting Film Music

A student of film music looking for a touchstone, a test case for any and every theory, could do worse than settle on Fritz Lang's *M* (1931). If film music appears anywhere in its bare essence, it appears here. The story concerns a child-murderer who wanders like a shadow through the streets of a modern city. The monster goes unrecognized because he looks like a harmless, pudgy nobody rather than like a hobgoblin. But he reveals his hobgoblin nature through music. The murderer, M, is a nervous whistler, and what he whistles—the only music we hear in the whole film—is hobgoblin music, Edvard Grieg's "In the Halls of the Mountain King," from the incidental music to Ibsen's *Peer Gynt*. Aside from its symbolic value with respect to the narrative, the restriction of music to just this whistling, and the whistling to just this tune, produces the "zero degree" of music in cinema: a few simple notes on the border between music and its absence.

One episode of this whistling deserves special attention. It occurs as we see the killer, Beckert by name, through a trellised mass of greenery as he sits in an outdoor café. The whistling strikes up, but just this once it does not seem to be coming from Beckert's lips, though it could hardly be coming from anywhere else. Always ominous, the whistling now becomes uncanny, disembodied. This impression comes fully into its own a moment later when Beckert, who is tormented by his compulsion, covers his mouth in an attempt to stifle the sound. It doesn't help; the whistling goes right on with no change of tone quality. Like the drive to kill, the music will continue against the will of the man who makes it—or doesn't. The moment is an odd one in a film whose genre, the police procedural, is conspicuously "realistic." Just what is the source of this music? Who is whistling it? Does it actually occur within the story at all? Or has it become a framing device, imposing itself from outside?

1

The film raises these questions only to render them unanswerable. Nonetheless, finding ways to answer just such questions is the aim of this volume. That the answers will be neither here nor there, yes or no, is very much to the point.

Music has traditionally been regarded as a subordinate element in the standard film genres. Although a solid body of research on film music has accumulated over the years, it is still a marginal part of the much larger field of study focused on image, narrative, the cinematic apparatus, and the history of film production. The film music literature, in any case, has tended to accept without serious challenge the status hierarchy that puts music on the bottom and treats film as above all a visual medium. But this assumption has little to support it historically, however commonsensical it may seem. It is now beginning to attract the challenges that may overturn it.

To be sure, cinema became possible as a medium because of technological innovations in the reproduction of images, which is why we still speak of "movies" or "motion pictures." But it is well known to film historians that movies have always wanted to do more than just move. Motion pictures went in search of music almost as soon as the projectors first began to roll in the nickelodeons. The quest for sound was in the first instance a quest for music, not for voices. Talk was cheap; when talkies finally arrived, their immediate success caught many people by surprise.

Perhaps the dominance of the image in our understanding of film is a reflection of the traditional association of knowing with seeing. Perhaps it comes from the capacity of movies to combine fictional narrative with photographic realism. Or perhaps it is a product of the role of glamour and star power in the classic Hollywood system and its heirs. These possibilities do not exclude each other, of course, nor do they forestall others not invoked here. It would be hard to imagine a more overdetermined scene of causation. The surfeit of possibilities tells us what we already know: we live in a world saturated by images. In a sense, the distance that was traditionally required to view an image has entered a state of seemingly permanent collapse. The image is now a proximate form, always almost too close. Images cling to us; our vision is cluttered with them. Music, meanwhile, has become more distant. Its ubiquity as ambient sound has made it more of an environment than an event. Listening is often displaced by being-heard; the phrase "background music" has almost become a tautology. If we have let image trump sound in the cinema, in our concept of cinema, it is hardly surprising.

Reviewing the foregoing possibilities, however, is also a way of gaining critical distance from them. The gesture is a familiar one: to historicize is to de-essentialize. Contingent forms are harder to mythify than perennial ones. The time thus seems right to stop winking an eye at the presence of music in cinema. That film is a visual medium goes without saying. What still needs saying, and is beginning to be said, is that film is also a musical medium.

As a result of this recognition, some scholars have begun to ask not how to conceptualize the use of music in film, but rather how to understand the ways in which film conceptualizes music. New questions on the table include how films imagine music, how films represent music as a phenomenon, and how films position music and musicality as parts of, or apart from, a fictional world. In social or ideological terms, these questions entail looking at film music not as a scarcely noticed background or an interpolated entertainment that sometimes delivers ideological messages while creating mood or atmosphere, but as an agent, a force, and an object engaged in ongoing negotiations with image, narrative, and context. So conceived, music operates very much on an equal footing with its negotiating partners. Its relationship to them is fully dynamic and reciprocal, rooted in a complex interpretive relationship to the semiotics of cinema rather than a simple encoded one.

To make good on this shift in conception, it is necessary to go where our title points: beyond the soundtrack. Strictly speaking, the term is a misnomer as applied to music; it originated in the 1940s as advertising lingo for recordings of music from the movies.[1] Still, the term seems to have stuck, and it may still have its uses. Perhaps it should operate the way "story" does in narrative theory as opposed to "discourse." The music of a film follows a narrative track, like the events of a story, but it also tends to take on a life or identity of its own, like the discourse that frames the story. The discursive dimension of film music lies beyond the soundtrack. The effect is familiar enough, but it has rarely been given its due. By recognizing it, we enable ourselves to ask what kind of life the music embodies, and how the life of the film as a whole is altered by it.

These questions bring several others in their wake. Traditionally, music in film has been understood as being either diegetic, a part of the film narrative, or extradiegetic, music without a source in the narrative, on which it serves as a layer of commentary or accentuation. Film composers tend to call diegetic music "source music" and extradiegetic music "underscore" or "dramatic scoring." In the first case, the musical sound is realistic and the scoring goes unheard as such, its discursive aspect subsumed by the naturalizing effects of giving the source a function in the story. In the second case, the scoring appears in its own right as a constructed discursive form at least partly disengaged from the "realistic" presentation.

This distinction is often useful and probably unavoidable. Sophisticated treatments of it have increasingly enhanced its usefulness by recognizing that it is not absolute; there are many cases in which the music's status is at least temporarily uncertain, and others in which the relationship between the types is transitional rather than oppositional: one flows into the other. Nonetheless, there are problems with the distinction, enough so that its value is an ongoing subtext, and sometimes an explicit topic, in this collection. The issue is not whether to scrap the distinction, which in any case film composers themselves have no inclination to do, but how to avoid being caught by its implicit worldview, the spontaneous philosophy that its unreflective use carries with it.

The diegetic-extradiegetic (or source-underscore) split maintains a more basic and far less tenable distinction between reproducing reality and signifying it. This is the familiar opposition of mimesis versus symbolization, of fact versus value, that is also basic to the idea of "realism" in representation. One result of maintaining this opposition is to mask the thoroughgoing inscription of social forces and values on *both* sides of the line it draws. It is not difficult to show that source music is not only heard in the story but also voiced in quotation marks, as if it were applied from without, or that the underscore penetrates the story and functions not only as accent but also as a tangible presence in the fictional world it envelops. It is not difficult to show that linking music and image produces a reciprocity of representation in which each responds to the forces and values inscribed on the other. Our paradigmatic moment from *M* does all these things. It dramatizes the effect of quotation by extracting the Grieg tune from simple allusive use and installing it in a space of impersonal intertextual agency; it transforms source music into an underscore by which the narrative has been subliminally penetrated from the beginning; and it crystallizes the overlay of the mythology of urban modernity with the folklore-derived monsters of traditional romance.

We hope to highlight inscriptions such as these and to develop new tools for recognizing and analyzing them. By doing so, we hope to advance the analysis of how music and image interact with each other as equal partners in the cultural work of film, as well as with the important contexts to either side of them: the cinematic apparatus, both technical and institutional, and the film audience.

Our initiative begins with another conceptual shift. We want to consider film as representing music, not simply as adding music as a supplement to a cinematic representation formed via image or narrative.[2] None of these representational modalities is to be accorded priority over the others. Such priorities exist, of course, but they exist as matters of practice, not of the character of film as a medium. The practice that subordinates music, or appears to, is often at odds with the medium, no matter whether the practice belongs to the films or to their critics. Cinematic rhythm—this is scarcely a new observation—has its own musical qualities of pace and flow, tension and release. Music has its own vocabulary of cinematic cuts, fades, jumps, dissolves, and shot sequences.

The relationship between theory and practice here is in any case more complicated and less obvious than it may seem at first. The fact that the dominant tradition in narrative film overtly subordinates music to image is a reason to theorize about this hierarchy, but it is *not* a reason to reproduce the hierarchy in the theory. There is no more reason to take films at face value than there is to confine literary interpretation to paraphrases of authorial intention. A film may suppose that it is using music as accent or inflection while actually deploying it as representation without acknowledgment or recognition. A film may incorporate music as representation at certain key points, only to find the usage subsumed under the reigning theoretical paradigm that reduces representation to accent. The problem is that these tendencies have rarely been well recognized, thus leaving representational usage in general less evident, less audible.

Another problem is that the question of how to understand film music is not settled, and cannot be settled, entirely on the basis of practice. Here again we encounter a feedback loop rather than a simple distinction. Theorizing film music as accent will dispose us to hear and interpret it as accentual; theorizing film music as representation will dispose us to hear and interpret it as representational. The theories will partly produce the phenomena they describe. They will, however, not do this arbitrarily, by fiat, but by mobilizing the possibilities latent in the juxtaposition of music with the moving image and by exposing the formal and historical contingencies behind the combinations that result.

This does not, however, mean that the rival theories do not make cognitive claims that may be weaker or stronger and may lead us to prefer one to the other, or, to be more precise, to subsume one under the other. With film music the representational theory is "stronger" in the logical sense. The notion of music as accent precludes music as representation because it assumes a prior representation to which the accent applies; narrative and image define cinematic content. Music can at best only intensify that content and/or duplicate it at the level of standardized codes. But the notion of music as representation includes the notion of music as accent because representation it-self has accentual capabilities; representations can be forceful or subtle, re-strained or exaggerated, involved or detached, and so on ad infinitum. Rep-resentations are performative. On this model cinematic content does not have a hierarchical derivation; it arises from the fluctuating interplay of nar-rative, image, and music in any and all combinations, including those in which narrative or image merely accent a musical statement. If film music can be shown to be representational at all, it must be representational over all and through all. The theoretical playing field is not level.

It should be added in passing that these relationships do not depend on, or at least do not vary directly with, the acoustic strength of the music, that is, the space it occupies in the viewer's attention.[3] The relationships involved are sensory in form, but epistemic in their determination. Acoustic strength may or may not be pertinent in the given case. When it is, it becomes so via a dialogical or dialectical interplay with representational values.

Taking music as an object of cinematic representation changes the critical agenda substantially. It immediately causes music to lose the transparency and simplicity that its role as mere accent imposes. As cinematic represen-tation, music becomes thickly textured, in the sense of demanding thick de-scription; it resonates with an intertextual polyphony that can no longer go unheard or unexamined. Like all representations, it exceeds its immediate purposes. The cinematic image provides it with a referential field but can-not determine what it does there. To revert one last time to *M:* in narrative terms the Grieg tune is only a tic, the sign of Beckert's compulsion to repeat his crime and an accent to fragmentary, off-center, or shadowy images. But any tune with a high degree of internal repetition could have served that purpose. The specific choice of "In the Halls of the Mountain King" trans-forms the genre of the film by associating it with narratives, and types of narrative, that are not represented in any other way. Without the music—and a bare scrap of music at that—*M* would be a different film.

What are the broader consequences of hearing cinematic music in these terms? At least three come quickly to mind. They can be roughly sorted (though not without overlap) into the categories of musical meaning, mu-sical agency, and musical identity:

1. *Meaning.* To represent music in film is to represent what the music represents. Film music depends on a representational value that music out-side film has often been wrongly denied to have. What is involved in this representation is not only "content," however defined, but also social posi-

tioning, the discursive construction of both subjects and objects, and the musical intertext embracing effects of performance, tradition, allusion, citation, and history.

2. *Agency.* To represent music, to take it as an object of interpretation, is to recognize it as a constituent part of a world and as an active force in the construction of that world rather than as a mere embellishment or appendage to a world the construction of which is otherwise complete. Music is not functional but substantive. It can express virtually any meaning, but alters any meaning it expresses.[4]

3. *Identity.* To represent music is to represent its self-representation. Music in film is not depicted, as action is; the music is heard. It is, indeed, heard in a fully real way that exceeds the "reality" of the visual images. Music in film represents itself via internal difference, a split between its acoustic and symbolic value, elicited by the cinematic-imagistic-dramatic context. This context, moreover, may already be partly shaped by the music. There is, accordingly, no simple origin for the representational process. The music may split itself (as the famous "barred subject" may in Lacanian theory) in a variety of ways and at a variety of times, not only from one film to another, but within the same film and even within the same scene.

The categories of musical meaning, agency, and identity form the basis for dividing this volume into three parts. In grouping the essays together, we have sought out—and inevitably brought out—the category with which each seems most strongly engaged. The result is not a uniformity, which we would not have wanted in any case, but a managed heterogeneity.

The chapters grouped in the first section, "Musical Meaning," focus primarily on how music drives and shapes, reflects on and transforms, cinematic narrative. These processes, situated in specific historical contexts, may operate at the level of either style (here Romantic, late Romantic, and minimalist) or individual musical works, especially classical pieces (Beethoven's "Eroica" Symphony, Chopin's G-minor Ballade). The essays in "Musical Agency" deal with the power of music in film to move or "transport" the audience into recognitions, subject-positions, and reflective understanding that could be accessed in no other way. Many of these essays trace cinematic voyages that, from a Western perspective, lead to remote landscapes and cultures—a jungle, a desert, the far north, the Far East, mysterious islands—that challenge the routines of confident self-understanding. Others stay closer to home to examine the shifting relations, now congenial, now vertiginous, between music and the image. The music these essays discuss is often discomfiting, somehow out of place, almost too independent of the image when not, on the contrary, too absorbed with it. Finally, the essays in

"Musical Identity" examine the influence of specific musical genres (using the term loosely) on filmmaking practice. These studies track how the generic identity that music always carries—classical extracts and film themes, jazz, opera, music for cartoons, piano music—has a signifying power that carries over into film, a carryover that also implicates musical identity with social identity.

We cannot promise that all our contributors will endorse everything said here in the introduction. What we can promise is that they all engage the issues raised, and others besides, in provocative, thoughtful, and surprising ways. The engagement was the point; the endorsement, if any, was a bonus. As in every collection of essays, the contributors understand the topic proposed to them in their own ways. We would not have it otherwise. The choice of music on which to focus we left entirely free, and the results are diverse. It is interesting to see that classical music looms rather large, a welcome surprise in the age of its cultural retrenchment. It is also interesting that source music tends to be more prominent than underscore—possibly a result of the way the topic was defined—though both are represented fully enough, as are the interstices between them.

In order to give the volume some genuine cohesion, however, we did restrict the contributions to the tradition of Western commercial narrative film, though one or two of our authors—how could they not?—slipped over the border into different territory. This decision recognizes both the worldwide influence of the tradition we've put under scrutiny and the simple fact that is it this tradition on which most theorizing about film music has concentrated to date. The attempt to think beyond the soundtrack has to start somewhere; this seemed the most logical place. We hope, of course, that the results will find a wider resonance as well, but those who want to can simply take this collection as an effort to re-engage the role of music in the dominant film genres, take the term "dominant" in as descriptive or ideological sense as you will.

In their original form, these chapters were presented at a conference with the same title as this book, organized by the editors and held at the University of Minnesota in April 2004, with the generous support of the University of Minnesota's Humanities Institute, the McKnight Endowment for the Arts and Humanities, the Department of Cultural Studies and Comparative Literature/Studies in Cinema and Media Culture, and the Samuel Russell Professorship in the Humanities. Needless to say, we could not issue speaking invitations to everyone we would have liked to hear from; it would have been easy to double the number of speakers without thinking twice. Our effort was guided by a desire to bring together representatives from two communities, those of musicology and of cinema studies, scholars who have not talked with each other as much as they might in dealing with the richly complex ground of their common interest. The conversation thus initiated is not a closed book, and neither, we hope, is this volume.

NOTES

1. This information comes courtesy of William Rosar (personal communication), who also explains that " 'film music' and 'music in film' are not industry jargon, whereas 'underscoring' and 'source music' are. . . . Film composers call what they write 'film scores.' 'Film music' is considered generic to include TV music, and is a term that really originated in the music world, not Hollywood. It mainly denotes music composed for films (underscoring). 'Film music' as a term has been used by academics since the 1930s, if not earlier."

2. The standard texts on music as a supplement to cinema include Claudia Gorbman, *Unheard Melodies: Narrative Film Music* (Bloomington: Indiana University Press, 1987), and Kathryn Kalinak, *Settling the Score: Music and the Classical Hollywood Film* (Madison: University of Wisconsin Press, 1992). Caryl Flinn, *Strains of Utopia: Gender, Nostalgia, and Hollywood Film Music* (Princeton, NJ: Princeton University Press, 1992), shifts the emphasis from normalizing theory to historical practice.

3. On the problem of acoustic strength, see Anahid Kassabian, *Hearing Film: Tracking Identifications in Contemporary Hollywood Film Music* (New York: Routledge, 2001), pp. 52–55.

4. On this looping effect between music and other media, see Lawrence Kramer, *Musical Meaning: Toward a Critical History* (Berkeley and Los Angeles: University of California Press, 2001), pp. 145–93.

PART I

Musical Meaning

1 The Boy on the Train, or Bad Symphonies and Good Movies

The Revealing Error of the "Symphonic Score"

PETER FRANKLIN

The goal of this chapter will be an examination of the opening title and credits sequence of *Gone with the Wind* (1939), but my subject takes in three larger, interrelated topics, namely, nineteenth-century European symphonic music, its fate in the era of modernism, and film as a site where that fate was to some extent worked out. My angle is an unusual one in that I shall be deliberately turning around the assumption on which Claudia Gorbman's valuable "unheard melodies" critical formula is based.[1] I shall not only be listening to cinematic melodies, but, flying in the face of all that we know about Hollywood scoring practices, I shall be interested in reading Hollywood movies as if they were musical in essence, on some level perhaps even *about* music and musical experience. The result may be an unstable intellectual compound that exists only impermanently within the confines of these pages, but the experiment will have succeeded if something is illuminated by the following proposals. First, that film historians might have overlooked a major historical source of cinematic narrative techniques in the practice and reception of nineteenth-century symphonic music. Second, that this could help us understand the peculiarly musical quality of early film—particularly of the sound era—in its more "art"-aspiring mode. Finally, that what have come to be regarded as "good" movies, tendentious and manipulative as they often are, tell us quite a lot about what is interesting about bad symphonies—and, by extension, what may be meaningfully suspect about good or "real" symphonies.

Let me begin with the boy on the train. Not long ago I found myself traveling from the southern suburbs of London into the city on a Saturday morning. On the other side of the carriage sat a boy of about seven with his mother. She had bought him a new toy, which could be effectively grasped even though it was still encased in its package. Looking like a carbuncular plastic version of Siegfried's Nothung (it was plainly labeled "Crystal Sword"), it produced a grim taped sound effect of synthesized clanging when the handle was pressed, as tiny bulbs briefly flashed like sparks along its cutting edge. It was nevertheless plain that the boy was thinking about light sabers. I knew this because he was singing softly to himself the *Star Wars* march as he gazed abstractedly in the direction of the serried gardens that were passing outside the window. Now and again he would look down at the sword as his barely audible singing took in other motifs from John Williams's score and finally the heavy-footed march first eerily adumbrated at the very end of *The Phantom Menace.* Not even the eventual replacement of the drab terraced houses and gardens by broader vistas and the great wheel of the London Eye distracted him from his contemplation. His gaze moved back and forth from the sword to the window, some version of a *Star Wars* movie evidently running in his mind's eye—probably *Episode II—The Attack of the Clones,* then relatively recently released.[2]

What interested me about this seven-year-old's reverie would no doubt have startled his mother. I noted that he was using music to accompany or even structure something seen in his mind's eye, a sort of virtual movie; that he was effortlessly exercising a culturally complex ability that might have enabled him to understand nineteenth-century operatic and symphonic narrative; that he had picked it all up from some popular Hollywood sci-fi movies. My insistence that his skill could have been applied to both opera *and* the symphony needs justification and clarification—and leads to rather more of my topic, which is historically broad and transnational in its wider ramifications. The operatic ancestry of popular Hollywood films has often been the subject of comment; the connection is implicit in the widespread tendency to hear in John Williams's scoring techniques an appropriation of the Wagnerian leitmotif and other characteristics of opera. My traveling companion's crystal sword standing in for a light saber is another reminder of more than accidental Wagnerism in the *Star Wars* films. But, perhaps more importantly, Williams is also associated with the revival of the so-called "symphonic score"—and this is where symphonies and symphonic experience of a particular kind are legitimately invoked. This is why I am able to suggest that the boy on the train, deprived of the actual movies that had inspired his daydream, was visualizing a musical narrative in a way that could have been equally appropriate to a symphony in the nineteenth century, if we attend to historical evidence of the popular reception of such music.

First, however, we must be prepared to apply critical pressure to the notion of the symphonic score, associated with composers such as Max Steiner and Erich Wolfgang Korngold from the classic film era. Were their scores ever truly symphonic? The inevitable cutting and pasting involved, and the music's reliance on atmosphere and thematic association, means that such scores could at best be allied only with what used to be considered "bad" symphonies, such as those in the Tchaikovsky-Rachmaninov-Gershwin vein that were scornfully dismissed by Adorno: "The sole remaining organizing factor is the schema, not work from within. The structures approximate the medley form. Song hits have become the heirs of nationally tinged thematics; the legitimate successor of Rachmaninov was Gershwin."[3] If film scores were symphonic, then we must accept that they were not so in the tightly organized, structurally unified sense of the Beethovenian model. They were Romantically, "decadently" symphonic, drawing on later constructions of the symphonic experience that were always edging into the popular arena. These film scores were consumer products, and accordingly vilified by idealistic critics. But we know what Adorno was up to in his passionately tendentious disapproval of the popular sphere and the culture industry that supposedly manipulated it. At least he clearly marks out the territory where what he thought of as "bad" symphonies lined up alongside the popular movies whose pseudo-symphonic underscoring he was no less exasperated by. Film was a cultural form that he deliberately and scornfully linked with Wagner, with withering critical intent.[4]

As always, though, Adorno offers a glimpse of a way out of the critical box he has constructed for us when he writes of the "reverse side" of Wagner's "apologetic, backward-looking relationship to the bourgeoisie":

> He is no longer able to accept the cosmos of bourgeois forms wholeheartedly. Nothing already existing is tolerated, no "standard forms." . . . Nowadays, compared to the Wagnerian *décadence,* the ground is being prepared for a new decay inasmuch as musicians have lost their sensitivity in this respect and actually thirst for the conventions which Wagner strove to discard. Few things illuminate his attitude better than his remark that, when listening to Mozart, he sometimes imagined he could hear the clatter of the dishes accompanying the music.[5]

Perhaps those lax, post-Wagnerian symphonic "medleys" themselves possessed some vestigial critical energy after all. That perception of a critical moment in the Wagnerian decadence might have prompted a question about modes of listening. Might Adorno's idealistically "musical" attitude to the "work from within" in Mozart's symphonies even deliberately *suppress* that ghostly historical sound of dishes? Concerns about the supposedly art-insensitive class, members of which were using those dishes, prompted the nineteenth-century's quest, Wagnerian or otherwise, not only for idealized autonomy, but also for a kind of musical experience that was more directly available to the expanding audience. This experience was ever more complex and engaging of subjective involvement rather than merely proclaiming its status as "culture" to all but the most "musical" of listeners (who could always conveniently tune out the clattering crockery).

We are forced to rely on literary evidence, on literary mediations of evanescent subjective experience, but when we view the subject from the perspective of film studies, it is striking how often nineteenth-century descriptions of musical experience involve the inner eye, from Wackenroder's Joseph Berglinger (1797) through Wagner's early elucidations of Beethoven, as far as (and probably beyond) Helen Schlegel's experience of Beethoven's Fifth in *Howard's End*.[6] Musical experience, and specifically symphonic experience, was frequently recorded and described in proto-cinematic visualized narratives of startling boldness. These arguably constitute a literary subgenre. Adorno himself was steeped in that tradition and can be at his most engaging when he indulges in untheorized visualization of symphonic music (think of the dancing oxen and forest-devoured cities Adorno sees at the end of Mahler's Third Symphony's Scherzo, or the dream village he glimpses in the first movement of Mahler's Fourth).[7]

Wagner's 1846 essay on Beethoven's Ninth is a locus classicus for its complex proficiency in filmic narrative, long before such a thing existed. Wagner cited extensive passages from Goethe's poetry to clarify his reading, which was in all other respects visual from the outset, as when Wagner describes the "great chief theme, which steps before us at one stride as if disrobing from a spectral shroud."[8]

Wagner's account of the first movement does not aim to correlate events and music in any detailed way (as he had promised he would not, in his introduction, with its standard formulas about "higher instrumental music" and things "unspeakable in words"),[9] but rather characterizes the kind of narrative that the music seemed to him incontrovertibly to perform. This is not a miming of events so much as a strategically constructed *narrative* of events, figured as stages in a spiritual "struggle for joy" whose generalized association with the individual subject Wagner takes for granted. Only in the cinematic era are we able to be more articulate about the strongly visual narrative rhetoric that we are dealing with—one marked, for example, by a rapidly cut montage in the central section: "we think we see two giant wrestlers. . . . In passing gleams of light we recognize the sad sweet smile of a happiness that seems to seek for us . . . force, revolt, defiance, new quest, repeated struggle make out the elements of a ceaseless motion in this wondrous piece."[10] Wagner presents the movement's close as a startling "dolly-back" shot to a panoramic view of the symbolic battlefield, dominated by the personified mood of joylessness, again *seen*: "expanding to colossal form, [it] appears to span the all, in awful majesty."[11]

Narrative accounts of the middle movements of symphonic suites, from Tchaikovsky to Mahler, would typically locate them in another time frame from that of the primary drama enacted in the outer movements, and would usually locate them in the past. Wagner's account of the Ninth's Scherzo is interesting for its internal cinematic "cuts" and suggestion of a kind of "flashback" to earlier events. He characterizes the movement's opening as the entry into a "new world" of breathlessly onward-rushing celebration. Particularly interesting is his description of the main structural articulation of the movement, for which no validating formal explanation is given (although it might have been): "With the abrupt entry of the middle-section there suddenly opens out to us a scene of earthly jollity."[12] Again Wagner cites lines from Goethe about feasting "folk" (often the nineteenth-century symphonic scherzo was located in an idyllic past or a bucolic realm). The account closes with a "cross-fade" and the flashback already referred to—here effected without the cumbersome stage machinery that would clutter Wagner's attempts to realize similar cross-fading or "dissolve" scene changes in the first *Ring* cycle at Bayreuth:

> We are not disposed to view this banal gaiety as the goal of our restless quest . . . our gaze clouds over, and we turn from the scene to trust ourselves anew to that untiring force which spurs us on to light upon that bliss which, ah! we never thus shall light on; for once again, at the movement's close, we are driven to that earlier scene of jollity, and now we thrust it with impatience from us so soon as recognized.[13]

Such descriptions open a valuable window onto mid- and later-nineteenth-century symphonic reception, and not least on the reception of the popular symphonies that catered to a growing audience of those seeking passionate, inward experiences in public places. The popular character of that experience was typically discursively feminized for reasons that might have seemed wonderfully and provocatively confirmed by Tchaikovsky's patron Madame von Meck, who wrote of his Fourth Symphony:

> These divine sounds embrace my whole being, excite my nerves, drive my brain to such an exalted state that I have spent these last two nights without sleep, in a sort of delirium . . . musicians can only appreciate it with their intellect, but I listen and feel and empathize with all my being. If I must die for listening to it, I shall die, but still I shall listen.[14]

What I am calling the "symphonic experience" seemed indeed to have given concert-goers license to think and feel the unthinkable, the transgressive, even to self-destructive ends. That experience was systematically scorned in official intellectual discourse on music, a discourse in which "merely subjective" or "extra-musical" associations were ever more influentially trashed in favor of "purely musical" responses that would create their own repertoires of both conservative and high modernist varieties. It was in the era of film, in the early decades of the twentieth century, that Madame von Meck's kind of music had its heyday in the movie houses.

I do not propose to solve here the question of whether entertainment film accompanied by what we broadly call Romantic or late Romantic tonal music in the nineteenth-century symphonic manner should be considered as a repressively "managed" version of musicalized narrative experience, or rather as an empowering permission to access such efficiently engaged modes of internal experience (what we readily write off as escapism). The surprising similarity of the forms of film and symphony, historically and socioculturally, can nevertheless be confirmed by the similarity of the discursive and critical operations that converge on them. This almost brings me to *Gone with the Wind*, a cinematic "great work" that exemplifies the complex issues involved in assessing whether films of that era were accompanied by music or rather *driven* by it. I am also interested in it as an exemplar of the way in which Hollywood in the 1930s and '40s mediated a whole constellation of issues, which might be imagined as arranged around a loose Adornian dividing line between high-culture-oriented modernism on one side and mass culture on the other. These issues inevitably included European immigration and cultural appropriation, the politics of American identity formation, and, yes, matters linking symphonic reception with the American Civil War and the impact of Margaret Mitchell's famously popular novel.

There is no single fixed term of reference here; the relevant cultural contexts and creative practices were in an evolving and historically shifting and developing relationship. The proximity of symphony and film in this period, however, is certainly attested by stories of classically trained musicians who so deliberately valued cinema's music that they adopted an "eyes wide shut" approach to film's overspecific and restricted image world. Readers of Brendan Carroll's biography of Erich Wolfgang Korngold will encounter the delightfully British composer and teacher Harold Truscott, who, at the age of twenty-eight, claimed to have written enthusiastically to Korngold about his 1941 score for *Kings Row*.[15] Carroll recalls the following: "He told me in 1975 that he saw *Kings Row* on more than thirty occasions just to hear the score, once with his eyes completely closed, and was able to memorize and write down the major portions of it."[16] Mozart's supposed subversion in transcribing Allegri's papally protected *Miserere* has given way to the passionate reclamation of music too "common" to be accorded the dignity of being considered works of art. The implications of this are confirmed by a more recent development in film-music culture and marketing that directly involves *Gone with the Wind*.

The liner notes for Charles Gerhardt's 1974 recording of what the CD cover calls "Max Steiner's Classic Film Score *Gone With The Wind*" included Rudy Behlmer's account of how the recording project developed out of conversations with Max Steiner (who had, however, died in 1971).[17] The aim was to produce something longer than the thirty-minute suite that Steiner had originally prepared and recorded in 1954. The terms in which Steiner discussed the project, and in which Behlmer presents it, reveal a specific concern to release a "real" symphony derived from the more operatic and inevitably fragmented film score (Steiner might almost have been reading Adorno on medley-symphonies and "work from within"):

> Recording the entire score Steiner felt would be totally impractical and unmusical because some of the melodies occur in incomplete or rearranged ways—sometimes as often as 20 times during the picture—and he saw no need for this repetition. . . . The objective was to offer a longer, more inclusive and permanent memento of the original film that would stand on its own and . . . present a substantial work in the form of a one-movement symphony or symphonic poem based on the music from "Gone with the Wind."[18]

The interesting ambivalence about whether the result is more a memento of the film or a self-sufficient "one-movement symphony" points forcefully to the congruence, or at least complementarity, of the two worlds of nineteenth-century symphonic music and twentieth-century film, where each reveals something important or otherwise hidden about the other. Current video and DVD versions of *Gone with the Wind* also valuably enable comparison of the experience of Max Steiner's functional overture—a genuine if rather downbeat medley of tunes from the main score, designed to accompany audience arrival (for seat banging if not dish clattering)—and the more operatic or, indeed, symphonically preludial title and opening credits music, which Gerhardt's recording enables us to hear "truly" symphonically. The boy on the train might have understood my ironic scare quotes. Musical purists would have to be warned to close their inner eye and concentrate on the voice-leading for fear of suffering a more authentic, if covert, symphonic experience that the movie itself (as we shall see) could be construed as "realizing," rather in the way that music students may be asked to realize a figured bass. Whether listeners know the movie or not, this music seems almost unavoidably to evoke episodic glimpses of a grandly visualized narrative to come and to summon a world of imagined cinematic experience. For us, now, this may largely be a matter of acquired cultural knowledge. My suggestion, nevertheless, is that the film could equally well acquire the force of an historical commentary on how to read musical narrative in the late nineteenth-century symphony.

My ironic dig at "pure" musical listeners, who, unlike Harold Truscott at the movies, must presumably keep their eyes wide *open* in order to avoid those unmusical inner-eye pictures, might be a cue to turn to politics, and the specific politics of musical meaning. Or might we, in fact, talk in the same way about the politics of meaning in *film?* Note the following two extracts from early reviews of *Gone with the Wind.* Here is one from the *Hollywood Spectator* in 1939; its writer clearly believed in pure film, if not pure music: "There is no flag-waving in the picture. It takes no sides in the controversies it records, preaches no sermons, points no morals—just lets us see humanity in action and uses a little group of wholly unimportant people as the symbols of what it wishes to express."[19] Compare this, by the black writer and dramatist Carlton Moss, from the *New York Daily Worker* (written in early 1940, it was titled "An Open Letter to Mr Selznick"):

> Whereas *The Birth of a Nation* was a frontal attack on American history and the Negro people, *Gone with the Wind,* arriving twenty years later, is a rear attack on the same. Sugar-smeared and blurred by a boresome Hollywood love-story and under the guise of presenting the South as it is "in the eyes of the Southerners," the message of *Gone with the Wind* emerges in its final entity as a nostalgic plea for sympathy for a still living cause of Southern reaction.
>
> The Civil War is by no means ended in the South, Mr Selznick. It lives on and will live on until the Negro people are completely free.[20]

The politics of meaning is here equivalent to a politics of reading, critical reading, in film as it is in music. This is true of the symphonic tradition above all, where, as I have already suggested, the passionate movies that ran before the mind's eye of the concert-goer were zealously trashed as crutches for the musically lame, even by those who indulged in and provoked them. That Hollywood movies may thus reveal something about the very cultural tradition to which they were reckoned to represent a debased coda is further emphasized not by Steiner himself—like Korngold and most big-name Hollywood composers of the period, he always had a hankering for the Old World and coveted the status of "great composer"—but by that interesting early critic of film music, Bruno David Ussher. In an extended essay on the *Gone with the Wind* score, published in 1940, Ussher celebrated Steiner's score as no mere accompaniment:

> Max Steiner's music adds motion and emotion to the long narrative of Civil War days in Georgia. It sets the atmosphere melodically and motivates the action before the picture itself flashes on the screen. It serves as a frame for sections of the picture, giving individual scenes rhythm and combining unity to their total of varied impressions. The score tells of battle where the spectator is spared the implied horror even of make-believe death and vast destruction.[21]

This reading comes close to validating my otherwise apparently eccentric suggestion that Hollywood movies might, from one angle, be about music and modes of musical reception as much as anything else. Steiner's music gives *motion* as well as *emotion* to the visualized narrative. More than just providing atmosphere, the music narrates the story "before the picture itself flashes on the screen"; it structures and binds together the movie; and, above all, it "tells of battle," showing us something of the Civil War's horror more directly than the film ever could (Ussher might have been referring specifically to the entr'acte and the striking montage sequence that opens part two, with the superimposed text: "And the wind swept through Georgia . . . SHERMAN!").[22]

This, of course, is not to bypass the question of politics. Should we regard this music, in Adornian fashion, as part of the tendentious "sugar smearing" to which Carlton Moss reacted so violently? Thereby, as ever, hangs a tale that is just one episode in a whole anthology about modernism and mass culture and the fate of late Romantic symphonic music in America (and perhaps in Europe, too). It is a tale that concerns the transgressive or empowering moment of the otherwise manipulative subjectivity of these movies, of this music; it constantly raises the question whether it *is* transgressive or simply manipulative—under the "orders of the determining ideology," as Adorno had suggested. This, once again, is a matter of the politics of how we read ambivalent meaning that flips readily from one side to the other of the interpretative line, like the brief but grandiose musical composition that accompanies the *Gone with the Wind* titles.

This music features and is structured by ever more expansive iterations of the score's main theme, the so-called "Tara" theme. Its shamelessly manipulative, critically anesthetizing, and thus more or less "hysterical" character has led to its coming to stand for almost the whole genre of classic-era Hollywood film music, just as the film's complex "heroine," Scarlett O'Hara, would come to stand emblematically all the starring female roles in classic-era movies. If we make the not-so-bold step of linking the two and suggesting that the leitmotif of place, of the land, is also a leitmotif of its owner, Scarlett herself, then we have a stronger purchase on how important our analysis of that theme might be. That association both invites and challenges the conventional critical tropes applied to such tendentiously and regressively persuasive music in the age of high modernism. The critical legacy of feminism might relevantly be invoked as we question what precisely the film *is* manipulating us to be persuaded of, just as we might now question the standard modernist or even Adornian line on the relevant symphonic models for the "Tara" theme. When we begin to consider such models, the relevance of such a comparison to the still little-charted territory of late-nineteenth-century symphonic meaning immediately becomes clear. The "Tara" theme speaks the language of engulfing late Romantic musical pleasure in its most grandiose and climactic mode. There are echoes in the theme, and in its orchestration, of the main "love" theme of Tchaikovsky's Fantasy Overture *Romeo and Juliet*—a theme that performs the utopian, but of course ill-fated, linkage of erotic fulfillment with an envisaged overthrow of repressively divisive cultural and social norms. We might also compare the "Tara" theme with the heroic finale theme of a more overtly nationalistic symphony like Sibelius's First, although the stoic insistence on the third degree of the scale in the Sibelius melody contrasts with the more jagged outline of the "Tara" theme, with its emphasis on the dominant (more energetic in its *preparation* for the tonic than in its arrival thereon). The similarly roller-coaster outline of the comparable theme in the finale of Rachmaninov's Second Symphony, conclusively and repeatedly descending to the tonic, more directly celebrates achievement and arrival, in however disheveled and overwrought a state.

It was these various shades and varieties of the state of being "overwhelmed" that attracted the gender-related tropes of elitist modernist criticism of such music and the kind of cinematic pleasure that it seemed to signify. And it is here that the complicating ambivalence of such pleasure, seen from an early twenty-first-century perspective, invites other observations, other kinds of critical assessment of films like *Gone with the Wind*. Beyond the specific historical context and political agenda of the movie and the novel, the character of the "Tara" theme, with its recurring and structuring significance (associated with key dolly-back shots to the celebrated silhouette of the house under a foregrounded tree), may be as difficult to assess in any conclusive way as is Scarlett O'Hara herself. The hysteric, the emblematic seducer who is never committed to her victims—perhaps committed only to the land and the outmoded, slavery-based class system that supported it—is also the strong, transgressive woman who overcomes her culturally constructed gender role to challenge and manipulate men, including Clark Gable; the threatened rape in part two demonstrates that she will also shoot them when necessary.[23]

In order to project that ambivalence out onto wider and more conventionally "political" issues, my concluding comments will focus on the close of the title sequence and the quotation of "Dixie." In his 1940 pamphlet, the enthusiastic Bruno David Ussher presented a picture of emigré Max Steiner—whom he interviewed while he was tending the fruit trees, artichokes, and strawberry beds surrounding his "quietly furnished villa in Beverly Hills" (does Ussher hint at a miniature Tara?)—as a composer who personally sympathized with people who, like him, had "felt the withering blasts of war." He also pointed out—in what is almost an aside in his essay, which stressed the extent of Steiner's musico-historical research and his concern to avoid anachronisms—that Steiner had lacked

> justification for the use of voices, the picture rarely depicting negro life or work in the field. Steiner employs a vocal background when "Dixie" is first heard in the opening title sequence, but he has wisely refrained from stressing the words. The human significance of the tune is brought home by the very presence of the voices.[24]

It is, of course, fascinating that this choral coda to the main titles is *not* included in Gerhardt's "symphony," as if in response to the implications of Ussher's nervousness about a song that had come to be known as the Confederate anthem and would be banned in many U.S. schools in the late 1960s as racist in its associations. These associations had less to do with the song's original folksy text about black cotton workers' loves and dreams than with the new words added by General Albert Pike ("Southrons, hear your country call you"), and perhaps with the song's probable origin in Dan Emmett's black-face minstrel song.[25] The song therefore suggests the white *construction* of a slave mentality, whose meaning in the movie depends very much on whether you hear the wordless voices as representing those of the briefly glimpsed slave workers, or of a patronizing choir of the United Daughters of the Confederacy, whose sentiments (and sentimentality) might be those of the tendentious and sugar-smearing text on the screen that accompanies the music (text that seems to have no source in Margaret Mitchell):

> There was a land of Cavaliers and Cotton Fields
> called the Old South.
> Here in this pretty world Gallantry took
> its last bow . . .

> Here was the last ever to be seen of Knights and their
> Ladies fair, of Master and of Slave . . .
> Look for it only in books,
> for it is no more than a dream remembered.
>
> A civilization gone with the wind . . .

By omitting the choral coda from the "symphony" version, Gerhardt oddly draws attention to its presence in the film at the end of the dazzling title and credits sequence. There it contributes to the realization of the nineteenth-century symphonic experience in a remarkable way, provoking involvement, a realignment of the passion aroused by the "Tara" theme, and, perhaps, a troubling moment of empathy or unease. The sadly humming singers of "Dixie" look back with complicatedly inflected nostalgia to a world whose heroism was misplaced, a world whose victims they may have been and which has indeed now gone. The retrospectively cleaned-up symphony of the "classic score" recording bypasses those problems, for reasons that may have been purely economic. Alternatively, the cleaning up could have as much to do with an unhistorical and uncritical notion of so-called "classical music" that the film seems much better, and more subtly, to understand, would we but listen *and* look.

NOTES

1. I am referring, of course, to the formula described in Claudia Gorbman's path-breaking book, *Unheard Melodies: Narrative Film Music* (Bloomington: Indiana University Press, 1987), and I am following in the wake of others who have responded to the challenge of Gorbman's formula and its rooting in psychoanalytic theory. See, for example, Jeff Smith, "Unheard Melodies? A Critique of Psychoanalytic Theories of Film Music," in *Post-Theory: Reconstructing Film Studies,* ed. David Bordwell and Noel Carroll (Madison: University of Wisconsin Press, 1996), pp. 230–47.

2. *Star Wars: Episode II—Attack of the Clones* was released by Lucasfilm Ltd. in 2002. My train journey took place in May of that year.

3. Theodor W. Adorno, *Introduction to the Sociology of Music,* trans. E. B. Ashton, (New York: Seabury Press, 1976), pp. 166–67.

4. See, for example, Theodor W. Adorno, *In Search of Wagner,* trans. Rodney Livingstone (London: NLB, 1981), p. 46.

5. Ibid., p. 48.

6. Wilhelm Heinrich Wackenroder's "The Remarkable Musical Life of the Musician Joseph Berglinger" (1797) is translated in Strunk's *Source Readings in Music History, Volume 6: The Nineteenth Century,* ed. Ruth A. Solie (New York: Norton, 1998); see, for example, p. 21. For a characteristic piece of Wagner's writing on

Beethoven, see "The Ninth Symphony (with parallel passages from the poems of Goethe)," originally published as Wagner's essay "Beethoven's Choral Symphony in Dresden" (1846); the Ashton-Ellis translation is reprinted in *Wagner on Music and Drama: A Compendium of Richard Wagner's Prose Works,* ed. Albert Goldman and Evert Sprinchorn (New York: Da Capo, 1988), pp. 167–76. The relevant section of E. M. Forster's 1910 novel *Howard's End* is in chapter 5.

7. See Theodor W. Adorno, *Mahler: A Musical Physiognomy,* trans. Edmund Jephcott (Chicago: University of Chicago Press, 1992), pp. 8–9, 44.

8. Wagner, "The Ninth Symphony," p. 167.

9. Ibid.

10. Ibid.

11. Ibid., p. 168.

12. Ibid., p. 169.

13. Ibid.

14. Alexander Poznansky, *Tchaikovsky: The Quest for the Inner Man* (New York: Schirmer, 1991), p. 347.

15. For the 1942 form letter sent out by the Warner Bros. Music Department in response to the many inquiries about the music for *Kings Row* (explaining that it remains unpublished and unrecorded), see Rudy Behlmer, *Inside Warner Bros. (1935–1951)* (London: Weidenfeld and Nicolson, 1986), p. 142. Harold Truscott (1914–92) was active as a composer and teacher in Britain until his retirement in 1979.

16. Brendan Carroll, *The Last Prodigy: A Biography of Erich Wolfgang Korngold* (Portland, OR: Amadeus Press, 1997), p. 306.

17. Charles Gerhardt, with the National Philharmonic Orchestra, *Max Steiner's Classic Film Score "Gone With the Wind"* (RCA Victor GD80452, BMG Music, 1974; remastered 1989).

18. Ibid., liner notes, p. 12.

19. Richard Harwell, ed., *Gone with the Wind, as Book and Film* (Columbia: University of South Carolina Press, 1983), p. 153.

20. Ibid., p. 157.

21. Ibid, pp. 161–62.

22. In its current DVD format (Turner Entertainment and Warner Home Video 2000), the entr'acte begins side B and was clearly intended as a curtain-raising overture to the second part of the movie, which opens with a black screen and a roll of drums before the montage (opening with slow-motion cannon smoke and flames) with superimposed text as described.

23. The issue of Scarlett's "hysterical" character was instructively addressed in a curious 1976 article by Dr. Charles E. Wells, "The Hysterical Personality and the Feminine Character: A Study of Scarlett O'Hara," reprinted in *Gone with the Wind, as Book and Film,* pp. 115–23.

24. Bruno David Ussher, in *Gone with the Wind, as Book and Film,* p. 165.

25. On the complex history of "Dixie," see Howard L. Sacks and Judith Rose Sacks, *Way Up North in Dixie: A Black Family's Claim to the Confederate Anthem* (Urbana: University of Illinois Press, 2003). The following observations must be

judged in the light of Lawrence Kramer's important chapter "Powers of Blackness," in *Musical Meaning: Toward a Critical History* (Berkeley and Los Angeles: University of California Press, 2002), p. 198, where he discusses citations of black music that do not identify with the "powers of blackness" but rather "enclose" them. According to Hilton Als in *The New Yorker* (26 September 2005, consulted online on www.newyorker.com/critics/content/articles/050926crbo), Jill Watts's recent book *Hattie McDaniel: Black Ambition, White Hollywood* (New York: Amistad, 2005) includes a reference to Martin Luther King Jr., aged nine, having sung "in the all-black chorus that sang in the movie theatre before the lights went down" at the premiere of *Gone with the Wind* in Atlanta.

2   **Representing Beethoven**

Romance and Sonata Form
in Simon Cellan Jones's *Eroica*

NICHOLAS COOK

INTRODUCING *EROICA*

The success of Milos Forman's *Amadeus* (1984) heralded a steady flow of
films about canonical composers of the classical tradition: Simon Cellan
Jones's *Eroica* (2003) might then be seen as following from Paul Morrissey's
Beethoven's Nephew (1985) and Bernard Rose's *Immortal Beloved* (1994).
But in some ways *Eroica* is so different as hardly to belong in this lineage
at all. Quite apart from being made for television (it was commissioned by
the British Broadcasting Corporation), it also focuses on the performance of
a single work, combining the genre of music video with that of period costume export drama. Though there is a romantic plot, a great deal of the film
consists of sometimes extended shots of different characters listening to the
music, shots that are intercut with performance footage. In this chapter I
shall suggest that the film's visualization of the listening process is both culturally revealing and the key to the film's success. In gauging the latter I
rely less on my own personal response to the film than on those of the many
viewers who posted their comments on the BBCi web site established at the
time of its original broadcast. The fact that *Eroica* existed from the start as
a web site as well as a film is another indication of its distinctive generic mix.

Eroica was broadcast by BBC2 on 4 October 2003, though it had been
screened a few months earlier at the Edinburgh Film Festival; it was released
in 2005 on the BBC's Opus Arte label.[1] The film revolves around the first
play-through of Beethoven's Third Symphony (the "Eroica"), and the synopsis on the web site reads as follows:

> Eroica unfolds over just a few hours of 9 June 1804. It begins with prepara-
> tions for the rehearsal; the musicians lugging their instruments, the servants

preparing the salon, Prince Lobkowitz, his family and guests anticipating a thrilling session, Beethoven's friends and lovers showing up to give support.

And then the bad-tempered maestro begins the rehearsal—the nature of the music is so different that it causes problems both for players and audience.

After the second movement has been played through the orchestra take a break and Beethoven persuades Josephine, the Countess von Deym, to accompany him to an ante-room to discuss their future together.

The whole of the symphony is played through. Beethoven goes home and has some fish for dinner. He likes fish.[2]

The structure of the film is very straightforward. The first fifteen minutes consists of a series of vignettes showing everybody getting ready for the rehearsal: the Lobkowitzes and their aristocratic friends, the servants, the musicians. We also see Beethoven and his pupil (and dogsbody) Ferdinand Ries, first at Beethoven's lodgings and then walking through the woods to the Lobkowitz palace; by the time they arrive, the orchestra is already in the hall where the rehearsal will take place (they are playing Mozart's *Eine kleine Nachtmusik*, which in the context of the film stands for the old aristocratic world of powdered wigs). So far the film has developed in a conventional narrative style, but from the moment the performance of the "Eroica" begins it is Beethoven's music that provides the plan, with the narrative action being grafted onto it. One has the impression (it can be no more than that) that the breaks between movements take place in real time, even in the case of the principal narrative interpolation, which comes between the second and third movements: as the synopsis says, Beethoven and Josephine go to another room, where in the course of a long conversation Beethoven asks Josephine to marry him and she turns him down. Toward the end of the film, however, there is a series of flash-forwards showing—in sequence—Beethoven and Ries walking home, the audience members leaving the hall and talking about the music, Beethoven and Ries having supper at a tavern[3] (more on this later), and Josephine and her children leaving the palace. All these are superimposed on the music, and this means that the film can effectively end with the symphony: after the music stops there are a few seconds of silence, the players put down their instruments, there are images of Beethoven and some of the listeners, then the composer curtly says "Thank you," picks up his score, and walks out, his footsteps echoing on the wooden floor. Appropriately, there are only ambient sounds as the credits roll.

The generic contribution of the music video is evident in the way in which the music, when it starts, provides the temporal framework for the film, as well as in the extensive performance footage, much of which (unlike the narrative sections) is cut to the phrase or beat, music video style: one might, for instance, draw a parallel between *Eroica* and Madonna's (and producer Mary Hunter's) "Material Girl" video, which also begins with a narrative introduction and combines narrative and performance footage after the song begins. Inevitably there are tensions in this generic mixture, perhaps most obviously in the soundtrack. Beethoven and Josephine are still talking while the third movement begins, and we hear it in the distance, muffled; there are other points, too, where the action takes place outside the hall (on the stairs, in the kitchen) and the music is muffled, so that the sound is being treated in a realistic style as an element of the diegesis. Yet this is contradicted by the sound quality of the music during the rest of the film, which is that of a music video: one hears a studio performance presented in the acoustic foreground, in the style of a CD. (The musicians on screen are in fact miming, just as they would be in a music video.)[4] There are also contradictions in the relationship between music and imagetext. At some points the music functions in a conventional film-musical manner: a particularly striking example occurs in one of the flash-forwards when Haydn, whom the film has attending the last part of the rehearsal (a cameo appearance by Frank Finlay), says, "Everything is different from today," and as if on cue the music—measure 380 of the last movement—rhetorically underlines the portent. In general, however, it is not the music that responds to the action but the action that responds to the music, simply because the film is largely about people's reactions to the music.

EROICA AND THE "EROICA"

The BBC press release for *Eroica* described the period-instrument performance, featuring L'Orchestre Revolutionnaire et Romantique under John Eliot Gardner, as "the first in modern times to replicate exactly the number of players and size of venue which the invited audience, on that historic day, experienced."[5] As an approach to historically informed performance, aiming in this manner to re-create the original event begs the question of whether what the composer heard was what he would have wished to hear. Alain Frogley observes that "Beethoven can hardly have relished the exact parity of the 15 strings and 15 winds employed in the first performance of the *Eroica* symphony in Prince Lobkowitz's palace."[6] What is interesting in this context, however, is that the BBC wished to emphasize the factual credentials of the film, as if it were as much a documentary as a drama[7]—and the film even re-creates the orchestral breakdown documented by Ries in his well-known, or at least much anthologized, memoir of Beethoven, although for some reason the breakdown has been relocated from the development section of the first movement to the exposition (bar 33).[8] Similarly, the film follows Ries's account of what continental scholars call the "Cumulus," just before the point of recapitulation in the first movement, where the horn appears to enter two bars early (it arpeggiates a tonic triad over dominant harmony)—except that Ries makes no mention of the orchestra coming to a stop, as it does in *Eroica*. He writes, "During the first rehearsal of this symphony, which went appallingly, the horn player did come in correctly. I was standing next to Beethoven and believing the entry wrong said: "That damned horn player! Can't he count?—it sounds terrible!" I believe I was very close indeed to having my ears boxed.—Beethoven was a long time in forgiving me."[9] In the film, though the words are changed, the event is conveyed accurately enough. But note Ries's use of the word "appallingly"! One of the contributors to the BBCi web site, signing as "Brian, Surrey," succinctly summarizes an obvious problem with the film, claiming, "My only criticism is that, after a faltering start, the orchestra was magically able to play the symphony perfectly on sight. Hardly likely! But then watching a rehearsal would not have been great viewing :-)"[10] The contradiction is insoluble, and perhaps emerges most forcefully with the breakdown at bar 33, which is as beautifully performed as the rest of the symphony: you have the impression that somebody scored it all out and that the orchestra carefully rehearsed it.

This tension, or compromise, between factual accuracy on the one hand and musical or dramatic satisfaction on the other pervades the film. Nick Dear, the screenwriter, claims that "Most of what you see is based on documented fact; a little bit is speculation,"[11] and this is basically fair comment (although, as we shall see, he might have mentioned a third category, that is, facts that have been relocated from their historical context). Indeed, it is testimony to the care Dear has taken that, of the three contributors to the BBCi web site who pointed out factual errors, only one was (probably) correct.[12] So, for example, modern sources such as Thomas Sipe's Cambridge Music Handbook on the symphony agree that the first rehearsal of the "Eroica" took place on 9 June 1804 at the Lobkowitz palace,[13] with members of the prince's orchestra playing and Beethoven conducting (whatever "conducting" means in this context, a question I shall not address).[14] It is questionable whether the rehearsal was quite the social event—as much a performance as a rehearsal—that *Eroica* depicts, but all the same, the protagonists—not just Beethoven and the lame Prince Lobkowitz and his wife and Josephine, but also Josephine's sister, Therese Brunsvik, and Count Dietrichstein—are real. Even the copyist, Wenzel Sukowaty, and Lobkowitz's *Kappelmeister*, Paul Wranitzky, are historical (Beethoven wrote a set of variations, WoO 71, based on Wranitzky's ballet *Das Waldmädchen*). Also real enough is Beethoven's infatuation with the young widow and mother Josephine, one of the also-rans for identification as Beethoven's "Immortal Beloved."[15] Surviving letters show that they were in touch in the summer of 1804, though the first hint of a romantic relationship does not appear until the end of the year.[16] The real Josephine is also known to have resisted Beethoven's advances, though it appears that the reason she actually gave was that she had taken a vow of chastity on her husband's death;[17] if that was true, then she did not keep it, for it has to be said that the demure Josephine of *Eroica* is not exactly in accordance with the reputation the real Josephine acquired, at least by a few years later.[18]

As I have already suggested, there are also details that, while factual in themselves, have been relocated in the film. An unobjectionable example is the point in the conversation between Beethoven and Josephine when he tells her that his heart is full of all the things he wants to tell her and that speech is a useless faculty; this is an almost direct quotation from one of his letters to her, dating from spring 1805.[19] Perhaps more questionable is Dear's habit of incorporating into the dialogue a number of famous quotations, some of which have nothing to do with the "Eroica." One example is when, in *Eroica*, Beethoven explains that "I've taken a new direction . . . a new path"; this is a reference to the "new path" that, according to Carl Czerny, Beethoven told Wenzel Krumpholz he was taking around 1803. Musicologists have been arguing about the meaning of this claim ever since, though they agree that the "Eroica" is a prime example of this new path.[20] If this reference is at least justified by its relevance to the symphony, others are not: examples include Beethoven's reference to himself in conversation with Dietrichstein as not a land owner but a brain owner (in reality a sarcastic rejoinder by Beethoven to a letter from his cousin Nicolaus Johann, who had put "land owner" after his signature),[21] and his remark that "as long as the Viennese has his beer and his sausage he won't cause any trouble and will go about his business."[22] There is something a little arch about these gratuitous displays of erudition on the screenwriter's part, though they create a certain thrill of recognition or at least amusement on the informed viewer's part, and perhaps should be seen as an integral component of the unstable generic mix of *Eroica*.

But there is one conspicuous case in which the relocation of events turns into surely conscious historical misrepresentation, and it is no accident that it bears upon a central topic of the film: the link between music and political context. The title by which the symphony is now known (in full, *Sinfonia eroica composta per festiggiare il sovvenire di un grand Uomo* [Heroic symphony composed to celebrate the memory of a great man]) dates from the publication of the orchestral parts in October 1806: in 1804 the work was explicitly named after Napoleon. This is the context for one of the most famous episodes in Ries's memoirs:

> I myself, as well as many of his close friends, had seen this symphony, already copied in full score, lying on his table. At the very top of the title page stood the word "Buoneparte" and at the very bottom "Luigi van Beethoven," but not a word more. Whether and with what the intervening space was to be filled I do not know. I was the first to tell him the news that Boneparte had declared himself emperor, whereupon he flew into a rage and shouted: "So he too is nothing more than an ordinary man. Now he also will trample all human rights underfoot, and only pander to his own ambition; he will place himself above everyone else and become a tyrant!" Beethoven went to the table, took hold of the title page at the top, ripped it all the way through, and flung it on the floor.[23]

The representation of this in *Eroica* is accurate enough, given the realities of dramatic adaptation. In the scene in Beethoven's lodgings at the beginning of the film we see a close-up of the score, marked precisely as Ries says, and then, in the final flash-forward to Beethoven and Ries at the tavern, Ries gives Beethoven the news about Napoleon and Beethoven crumples the title page and tosses it away. There are factual inaccuracies, of course: not only Beethoven crumpling the title page instead of tearing it in two (why, one wonders?), but also Beethoven and Ries being at the tavern at all (Ries says that Beethoven played another concert that evening).[24] Another factual inaccuracy, this one involving chronology, is not trivial. Napoleon's proclamation of himself as emperor took place on 18 May 1804, and, as Thayer says (though he is making a different argument), "Even in those days, news of so important an event would not have required ten days to reach Vienna."[25] The action of *Eroica*, however, is set on 9 June 1804, more than three weeks after Napoleon's proclamation. Not only was the event by then common knowledge in Vienna, but it also resulted in a significant shift in Viennese perceptions of Napoleon (as Sipe puts it, the "compounded mutual distrust between the two regimes").[26] Under such circumstances the kind of sympathetic, openly political discussions of French republicanism pictured in *Eroica* would be downright implausible.[27]

According to Carl Dahlhaus, "Actual facts can be converted into myth by being isolated from their historical context and transferred to a symbolical one."[28] The film's conjunction of the first rehearsal of the "Eroica" with the news of Napoleon's proclamation, so much at odds with the prevailing concern for historical accuracy, reflects the film's own myth-making process and the values that inform it. The relationship between music and politics is one to which the protagonists of *Eroica* repeatedly refer, starting with Beethoven himself, who arrives at the palace at the same time as Otto Fisher, the horn player, and says, "You're late for the revolution, Otto!" Again, after Ries tells Marie Lobkowitz, rather apologetically, about the symphony's dedication to Napoleon, she asks him, "Can music exist independently of politics?" When he replies that he couldn't say, she responds, "*I* could." By contrast, when, a few minutes later, Lobkowitz whispers to Dietrichstein, "My wife says it's about Boneparte," Dietrichstein—who serves throughout the film as the voice of aristocratic reaction—replies, "How may a piece of music be said to be *about* something?" That is a question to which the women have the answer. Near the beginning of the second movement Marie whispers to Therese, "I can just see the death cars in the boulevards, can't you, Therese?" and Therese replies, "Black plumes on the horses and gold epaulettes." Again, at the end of the previous movement, Marie says to Beethoven, "I thought of a battle, I thought of a general, the horse rearing, the saber shining, columns of men streaming through the mountains. . . . I was meant to, wasn't I?" to which the composer replies with uncharacteristic judiciousness, "If you like."

It is one of the attractions of a dialogic medium like film that it effortlessly achieves a mobility of viewpoint that can be replicated only with difficulty in a monograph: the issue of whether music can have specific meaning, political or otherwise, is represented as a matter of contention, which is exactly what it was at this time. With the possible exception of Beethoven, whose authority, however, derives from his music rather than his words, *Eroica* avoids setting up some characters, and therefore some views, as obviously more authoritative than others. Marie is prone to superficiality (having had the meaning of *sforzando* explained to her, she delightedly replies, "How modern!"), her husband is a sympathetic aesthete who lacks any comprehension of the real world of politics, and Ries is tongue-tied, unwilling to commit himself, afraid of saying the wrong thing.

Curiously, the only character that shows any real development or complexity is Dietrichstein, the voice of aristocratic reaction, who is initially presented in the most unsympathetic light. Thus when Josephine and Therese, who have arrived late, apologize to Beethoven at the end of the first movement, Dietrichtsein says in the composer's presence, "Well, you didn't miss very much, my dear—tasteless intermarriage of the diatonic and the chromatic—hardly worth hurrying for" (to which Josephine replies, "Well, what we heard was splendid!"). The aristocratic disregard for feelings and the readiness to deliver judgment go hand in hand, yet during the second movement it is Dietrichstein who, of all the listeners, is most deeply affected by the music. (It is as he listens that we gain the sense of character development, and I shall come back to this.) By the end of the movement, however, he has recovered his poise, striding forward to Beethoven as soon as the music stops and saying in measured tones, "That wasn't bad. It's not a symphony, though." When Beethoven responds in the predictable manner, Dietrichstein explains: "The symphony has a structure; this is a formless mass, a mere arrangement of noise, a great piling up of colossal ideas. It's very moving. In parts it has elements of the sublime. But it is also full of discord, and it lacks rounding out. It is not what we call a symphony." In this historically quite plausible commentary (it becomes clear that Dietrichstein's ideal is Haydn), the "we" is telling, with its suggestion of a closed aristocratic circle of those qualified to deliver aesthetic judgment—a circle from which the youthful Beethoven appears to be excluded.

But it is here that the film begins to take sides. It is not only that, as we know, Dietrichstein is on the wrong side of history, both musically and politically (there is a network of references to the incipient collapse of the old order, linked to Lobkowitz's squandering of the family fortunes on his orchestra—and it is a fact that he went bankrupt in 1814).[29] At measure 573 of the first movement—just a few bars into the giant coda that represents the movement's most unconventional formal feature—the butler whispers to Ries, "A Haydn would be over by now, sir, wouldn't it? He's buggered around with the whole thing, hasn't he—the shape of it and that?" (Ries, of course, doesn't know what to say, though one suspects he secretly agrees.) The butler's aesthetic position may in essence be the same as Dietrichstein's, but it gains credibility from being expressed in ordinary language instead of the rather pretentious connoisseur's terminology that Dietrichstein employs (and its analytical acuity is a further bonus). While the film sides against Dietrichstein's model of aesthetic judgment, however, it does not present a consistent one of its own: whereas the butler's measured enjoyment of the music is based on his evident experience as a listener, a young lady's maid is presented as a totally naive listener[30] who is nevertheless enthralled by this difficult music. Beethoven's music, it seems, can speak to all classes and conditions of humanity, and it is hardly the film's job to explain how that might be.

I would argue, then, that *Eroica* presents a diversity of aesthetic responses to the "Eroica," responses as well grounded in historical fact as one could reasonably expect. It combines these, however, with approaches that developed over the two hundred years following the symphony's first performance. Some of the latter are, or appear to be, incidental references rather similar in nature to the relocated quotations I discussed earlier. For instance, when in the first movement Marie says, "My God, it's like a dam bursting," there is an echo of Romain Rolland's early twentieth-century description of the opening measures as "the bursting of a dam," while Lobkowitz's likening of the movement to "a hero of antiquity—a Greek perhaps . . . Achilles" reflects a widespread nineteenth-century critical tradition of comparing the "Eroica" to the works of Homer. (I take it to be no accident that both of these sources are mentioned in Sipe's handbook.)[31] But there is one far more important example of critical anachronism, which is spelled out by Haydn in the flash-forward I referred to earlier. Beethoven, he says, "has done something no other composer has attempted. He's placed himself at the center of his work. He gives us a glimpse into his soul. I expect that's why it's so—noisy. But it is—quite, quite new—the artist as hero. Quite new. Everything is different from today." And here there is much that can be said from the standpoint of musicology. The idea that, in Scott Burnham's words,[32] "Beethoven himself is acknowledged as the hero of the *Eroica* Symphony" is so familiar, so ingrained in our experience of Beethoven's music, that it is easy to forget that it is a strictly historical construction. When he says this, then, Burnham is not stating a universal truth, but rather glossing Wagner's suggestion in a short story of 1841 that the symphony constitutes not just a representation of heroism, but an act of heroism in itself. According to Wagner, Beethoven "must have felt *his* powers aroused to an extraordinary pitch, his valiant courage spurred on to a grand and unheard-of deed! He was no general—he was a musician; thus in his realm he saw before him the territory within which he could accomplish the same thing that Bonaparte had achieved in the fields of Italy."[33] But this style of interpretation began to reach a wide audience only with the writings of Beethoven's biographer Ludwig Nohl in 1870s, thereafter being circulated by—among many others—Hans von Bülow, Sir George Grove, Romain Rolland, and J. W. N. Sullivan.[34] The result, to quote Burnham again, is that

> with the *Eroica* symphony, Beethoven becomes the hero of Western music, "The Man Who Freed Music." With this one work, Beethoven is said to liberate music from the stays of eighteenth-century convention, singlehandedly bringing music into a new age by giving it a transcendent voice equal to Western man's most cherished values. . . . We have moved from Beethoven's hero

to Beethoven Hero; the hero with whom we identify becomes subsumed within the figure of a demigod we can only serve.[35]

In this way, if, in Dahlhaus's words, "What the 'Eroica' realizes aesthetically is not the image but the myth of Napoleon,"[36] then what *Eroica* represents is the myth of Beethoven as it was constructed during the century after his death. Or rather it represents a series of not always compatible myths about Beethoven and his music—or about music in general, if Burnham is right when he claims that "The values of Beethoven's heroic style have become the values of music."[37] One perhaps shouldn't expect more, or less, from a film like *Eroica*.

WATCHING *EROICA*, HEARING THE "EROICA"

I have already mentioned the BBCi *Eroica* website (still accessible at the time of writing), which consists of separate sets of pages on the film, the music, and Beethoven himself, including video interview clips with Ian Hart (Beethoven), Peter Hanson (Wranitzky), and the producer Liza Marshall. There is also a quiz (with questions like "Beethoven was the favourite composer of which Peanuts character?") and, more interestingly, a bulletin board where viewers could—and did—post their comments; many of them identified themselves with nicknames, rather like the names people give themselves on eBay. The result was to heighten the sense of participation in a virtual community. Put together with other critiques and commentaries available on the web, these postings make possible a sort of instant reception history of the film.

Behind a number of the postings lies the issue of *Eroica*'s genre, though it is not put that way. One viewer, for instance, comments on the way in which "the music, quite rightly, took centre stage" (Jen, Scotland), while another writes that "the music dominated the film, as it should" (S., London). Other viewers elaborate on the same idea, writing "I loved the way the music was the main focus with the characters boosting the story, not the other way around" (Amy Whitwam, Huddersfield), "its unique character seems to be in a novel, subtle, but crucial shift of emphasis whereby the 'play' is experienced as an extended footnote to the Symphony" (Chris Nash, Leominster), or "The sheer audacity of it! Playing the symphony 'in its entirety' . . . extended periods with no dialogue whatsoever" (Swee'pea, London; ellipses in original). In a way what is surprising about these comments is the surprise they convey, since what is at issue in them is simply the transference to classical music of the generic conventions of the (pop) music video. The unequal blend of music and narrative that turns the latter into a mere footnote is, after all, a commonplace feature of music videos. Perhaps the classical music video is not as yet sufficiently established to be understood as a genre in its own right.

The most interesting perspective on this issue comes from Liza Marshall in her website interview:

> The actors all found it a very unique job, because . . . there wasn't very much dialogue, so they were pretty much on set all the time, reacting to the music, and while when you normally do a drama, often if you do a close-up the other side of the shot might have disappeared, but they were acting against a 30-strong orchestra.[38]

In an interview included with the press pack distributed by the BBC, Jack Davenport (Prince Lobkowitz) confirms that "our job as actors was to respond to the music, and it seemed more important to me to keep one's responses as fresh as possible. . . . [The] emphasis is very much on what you're hearing rather than what you're seeing."[39]

The approach to *Eroica* that this suggests—that at the film's core lies the visualization of the listening process—has a strong historical grounding in the appropriation of the "Eroica" as the paradigm of a new way of hearing music. Indeed, this emergent listening practice forms an integral component of what Burnham understands as the "heroic" style. Following Burnham, I mentioned the Wagnerian interpretation that turns the "Eroica" into not a representation of Napoleon's heroism but an act of heroism in itself, and the same idea can be taken a step further. As the music unfolds, the listener retraces Beethoven's act of heroism, internalizes the psychological journey that Beethoven traverses, and experiences the growth of character embodied in that heroic journey as the growth of his or her own character. In Burnham's words, "It is here that we start to understand the power of Beethoven's heroic style as an expression of the conditions of selfhood. Of primary importance in this music's projection of the experience of self-consciousness is its ability to enlist our identification, to make us experience its surging course as if it were our own."[40]

Precisely because of its influence on subsequent music, this dynamic quality of the new listening constructed by the "Eroica" is very hard to recapture today. It is reflected in a watered-down form in *Eroica* when, following the breakdown in the first movement, Beethoven tells the orchestra that "the mood shifts all the time," but a famous contemporary review of the symphony by Heinrich Hermann conveys what is at issue much more vividly: "In these extremes and in the frequent and abrupt exchanges of fearful, violent, percussive rebukes with the most ingratiating flowers of melody lies a great part of Beethoven's humor."[41] Although the Romantic subjectivity that Burnham is talking about, with its interiority and sometimes bizarre imagination, is depicted in such contemporary images as Eugène Lami's "On hearing a Beethoven symphony" (1840), Albert Graefle's "Beethoven playing for his friends" (ca. 1877), and Fernand Khnopff's "Listening to Schumann" (1883), it stands to reason that the specifically temporal aspect fundamental to Burnham's argument can be embodied only in *moving* images. We can therefore think of *Eroica* as a reimagining of the new modes of listening that the "Eroica" adumbrated—or of the difficulties it created for contemporary listeners.

Occasionally this surfaces in the dialogue. Josephine, for example, tells Beethoven, "It's so loud, so warlike, the transitions are so abrupt. . . . It frightens me, to be honest." But these modes of listening are primarily conveyed through the many, sometimes very extended shots of individual listeners that form so striking a feature of *Eroica*. The listeners are represented not as a collective, an audience, but as figures isolated from one another and lost in their own experience, in a manner again reminiscent of the contemporary images to which I referred. Not surprisingly, these visualizations of listening loom large on the online bulletin board. Swee'pea refers to "the characters and their relationships entirely conveyed through body language and facial expressions." Peter Wells comments, "I was very impressed with the method used by the director of minimal dialogue and making full use of the actors expressions to show the characters differing emotions—shock, surprise, wonder and an incipient understanding—as the music unfolded" [original spelling]. And Derek Eley, a reviewer of the Edinburgh Film Festival screening, writes that "music, ideas and personalities blend as one, with expressions on the faces of the players and protags transforming the picture into a kind of character ballet."[42]

Eroica goes some way toward providing a complete taxonomy of Romantic listeners, depicting every response from the thoughtful introspection of Lobkowitz to his wife's incessant, wide-eyed bobbing up and down and smiling, from the butler's measured appreciation to the lady's maid's alternation between dolefulness and radiance. As I suggested above, however, Dietrichstein, played by Tim Piggott-Smith, is the only character who really develops in the course of the film, his development taking place as he listens (though for Eley, the association between character development and listening is more general: "While the characters continue to speak like handbooks in the pauses between the movement, their real development takes place when Dear's didactic dialogue stops"). There is one particularly striking shot, lasting more than one-and-a-half minutes, which coincides with measures 124–53 of the second movement. The camera pans to Dietrichstein, who starts walking behind the orchestra, taking up a position behind an oboist (figure 2.1). From now on Dietrichstein stands still, though he occasionally moves his head from side to side; his gaze is abstracted and his eyes are moist. All this while the camera is slowly zooming in. Dietrichstein's epaulettes come into prominent view just as the strident tones of the brass come to dominate the orchestra (around measure 142), perhaps suggesting that it is the catastrophe and vainglory of war that he is thinking of. As the camera continues zooming, Dietrichstein blinks repeatedly and his breathing becomes labored; by the end of the shot he is visibly swallowing back tears (figure 2.2). The depth of emotion embodied—that is, constructed by the signifying body—in this shot makes the recovery of Dietrichstein's aristocratic poise by the end of the movement (when he lectures Beethoven on what a symphony is) the more chillingly impressive.

Liza Marshall specifically comments that "Tim Piggott-Smith . . . has that amazing long close-up where he almost starts crying and then holds it back, which I think was fantastic, and . . . he did that off his own bat."[43] What the camera captures is not something scripted, not something directed as such, but a purely performative act: perhaps not so much Tim Piggott-Smith playing Dietrichstein listening as Tim Piggott-Smith listening right before us, his face becoming a vehicle for the music (when writing the previous paragraph I really wasn't sure whether to refer to "Dietrichstein" or "Piggott-Smith"). There's something uncanny about the transition, during the course of this shot, from the diegetic to what is sometimes called the metadiegetic, as the focus changes from the music being played to the music in Dietrichstein's head. Phil in Glasgow writes, "It has been over a month now since I saw EROICA and I am still haunted not only by the music, but also by the enigmatic facial expressions of the composer, by the perpetual smile of the hostess [Marie], the bewildered and confused expressions of the guest [Dietrichstein]." Almost as if you were looking at yourself in a mirror, watching the full-frontal close-ups leads you to identify with the subjectivity of the actor-listeners, just as they identify with Beethoven's. Rather than the music mediating identification with the characters, as in conventional film music, in the inverted world of *Eroica* the characters mediate identification with the music. (Maybe in reality it works both ways—not only in *Eroica*, but also in conventional film, for we are, after all, equally adept at reading the nuances of facial and musical expression). But of course it is only the comparison with film conventions that makes this identifica-

Figure 2.1 Count Dietrichstein listening to the second movement (m. 125), in *Eroica*.

Figure 2.2 Dietrichstein at measure 149 (*Eroica*).

tory structure seem out of the way. Pop music in the multimedia age is often presented in this manner, with the singer's face (the listener's admittedly less often) being brought into close-up by the camera just as the voice is brought into close-up by the microphone.

Even if one should know better, it is hard not to feel that the close-ups of listening provide a direct access to the historical experience of the "Eroica" in 1804 in a way that Nick Dear's dialogue, enunciated in the impeccably English middle-class tones of BBC costume drama, cannot. (This feeling, as well as the possibly extraneous historical references I discussed earlier, may lie behind Eley's reference to "Dear's didactic dialogue.") It is also tempting to claim that Beethoven's music reveals the real Dietrichstein, as opposed to the disdainful aristocrat who resumes control so quickly after the music stops. (Eley is thinking along similar lines when he claims that Dietrichstein "verbally spars with the young composer while secretly acknowledging his talent.") But maybe these claims seem plausible just because they are part of the mythology that *Eroica* helps to perpetuate. It would, after all, be at least as logical to claim that, just as Dietrichstein's gaze invades the viewer, so the music invades Dietrichstein as an alien presence, and that he becomes himself once again only as the music stops. Seen this way, the film becomes a visualization of music's agency: the music scripts the actors and their interactions, and in doing this it may be seen as creating a utopian community that lasts while the music lasts. There is a telling moment early in the film following on the exchange in which Beethoven claims he's not a land owner but a brain owner. Marie apologetically explains to Dietrichstein that "Our friend thinks his talent exempts him from everyday customs of deference," and Beethoven asks Lobkowitz, "It does, doesn't it?" Lobkowitz replies, "It does, it does," and then adds, "Here it does, anyway." But of course, as long as they are talking, it *doesn't*, even in the Lobkowitz palace, as the various spats between Beethoven and Dietrichstein show only too clearly. It is only when the music begins that the nobility of spirit that Beethoven considers to be conferred on him by his talent becomes equivalent to the nobility by birth that was such a crucial factor in Viennese society at this time; only as long as the music plays can class and social barriers be transgressed. This perhaps explains the uncomfortable transitions from music to silence at the end of the movements, as imagined community gives way to the administered world.

One of the most attractive aspects of *Eroica* is the socialized model of musical listening that it presents. Images like Lami's might be read as depicting a dysfunctional society, as if the price of Romantic subjectivity were solipsistic isolation, which, after all, is precisely what the Romantic/modernist concert hall promoted. There are, as we have seen, extensive passages of introspective listening in *Eroica*, but there are also many instances of interaction between the listeners. By re-creating the aristocratic salon, *Eroica* offers a complementary model of the construction of subjectivity, in which listeners are engaged in a series of ongoing interpersonal negotiations of self that are as much scripted by the music as their more solipsistic experiences. One reviewer refers to "a language of raised eyebrows, sly smiles, and knowing glances," while another writes that "Clandestine meetings and meaningful glances support the music in building bonds between characters, which ebb and flow with the strings and drums, also showing the personal effect the music has on each character as an individual."[44] But I am also talking about something as simple as the way the actor-listeners are constantly walking around during the performance, not only among one another but also among the players. In what might in another context seem an oddly unmotivated comment, Sylvia Morgan of Broadstairs, Kent, writes, "How enjoyable it was to see the actors walking around the musicians as they were playing."[45] At an abstract level one might see this as a visual correlate of the acoustic motions of the music, but it is also (to borrow Eley's word) a kind of ballet in that it gives embodied expression to the musical motions and emotions—it draws out, so to speak, the embodied dimension that is inherent in all music. The effect of dynamic motion is also constructed for the viewer by the constantly moving handheld camera, opening up different paths through both the orchestra and the listeners. D Treasure comments on "the wobbly camera shots giving a sense of events unfolding in the present," while Jasper Huizinga of Groningen writes that "being a TV-maker myself, I was completely blown away by the beautifully fast editing, the quick close-ups, the whirling moves of the camera."[46]

The effect of this constantly dynamic quality—which again might be seen as a more or less straightforward translation to a classical-musical context of the commonplace practices of pop music videos—is to draw the viewer-listener into the film and into the music, encouraging identification with the actor-listeners on the screen, and so creating the sense of really being there, of being part of the music while the music lasts. This is an experience that many of the BBCi commentators want to convey: "the effect was of actually being amongst the orchestra" (Joy Brice, Headcorn, Kent), "It felt as if you were actually there" (Wilf Fenton, Rochester, Kent), "I felt I was actually there" (Peter Sheldon, Milton Keynes). Others combine this experience with the dimension of historical construction to produce a more complex but equally positive judgment: "Best thing was how it made you listen afresh," comments Jonathan Bushrod, and David Morris (UK) speaks of "hearing this wonderful 'new' music for the first time," while Christine Warren (Devon) says—with an ambiguity that I don't think is intended—"I can imagine that at the time it was extraordinary music. Well done. More please."

And this takes me to my final point, which is quite simply how positive the great majority of judgments were. Naturally there were some negative responses, which I reproduce in their entirety: "there was too much in the way of facial expressions and silly grins whilst the music was being played";

"could have done with the countess [presumably the princess] smiling a little less"; "atrocious acting, simpering women, detracted from and added nothing to the sensational music"; "the orchestra held the attention for a slightly longer spell than the dialogue and dreadful acting! Who on earth is the individual playing Beethoven? Beethoven could at times use crudity, but that was in an extremely controlled situation and that was for a specific purpose. There is no record of him blaspheming in front of an orchestra. Of course, I suppose we should be grateful for small mercies that this film was at least one rung up from the evolutionary scale for the BBC from East-enders." But against these four negative responses one can set 122 positive ones, 45 of which included a request that *Eroica* either be rebroadcast or issued on DVD. The following is just a small sample of these responses: "what a masterpiece (and I mean the film)"; "*Eroica* was amazing"; "I would like to say that the film was amazing. It was one of the best dramas I have seen in a long time"; "without doubt the best music film I have seen"; "the best film about Classical Music I've ever seen"; "this is the greatest musical dramatization I have ever seen"; "quite the most brilliant film I've seen in ages"; "undoubtedly the best programme on TV this year"; "this may well be the best thing I've ever seen on TV"; "worth my TV license money for the entire year!"; "once in what these days feels like every millennium or so, something comes up on TV that reminds you what it's like to be human."

Even allowing for the small size and self-selecting nature of the sample, the tone of these comments is striking (which is why I have quoted them verbatim), the more so because many of the viewers were evidently not classical music lovers: "I wasn't expecting to be so entertained by classical music. It was spellbinding"; "I know absolutely nothing about classical music, and hardly ever listen to it . . . but by the end of *Eroica*, I was in tears . . . literally. Unique, revelatory, astounding"; "I loved it, it has made me adore classical music!!!! Thank you BBC!!!"; "I have misjudged such music. Many thanks." Yet I have made no claim that *Eroica* is an exceptionally good piece of cinema in any conventional film-critical terms, let alone a work of particular musicological or critical insight. The conclusion I draw is that this kind of through-the-looking-glass film is a highly effective genre not only in its simultaneous satisfying of musical and narrative desire, but also in its drawing on viewers' literacy in film to support their reading of the now less familiar genre of classical music—as well as its blending of aspects of popular and "art" musical traditions, including the socialized, embodied image of musical listening that it projects. It exactly inverts the method of traditional approaches to music appreciation, with their grounding in Kantian ideas of aesthetic distance. Instead, *Eroica* draws you into the music, transforming passive listening into a kind of virtual participation, and in this way constructing a technologically mediated equivalent of the concert that is arguably more appropriate than the traditional audio recording to a society in which music is predominantly consumed in a multimedia context. If, as Burnham claims, the "Eroica" "stands in a uniquely influential position in the history of Western music,"[47] then maybe *Eroica* can serve the more modest but still significant role of showing how old music may be newly experienced, and so contribute to the classical tradition's continuing search for a viable presence in today's society.

NOTES

1. Catalogue no. OA 0908 D.

2. www.bbc.co.uk/music/classicaltv/eroica/film/. The homepage for *Eroica* is www.bbc.co.uk/music/classicaltv/eroica/. All web materials were accessed on 14 April 2004 unless otherwise noted.

3. Not at home, as stated in the previously quoted synopsis.

4. BBCi interview with Liza Marshall, the producer of *Eroica:* www.bbb.co.uk/music/classicaltv/eroica/film/ (7 July 2006).

5. www.bbc.co.uk/pressoffice/pressreleases/stories/2003/05_may/19/eroica.shtml (19 May 2003).

6. Alain Frogley, "Beethoven's Music in Performance: Historical Perspectives," in Glenn Stanley, ed., *The Cambridge Companion to Beethoven* (Cambridge: Cambridge University Press, 2000), p. 337 n. 11. Not all scholars are quite so sure about the exact numbers; see Tomislav Volek and Jaroslav Macek, "Beethoven's Rehearsals at the Lobkowitz's," *Musical Times* 127 (February 1986), p. 78.

7. The Opus Arte catalogue similarly categorizes *Eroica* under "documentary" and "film" as well as "concert." There is an institutional dimension to these categorizations: according to the press release, *Eroica* was "a unique collaboration between the BBC's Classical Music and Drama departments."

8. It appears that Nick Dear, the screenwriter, follows the account in Thomas Sipe, *Beethoven: Eroica Symphony* (Cambridge: Cambridge University Press, 1998), p. 27, which ascribes the breakdown to Beethoven's syncopations rather than his conducting, as claimed by Ries in *Remembering Beethoven: The Biographical Notes of Franz Wegeler and Franz Ries,* trans. Frederick Noonan (London: André Deutsch, 1988), pp. 68–69. *Eroica* has Beethoven sitting at this point.

9. Ries, *Remembering Beethoven,* p. 69.

10. Wesley, Kent, makes a similar point. All viewers' comments are taken from www.bbc.co.uk/music/classicaltv/eroica/film/comments.shtml. This is the same issue that arises in relation to Wladik Szpilman's performance of Chopin's G-minor Ballade in Polanski's *The Pianist.*

11. BBC press release, www.bbc.co.uk/pressoffice/pressreleases/stories/2003/08_august/ 26/ bbc2_drama_eroica.pdf, p. 31.

12. W. Fenton (Rochester, Kent) asks how Mendelssohn could have been in the tavern at the end when he wasn't born until 1809 (in fact the character in the movie was Johann Mälzel); Paul Rottenberg (USA) complains that Beethoven is seen crumpling up his dedication whereas in reality he scratched through it with his pen (the title page that Ries said was torn in two—not crumpled—has generally been assumed to be from a different copy than the copyist's score Rottenberg is referring to, as discussed as early as the 1860s by Beethoven's biographer Alexander Wheelock Thayer [*Thayer's Life of Beethoven*, rev. and ed. Elliot Forbes (Princeton, NJ: Princeton University Press), 1: 349], though for a dissenting view see Tomislav Volek and Jaroslav Macek, "Beethoven's Rehearsals at the Lobkowitz's," *Musical Times* 127 [February 1986], p. 79). Guido Devos (Vilvoorde, Belgium) claims that "the conversation with Josephine von Deym . . . can't have taken place in that period," which is probably true (see below).

13. Sipe, *Eroica Symphony*, p. 26.

14. According to the BBCi interview clip (www.bbc.co.uk/music/classicaltv/eroica/rams/inthanson3.ram; 7 July 2006) with Peter Hanson, who plays Wranitzky in the film and in real life is leader of L'Orchestre Revolutionnaire et Romantique, the working principle developed during the filming of *Eroica* was that the leader was basically responsible for timekeeping and Beethoven for expression; this is in fact quite plausible historically.

15. This identification is proposed by Siegmund Kaz Nelson and incorporated into Horst Seemann's 1976 film *Beethoven: Tage aus einem Leben*. For more details of Josephine, see Maynard Solomon, *Beethoven Essays* (Cambridge, MA: Harvard University Press, 1988), chapter 11.

16. In a letter of 19 December from Josephine's sister, Charlotte Brunsvik; see Maynard Solomon, *Beethoven* (London: Cassell, 1978), p. 152.

17. Letter 100 in Theodore Albrecht, ed. and trans., *Letters to Beethoven and Other Correspondence*, 3 vols. (Lincoln: University of Nebraska Press, 1996). The letter is undated but assigned by Albrecht to late winter 1905. In *Eroica* Josephine says that if she were to marry Beethoven she would lose custody of her children, since Beethoven has no title. I do not know of a historical source for this assertion (although it nicely links with the theme of nobility of spirit invoked elsewhere in the film), and it is at odds with the general but mistaken belief—largely fostered by Beethoven himself—among the Viennese aristocracy that the Dutch "van' " was equivalent to the German "von," so that Beethoven *was* titled. This misconception was publicly exposed in 1818, when Beethoven's suit against his sister Johanna over the guardianship of his nephew Carl was transferred from the Landrecht (which heard cases involving the aristocracy) to the Magistracy; Solomon, who has written at length on what he calls Beethoven's "nobility pretense," describes this humiliation as "probably a factor in the withdrawal from society that marked his last years" (*Beethoven Essays*, p. 53).

18. Solomon, *Beethoven*, p. 152.

19. Letter 110 in Emily Anderson, ed., *The Letters of Beethoven*, 3 vols. (London: Macmillan, 1961).

20. Carl Czerny, *Erinnerungen aus meinem Leben*, ed. Walter Kolneder (Strasburg: Heitz, 1968), p. 43. Cited in Carl Dahlhaus, *Ludwig van Beethoven: Approaches to His Music*, trans. Mary Whittall (Oxford: Clarendon Press, 1991), p. 167.

21. For this story see Alan Tyson, "Ferdinand Ries (1784–1838): The History of His Contribution to Beethoven Biography," *19th-Century Music* 7 (1984), pp. 218–19.

22. Letter 12 (2 August 1794), in Anderson, ed., *Letters of Beethoven*.

23. Ries, *Remembering Beethoven*, p. 68.

24. Ibid., p. 69.

25. Thayer, *Thayer's Life of Beethoven*, p. 349.

26. Sipe, *Eroica Symphony*, p. 49.

27. Solomon, *Beethoven*, p. 137, writes that in 1804, "To have kept 'Bonaparte'—either as title or as dedication—at a moment when renewed war between France and Austria was imminent would have marked Beethoven as a philo-Jacobin, a supporter of a radical cause and of a hostile power. It would have led not merely to the loss of a patron—for Lobkowitz was an ardent patriot who later raised a battalion of troops to fight the French—but to the probability of reprisals in anti-Revolutionary Austria as well." All this makes Marie Lobkowitz's overt avowal in *Eroica* of everything French even more implausible.

28. Dahlhaus, *Ludwig van Beethoven*, p. 19.

29. According to Countess Lulu von Thurheim, "from morn to night he was occupied by music and squandered a large fortune in order to maintain the most outstanding musicians. . . . He died quite young and left his seven small children nothing but a load of debts." Quoted in Tia DeNora, *Beethoven and the Construction of Genius: Musical Politics in Vienna, 1792–1803* (Berkeley and Los Angeles: University of California Press, 1996), p. 196 n. 5.

30. At the Cumulus, when the orchestra stops, a young footman asks the lady's maid what is going on; she has no idea, but the butler explains, "Horn came in too early."

31. Sipe, *Eroica Symphony*, pp. 76, 85, and elsewhere.

32. Scott Burnham, *Beethoven Hero* (Princeton, NJ: Princeton University Press, 1995), p. xv.

33. Translated from "Ein glücklicher Abend' " in Burnham, *Beethoven Hero*, p. xv.

34. For all except Sullivan, see Sipe, *Eroica Symphony*, pp. 63–77; for Sullivan, see John William Navin Sullivan, *Beethoven: His Spiritual Development* (London: Jonathan Cape, 1927).

35. Burnham, *Beethoven Hero*, p. xvi.

36. Dahlhaus, *Ludwig van Beethoven*, p. 25.

37. Burnham, *Beethoven Hero*, p. xiii.

38. www.bbc.co.uk/music/classicaltv/eroica/rams/intliza_actors.ram.

39. BBC press release, www.bbc.co.uk/pressoffice/pressreleases/stories/2003/08_august/26/bbc2_drama_eroica.pdf, p. 36.

40. Burnham, *Beethoven Hero*, p. 24.

41. Quoted in Sipe, *Eroica Symphony*, p. 58. The review was published in the

Morgenblatt für die gebildete Stände under the pseudonym Ernst Woldemar; this passage refers specifically to the E-minor "new theme" in the first movement.

42. www.keepmedia.com (subscription required).

43. www.bbc.co.uk/music/classicaltv/eroica/rams/intliza_actors.ram.

44. Reviews by Trinity, www.iofilm.co.uk/fm/e/eroica_2003.shtml, and Terresa Gaffney, www.thezreview.co.uk/reviews/e/eroica.htm.

45. This, perhaps regrettably, is one of the film's less historical aspects. Volek and Macek ("Beethoven's Rehearsals at the Lobkowitz's," p. 77) document that in the Lobkowitz hall the musicians' area was divided from the audience's by a balustrade with grilles. There were twelve large and six small benches, with backrests, for the audience.

46. Inevitably, what one viewer particularly likes another particularly dislikes: jocelyne-4, another reviewer of the Edinburgh Film Festival screening, writes, "If only the Director had resisted the temptation to spin round the viewers as they watched!" (www.imdb.com/title/tt0369400/usercomments). The director of photography was the well-known Barry Ackroyd, who himself writes of *Eroica* that, "We wanted a nice period look but there's some quite jagged camera work using zooms and tracking and wild, free-form camerawork. I worked closely with the grip and the focus puller and just went with the music" ("Words & Music: Barry Ackroyd BSC Reflects on Two Very Different New Projects—*Eroica* for TV and *Ae Fond Kiss* for cinema," *Exposure* 26, Autumn 2003 [Fujifilm Motion Picture and Professional Video], p. 17, www.motion.fuji.co.uk/resources/pdf/EXPO%2326%20p16–17%20Ackroyd.pdf).

47. Burnham, *Beethoven Hero*, p. xvi, referring specifically to the first movement.

3 Minima Romantica

SUSAN McCLARY

About fifty minutes into *The Hours*, the luxuriant strains of Richard Strauss's *Four Last Songs* suddenly intrude on what had established itself as a minimalist soundtrack. The scene begins as Louis (Jeff Daniels) rings a doorbell, and the cut that takes us into an apartment belonging to Clarissa (Meryl Streep) coincides with the full-volume sound of a soprano who has just reached the middle of the third song, "Beim Schlafengehn" (Going to Sleep).[1]

Clarissa is preparing a party for her dying friend, Richard (Ed Harris), and her choice of background music helps establish her cultivated tastes, even as it resonates thematically with the existential questions that hover over the film as a whole, and with the hope to which she still clings in the face of impossible odds. For a while, the two characters try to converse over the ecstatic music, their mutual discomfort discordant against the sounds that engulf them. But Louis's untimely intrusion has effectively shattered Clarissa's carefully constructed cocoon. She snaps off the CD player just as Strauss's Soul gets ready to take its final flight into the beyond—at the end of measure 55, to be exact—and both her character and those of us who observe her find ourselves unceremoniously dumped back into the real world that refuses to ratify such illusions as Strauss's music offers.[2]

This brief and purposely disorienting moment explicitly recalls how subjectivity used to sound in films. We have long counted on those surging melodic lines to produce a sense of infinite longing; they enable us to believe we can transcend present conditions, spiraling ever upward toward a promise of perfect bliss. The passage excerpted here (ex. 3.1) comes on the heels of a tonally fraught passage with lyrics that describe the workaday world, in comparison with which the image of soaring seems extraordinarily effortless and confident. Although the orchestra revels in ever-rising

Example 3.1 Richard Strauss, "Beim Schlafengehn," mm. 38–60.

arpeggios during these measures, the harmonies change but rarely—and almost always in ways that trace the most basic of cadential patterns. Twice (in mm. 48–49 and m. 56) the chords swerve temporarily into chromatic inflections, thereby producing a quality of mystery (we cannot arrive at transcendence by our own hook) and endowing the reappearance of diatonic certainty with an even greater sense of plenitude. And it is that all-but-guaranteed arrival at plenitude that Clarissa so rudely disrupts.

Musical procedures such as Strauss's reached film by way of émigré European musicians, who drew pragmatically on their training in nineteenth-century German symphonic composition when they came to writing soundtracks. But their music's grounding in Romanticism also offered spectators a means of escape into a mythologized and culturally elite past. Think of the very ordinary lovers in David Lean's *Brief Encounter,* whose location in a grimy railway-station tea shop is transformed for the spectator with the entry of Rachmaninoff's Second Concerto: the dreariness of modern industrial life—the commuter train for Lean's lovers, a mechanically reproduced medium for their viewers—drop from consciousness with those strains of utopia. If Lean maps those sounds onto erotic desire, mainstream cinema employs them to back up and intensify all manner of aspirations: the child striving to make his bicycle take off into the air in *E.T.* or Whoopi Goldberg struggling for human dignity in the rural South. (*The Color Purple,* incidentally, owes its soundtrack not to some displaced central European but to Quincy Jones, who started his career working with Ray Charles but who here demonstrates that he can also construct standard cinematic interiority through gestures closer to those of Mahler's *Songs of a Wayfarer* than of "Hit the Road, Jack.")

Nineteenth-century symphonies and narrative fiction share many structural and ideological values, making their collaboration in multimedia cinema seem nearly predetermined. Both aspire to deliver the illusion of seamless continuity, to portray the trajectory of a subject overcoming obstacles and securing ultimate goals as though by inevitable means of cause and effect. But, as many critics have pointed out, this apparent inevitability results from the careful imbrication of fragments, none of which boasts anything resembling continuity. With respect to film, we often find long gaps intervening between snippets of music, images on the screen that jump between scenes, and even rapid-fire camera reversals that signal shifting points of view. But a skilled filmmaker, like a composer or writer, works to make us unaware of the discontinuities: music fills the spaces between visual cuts, dialogue covers up the gradual fading out of musical passages, and the sound of the orchestra swells to enhance the approach of narrative climax. Taken together, sound and sight in film still follow the standard nineteenth-century model of centered subjectivity in both protagonists and spectators.

I hasten to mention at this point that neither the music nor the fiction of the nineteenth century held exclusively to the convention described here; indeed, much of the art we most respect deliberately rebelled against it. Franco Moretti and Fredric Jameson, for instance, have traced the ways nineteenth-century novelists explored other possibilities.[3] Moreover, composers as far back as Beethoven and Schubert (to say nothing of Schumann with his ironic fragments) recognized the mendacity of such narratives and experimented with alternatives.[4] But Beethoven would not have found it necessary to dismantle the ideals of his own heroic period nor Flaubert to sling mud at sentimental novels if both artists had not realized how firmly entrenched and deeply internalized those paradigms were. And despite their now-canonized attempts at deconstruction, those very conventions have survived intact in genre fiction and mainstream cinema.

Except for the brief moment of diegetic music in *The Hours* analyzed above, the film scores discussed in this chapter avoid the direct channeling of the Romanticism that has long stood as the lingua franca of mainstream cinema. Indeed, all three do so even though their express mission is to provide the backdrops for stories set in the nineteenth or early twentieth centuries. If film-music composers have long been transporting us aurally back to the nineteenth century to guarantee the authenticity of modern interiority, the musicians I consider here—Alexander Balanescu in *Angels and Insects*, Michael Nyman in *The Piano*, and Philip Glass in *The Hours*—reinterpret their historical periods with the musical procedures of contemporary minimalism.

More than one professional musician has assured me that these composers do so because, as minimalists, they simply do not know any better. I find that explanation difficult to endorse, given the obvious sophistication of all three scores. Yet the ubiquity of minimalism in the soundtracks of our present lives—in everything from hip-hop and electronic dance music to advertisements and the environmental sound piped into upscale restaurants—suggests that we have come to accept such musical processes as natural;[5] indeed, we may not even hear them as meaning anything at all, just as fish fail to notice the water that surrounds them. A more interesting version, then, of the skeptical position presented at the beginning of this paragraph might have it that minimalist composers just make use of the current lingua franca, just as their predecessors relied automatically on their most familiar idiom—that of German Romanticism. The symphonic tradition drawn upon by Max Steiner and his contemporaries, however, came already equipped with shared codes of signification and implicit ideals of selfhood. The flat-line procedures of minimalism frequently seem to have pulled the plug not only on that particular outmoded language, but also on the very notion of signification in music. Can one—better, *should* one—hear such procedures as meaning anything other than refusal?

I believe quite firmly that all cultural practices—minimalism included—engage with meaning, even if those involved persist in denial.[6] A minimalist score that wants to retreat to the status of wallpaper (for instance, Brian Eno's *Music for Airports,* 1978) still has cultural implications. Moreover, none of the scores that concern me in this chapter aspires to self-erasure. Instead, each foregrounds other aspects of those earlier times and their inhabitants, even as they also shed light on our own reflex reactions to the Romantic idiom that film music has rendered virtually universal. This agenda is not restricted to film music, for the composers I am dealing with here have also produced concert music that comments upon or deconstructs the earlier idiom by means of minimalist procedures—in, for instance, Nyman's reworking of Schumann's *Dichterliebe* in his opera *The Man Who Mistook His Wife for a Hat;* the collaborations between Nyman and Balanescu; or countless pieces by Glass, especially *Glassworks,* the tactics of which reverberate in all three soundtracks.[7]

In *Glassworks,* Glass simulates the bruised interiority and the longing for transcendence treasured in both nineteenth-century music and its film-music descendents—note the way the A$^\flat$ in Strain 3 of "Opening" (ex. 3.2, second measure)[8] produces a dominant seventh that should resolve to E$^\flat$ major. Instead of proceeding down to G, however, the A$^\flat$ becomes a new point of reference, allowing the entire complex to surge upward—now perhaps aspiring toward D$^\flat$ major. The B$^\flat$ in the bass of the final measure yearns to incite another move forward. But rather than pursue that trajectory, Glass just circles back mechanically, always just at the moment where the Soul ought to take flight. In contrast to Clarissa, who just snaps off her recording, he constructs a loop of causes that do not yield their promised effect. As he simulates those pleasures and longings but refuses to grant their final assurances, he positions us as heirs to the great tradition, now woefully bereft of its comforts.

Angels and Insects (1995), a film directed by Philip Haas based on a novella by A. S. Byatt, follows the unhappy encounter between an entomologist fresh from research in the Amazon basin and an inbred family of English aristocrats. Both novella and film carry a burden of heavy-handed symbol-

Example 3.2 Philip Glass, *Glassworks,* "Opening" (Strain 3).

[con Ped.]

ism—clothing made to resemble the markings of butterflies, domestics who swarm silently about the house, a matriarch who looks like a bloated maggot, mutant children, and the open secret of incest. Alexander Balanescu's music underscores the self-absorbed, instinctual, insectlike culture of this elite but decadent family, tipping us off aurally to the fact that we're dealing here with a human ant colony. Whether in scenes involving courtship or those merely showing the bustling servants, a motive made up of sighing two-note appoggiaturas creates a quality of obsessive desire that seeps from the walls, that permeates everything.

Of course, this musical sign of desire dates back at least as far as eighteenth-century representations of sentiment, and it throbs throughout Romantic scores (recall especially the horns in Tchaikovsky's *Romeo and Juliet,* deftly parodied by Marty Feldman's melancholy horn solo in Mel Brooks's *Young Frankenstein*). At times, for instance, when the music accompanies the hapless scientist as he falls in love with the daughter of the manor, the music functions in standard ways to suture the spectator to his aspirations; we are encouraged by the appoggiaturas to long for the (standard) satisfaction of his (standard) desires.

But in Balanescu's minimalist saturation of his score with the two-note appoggiatura, the figure also calls attention to itself as a musical trope. As it intrudes into apparently neutral scenes, we might well wonder why the music keeps insisting on "desire" when we see nothing but children playing or servants going about their menial tasks. In fact, we might even start to wonder whether or not the music is intended to signify *at all,* so prevalent are its gestures.

Adorno once described gesture in Wagner's music as producing "the embarrassing feeling that someone is constantly tugging at [one's] sleeve,"[9] and Balanescu's score produces just this effect. Are we supposed to be yearning urgently for something—or are we supposed to ignore that obsessive pattern as so much sonic filler? Postmodernist modes of consuming classical music (Beethoven's "Eroica" thundering forth its heroic struggle on deaf ears as we sip lattes at Starbucks) reward us for writing the music off as mere sound devoid of significance. Don't say Adorno didn't warn us![10]

Balanescu apparently wants it both ways, however. If his strategies sometimes incline us to bracket the music off as simple minimalist background, he also rewards the listener who continues to assume that it *does* signify something. As the entomologist begins to figure out what everyone else has always known—that his wife's brother has sired all those albino children he calls his own (insect = incest, which has to be spelled out for him explicitly in the course of a Scrabble game)—the odd ubiquity of desire mechanisms throughout the soundtrack suddenly becomes terribly meaningful. Anyone who has chosen to tune the music out thus becomes a dupe along with the protagonist. The hermeneutic paranoid who always suspects a hidden web of connections is here (as so often) fully justified.

Balanescu also allows this obsessive motive to worm its way into the tunes played at the party in the opening sequence and at the later wedding scene. For these occasions, the composer delivers identifiably nineteenth-century music genres, though he pulls them into the symbolic economy of the film through their minimalist reworkings. Played by an actual string quartet in full view of guests, these waltzes and marches both signal period music and also remind us of the repetitive, ritualistic, and alien world here depicted—no less repetitive, ritualistic, and alien, by implication, than the drumming that accompanies the orgiastic ceremonies of Amazonian tribes shown during the opening credits.[11] Just as the stylized, buglike costumes deny us the fantasy of a sumptuous Merchant Ivory past, so even the presumably diegetic music in the soundtrack prevents us from escaping the claustrophobic setting of *Angels and Insects*.

Michael Nyman's score for Jane Campion's *The Piano* (1992) similarly blurs the distinction between the diegetic and nondiegetic, but for a more particular reason: Ada (Holly Hunter), the mute principal character, refuses to communicate in sound except by means of her piano—that most weighty of bourgeois cultural signifiers, which she has brought with her to the wilds of New Zealand in the mid-nineteenth century. At times her playing represents only the aura of household civility expected of nineteenth-century women; she accompanies her daughter's singing and contributes entertainment for social occasions. But Ada's music also serves as her only expressive outlet, and it hints at the passionate interiority that seethes behind her impassive face. Much of the film's plot turns on the ambiguous status of her performances. Is Ada just making music? Or are we supposed to hear her playing as aural evidence of her literally unspeakable desires? Again, our experience with cinematic underscores predisposes us to respond to her performances as offering emotional cues, especially when Nyman allows her music to slip its leash and flood the soundtrack with orchestral elaboration. Moreover, the characters within the film also express confusion over the meaning of her playing.

In one hilarious scene, the unexpected vehemence of her playing unsettles the priggish church ladies who surround her in her new alien setting. As the ladies scurry home through the forest, the one they call Auntie has her Maori servants surround her while she squats to piss, during which activity she opines:

> You know, I'm thinking of the piano. She does not play the piano as we do, Miss. (Up! Up!) [She frets at her servants to keep their screen up.] No, she is a strange creature. And her playing is strange. Like a mood that passes into you. (Up!) Now your playing is plain and true, and that is what I like. To have a sound creep inside you is not at all pleasant. [A bird flies up suddenly, frightening her away as she struggles to pull up her undergarments.][12]

A trenchant cultural critique if ever there was one!

More important, Ada's new husband (Sam Neill) and his foreman, George Baines (Harvey Keitel), find it difficult to distinguish between her performance and her essence. George gets his first glimpse of Ada's rich interiority when he takes her back to the beach where her Broadwood piano sits abandoned; for the first time, this sullen, withdrawn woman smiles and surrenders herself to sensual enjoyment. And here we hear the movie's principal theme—the one everyone bought on CD or even in sheet-music form so as to play it over and over again in the living room.

Similarly, George cannot get enough of the tune: he purchases the piano and has the Maoris drag it home so that he might have private access to Ada's playing and its implicit physical analogue. Their courtship advances as a carefully structured erotic game in which she gets access to her piano in exchange for escalating sexual favors. As Nyman puts it, Ada's music "has to convey the messages she is putting across about her feelings towards Baines, during the piano lessons, and these differ from lesson to lesson as the relationship, state of sexual bargaining and passion develop."[13] As the relationship escalates, she shakes her head in refusal even as the metaphors conveyed by her music, surpassing George's wildest longings, cry "yes." In this, the film's positioning of music as an irresistible aphrodisiac recalls Tolstoy's "The Kreutzer Sonata."[14]

Although Nyman may be best known to film aficionados through his contributions to Peter Greenaway's austere postmodernist films, he composed Ada's music (actually played in the film by Hunter herself) with the express intention of simulating period music.

> Initially I was unsure as to how precisely to pitch the style: it had to be a "possible" mid-nineteenth century music but not pastiche and obviously written in 1992. But then I had the perception that, since Ada was from Scotland, it was logical to use Scottish folk and popular songs as the basis for our music. Once I hit on that idea the whole thing fell into place.[15]

Yet Nyman's circular procedures—however much they throb with passion—also sound obsessive and trapped. In many respects, his music for Ada recalls Glass's *Glassworks,* down to its self-divided, two-against-three figuration in the accompaniment and its futile attempts at escaping into a different reality.

Still, Ada's tunes stand as explicitly nineteenth-century artifacts up against the even more severely minimalist music that surrounds her—music that registers with Ada's mundane existence, with the drudgery that drives her into the refuge of her piano. We hear this contrast right at the beginning of the film when her voice-over describes her refusal to speak and her arranged marriage to an unknown man in New Zealand. A low, dissonant blur, reminiscent of Brian Eno's meltdowns,[16] and a passage of agitated appoggiaturas proceed until Ada pierces that drab sonic background with her practicing, thus affording both herself and us some relief. Schubert's "An die Musik" speaks precisely of this function of domestic music making: "Thou holy art, in how many grey hours have you brought my heart into a better world!" Except that Ada's music lacks the ability—even when it expresses yearning—to produce transcendence or repose. In weaving together various dialects of minimalism and gestures reminiscent of the Romantic piano repertory, Nyman effectively produces a contemporary critique of nineteenth-century aesthetic ideals and illusions.

At the end of the film, after her husband has chopped off one of her fingers to silence her means of communicating aurally with her lover, Ada departs with George in an open boat rowed by Maoris. Suddenly she demands that the piano be cast into the sea, and as it plunges to the depths, its ropes pull her down with it. She appears to choose her instrument and death as an alternative to a fraught, tedious existence stripped of dreams. But then she opts for life and, kicking the ropes off, she rises to George, a prosthetic finger, and even a brave reentry into speech and normal social interactions. For the piano had ultimately granted not escape but rather imprisonment of a different kind, and its music had always implied as much. Still, as the final credits roll, we are immersed in the lushly orchestrated strains of the minimalist Romanticism that made this soundtrack a best-selling album. Who said false consciousness—even when marked as such—wasn't profitable?

As an epigraph to his novel *The Hours,* Michael Cunningham quotes Virginia Woolf in one of her diaries: "I should say a good deal about The Hours, & my discovery; how I dig out beautiful caves behind my characters; I think that gives exactly what I want; humanity, humour, depth. The idea is that the caves shall connect, & each comes to daylight at the present moment."[17] And in the final voice-over in the film, Woolf refers again to "the hours" as those units of time human beings strive to endure and yet somehow treasure. When Cunningham's book went into film production, the author requested that Philip Glass, a longtime favorite of his, compose the soundtrack. To Cunningham's delight, Glass accepted the commission (he received his second Academy Award nomination for his efforts).[18]

Glass saw his job as lending cohesion to the film's three tangentially connected stories concerning women from three historical moments:[19] Woolf herself during the 1930s and '40s (Nicole Kidman), a housewife in 1950s suburban Los Angeles (Julianne Moore), and a contemporary book editor living in New York (Meryl Streep). It is Glass's music that gives the caves behind the characters affective depth and that also connects them, as all three pass through existential crises that force them to weigh the value of staying alive or choosing death. As did Nyman, Glass opted for the luxuriant orchestra of classic cinema, along with the piano in a concerto texture that pits the heroic, slightly alienated solo instrument against the social group. The sounds themselves, in other words, satisfy the traditional expectation for period trappings, even as his minimalist procedures constantly deny the comfort offered by conventionally romantic film scores. Indeed, the redundancy of the score—however much it might simulate nineteenth-century emotional qualities—grounds us in the quotidian, in the present moment of duration rather than trajectories aimed at transcendence.

Like Cunningham and his characters, Glass's music suggests that we have nothing beyond sheer survival of the hours that measure out our lives. His score works from the same set of harmonic gestures in *Glassworks* discussed earlier: concentrated references to the Romantic signs of hope and yearning, always doubling back to resignation. In fact, in one of the most poignant scenes in the film, he has Richard give Clarissa and us a lesson in postmodernist semiotics, as Glass's harmonic changes match precisely with the alternations between aspiration and despair in Richard's speech, making it function like operatic recitative.

I have devised a notational schema below that tries to capture the interactions between the dialogue and music during this scene. Glass relies on three very simple—indeed, minimal—yet affectively potent tactics. First (ex. 3.3), a baseline of G minor, which registers as a constant throughout the entire scene, enters in layers. When Richard states, "I seem to have fallen out of time," the figure of a rising fourth appears, then persists as an ostinato. These fourths could function in either major or minor contexts, and their ascending direction even produces a literally upbeat feel, though this same gesture also resembles the sound of fretful anxiety, much like that associated with Richard as a child ("Bug") in the Los Angeles segments of the film. When Clarissa responds to Richard, a drone on the lower octave appears—perhaps to calm Richard's implicit panic, but also planting the inexorable keynote. With the innocuous phrase "S'only a party," the determining mediant enters, confirming G minor—not G major (an equal possibility until now)—as the emotional world within which the rest of the scene will unfold. (I have marked "Gm" on the right edge of the page wherever this G minor pedal obtains.)

Glass's second pattern (ex. 3.4) presents a slight inflection of the pervasive G-minor backdrop. An inner voice moves from D to E♭, thus producing a major-triad sonority and thus a brief ray of hope. Either chord—G minor or E♭₆—harmonizes perfectly well with the very slight melodic fragments that weave above it, but even so minute a change brings relief to this unbearably depressed scene. We hear this maneuver clearly when Richard delivers his line (so central to helping us link this story with the one featuring Virginia Woolf): "Ah, Mrs. Dalloway!" The inflection marks his ironic attempt at levity, but he comes right back to G-minor reality with the word "silence."

Every time it appears, this alternation offers some modicum of comfort before collapsing back, for neither of the characters believes at all in the hope they try to convey to each other in their voices and faces. After a while, the alternation begins to sound almost like the intake and release of air in a dying patient. Note especially how this musical strategy operates in its setting of Clarissa's apparently optimistic line, "This is a group of people who want to tell you your work is going to [sudden plunge back to G minor] live." No wonder Richard responds with such cynicism!

The third pattern (ex. 3.5) seems more dramatic compared to the other two, neither of which offers any actual motion in the bass. Just after Rich-

Example 3.3 Pattern 1.

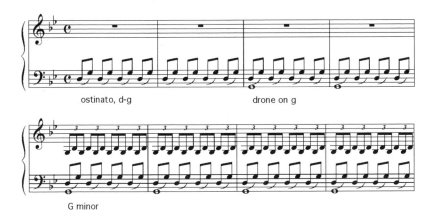

ostinato, d-g   drone on g

G minor

Example 3.4 Pattern 2.

G minor   E♭₆   G minor   G minor   E♭₆   G minor

ard's "Mrs. Dalloway" line, the music announces a change in topic. The bass moves forthrightly down from G to F, set as a major triad. That harmony could function to take us to, say, B♭ major or any number of other places. In any case, it uproots us from the paralytic state the music had fallen into before this moment. After a short while, it moves on through a chromatic twist to a chord on D—also major in quality but now pressured with a lingering seventh toward resolution . . . to G minor. In other words, despite what initially seems like genuine progress, the pattern loops back quickly and as if inevitably to the place from which it had seemed to rescue us. Although Clarissa first introduces this pattern, it appears most consistently in Richard's extended speech, its principal meanings most clear in his description of his aspirations as a writer. Perhaps most poignantly, Glass brings it in yet again right after Richard has said, "I failed." And here Richard turns the full force of this set of harmonic tricks against himself. Glass pulls the plug on the musical respirator as the music stops cold halfway through Richard's last sentence: "We want everything [end music], don't we?"

Example 3.5 Pattern 3.

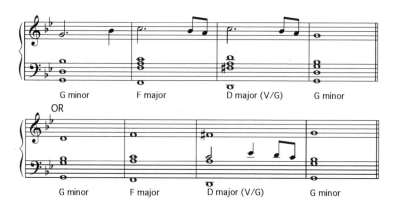

G minor   F major   D major (V/G)   G minor

OR

G minor   F major   D major (V/G)   G minor

R: I seem to have fallen out of time.   [ostinato, d-g]

C: Richard, Richard! It's a party.   [add drone on g]

    S'only a party.   [add triplets, g-b♭]

    Populated entirely by people who respect and admire you.   [Gm]

R: Uh! Small party, is it? Select party, is it?   [Gm]

C: Your friends.   [Gm]

R: I thought I had lost all my friends. I thought I drove my friends crazy.   [Gm]

C: [chuckles wearily] Jesus . . .   [Gm]

R: Ah, Mrs. Dalloway!   Always giving parties to cover the silence.

    Gm_____ E♭₆_____ Gm___

C: . . . . Richard! You won't need to do anything.

    F_____ V/G_____ Gm_____

    All you have to do is appear, sit on the sofa. And I will be there.

    (Gm)_____

    This is a group of people who want to tell you your work is going to live.

    E♭₆_____ Gm__

R: Is it? Is my work going to live? I can't go through with it, Clarissa.

    (Gm)_____ E♭₆_____

C: Oh, why do you say that?

    (E♭₆)_____ Gm_____

R: I can't.   [Gm]

C: Why?   [Gm]

R: Because I wanted to be a writer. That's all.   [Gm]

C: So?   [Gm]

R: I wanted to write about it all.   Everything that happens in a moment.
(Gm)_____ FM_____ V/G__
The way the flowers looked when you carried them in your arms.
(V/G)_____
This towel, how it smells, how it . . . feels, this thread.
(V/G)_____ Gm_____
All our feelings, yours and mine.   [Gm]
The history of it, who we once were.   [Gm]
Everything in the world,   everything all mixed up, like it's all mixed up now
(Gm)_____ E♭₆_____ Gm_____
. . . . . And I failed . . . . I failed.
E♭₆_____ Gm_____ FM_____
No matter what you start with, it ends up being so much less.
(FM)_____ V/G__
Sheer fucking pride.   And stupidity. We want everything, don't we?
(V/G)_____ Gm_____//

The situation may recall another famous AIDS aria in recent film: Tom Hanks's tour-de-force *scena* in *Philadelphia*.[20] In *Philadelphia*, however, the character inhabits an actual Romantic operatic excerpt—an aria from Umberto Giordano's *Andrea Chenier* as sung by Maria Callas—that produces the standard catharsis Hollywood has conditioned us to expect. (Within the film, this excerpt has the effect of purging the Denzel Washington character of his homophobia, as its haunting strains follow him home, causing him to see even his relationship with his own wife and child with fresh eyes.) If *The Hours* had followed suit, Richard would have had Strauss's "Beim Schlafengehn" playing in the background to amplify his essential heroism in the face of death. Instead, Glass inflects Richard's speech with the music that runs throughout the rest of the soundtrack; the music acknowledges his emotional contradictions, but it withholds the catharsis both we and the characters so deeply crave.

Only one instance in the soundtrack to *The Hours* violates the stoic minimalism it otherwise espouses. Near the end—after we have witnessed over the course of the film so many temptations to suicide—Clarissa retreats to her bedroom. Her lover (*West Wing*'s Allison Janney) enters to comfort her, and the two suddenly join in an intense, life-affirming kiss. As they do so, the music subsides into a kind of resolution, the major-key ending so loved by the Romantics and traditional filmgoers. Alas, the next scene and its music take us back into the film's ambiguities. But, for that brief moment, the vacillation halts and the power of domestic love triumphs. That Glass bends his own stylistic rules in order to give us this slight glimpse of repose (and does so in the context of a lesbian household) makes it all the more remarkable.

The final sequence of *The Hours*—brief moments focusing on each of the women followed over the course of the film—is stitched together affectively by means of Glass's music, which forges links (to use Woolf's image) between their individual caves. Two of the characters choose life, two choose death, but all of them live inevitably in that ambiguous emotional world articulated first in *Glassworks*. At the conclusion of the credits, the music subsides again to that sustained minor-key triad that has made up so much of the soundtrack throughout. It ends, in other words, with the musical equivalent of an ellipsis.

So how does subjectivity sound (or feel) today? Audiences have not outgrown their fondness for over-the-top climactic fervor, which still appears with great regularity in contemporary film (recall the scores for *Lord of the Rings* or *The Last Samurai*, for example). But even if we still respond like Pavlov's dog when we hear a rising sequence, most of us also know that such music and its gestural vocabulary date from a bygone era. Much cultural water has flowed under the bridge in the last hundred years, and other ways of experiencing the Self came along with twelve-tone music and minimalism, to say nothing of blues, jazz, and rock. Consequently, we have learned how to respond to, say, atonality in films set in angst-filled Prague or hip-hop in south-central Los Angeles.

But all three of my films fly in the face not only of the music usually identified with romance, but also of the conventions connecting historical period with musical genre. The composers thereby perform translations between contemporary musical sensibilities and the very era that gave us full-blown Romantic scoring. In cloaking their historical characters in minimalist garb, they invite us to rethink deeply ingrained notions of the nineteenth century, conditioned responses to sound in cinema, and even our conceptions of selfhood.

Of the three films discussed in this chapter, *The Hours* would seem to be the one most concerned with bringing narrative and musical structures together in ways that modify standard assumptions concerning selfhood. It is no coincidence that Nyman's lush score for *The Piano* plays into traditional cinematic values, for Campion's Romantic script does as well. So closely does Nyman's music mimic nineteenth-century idioms that few viewers even identified it as minimalist. He produces, in other words, a very effective hybrid between period music and contemporary styling, reveling in postmodernism's overturning of serialism's prohibition against tonality and its gestures. Balanescu's ingenious score might have fared better in a film a little less committed to symbolic overkill. He tempts this viewer, in any case, just to shout: "Yes, I get it!"

Glass's score for *The Hours*, however, constantly invites us to wish for a deus ex machina to deliver us from the existential dilemmas of everyday existence. It draws on those strains of utopia we have internalized to induce hope. But like Cunningham's novel and Daldry's film, Glass's music makes us aware of the impossibility of having those dreams ever truly realized. Still, like Richard in his monologue or Virginia Woolf at her desk, he encourages us to believe in the need for aspiration, without which life would be genuinely unbearable. Richard and Virginia do not commit suicide to the blazing glory of Strauss's "Beim Schlafengehn," and perhaps that makes their range of choices all the more resonant with our own.

John Mowitt has suggested that the arch cynicism of postmodernism might count as yet another variety of transcendence. Although this attitude does not promise the escape from everyday reality that Romanticism does, it certainly qualifies as a stance that confirms the anti-Romantic toughness to which many of us now subscribe. In the words of Argentine novelist Ernesto Sabato, in his classic *Sobre Héroes y Tumbas* (On Heroes and Tombs):

> Pessimists are recruited among former optimists, since in order to have a black picture of the world it is necessary to have previously believed in that world and its possibilities. And it is an even more curious and paradoxical fact that pessimists, once they have been disillusioned, are not constantly and systematically filled with despair, but rather seem prepared, in a manner of speaking, to renew their hope at each and every instant, although by virtue of a sort of metaphysical modesty they conceal this fact beneath their black envelope of men suffering from a universal bitterness—as though pessimism, in order to keep itself strong and ever-vigorous, needed from time to time the impetus provided by a new cruel disillusionment.[21]

NOTES

1. Text by Hermann Hesse: "And my soul, unguarded, will soar on widespread wings, to dwell deeply and thousand-fold in the magic realm of night." Strauss composed these songs in 1948, the year before his death. The song is here performed by

Jessye Norman (soprano), with the Gewandhaus Orchestra, Leipzig, conducted by Kurt Masur. The orchestral reduction is mine.

2. *The Hours,* directed by Stephen Daldry (Miramax, 2002), track 11.

3. Franco Moretti, *The Way of the World: The* Bildungsroman *in European Culture* (London: Verso, 1987), and Fredric Jameson, *The Political Unconscious: Narrative as a Socially Symbolic Act* (Ithaca, NY: Cornell University Press, 1981).

4. For a more extensive treatment of this issue, see my *Conventional Wisdom: The Content of Musical Form* (Berkeley and Los Angeles: University of California Press, 2000), chapter 4.

5. See Robert Fink, *Repeating Ourselves: American Minimal Music as Cultural Practice* (Berkeley and Los Angeles: University of California Press, 2005).

6. See my "Rap, Minimalism, and Structures of Time in Late Twentieth-Century Music," *The Geske Lecture* (Lincoln: University of Nebraska Press, 1999), and *Conventional Wisdom,* chapter 5.

7. Michael Nyman, *The Man Who Mistook His Wife for a Hat* (1987); Nyman with Alexander Balanescu, *Zoo Caprices* (1986); Philip Glass, *Glassworks* (1982). For more on these effects in *Glassworks,* see my *Conventional Wisdom,* pp. 142–45.

8. Dunvagen Music Publishers.

9. Theodor W. Adorno, *In Search of Wagner,* trans. Rodney Livingstone (London: NLB, 1981), p. 35.

10. Adorno's critiques of music in the age of mechanical reproduction center on his position that too easy access has the effect of rendering music meaningless. See, for instance, his "On the Fetish-Character in Music and the Regression of Listening" (1938), in Theodor W. Adorno, *Essays on Music,* ed. Richard Leppert (Berkeley and Los Angeles: University of California Press, 2002), pp. 288–317.

11. The minimalist "tribal" music is provided by Mauro Refosco.

12. *The Piano* (Miramax, 1992), track 28 (1:28:30–1:30:10).

13. Michael Nyman, "The Composer's Note," in *The Piano, Original Compositions for Solo Piano* (London: Chester Music, 1993), p. 5.

14. See Richard Leppert, *The Sight of Sound: Music, Representation, and the History of the Body* (Berkeley and Los Angeles: University of California Press, 1993); and Lawrence Kramer, *After the Lovedeath: Sexual Violence and the Making of Culture* (Berkeley and Los Angeles: University of California Press, 1997).

15. Nyman, "The Composer's Note," p. 5.

16. Compare this, for instance, with Eno's treatment of the Pachelbel Canon in D in his *Discreet Music* (1975).

17. Michael Cunningham, *The Hours* (New York: Picador, 1998), epigraph; *The Diary of Virginia Woolf, Vol. II (1920–1924),* ed. Quentin Bell and Angelica Garnett (New York: Harcourt Brace & Company, 1978), entry for August 30, 1923. Cunningham's claims that Glass's "music is, to some degree, part of everything I've written."

18. Notes by Cunningham in CD of the soundtrack for *The Hours* (Nonesuch 79693–2, 2002).

19. Interview with Glass on the DVD for *The Hours.*

20. *Philadelphia,* directed by Jonathan Demme (Columbia Tri-Star, 1993).

21. Ernesto Sabato, *On Heroes and Tombs*, trans. Helen R. Lane (Boston: David R. Godine, 1981), pp. 22–23.

Los pesimistas se reclutan entre los ex esperanzados, puesto que para tener una visión negra del mundo hay que haber creído antes en él y en sus posibilidades. Y todavía resulta más curioso y paradojal que los pesimistas, una vez que resultaron desilusionados, no son constantes y sistemáticamente desesperanzados, sino que, en cierto modo, paracen dispuestos a renovar su esperanza a cada instante, aunque lo disimulen debajo de su negra envoltura de amargados universales, en virtud de una suerte de pudo metafísico; como si el pesimismo, para mantenerse fuerte y siempre vigoroso, necesitase de vez en cuando un nuevo impulso producido por una nueva y brutal desilusión. (*Sobre Héroes y Tumbas* [1961] [Barcelona: Editorial Seix Barral, 2003], p. 32)

4 Melodic Trains

Music in Polanski's *The Pianist*

LAWRENCE KRAMER

In short any stop before the final one creates
Clouds of anxiety, of sad, regretful impatience
With ourselves, our lives, the way we have been dealing
With other people up until now.

John Ashbery, "Melodic Trains"

Roman Polanski's *The Pianist* (2002) was much praised for refusing the consolations of tragedy. Its protagonist, a Polish musician who survives the Holocaust, is not a hero. His survival amid the deaths of countless others is just something that happens; his story has no higher significance. Unlike Steven Spielberg's *Schindler's List* (1993), *The Pianist* does not leaven atrocity with nobility. But unlike Claude Lanzmann's *Shoah* (1985), it does not regard cinematic narrative itself as false witness. Instead it allows atrocity to deform the narrative into a chronicle of random chances and small, infrequent acts of decency observed with the cinematic equivalent of a hardened stare. The film's visual style is detached, cold, devoid of subjectivity; it simply watches and records, often from a fixed standpoint, at a distance, unwilling to interpret or edify. It will turn out that only a certain music can do that.

Not only can, but must: for it will also turn out that in this film the demands of witnessing constantly exceed the powers of sight. Consider an exemplary scene. Picked out at random, men from a line of Jewish laborers are ordered to lay face down and then shot in the head one by one while the camera remains steady and unblinking. Composed in bleached-out tones, the scene tells us that its victims are already ghosts. That they are dead in human terms before they die is shown by their surrender of the power of witnessing. Those killed obey the command and die with their eyes downcast; those spared stare rigidly ahead lest they be killed for watching. The responsibility to see is transferred to the audience by the camera's unblinking gaze. But there is no reward for bearing witness to the unbearable except the act itself.

The viewer perhaps senses this even more acutely by ear than by eye. Though it becomes speechless, the scene of serial execution is anything but soundless; it is punctuated by the rapid rhythmic alternation of loud gunshots and the soft crunch of the executioner's boots on the ground. The pattern breaks on an anguished silence (and a more intimate view) as the ammunition runs out and the victim steals a furtive upward glance as the gunman calmly, methodically reloads before squeezing off the last shot. The detail of reloading the gun acts as a riposte to a cognate scene in *Schindler's List* in which, with grotesque comedy, the appointed victim survives because three jabbering SS men cannot manage to fire either of two jammed guns. Spielberg observes the exception, Polanski the rule. In so doing, he also shows the rule *of* the exception, epitomized by the men left standing, Szpilman among them: survival may happen, but never for a reason.

Polanski thus seems to take to heart another rule, widely attributed to Theodor Adorno: No poetry—that is, no pretty fictions, no aesthetic alibis— after Auschwitz.[1] Yet in one respect the film seems to belie this resolution. If the pianist, Wladic Szpilman, is no hero, his and his nation's iconic composer, Frédéric Chopin, may take over the role in the form, almost literally in the person, of his music. The music even contradicts the random character of the narrative, which is framed symmetrically by performances of Chopin's Nocturne in C♯ Minor, the second of which makes restitution for the disruption of the first by Nazi bombardment. The performances are symbolically identical: live radio broadcasts by Szpilman that devote the power of the mass media, the Nazis' favorite propaganda tool, to the dissemination of music as high art. The film thus seems to reaffirm two ideas often denied on grounds of the Holocaust itself: that art, and above all music, speaks a transcendental, universal language, and that art, and above all music, is a profoundly civilizing force, both what saves us from barbarism and what is worth saving from it. Polanski here seems to flout Adorno's rule and fling it back in its author's face: Chopin's music, Europe's art music, has not been falsified by history. If not such poetry after Auschwitz, then what?

More directly, perhaps, Polanski's antagonist is Spielberg. Classical music figures in *Schindler's List* when one of the storm troopers "liquidating" the Lodz ghetto frenziedly plays Bach on an abandoned piano. (Two other SS men argue about the piece. "Bach?" says one. "Mozart," proclaims the other.) The music subsequently detaches itself from this scene and appears as underscore to a long nocturnal shot that represents the horrors within the ghetto walls by random flashes of light in the windows. Polanski, who survived the Krakow ghetto as a boy, will have none of this. His response, taking a pianist as protagonist, turns Spielberg's scene against itself: if this music is not the foe of such atrocity, what is?

But it is not that simple. Not quite. Of course not.

On the one hand the film's plotting and frame structure idealize classical music. As a pianist, Szpilman is marked for survival by everyone though there is nothing to distinguish him otherwise from anyone else. If he lives, the music lives. No one even remotely suggests that the music enshrines a fantasy of civilized life that history has shattered. On the other hand the music we actually hear tends to falter on the conditions of moral and physical devastation that call it up. As Adorno might have said, history has falsified it after all, and precisely by exposing the falsity immanent in it.

There is no exact way to gauge the deliberateness of this contradiction, and no apparent way to reconcile its turnings. On the one hand the film seems oblivious of it and seems to want the audience to be oblivious too. On the other hand the narrative is built on it, drawn inexorably by it to stake the film's meaning on the meaning of music in a few key episodes.

On the one hand; on the other: it sounds like piano music. Let me continue to reel off these ambidextrous gestures, which at the film's climax will literally resolve—or not—at the pianist's hands.

On the one hand, there is the large redemptive circle drawn over the narrative, the restoration of the interrupted nocturne. And as if the closing of the circle were not quite secure, a supplement is added to latch it shut: a full concert performance of Chopin's Grande Polonaise Brillante in its original version for piano and orchestra. The music is incongruous in its pleasantry and glitter; Szpilman's performance of it is an epilogue, placed under the closing credits. On the one hand, too, there is the embodiment of the spirit of music, even the pure source of German music—J. S. Bach—in an idealized feminine figure, a beautiful blonde cellist, herself not Jewish, with whom Szpilman might have had a romance had the Nazis not stormed in. And then there is the fact that the only good German in a film that portrays Germans as either cold brutes or fat slobs is a music lover: the handsome, civilized officer who enjoins Szpilman to play and saves him in the end— feeds him, hides him, acknowledges his humanity, asks his name.[2]

Unlikely as it is, Szpilman's encounter with the officer (also a historical figure, Wilm Hosenfeld) has an even more unlikely counterpart, or rather counterpoint, since the event is musical. The encounter takes place in a ruined house where Szpilman also, one night, hears to his amazement the Adagio from Beethoven's "Moonlight" Sonata floating mysteriously through the air. Its presence is never explained. The film thus addresses the clichéd question, how could the people of Goethe and Beethoven . . . ?

When the officer later appears—ominously at first, via the tips of his black boots—the question becomes personified. The good German is a remnant, as the music is an echo, a phantom, of the good Germany that the Nazis have brought to ruin.

But on the other hand: music, both heard and unheard, haunts the film as the spirit of a lost, void, or hopelessly inadequate ideal. In one scene Szpilman finds a piano in a safe house and reverently exposes its keyboard. The shot sequence momentarily fools us into thinking that he starts to play, with the sound of the orchestra, which sneaks in from nowhere, in his mind's ear. But to play is to risk discovery and death, and a shot of his hands quickly corrects our impression. Unable to make a sound, Szpilman is playing silently over the keys while we hear the music—the frothy Grande Polonaise—on the soundtrack, an acoustic reality but a symbolic phantasm.

Later the same thing happens in a ruined hospital where Szpilman has taken refuge. But this time there is no imaginary orchestra—and no piano. The music, a fragment of Chopin's G-minor Ballade that we will soon hear again under different circumstances, is more serious, more appropriate, than before, but also more phantasmal. It begins to drift acousmatically through the corridors, finding its source—but is the pianist playing what he "hears" or hearing what he "plays"?—in a shot of Szpilman sprawled listlessly in a hard chair, his fingers moving in air over a purely imaginary keyboard. More starkly than the first, and more surely, this phantom performance hollows out the cultural ideal it invokes; its gesture of fidelity to music cannot help turning into a travesty. Even the music seems to concede as much, as it overlaps into a lingering shot of dead leaves drifting through an empty street.

More devastating still is a moment during Szpilman's secret stay with his cellist friend, Dorota, and her husband. Dorota, now pregnant, snatches a moment of solitude to play the Prelude to Bach's Suite in G Major for solo cello. The music is both tranquil and self-contained, like Dorota herself in her little room, tightly framed by the screen space. The solo instrument provides both melody and bass in a symbiotic fusion that encapsulates the cultural ideal of music as an expression of spirit and embodies it in the resonant communion between the mother and the unborn child. Awakened by the sound of music in the air (as he will be later, in another sense, by the "Moonlight" Sonata), Szpilman seeks its source. At first what he finds is not Dorota, but her symbolic equivalent in a cinematic still life: a transparent vase, filled with flowers, at the center of a table. Both the table, where meals are shared, and the fragile but unbroken glass have symbolic values that resonate throughout the film, as we will see shortly.

Following the sound, Szpilman discovers Dorota behind a half-opened door and gazes at her intently. He, and we, see her in profile, surrounded by light but framed in darkness, the threatened but still intact embodiment of music, life, and culture. He watches and listens, visibly tempted to make himself known. But he holds back, unwilling to shatter the illusion by reaching out for it. The gesture is doubly ironic. In protecting Dorota's waking dream, it marks the first and only time in his odyssey, perhaps in the whole film, that Szpilman makes an honest recognition of another's personhood. But the recognition is moot. Dorota has no part in it, and for Szpilman it is a step toward internalizing the concealment, the breaking of human connection, that his fugitive existence demands. Only by intruding on the music could its truth have been upheld.

The scene epitomizes the pervasive irony that the cultural treasure of music has been entrusted symbolically to this unheroic figure focused on his own survival and nothing more. Szpilman, we gradually come to understand, is a man who sees without witnessing, in part just because he lives only for music. Hence he is reduced near the end to a craven voyeur watching death in the street through a broken hospital window. Shards of translucent glass surround the hole through which he peers. Their edges gleam like the edges of cut crystal; the incisions of light form a visual echo of the *Kristall* in the German *Kristallnacht*, Crystal Night, the name given to the night of 9 November 1938. Known in English as the Night of Broken Glass, this state-sponsored pogrom was the point of no return from which the Holocaust inexorably proceeded. It literally bestrewed all of Germany with shards from the broken windows of Jewish shops.[3] Its visual trace in the film forms a symbol of the horrors that the night foretold but did not yet comprehend, and that Szpilman, from his own limited perspective, never does comprehend.

The perspective itself is shattered by this failure. What Szpilman first sees through his broken glass is a pile of bodies doused with gasoline and set aflame, a fragment of a literal holocaust. Later a sheet of flame bursts through to his point of vision as more glass shatters, and he takes flight onto the main street of a vast necropolis, a city reduced to rubble into the endless vista of which he slowly recedes.

The shards at the window remind the eyes watching the film of their own vulnerability and define even their purely fictitious act of witnessing as cut by the field of vision. Hovering allusively in the background may be a pair of famous scenes from Luis Buñuel's *Un Chien andalou* (1928), one in which an eye is sliced open with a razor, another showing donkeys lying dead across the tops of pianos. The shards of vision constitute Polanski's self-reflective posing of the question that has been central to Holocaust studies, that of whether it is either possible or proper to represent traumatic events of such magnitude. Although the film does not show the death camps, only the trains that go there, what it does show is more than enough to force the question.[4]

One hand and the other. These tensions peak, and perhaps resolve, when Szpilman and the German officer meet in the ruined house. As already noted, the prefatory sound of the "Moonlight" Sonata revives the old question about the people of Beethoven becoming Hitler's minions. But the question is posed ironically, indecipherably, because the officer acts mercifully for equivocal reasons, never quite explicit: because he knows the war is lost, because he is tired of all the killing, or, most likely, because Szpilman is a pianist. Szpilman himself acts just as equivocally. He plays when commanded to, plays Chopin in a darkened room while the officer's military hat and overcoat sit ominously on the piano. Why? Because it is what he does? Because he is craven? Because he just needs to play one more time? He literally plays for his life, symbolically sings for his supper. When he finishes he swiftly withdraws his hands from the keyboard to his lap, as if terrified at what he has done. The scene is composed principally of medium close-ups of Szpilman and the officer and tight close-ups of Szpilman's hands, which weave the two men together into a knot of musical destiny that is both a bond and a riddle.

We will keep circling back to this scene, crossing hands, seeking a close. But to make our circling effectively hermeneutic it's necessary to situate the scene within the narrative it both consummates and contradicts.

Szpilman's life as a fugitive begins when, for no good reason, he escapes the rail yards from which the boxcars are departing for the death camps. Yet another music-lover yanks him away from the line for Treblinka. His being passed over is rendered the more ironic by his family's last meal together, which they share in the train yard. The meal consists of a single piece of candy bought at exorbitant cost and painstakingly divided into tiny pieces. In the Jewish context, this communion meal, like the Last Supper, is a Passover Seder. And Szpilman, in the arbitrary inverse of a miracle, is as if marked with the blood of the lamb. His odyssey can be mapped as an ironic trip in another direction, a transport to life reminiscent of the "different trains" in Steve Reich's composition of the same name.

The trains Reich has in mind are those he rode between New York and Los Angeles when he was a boy during the war years, and those that, as a Jew, he would have had to ride if he were in Europe. *Different Trains* (1988) incorporates the taped voices of Holocaust survivors and makes music of them by imitating their vocal melody on stringed instruments. The instrumental sound thus assumes the trace of trauma and the burdens of testimony and saturates the piece with them. In contrast, *The Pianist* allows events to affect music in its essence only once, during the episode in the ruined house to which the whole film builds. Otherwise there is a strict separation between music and historical trauma. The music is held in reserve or doled out like the bits of communion candy, holding the place of life and civilization until they can be narratively restored. The film's imagery repeatedly exposes this restoration as futile or absurd, but the music insists it is neither. The circular movement of the narrative from an exploded recital to its restored completion brushes critical reflection aside by uniting the narrative with the primal musical rhythm of return. The music, especially Chopin's music, is the melody of the different train that does not go to Auschwitz or Treblinka.

Szpilman is spared the final (and only) stop on the route to death and so is granted the ambivalent gift described in John Ashbery's poem, the marking of the ancient metaphor of life as a journey with station stops of anxiety, regret, impatience, self-doubt, all of which, nonetheless, constitutes life. The film tends to mark these stations with music, but music in some truncated form, in a truncated scene. We've glanced at them all: the untouched and phantom keyboards under moving fingers, the Bach in the doorway at Dorota's, the invisible "Moonlight" Sonata, and Szpilman's playing Chopin for the officer at the final "stop" before all "starts" again with the resumption of the interrupted nocturne. The nocturne, however, is not a true destination. It is, all too literally, a curtain-raiser.

The true destination, which proves false, is the performance of the Grande Polonaise tacked on under the credits. Its falsity is a direct consequence of the nocturnal meeting of the German officer and Jewish fugitive, and their spectral surrogates, Beethoven and Chopin—a meeting we are almost ready to confront ourselves. The "Moonlight" Adagio, which Szpilman hears but never plays, represents a lost ideal of romantic melancholy; the Chopin he chooses, the G-minor Ballade, acts as both appropriation and critique, turning the melancholy into rage, passion, indignation, and defiance. That it prompts an unexpected act of mercy is ironic: Szpilman plays like a Jewish Scheherazade on the thousand and first night, meanwhile fully expecting the night to be his last. The use of the C♯-minor Nocturne as a frame in the film may represent an attempt to synthesize melancholy and protest, the spirits of the Adagio and the Ballade, in order to reaffirm romantic anguish in a reflective mode: to reaffirm it both as a cultural treasure, a part of the history of feeling, and as a meaningful mode of suffering, capable, like Szpilman, of surviving the Holocaust that threatens not only its empirical existence but its very ontology.

It may be relevant, though only as a layer of esoteric meaning that would escape most viewers, even those who know their Chopin, that the C♯-minor Nocturne was the last piece that Chopin composed before leaving Warsaw; in that sense, it's his most acutely Polish piece, poised between homeland and diaspora. It's interesting, too, that in the Hollywood thriller *The Peacemaker* (1997), the villain, a Bosnian piano teacher who wants to inflict a nuclear holocaust on the West to match the pain he has endured, is shown playing this same piece, the sign of a sensitive spirit gone rotten.

Neither of the framing devices provides an adequate reckoning with the climatic scene. They may not be meant to; it's hard to tell. The return to the C♯-minor Nocturne is too pretty, too dressed up, and the whole gesture is too pat: it simply observes the Hollywood rule of moralizing by making a big repetition, something as often done with music as with words. The scene is also too easy to see, as the intact pane of glass on the radio booth makes evident. The interruption of the first nocturne was marked when a bomb blast shattered the glass in the same place, an event replicated in frozen, seemingly fixed form by the shard-beset hospital window that epitomizes the film's vocabulary of witnessing. It is not so easy to fix such broken glass.

In this context the addition of the extra frame, the Grande Polonaise, becomes an act of bad faith: evasive, sentimental, hypocritical. Yet on the night I saw the film it was just what the audience wanted, or perhaps needed, and I am not overeager to criticize them for it, even if I did walk out myself while the others eagerly stayed until the last note. Chopin's iconic standing formed a seductive veil over the proceedings, and so did the visual paraphernalia that it commanded: the rebuilt studio, the plush concert hall, the pianist's healthy appearance and new tuxedo, the gleaming piano. Even the music is refurbished, retrieved from the silent keys in the safe house that the fugitive dared not touch.

The studio and concert hall, impossibly spiffy in their renovation, lie a world away from the ruined house of Szpilman's encounter with Hosenfeld and the keys there that he does touch. That is the real center of gravity: the ruined, haunted palace of European civilization. The music heard there is not repeated within the film, nor could it be; it is too deeply rooted in its occasion. Let's go back.

The scene begins with the irony of the "Moonlight" sequence. The disembodied sounds of Beethoven's C♯-minor Adagio, first cousin to the C♯ minor of the framing nocturne, fill the ruined house and Szpilman's ears. But the house cannot contain the sound, and neither can Szpilman's senses.

The music continues under a shot of the nocturnal street, producing the nostalgic sound of romantic melancholy over the utter wasteland that Warsaw has become. The scene is almost abstract, cruelly beautiful, a static composition of blues and blacks as baffling to the eye as the music is to the ear. This sequence, as both the audience and Szpilman listen, forms the film's moment of self-reflection. Each listener is pressed to find edification in this "classical," this German, this pan-European music in the absence, so far, of any good reason to do so.

But the music is as symbolically unreal as the imaginary sound of an untouched or phantom piano. It is nominally acousmatic, source sound without a visible source, but as presented in *The Pianist* it has no source at all. Or if it has, the source is not acoustic but symbolic: the cryptic ruined landscape of the city under moonlight. Szpilman's ear cannot trace the vagabond sound to its origin. It might just as well be hallucinatory, though it is not; in both a moral and an acoustic sense, it simply shouldn't be there. For all we know it might be the lament of Walter Benjamin's angel of history, "irresistibly [propelled] into the future to which his back is turned while the pile of debris before him grows skyward."[5] The "Moonlight" Adagio thus becomes a phantasmal object inextricable from but not identifiable in or with the cinematic image. Its impact may equally well be read as ironic, bitterly so, or elegiac.

Szpilman's subsequent performance of the G-minor Ballade constitutes that reading. It forms both an acknowledgment that Szpilman has thus far failed to grasp the enormities around him and an attempt to compensate by letting the music articulate what the musician could not. But the music, like its occasion, is fraught with ambivalence. Its very identity is self-divided, for the music we hear in this scene is neither a brief extract nor the whole Ballade but an abridged version: a whole that is not whole.

This fragmentation is important. It is impossible to explain on a purely pragmatic basis; a shorter piece could have been used here and played through. The contrary choice is just the point. Nowhere in the film do we hear a piece of music whole. Like Szpilman, the listener is forced to sift through the rubble: "These fragments I have shored against my ruin." One of those fragments we have heard haunt the empty hospital, but its recurrence here is itself fragmentary, even abortive; the Ballade, like the glass in the hospital window, appears as a group of shards held together around, even by, an empty center. In a broken world there is nothing but broken music. Wholeness comes only with the Grande Polonaise under the closing credits, music whose presence we have already recognized as more than dubious.

Insofar as what we hear of the G-minor Ballade is only a substitute for what we don't hear, this music is not itself; it comes from nowhere. Despite its visible source, it is as vagabond as the "Moonlight" Sonata. It floats in the same liminal space between presence and absence, inside and outside, narrative and frame. Like the sonata, the Ballade as heard here cannot be contained by its nominal cinematic category; the category founders on it. As source music, the Ballade is certainly less ghostly than the sonata, but it is no less strange, and self-estranged. True, it is a famous piece that Szpilman, the Chopin specialist, would be likely to know by heart. But the piece he plays is not *that* Ballade, but a displaced and even deformed fiction of it. Asked by the officer what he does for a living, Szpilman replies, "I am—I *was*—a pianist," and if the music could speak it might say with equal justice "I am—I *was*—the G-minor Ballade."

The performance of this Ballade in ruins permits Szpilman and the officer to meet outside the relations of German and Jew, victimizer and victim, from which at the same time neither can escape. But it does not do so by invoking an ideal of musical beauty that the circumstances would immediately discredit, nor even the idealized form of sorrow or remorse embodied by the "Moonlight" Sonata. On the contrary: the performance voices everything that must remain unsaid between the two men in order for a fragile, transient reconciliation to form between them.

The scene at the piano literally places that reconciliation in Szpilman's hands, which bear out both what lies within reach and what lies beyond it, a limit later marked in narrative terms when Szpilman fails to receive a plea for help sent by the officer. The performance is a kind of testimony, at once liberating and agonizing. As Maurice Blanchot observes, thinking of music in the death camps, "The power of music seems, momentarily, to bring forgetfulness and dangerously causes the distance between murderers and victims to disappear. But . . . [t]here is a limit at which the practice of any art becomes an affront to affliction. Let us not forget this."[6] Szpilman's performance conveys a similar admonition, insisting on the recognition that the officer's invitation to "play something" is actually a command backed by the possibility of murder, despite the fact that the officer has no malign intentions, but to all appearances just wants to hear some music—"to bring forgetfulness." This, however, does not mean that the music entirely fails to relieve the affliction it affronts. There is no untangling its ambivalence, which the film perhaps just stumbles into, laudable not so much for grasping as simply for yielding to the intractability of its subject matter.

How is such music to be heard? How *can* it be heard without falling into fatuous art worship or high-toned dismissiveness, the one attitude as morally blind as the other? I propose to theorize one possible answer while Szpilman's disused hands still hover over the keyboard. We will soon circle back one last time to the ruined house, but we need an intermission first, an interlude.

In *The Gift of Death*, a meditation on ethics, Jacques Derrida distinguishes between two modes of invisibility. Some invisibility is temporary, as my hands—the example is Derrida's—may be hidden under a table until I reveal them. Some invisibility is permanent, an invisibility in principle. Such is the invisibility of human inwardness, and, incidentally, of music. Derrida's reference to music is made in passing, even a little carelessly; I want to take it seriously, especially in relation to the idea of inwardness. The remoteness of this issue from cinema, and from *The Pianist*, is only apparent.[7]

Of course, there is a sense in which music is not invisible in the least. As Richard Leppert in particular has taught us, the sight of sound is as important to its meaning as the sound itself.[8] But the fact remains that you can close your eyes and the music will still be there. In that sense it is invisible in principle. And for that reason it maintains a close likeness to the idea of inwardness, which develops alongside the concept of music from at least the Enlightenment onwards. Derrida suggests that the ethical arises when inwardness, though invisible, becomes apparent to the gaze of an absolute otherness, identified in the first instance with God. But since, as he puts it in a formula meant to embody its own meaning as the French words change their meaning upon repetition, *tout autre est tout autre*, all others are all other, the ethical is fully present in every human encounter. And insofar as I treat music as an expression of human inwardness, as historically I have been taught to do; insofar as I install my own invisible inwardness in a subject position made available by the music, the act of listening reenacts the equally invisible gaze in which the ethical is grounded. Perhaps that's why a common love of music can bind people to each other so strongly. Perhaps that's why so many in *The Pianist* act spontaneously to protect Szpilman.

Not every act of listening, however, makes this relationship audible, nor is it audible in every piece of music. It tends to reverberate in film when music goes vagabond, in grave or uncanny or perplexing moments like those in *The Pianist*. These are moments in which categories fail, boundaries blur, and listening assumes the value of a symbolic debt I did not know I owed, and for which I must thus answer all the more. Under such conditions the coalescence of music and inwardness may at times be heard as an exposure of and to the gaze of the other. It follows that in listening the gaze must be inwardly answered and returned. When this happens in music alone the gaze is felt, not seen; the exact terms of the symbolic debt are left to the listener to discover. In a film the terms become almost too clear. The cinematic image becomes the scene of the acoustic gaze, which must be answered by seeing the image as if it were being cast by the music: not as a visual form to which the music is joined, but as the music visualized.

The wandering whistling from *M*, discussed in the introduction to this volume, is a classic example; the murderer's hands over his mouth, failing to capture the vagabond sound, are as frighteningly ineffectual as the hands that Edvard Munch's screamer places where his ears should be. A more recent example occurs in Jane Campion's *The Portrait of a Lady* (1996), based on the novel by Henry James. The film's musical plot includes a vagabond rendition of the melancholy slow movement from Schubert's "Death and the Maiden" Quartet. The movement becomes an apparitional form, a penumbra cast by four different, discontinuous fragments scattered at intervals along the narrative arc of a failing marriage. With the final fragment, the cinematic image blurs and splits, rendering the protagonist's face as apparitional as the music that charts its destiny.[9]

In *The Pianist* the "Moonlight" Sonata demands a gaze as clear and pitiless as the moonlight that falls on the ruined city. The sight demands that we listen more acutely, that we hear the music both as a ruin itself and as the knowledge of what has ruined it. The Chopin Ballade calls for a recognition of humanity that can animate the spectral overcoat on the piano. Part accusation, part *cri de coeur*, the music wills the uniform to be not the cloak of power, but a garment men wear against the cold. The sound demands that we hear more than we can see, the more so the more acutely we listen.

When you listen to the invisibility of music, the music listens back. That's what it does in the ruined house; it listens to see if our listening is an act of witness. The officer seems to grasp this as he drifts slowly across the room, then turns and backs unsteadily into a chair, as if stunned by what he hears.

Like the music that fills it, the scene of the Chopin Ballade is shaped by Szpilman's hands, which he must loosen up, rehumanize from their gnarled, clawlike state, in order to play, and with which he ultimately either surrenders his life or takes it back "into his own hands"—it's impossible for him to know which. The music as excerpted traces this action deliberately, followed closely by the camera. It moves from the tentative monotone opening through complex melody-and-accompaniment textures to the increasingly virtuoso coda. Szpilman's hands are shown from a distance during the opening, as if to measure their self-alienation. Thereafter we see them in close-ups as they attack the keys with ever-increasing confidence—and violence.

But there is more. We hear a lot of this music, more than enough to make a symbolic whole, and the compositional pattern produced by the abridgment we hear forms a complex layer of commentary on the film and at the same time the medium for its narrative turning point, its classic peripeteia. The music here acts neither generically nor atmospherically; it acts in detail, as a musical utterance dense with musical meaning.[10]

The abridged Ballade consists of the original's quasi-improvisatory introduction, the first statement of its brooding refrain, a slightly cut statement of the quasi-developmental episode that follows (the source of the hospital fragment), and the whole of the fiery Presto coda, to which the episode segues. The first two segments invoke both the pathos of loss and the ethos of balladry, both associated in Chopin's day with exile and the oppression of Poland. The introduction restores "arpeggio" to its literal meaning as the pianist's tentative octaves imitate a bard's sweeping the strings of his harp. The refrain, in a parlando style punctuated by "strumming" notes or chords, not only sustains the ballad mystique but also continuously asserts the presence of a narrative voice—in the context of the film, the mark of the humanity of which the Jews have been deprived. In this one respect Szpilman's odyssey is exemplary; its later stages are punctuated by the noises of destruction but enveloped by the absence of speech. As we watch Szpilman's hands become more limber, their movement on the keys becomes a kind of signing, a voice in the hands. But the coda abandons the illusion of voice for a display of violent action, culminating in the wrist-busting final run of chromatic double octaves with short appoggiaturas, a fantasy of revolt, revenge, defiance, and a confession, like it or not, of desperation.

These feelings are indexed by the coda's explosive emphasis on a tonic key to which no perfect cadence is possible. In the original work, the final statement of the refrain rises through a massive crescendo to an imperfect cadence with which the refrain ends and the coda begins (m. 208). The effect is cathartic, but it is also self-consuming. The harmony is lucid and powerful, but it is not conclusive, and it becomes less rather than more so as the coda proceeds. The music's rampaging energy feeds on itself, lurching from one impassioned outburst to another with no promise to end and, when the end comes, refusing to accept it as inevitable. When what seems to be a pre-cadential dominant finally appears (m. 248), it devolves violently onto a single accented G struck deep in the bass and held for a full measure; the third and fifth of the tonic triad are reduced to overtones. The full triad does come back thereafter, but not in a cadence, not even at the last minute. The ending is not a cadence at all, just a surrogate—a high G-minor chord falling to a low G in octaves—voiced in the cadential manner.

The film actually manages to make this situation worse. The small cut in the episode eliminates an extended dominant preparation; what remains of the passage is all tonic, a static plateau. When the coda erupts immediately thereafter, the shock does nothing to jar the music from that plateau. The harmonic movement is emphatically not from dominant to tonic but from tonic to tonic. There is no effect of catharsis. The big imperfect cadence never happens. The coda does not even begin with its own downbeat, and it begins without a note in the bass. The Presto con fuoco thus sounds more unanchored than ever, its fury and desperation more absolute.[11]

The visual correlative of these feelings is an extended close-up of Szpilman's hands tearing into the keyboard, over which they tremble after striking the last chord with maximum force. In its expressive intensity, the image underscores the sheer unreality of what it represents. No one in Szpilman's condition could possibly have played this music. (In fact, the music the real-life Szpilman played for the German officer was the C#-minor Nocturne: a melancholy plea, not a defiant affirmation, and a relatively easy piece whose presence in the film is a tacit restoration of the historical truth.) The significance of the scene is allegorical, not historical; its impossibility is part of its point.

As allegory, as a fantasy that goes reality more than one better, the Ballade scene invites us to take pleasure in this music and in the values it enshrines. The harrowing scenes that have led us to this point have left such things far behind; feeling them can seem a recovery and a relief. Early in the scene, coming dangerously close to a kitschy affirmation of transcendence, a ray of light even falls on Szpilman as he plays. But the light is as accidental as the meeting with the officer, and as ordinary as the can of pickles that the starving pianist brings with him to the piano; it veils Szpilman in a cloud of dust motes more than it illuminates him. Nor does the light prevail. The scene is intercut with a lengthy single shot of the dark ruined street outside, where a faceless German soldier stands by a hulking car. The image echoes the shot of the ruined city that earlier overlapped the "Moonlight" Sonata; the music may fill the darkness, but cannot redeem it.

The pleasure offered by the music thus brings with it a question of responsibility. To enjoy is to endorse, and no endorsement here can be untainted. The soundtrack of *The Pianist* is heavy with sounds that are as painful to hear as its scenes are painful to watch: the crunch of the executioner's boots on gravel and the loud report of his gun, the splintering of glass, the violent *whoosh* of a flamethrower. Yet this painfulness, which is surely necessary, is just for that reason less challenging than the pleasure the film invites when music is at stake.

That pleasure is why you are reading about *The Pianist* here. It is the reason for choosing this one film in particular to illustrate the general thesis of *Beyond the Soundtrack*, that music is not a mere auxiliary to the image but a fully imagined and active part of a cinematic world. In a sense the film asks precisely the questions that this book does. What kind of world do we imagine with our music? And for our music? And can that music sustain us, or itself, when that world collapses?

The film addresses itself to extreme circumstances in part to rattle the complacency of normal ones, and not just in cinema. What is at stake, it asks, when and whenever we call on music to represent us? How and why might it happen that music no longer sounds in the background, as it were on the soundtrack of experience, but comes to the fore as a literal matter of life and death? What does that tell us about how and why we listen, and what we hear? Or does it tell us anything at all? *The Pianist* is exemplary for the way it implicates itself in these questions. Its form as utterance is evidence for its claims as discourse. It records an aesthetic crisis on which its own claims as art stand or fall.

The pivot of this crisis is the sound of Chopin's G-minor Ballade; my comments have all gravitated around it, and so does the film. For anyone whose feelings are engaged by the narrative, it is virtually impossible not to take pleasure in Szpilman's performance of this music. Yet there must be a sense in which it is painful to take this pleasure. That sense defines the ethic of witnessing here, the acoustic equivalent of cut vision. The one who looks on and listens in is asked to join these acts with the symbolic sacrifice, the desacralizing of music, that Szpilman is never able to make.

This mandate takes specific form in what the music lacks. Missing from the abridged Ballade are a theme of great lyrical beauty and the complex vicissitudes it undergoes. Of course only a fraction of the film audience can be supposed to know this; this dimension of the scene is necessarily esoteric. Yet what we do not hear of the Ballade is just as important as what we do hear. The lyric theme first occurs as a frail, whispered dream; it returns as an ecstatic apotheosis, its fullness of texture bought at the cost of an impossible harmonic remoteness; and it returns again in a compromise between these two forms, as if to bring the dream closer to reality by sacrificing part of its ideal, ecstatic version. In all its versions, the lyric theme suspends the pathos of tragic narration carried by the refrain and replaces it with glimpses of beauty, romance, sensuousness, pleasure. The film scatters traces of these things elsewhere, in its other music; here it demands that we feel their absence, and feel it as a specific lack even if the music is unknown to us. We can hear what Szpilman does not play in the splices, the ellipses, audible in what he does play.

The vicissitudes of this phantom melody are worth pursuing more closely. The film, with its phantom version of the elegiac "Moonlight" Adagio, seems to invite just that.

The lyric theme and the refrain have intertwined destinies, although they meet only once. On the first and last of its three statements, the lyric theme segues into a transitional passage that leads inexorably back to the refrain, the foreordained destination of all attempts to escape the refrain's gloom. This fatality is avoided only in the harmonic never-never land of the central lyric statement. The refrain has returned on the dominant of A minor, with a pedal point on E and recurrent six-four harmony that make it edgy as well as gloomy. It is on this harmony that the two themes meet—and part. As the refrain evolves into a markedly dissonant crescendo, the lyric theme steps in and transfigures it. The theme takes the prevailing harmony as its own dominant and breaks through to its ecstatic form in A *major*, effortlessly sublimating the minor mode to which the refrain clings and apparently reversing the sense of irreparable loss that impels the clinging. The key of A major is quite remote from the G-minor tonic in whose sphere the refrain otherwise moves and even more remote—as remote as possible, a tritone away—from the E♭ major of the first and third lyric statements, the lyric frame. It is in this otherworldly tonal space that a free elaboration of the lyric idea becomes possible.

But this is precisely the space of the lyric's unreality, which is the condition of possibility for its transfigured and transfiguring presence in the central statement. Reality will reclaim its authority soon enough, and with a vengeance, when the refrain returns in the aftermath of the third lyric statement trailing the very features that the central statement seemed to dispel. Again over a pedal point supporting recurrent six-four harmony, the refrain now poises itself on the dominant of G minor, the point from which worse will come in the form of the raging coda. The abridged composition that Szpilman plays in the film goes to that worse without a detour. The world of the film has no room for detours, let alone for lyrical fantasies. The abridgement forms an interpretation of the void that results. It does literally what the original music does figuratively: it dissolves the illusion of hope into the reality of rage and despair. But this interpretive fidelity is also a spiritual betrayal, through which the music, like Szpilman, survives only at the cost of the very values that might make survival meaningful.

All three statements of the lyric theme sustain the effect of lyric voice, of song rather than of narrative, the ultimate fragility of which prompts the fantasy of violent restitution that closes the piece. The violence is justified, or at least dialectically grounded, by the utopian dream that the original music cannot give up but cannot keep. In the film, the violence is stripped of this rationale and left to stand naked. The result is a knot of ironies that cannot be undone, not even cut. The music defies the symbolic authority of the empty hat and coat on the piano, the power of which is real in precise proportion to its human emptiness. Yet the garments' owner, though Szpilman does not yet know it, will behave humanely; he will even give the coat to Szpilman as a parting gift (which, ironically, will almost get Szpilman shot as a German). The pianistic skill reflecting civilized cultivation at its supposed highest thus becomes the imaginary means for striking down, with the utmost brutality, the brutality that has all but destroyed civilization. The hands here are as important as the sound they produce. Yet the effect of catharsis is real, and surely no one could grudge either Szpilman or the film's audience the relief, however inadequate, that it provides.

Listeners who don't know the music will certainly get the point of the abridged version—cut, as by a shard of glass. They will hear the musical enunciation of survival at any cost, even of the values that music itself holds most dear. They will hear the movement from grief to rage in the cut Ballade cancel out the reflective mourning of the "Moonlight" Adagio. They will hear that defiant survival may be compromised by its own extremity and amorality. But listeners who do know the music will feel a deeper cut. They will grasp that the power of what they hear rests on the near absolute loss of all foundations. They will grasp that this collapse of the edifices of music and of civilization as a whole also entails the loss, not even of the possibility of happiness, but of its mere dream or hope, which seems to have been swallowed up permanently by the abyss that is the ruined city. And they will grasp this city of the dead as the material form of the civilization in ruins whose music we are hearing, the eternally mute world of shattered stone and broken glass that can be rebuilt, if at all, only if it is shattered again by the hands of a phantom, truncated Chopin in a night that no nocturne can penetrate.

NOTES

The epigraph is from John Ashbery's "Melodic Trains," from the collection *Houseboat Days* (New York: Viking, 1977).

1. Adorno's exact words were "Writing a poem after Auschwitz is barbaric," a statement he later revised, though not by much: "Perennial suffering has as much right to expression as the tortured person to scream, so it may have been false that after Auschwitz writing a poem was no longer allowed." My translations from Adorno, *Gesammelte Schriften in zwanzig Bänden,* ed. Rolf Tiedemann (Frankfurt am Main: Suhrkamp Verlag), vol. 10, *Kulturkritik und Gesellschaft* (1977), 30, and vol. 6, *Negative Dialektik. Jargon der Eigentlichkeit* (1973), 355. For discussion, see Elaine Martin, "Re-Reading Adorno: The 'After-Auschwitz' Aporia," http://forum.llc.ed.ac.uk. As we will see, Polanski dissents as much from Adorno's second statement as from his first.

2. The name is worth reflecting on. When the two part, the officer asks Szpilman's name and calls it a good name for a pianist, punning bilingually on *Spiel* (play) and *Mann* (man). The pun indirectly reflects the allegorical nature of Szpilman's artistic identity. Also worth noting in this context is the odd fact that the officer waits until after hearing Szpilman play to confirm the unsurprising fact that the pianist is a Jew. It is as if it were necessary to restore a measure of cultural mediation, however artificially, before the two men could meet on terms of mutual recognition.

3. For a brief account of the event and its recognition at the time as "a quantum step . . . the real thing," see Deborah Dwork and Robert Jan van Pelt, *Holocaust: A History* (New York: Norton, 2002), 99–102. *Kristallnacht* was apparently coined as an ironic euphemism; the symbolic value of broken glass seems to have been lost on no one. As one victim recalled, in this case of a home invasion, "[My parents] had a glass display cabinet with a lot of pretty things in it, and also glasses and so on. [The Nazis] had just taken it and thrown it over. I mean, every little tiny last bit of it was broken" (100).

4. The literature on this subject is extensive and overlaps with a more general literature on history and trauma. Important texts include (among many others) Primo Levi, *The Drowned and the Saved,* trans. Raymond Rosenthal (New York: Random House, 1989); Shoshana Felman and Dori Laub, *Testimony: Crises of Witnessing in Literature, Psychoanalysis, and History* (New York and London: Routledge, 1992); Cathy Caruth, *Unclaimed Experience: Trauma, Narrative, and History* (Baltimore, MD: Johns Hopkins University Press, 1996); Dominick LaCapra, *History and Memory After Auschwitz* (Ithaca, NY: Cornell University Press, 1998) and *Writing History, Writing Trauma* (Baltimore, MD: Johns Hopkins University Press, 2001); and Giorgio Agamben, *Remnants of Auschwitz,* trans. D. Heller-Roazen (New York: Zone, 1999). For a useful overview, see Debarati Sanyal, "A Soccer Match in Auschwitz: Passing Culpability in Holocaust Criticism," *Representations* 79 (2002): 1–27.

5. Walter Benjamin, no. ix of "Theses on the Philosophy of History," in Benjamin, *Illuminations*, ed. Hannah Arendt, trans. Harry Zohn (New York: Schocken, 1969), 258.

6. Maurice Blanchot, *The Writing of the Disaster*, trans. Ann Smock (Lincoln: University of Nebraska Press, 1996), 83.

7. Jacques Derrida, *The Gift of Death*, trans. David Wills (Chicago: University of Chicago Press, 1995), 90.

8. Richard Leppert, *The Sight of Sound: Music, Representation, and the History of the Body* (Berkeley and Los Angeles: University of California Press, 1993).

9. For more on *M* and *Portrait*, see, respectively, my *Musical Meaning: Toward a Critical History* (Berkeley: University of California Press, 2001), 179–83, and "Recognizing Schubert: Musical Subjectivity and Cultural Change in Jane Campion's *The Portrait of a Lady*," *Critical Inquiry* 28 (2002), 25–52. As my examples may suggest, classical pieces are particularly prone to vagabond movement because a certain self-division and reflexivity are often built into their genres. But the affinity is not exclusive. Near the beginning of *Shoah*, for example, and all the more pointedly because of that film's rigor about testimony, a Holocaust survivor sings a folk tune while boating on the same river where he had sung the same tune as a death-camp inmate. As we look on from a distance the tie between the man and the music loosens; the tune grows progressively softer, fading from source music to acousmatic sound and finally lapsing under the off-screen sound of spoken testimony. It is not clear which is more painful, the persistence of the sound or its loss, but the listener must somehow account for both.

10. This account of the Ballade, developed in the paragraphs to follow, should be read in tandem with the account in Michel Chion's contribution to this volume. Chion observes that neither Szpilman nor the officer identifies the music Szpilman plays, and suggests that what we hear is no longer music at all, properly speaking. Chion gives this idea a fascinating development, which I will not attempt to repeat. But it remains a little puzzling that we are asked to hear so very much of this non-music. That we really are called on to listen, and listen closely, suggests another layer of ambivalence in a film, and a scene, already laden with it in every connection with music. At one level, the scope of the historical catastrophe makes musical chitchat insupportable and corrodes the very substance of music itself. At another, the identity of the G-minor Ballade and its composer simply goes without saying, as it always has—and that it can still do so becomes the frail medium in which even a shattered ideal can still do a modicum of good. At this level the concrete identity of the music, especially in its distorted form, is stronger than ever. On either reading, the key point about this scene is that although it can pass for uplifting (and of course the film was marketed as uplifting), the uplift is a disguise; every note, every shot, is riddled with ambivalence.

11. The musical details are these. The cut in the episode starts after a V–I progression that does not quite rise to the level of a weak imperfect cadence. The omitted material runs from the second beat of m. 40 through the downbeat of m. 44; the passage resumes on the second beat of m. 44 and continues to the downbeat of m. 48, at which point it jumps to the second beat of m. 208. Measures 44 and 46 stay on

the tonic; mm 45 and 47 prolong it with a streak of subdominant color over a tonic bass. The downbeat of m. 48, which substitutes for that of m. 208, represents a tonic whose ties to the dominant have frayed and, if heard without mm. 40–44, have thinned to the vanishing point. What follows in the original Ballade is a recovery of the tonic-dominant bond, but you would never know it from the film version. The coda in *The Pianist* could scarcely have a more attenuated context.

5 Mute Music

Polanski's *The Pianist* and Campion's *The Piano*

MICHEL CHION

At the age of fifteen I read a German novel that had a profound influence on me. This novel, which I found in the library of my boarding school dormitory, was Thomas Mann's *Doctor Faustus*, written in the United States and published in 1947. I was fascinated by Mann's description of pieces of music that could not be heard since their "composer" was the fictional hero Adrian Leverkühn, and they did not exist. This did not prevent the narrator from describing the music in great detail. When I started composing music several years later, I got the urge to bring one of Adrian Leverkühn's imaginary pieces into existence. In 1973 I composed a work that might have been his own, a condemned man's *Requiem*, ironic and despairing like Mann's hero. My *Requiem* was made as *musique concrète*, on audiotape, with "fixed sounds." There cannot possibly be a score for *musique concrète*, since it is a kind of music that cannot be notated and whose performance itself cannot be represented. In a word, it is the most invisible sort of music.

While reading *Doctor Faustus* I was listening to a lot of classical music on the radio and on records. I was also reading biographies of composers, but I did not yet know how to read or play music, much less write it. All those marks on sheet music remained silent to me, a bit like Chinese or Hebrew for those of us who don't know such languages. I was thus encountering at the same time three different sorts of music that did not intersect: a first sort that I imagined in my head without hearing it as I read an author's work; a second kind that I listened to on the radio and on records, or watched musicians play at concerts, but which for me had nothing to do with written signs; and a third music consisting of written signs that for me had yet to bear any relation to what I heard.

Toward age sixteen or seventeen—rather late for a musician—the floodgates opened. I learned to play piano, to read music, and even to write music (harmony, counterpoint) before gravitating to *musique concrète,* music that is neither written nor seen. From this experience of delayed apprenticeship in reading and writing music, there remains for me a gap between seeing, hearing, and words. What is seen in the form of printed music, what is heard by the ears, and what is imagined from reading Thomas Mann or Proust (Vinteuil's sonata in *Remembrance of Things Past*) constitute three different faces of music—three different paths that for me were destined never to cross—and each was in itself incomplete.

In the cinema these different dimensions can either be combined or exist in isolation. That is no doubt why I am very sensitive to the way films allow for the existence of what can be called *mute music,* which I would now like to consider. But first, let's agree on what we call music and reexamine the issue of whether a fragment of music—since cinema often plays excerpts of thirty seconds—is still worthy of the term. If, for example, we take a coda from a Mozart sonata, or a transition from the sonata consisting of a series of modulating scales, are we dealing with music? In a piece of classical music, not everything constitutes music. A Mozart composition, for example, involves residue such as the connective tissue of scales or ornamental passages. The cinema often uses this kind of nonthematic material, calling it *music.* So when a bit of what we call music occurs in a film, this does not mean that *music* and all it normally entails is involved. A chord, a flute melody, or a sound made for emphasis is nothing more than what it is. A film need not necessarily deploy an entire musical system and everything that music represents in culture and discourse.

When a writer such as Faulkner, Prévert, Handke, or Guerra writes for the cinema, we call what he writes a screenplay or dialogue; we don't call it *literature,* nor do we regard it using the same criteria we apply to that form. Similarly, when a painter works for the cinema we conventionally call what he does *production design* or *set design.* But when a composer produces work for the cinema, it is customary to retain the term *music* for what he writes, even though it normally appears in another form—that is, a fragmentary form—in a wholly different role, with a wholly different logic, and, above all, in an entirely different context than musical works have traditionally appeared in Western culture.

Consider that a piece of music may be present in a film in at least four forms:

Heard in excerpts (frequently) or in its entirety (rarely in fiction films, save for short pieces), without our seeing its performance

Heard simultaneously with the depiction of its instrumental and/or vocal performance

Verbally evoked through the means of a title of a work or a composer's name

"Shown" in the form of music on the page (when it's a work that can be notated).

These four forms can occur separately or in combination.

We ought to consider the pertinence of the term *music* beyond the framework of cinema, too. That single word, *music*, is often employed by scholars, historians, and music lovers whether they are referring to melodies, lieder, opera, oratorios, cantatas, songs, or choruses (that is, music with lyrics), or to music without text such as symphonies, concertos, piano works, or string quartets (all types of instrumental music). Incidentally, how should we define this latter term? The designation *instrumental music* is purely material and pragmatic, referring to music played on instruments, but at the same time it is purely negative, referring to music that doesn't involve voices either singing or uttering a text. Something having a purely pragmatic and negative (by elimination) definition does not strictly constitute a unified domain.

Furthermore, in a certain era in the history of music, even when a piece was written solely for instruments and no text was heard, a text was frequently understood. This occurred either in the case of instruments executing a known song, evoking in listeners the lyrics that had formerly been sung to that tune, or, in more than one Romantic symphony, when the music evokes or even imitates a Lutheran choral theme.

In the nineteenth century in particular, music whose sounds were intended to evoke other sounds unheard in the piece—sometimes the sounds of voices—held a position of considerable importance. Amateur musicians often played transcriptions of symphonies, but they also played evocative piano pieces in which, in the right-hand melody, one was supposed to imagine a horn, a harp, a flute, a gondolier's song, a chorus. In the central section in E-flat major of Chopin's Nocturne in G Minor, op. 37, no. 1, a listener or a pianist of the era would immediately "hear" or imagine, beyond the piano, a Lutheran-style chorale, sung by a choir to imaginary words or played on an organ. The sound of the piano thus referred to other sounds and to absent words. This aspect of music listening has disappeared today for most listeners. In the sounds of the piano they hear nothing but the piano, and only Chopin in the music of Chopin. An entire highly coded dimension of music has been lost.

When Frédéric Chopin composed the first of his four ballades for piano in 1836, the ballad was a popular genre in the domains of literature and poetry. Any cultivated person in Europe knew, either in German or in the numerous English or French translations, the ballads of Gottfried Bürger such as "Lenore" (1773) and Goethe's "Erlkönig," or "Alder-King" (1782), which inspired several composers, of whom Schubert remains the best known.

Interestingly enough, these two poetic ballads allude to acousmatic sound impressions, which is to say purely aural ones, without the support of sight. In Bürger's poem (translated into French by Gérard de Nerval), a woman listens to the sounds made by the ghost of her husband who went off to war, and then she hears his voice outside her door. In Goethe's "Alder-King" the little boy hears a voice, while his father hears only dry leaves *(dürren Blätter)* rustling in the wind—but both father and son are reacting to a noise that has no visible source. In both poems, since sound is acousmatic, it fosters doubt and ambiguity.

During the first half of the nineteenth century, then, the title "Ballade for Piano" clearly referred to a ballade for the piano without words, but suggesting at certain moments unspoken, imaginary words. Two years before Chopin's Ballade in G Minor, Felix Mendelssohn composed for solo piano the first set of pieces in a cycle he dubbed *Lieder ohne Wörte,* "Songs without Words," but after Mendelssohn it would seem that it was no longer necessary to state explicitly "ballade without words"; this became implicit. Thus the wordlessness of this new piano ballade genre was reinforced, because the specification "without words" could itself be omitted and remain unspoken.

More generally, during the post-Beethoven period, European instrumental music, especially music for solo piano, was often twice mute. This repertoire often suggests unspoken words and imaginary lyrics—not only through the titles, but also through the *recitativo* and declamatory character of certain passages (particularly in the piano works of Liszt). What's more, the title of the work was often mute regarding its own muteness.

I am pointing out this aspect of Romantic music because although at the beginning of the twenty-first century we are accustomed to listening to music by Chopin, Liszt, and Mendelssohn as pure or absolute music, this was not the way composers produced it and listeners heard it at the time. Even if it is not true that Chopin's ballades were (according to Schumann) inspired partly by ballads by the Polish poet Adam Mickiewicz, we can still hear in them something like a declamation without words—mute music. Romantic music for piano, particularly that of Chopin, Schumann, and Liszt, is, in fact, often similar to the voice of someone humming a poem or a melody with mouth closed: a melody with unheard words.

I'd like to explore this phenomenon by comparing two scenes from two similarly titled films, both of which confront or associate *music* (if I may use this word) with *muteness*.

In Roman Polanski's *The Pianist* (2002), the hero Szpilman is a Polish Jew who has escaped from the terrible massacre of the Warsaw Ghetto and must hide out for months with no possibility of playing the piano. In his imagination, though, he does play: he moves his hands without creating physical sound, which we hear on the film soundtrack as if the music is heard inside his head. Fifteen minutes before the end of the film, while the protagonist is trying to open a can of preserves, he is discovered by a German officer. It should be mentioned that Polanski, intent on making a popular film for a broad global audience, adopted a certain linguistic convention: the Poles speak in English, while the Germans speak in German. In the scene where the officer finds Szpilman, the two characters speak German; here both the words that are said and those not said are very important, as is the case in any film.

> THE GERMAN: *Was machen Sie hier? Wer sind Sie? Verstehen Sie nicht?*[1] What are you doing here? Who are you? Don't you understand?
>
> SZPILMAN: *Ich wollte diese Büchse öffnen.* I was trying to open this can.
>
> THE GERMAN: *Arbeiten Sie? Wovon leben Sie?* Do you work? What do you live on?
>
> SZPILMAN: *Ich bin . . . ich war Pianist.* I am . . . I was a pianist.
>
> THE GERMAN: Pianist. *Kommen Sie her. Spielen Sie mal.* Pianist. Come here. So play.

Then, without saying anything, without announcing the title of what he's going to play, Szpilman sits down at a grand piano and plays. When he has finished, the German officer says, *"Sie haben sich versteckt"* (You hid). Then he pronounces the fatal word that could get Szpilman killed: *"Jude"* (Jew).

How can what happens in this scene be described? As I see it, you can't just say "Szpilman plays Chopin's Ballade for Piano in G Minor," or "the German officer listens to Chopin," or "he listens to the G-minor Ballade," or even "he listens to music," for neither of the two characters says the word *music,* nor does either pronounce the name of Chopin or the title of the composition. The cinema creates a space in which things presented to our senses can return to being enigmas, their original state before we had names for them, and these things can be redefined at any moment.

The German officer makes no reference to what we have just heard, nor does he say the word *music,* but he continues his interrogation as if nothing had happened, thus annihilating through speech what we have just seen and heard. Szpilman says nothing either, but then he is in a weak position and his life is in jeopardy.

At the very end of this lengthy film, when the war is over and Szpilman—whom the German did not denounce—has survived all these horrors, we see him once again, dressed in tails, giving a concert in a large hall. The piece is the Andante spianato for piano and orchestra, again by Chopin, the Polish national composer. The context has changed: Szpilman no longer performs before a German officer but in a big concert hall, for benevolent listeners, no longer in danger of losing his life. But once again, no one in the scene says anything before or after the musical performance. Although this final scene that plays under the end credits should constitute a "happy ending," for me the emotion it produces is terror. Why? Perhaps because it suggests that after the horror of the Holocaust everything can go on as before, as if the music remained absolutely intact, untouched by events, and in this capacity were a symbol of the indifference of the universe. Unlike painting, for example, music is something that carries no traces, that cannot be marked, and that has no scars. It remains untouched by history, by events, by horror.

I have used the word "music," and at the end of the film we can also speak of music, for we see a normal concert in its ordinary setting, with an audience, a stage, an orchestra, and a conductor. But in the previous scene, when Szpilman plays the piano before the German officer who says not a word about it, the film allows me, it even *asks* me, to forget that it's music. Even if I know the Ballade in G Minor, op. 23—one of Chopin's best-known works—in that scene I have to hear it as a collection of sounds, not knowing if they belong to a piece, if they are music. Szpilman starts out with an arpeggio, a succession of notes, as if he were testing the instrument, and as if he were also testing a key. Then he tries out something that could be the main motive of a melody, although it's too short to be a melody: C–D–F♯–B♭–A–G. Of course I know that the notes are part of an existing composition, but I must forget this; it must be as if I were hearing it for the first time. It is no accident that Polanski chose that particular piece from among all the ones Szpilman could have played. The G-minor Ballade does not begin with a strong affirmation that it's music; it begins tentatively, as if feeling its way, like a poem that begins with disconnected words.

What we hear is just an idea, a sketch that was written down quickly during a voyage. Imagine Chopin in a carriage, scribbling onto a scrap of staff paper a short tune—a fragment of a few notes that's perhaps a memory or echo of something he has heard—not knowing what he's going to make out of them. This is what the composer gives us to hear at the beginning, before developing an entire piece from the fragment.

When Szpilman finishes playing, we also don't hear what is ordinarily called music, but a series of notes struck violently from the highest to the lowest registers of the piano, resembling a sentence spoken with violent force. It is a sentence, however, that one couldn't manage to speak. It is as if the music were a person with no mouth or throat to speak, and as if the performer were able only to imitate speech, like a parrot.

What Szpilman plays at the end, which of course consists strictly of the notes that Chopin wrote, also resembles a struggle, the struggle of someone who strains against being gagged or against his own body, someone who is trying to say something and cannot. Here the music, or rather the notes that Chopin wrote for the end of his piece, is mute, the way we call an animal mute when it appears to be trying to say something. In the same way that the two characters are mute regarding the music that Szpilman is going to play or has just played, there is no hope of establishing a connection, a relationship, between what is played on the piano, what is happening visually in the scene, and what is said by the characters.

We have here a typical example of what I have called the gulf-effect between the *said* and the *shown.* I call the *said,* in a film, everything that belongs to verbal language: words read or heard, uttered by a diegetic or nondiegetic voice. The *shown* is everything that is concretely seen and heard; beyond merely surrounding, coloring, and giving visual form to what is said, it is the very stuff of cinema.

A film is a closed system, demarcating what is in the work and what is not. The film's visual frame, sound, and temporal *durée* encompass a series of *saids* and a series of *showns,* and in this closed milieu, this ecosystem where everything interacts with everything else, anything that is not verbal is liable to "mean" something in relation to what is literally verbalized through dialogue, voice-over, or written language. "Anything" can mean a texture or a shadow, a car passing, a camera movement, a breath, or a thunderous crash.

In analyzing possible relations between the said and the shown in cinema (remember that the shown may be visual or aural), I have outlined five possible cases that can exist separately or in combination in any scene.[2] The gulf-effect is one of these five situations; it designates a case where the dialogue or voice makes no reference to something significant that occurs or arrives in the characters' space. In Polanski's film, the gulf-effect—which creates mystery, discomfort, the sign of an impossibility—is at its greatest.

We can say that what we see and hear in the *shown* is just a pianist playing the piano. The function of a piano—its usefulness—consists of its ability to be played by a pianist. But as we know, it also makes sounds if the keys are struck without intentionality; someone who doesn't know how to play the piano—a cat walking across a keyboard—can certainly produce sounds.

In Polanski's film, Szpilman chooses to play a piece marked by many interruptions and silences. It resembles an improvisation or a poem although it is neither. The piece suggests muteness, not as if it were the result a physical handicap (such as the lack of organs for speaking) or the organic malfunctioning of these organs, but rather as if speaking were simply an impossibility.

Perhaps uniquely, cinema, through the dialectic of the said and the shown and through the use of the gulf-effect, permits the expression of this impossibility of speaking, and the revitalization of this forgotten dimension of Romantic music.

The other scene I wish to examine comes from Jane Campion's *The Piano* (1993). At the film's very outset, Ada says in an internal voice with a Scottish accent, "The voice you are hearing is not my speaking voice. I don't think myself silent; that's because of my piano." As these words are heard we see her walking outdoors, then watching her daughter sleep, then sitting down at the piano, which she proceeds to play.

Because of *my piano*. Again, as in Polanski's film, the character speaks not of music, but of a piano. Ada does not say "because of the music," or "because I'm playing music," nor does she say "because of *the* piano." The terms used announce the film's theme: dispossession, partial drives, the alienated feminine condition. This piano she calls hers is a part of her that she will lose. She does not use the term "play." Does she play? I don't know. Her hands, as we can see, are very active, moving like differentiated and autonomous parts of her body on the piano, which is like a part of herself. And the film chooses not to specify for us the nature of what we are hearing; it chooses not to tell us if she is playing a piece by heart or if she is improvising. Both are possible: it could be a piece in an improvised style, like some toccatas or preludes in the keyboard repertoire, but it could be an improvisation by the character, too. The film chooses to leave doubt as to what she is playing, but then again, we don't have to choose. In fact, it is our duty, a rule of the game, *not* to choose, not to decide in the place of the film. We can only say that we don't see any manuscript or printed music.

Obviously we must forget, or rather we must not know, that the music was specially composed for the film by Michael Nyman in a strange and partly anachronistic style, dating from twenty to thirty years later than the film's temporal setting. We don't hear a recognizable music, nor is it recognizably anti-music (e.g., random plunking on keys) or a passage of improvisation; it is only a flood of notes. We see Ada stop suddenly when a woman enters the room, but notice that Campion has avoided showing us Ada's face while she "plays" the piano; we see it only when she has stopped "playing." Polanski, on the other hand, showed Szpilman's face while the latter played, but as we know, nothing is visible on the face of a pianist while he is playing; we cannot know to what extent he is conscious of what he is playing. The face of a musician in the process of playing a piano, violin, harp, or any other instrument that does not involve the mouth or breath is a mystery. It's like a closed box, and we cannot know if the hands are moving with or without the participation of the mind and emotions. The face of a pianist represents the face's right to be impenetrable, its right not to be in contact with others.

There are other differences between *The Piano* and *The Pianist*. What is produced by Ada's hands in collaboration with the piano sounds sweepingly self-assured. The young woman's hands seem familiar with the keyboard as a whole, and they navigate all the octaves with utmost confidence. On the other hand, Szpilman's hands, when he attacks Chopin's work, hesitate as if on the threshold of a void. They play one note, and then the next, and each of these notes seems solitary. After all, Szpilman cannot say, "this is *my* piano."

Let us not descend into oversimplification, however. What Ada produces with "her" piano is not just a flood, a liquid flow; we can distinguish real forms and phrases in this flow of forms, like a fish one might see swim by in the water. And conversely, what Szpilman begins playing on this piano that isn't "his" also succeeds in flowing, after it has begun in such a different manner. In both cases, we must occupy two places at once. One part of ourselves knows the conventions of film, and knows the music of Chopin; the other part of us has to rediscover the music anew, or rather experience the sounds as they come to us, giving the music a new chance to be born.

It is often characteristic of classical music that it narrates its own genesis. A musical piece might begin with notes, a chord, a rhythmic idea, a sort of chaos or raw material, or else with isolated sounds before the whole thing gains complexity and organization. Music often begins with what the book of Genesis calls the original formlessness and void, the initial confusion. A book will rarely begin with the letters of the alphabet or with isolated words. At the beginning of a novel or a poem we are immediately in the world of language. A musical work, however, often tells us the story of its own creation, its own birth, and, even in the hands of classical composers, it might commence by teetering on the borderline between noise and organized sound, nonintentional and intentional sound, inchoate elements and patterned organization.

This is something that the cinema allows us to hear afresh. In a way, the cinema gives us the ability to rediscover what we call music, what we have heard thousands of times, in conditions that approximate the first time by virtue of creating its own new context. Of course, I know that this "first time" is illusory. We cannot repress or undo our own understanding of music, of our culture, and it is useless even to try. But let's say that we can pretend to do so.

In Polanski's film what happens, and what do we experience? All we have to do is listen to the words that are actually spoken—*spielen* (play) or *piano*—as well as to notice what words are not said, such as *music* or *Chopin*. We must be aware of speech that is suggested in the music even while it remains mute. We must watch what is on the screen and hear what is in the loudspeakers: faces or, on the contrary, no faces; notes on the piano, one after the other. What we need to do is be aware of the *cinematic reality* and the *diegetic reality* at the same time, knowing that they are not mutually exclusive but rather superimposed. It's not one instead of the other, but rather one *and* the other.

I call *diegetic reality* that which occurs in the action, based on what we can see and hear. *Cinematic reality* is what is literally before our eyes and ears, and which corresponds to another reality of a "magical" quality, if you will, but is every bit as important.

A simple example of the coexistence of diegetic reality and cinematic reality in the cinema is the telephone sequence—what I'll call a "telepheme" after an old French word invented around 1900.[3] Two characters speak on the phone without seeing each other (this is *diegetic reality*), but in the editing, through crosscutting, the directions of the characters' gazes intersect, one looking to the left and one to the right. In diegetic reality they do not see each other, but in cinematic reality they do. This latter reality does not destroy the former and is not nullified by it; rather, the two are superimposed.

The diegetic reality of the scene between Szpilman and the German officer, of course, is that the former plays for the latter a piece of music that is a Chopin ballade. The cinematic reality is that he plays a nameless fragment, made up of notes that are seeking a theme, a center.

With cinema we can also dispense with naming and judging the music as well as the manner in which it is performed. Is Szpilman doing a "good" rendition of the ballade? This is not the question. Did Michael Nyman write good or bad music for Jane Campion's film? That isn't the question either. The mystery of what we call music—and especially the mystery of the relationship between instrumental music and the language it sometimes seems to proffer in silence—can be rediscovered thanks to the cinema.

Translated by Claudia Gorbman

NOTES

1. In German, the officer uses the second person formal, a sign of respect, and not the second person singular *(Was machst du?)*, a mark of familiarity, superior rank, or disdain.

2. Translator's note: These five figures that define relations between the said and the shown are scansion, the gulf-effect, contrast, counterpoint, and contradiction. See Michel Chion, *Un Art sonore, le cinema: histoire, esthétique, poétique* (Paris: Cahiers du cinéma/essais, 2003), pp. 340–47.

3. See ibid., pp. 324–29.

PART II

Musical Agency

6 Opera, Aesthetic Violence, and the Imposition of Modernity: *Fitzcarraldo*

Richard Leppert

> I consider opera a universe all its own. On stage an opera
> represents a complete world, a cosmos transformed into music.
>
> **Werner Herzog**

> The operatic world is, whatever else, a world of magic invocations.
>
> **Siegfried Kracauer**

Werner Herzog's *Fitzcarraldo* (1982), set in the Peruvian Amazon some-time near the turn of the last century, tells the story of an Irishman of un-certain class standing, a passionate lover of opera who wants to build an opera house in the frontier town of Iquitos—a theater to rival the opera house in Manaus, the product of European rubber-baron largesse.[1] Fitzcar-raldo intends for Caruso to inaugurate his theater. First, however, he's got to make some money. In the remote jungle, far from Iquitos, there lies a vast and heretofore inaccessible tract of land rich in rubber trees. One impedi-ment stands in his way of reaching it: the wickedly impassable Pongo das Mortes rapids, deep in a gorge of the Ucayali River, an Amazon tributary. Fitzcarraldo hopes to overcome this challenge by first traveling upstream on the Pachitea River, another Amazon tributary that closely parallels the Ucayali; indeed, at one point the two rivers virtually meet, save for a steep hill separating them. Fitzcarraldo will pull his riverboat up this hill and down the other side, thereby reaching the Ucayali. By this means having bypassed the rapids, he will then steam downstream to his rubber-tree tract and its awaiting fortune. The engineering challenge of moving a 350-ton riverboat overland[2] is surpassed by the challenge of pacifying a dangerously hostile indigenous population. The raison d'être of the endeavor is opera, and the means to this end is opera as well, not only because it provides the inspiration for meeting the engineering challenge, but also, and more im-portant, because it is the means by which the Indians are subdued.

There are four kinds of music employed in the film, two of which are used nondiegetically and two diegetically, with virtually no overlap between the pairs. The principal nondiegetic music is provided by a purpose-composed score by Florian Fricke and his ensemble, Popol Vuh, a team that is also responsible for the music in several of Herzog's other films, including *Aguirre, der Zorn Gottes* (1972) and *Nosferatu—Phantom der Nacht* (1979). Popol Vuh's music comes off as a kind of ambient wall of sound whose acoustic vastness is matched by the vagueness of its cultural sources. The rampantly hybrid (not to say pastiche) quality of the music, something like New Age meets Orff, has an air of the ritualistic tempered with an off-the-shelf mysteriousness that is at once worldly and not. The music affects timelessness, if only on account of the mix of sounds that cancel out historical and cultural specificity. Throughout the film Herzog uses Popol Vuh's music as a discursive accompaniment to nature, nearly always represented in dire opposition to culture.

The only other nondiegetic music in the film is heard only fleetingly. When the riverboat heads upriver for its fateful encounter with "nature"—setting out for, and later departing from, the last European settlement, a missionary outpost—brief excerpts from Richard Strauss's *Tod und Verklärung* play softly as background accompaniment.[3] The choice is apt, to the extent that Fitzcarraldo has now entered into the lived space of the Indians. As Fitzcarraldo proceeds, the threat of physical *Tod* (death) becomes increasingly real; but the actual *Tod* will be that of Fitzcarraldo's dream, which becomes the inadvertent vehicle for the *Verklärung* (transfiguration) of the Indians' dream, one entirely different from his. As the riverboat leaves the mission outpost, and hence approaches the last remnant of "civilization," Strauss's music is accompanied by a thunderstorm and lightening as the sky darkens and the sun sets. In short, the trope announced by the composition's title is both aurally and visually overdetermined.

Throughout the film, Fricke's nondiegetic score is often abruptly intercut with the diegetic music principally provided by Italian opera. These two sound masses, radically different from one another, establish an acoustic binary that in turn underscores the design of the film's nature/culture narrative. Herzog also uses small bits of indigenous and pseudo-indigenous music, but it's opera that matters most. Opera determines the narrative, defines the antiheroic hero, and, not least, provides a commentary to the story of which it is a determinant. Opera is staged, "live" ("live" in scare quotes), at the beginning and end of the film. At six other points opera is referenced, and almost exclusively so as part of the narrative action, via a windup, lotus-horn gramophone. (There is only one instance where the diegetic use of gramophone briefly morphs towards the nondiegetic, and only one instance, also brief, where operatic music is used nondiegetically.) For the purposes of this chapter, I will say nothing more about Popol Vuh's music, though there's a good deal to be said; I will comment on Herzog's use of nativelike music. Most of what I have to say will concern Herzog's use of opera in *Fitzcarraldo,* concerning which I'll restrict the discussion to the live-action staged scenes that open and close the film, and to just two of the six episodes where the gramophone is employed.

Herzog's story for *Fitzcarraldo* connects the Peruvian Amazon to an incomplete, timeless space seemingly caught in the ahistoric moment of its creation. The film's first visual is a static distance shot of the jungle, darkly green, functioning like a curtain that is about to be raised on the epic stage of the Amazon basin, where a romantic parable will be played out in quasi-documentary style. The first "event" is acoustic—audible but invisible: thunder, in sonic allusion to trouble and change. The electrical discharge has no visual referent; we can hear what we cannot see, a hint that the film is literally about acoustic realities. Visual stasis is succeeded by a slow pan of the jungle shrouded in fog; the curtain, as it were, becomes a scrim. We see enough to know that we're not seeing what is there to be seen. The camera moves from the pan to a slow zoom into the "face" of the jungle, only to confirm its visual impenetrability, an effect that overdetermines the sense of the invisibility that plagues seeing.[4] Herzog then cuts to the façade of the Manaus opera house, shot from below from the bottom of a long stairway. The opera house sits high like a gigantic altar, a site of art worship, whereupon the sacrifice of nature to culture will be celebrated.

The logical impossibility that lies at the heart of opera organizes the film's logic. Opera is the film's form and its content. Opera as both an institution and sonic manifestation defines the film's narrative structure, particularly its overtly exaggerated situations, as well as the character of its principal protagonist. Fitzcarraldo himself is operatically larger than life, and a man obsessed to hear life sung; every narrative element in the film revolves around this urgent need. As Fitzcarraldo puts it, "Opera gives expression to our greatest feelings."[5] Indeed, the function of spoken language in the film is wholly instrumental; its purpose is to lead to song.[6]

As the action begins, Fitzcarraldo, together with his lover Molly, is furiously paddling his small boat into Manaus, after traveling 1,200 miles on the river, including two days at the end with a broken-down motor. He reaches the opera house and begs his way in, just in time to see the performance conclude. It's *Ernani.* Caruso is performing the title role, and it's Caruso whom Fitzcarraldo came to hear, and for the first time in his life. It's obviously a special performance, all the more so because the role of Elvira is performed by none other than Sarah Bernhardt, who mimes her part.[7]

(The "soprano," whose voice Bernhardt lip syncs, is visible, in concert attire, well off to the side, though she too attracts some attention with her gesturing.)[8]

This scene was staged for Herzog by Werner Schroeter, who, besides being a filmmaker, already had experience with directing opera, unlike Herzog at the time. Schroeter created a surreal, multiply overdetermined dream world on a stage illuminated in luridly saturated colors, and peopled by actors who perform with intense emotion the ridiculous text Verdi has assigned them.

Ernani (1844) is early Verdi, his fifth opera, premiered five years after his first. Herzog's original plan had called for *Un ballo in maschera* (1859), a mature work, whose plot—itself fairly ridiculous—is nonetheless positively Shakespearean by comparison with the abundantly ludicrous goings-on of *Ernani*. For that matter, the plot of Bellini's *I Puritani*, used for the film's final scene, is equally absurd.[9] Indeed, epic-quality improbability constitutes the film's cultural logic, a point Herzog is keen to establish from the very start.[10] *Ernani*'s tragic story is a triumph of nearly cosmic absurdity, no less than its score is often stunningly beautiful, and a perfect vehicle for a great singer—here Caruso—but one whose acting abilities are limited to stock gestures signaling the intensity of his passions. The now-ancient nonsinging Bernhardt, who not incidentally lip-synchs atrociously (hinting that she barely knows her part), does everything within her powers of pantomime to draw attention to herself and away from Caruso.[11] She grandiosely performs the part of Elvira, a would-be bride, many decades after any amount of lighting and cosmetics could achieve her credibility. Bernhardt, in life rail-thin and just over five feet tall, here physically dominates the short Caruso. In sum, Schroeter represents her as a consummate ham, a character more fit for music hall than a star of the legitimate stage.[12]

The mute actor playing the aged Bernhardt is a cross-dressed male,[13] poorly disguised, and that's exactly the point. Bernhardt essentially proclaims her transvestism, as it were, as the open secret of the surface foundation of opera's dream world.[14] Opera, especially as staged here, drives home the point that what we see (real fakery) claims little authority over what we can hear (the centrality of song). Thus the performance of *Ernani* is live, but all of it is *obviously* in playback. Bernhardt's mouth doesn't come close to fitting the text she purportedly sings (this is part of the diegesis); but then neither does the mouth of Caruso or that of the "real soprano" performing Elvira's role offstage. (The ventriloquism of Caruso and the offstage soprano is nondiegetic, to be sure, yet plainly visible and hence discursive.) To complete the point, an actor plays Caruso playing Ernani; the actor's voice is neither Caruso's nor his own, but that of another singer whose performance he mimes.

We have our first look at the performance, in medias res, as the aged Bernhardt, portraying one half of a romantic couple, missing her cue, enters the scene too soon at the top of a very long and curved staircase; she checks herself, backs out of sight momentarily, and then reappears, but with arms outstretched as though she were confusing Elvira with Lucia and about to do a mad scene for the benefit of its heightened dramatic impact. Bernhardt's right leg was amputated in 1914, a biographical fact that Schroeter vigorously exploits. On the way down the stairs she moves haltingly, nearly stumbling, troubled by her prosthesis, but averting disaster, if barely. Her exaggerated clumsiness visually degrades to near slapstick the overwrought drama of the approach to her lover, where, shortly thereafter, she will enact her own death. Verdi gives Elvira a faint at the end of *Ernani*, but Bernhardt, not to be upstaged by Caruso's text-authorized death scene, seizes his exceedingly large dagger after he stabs himself and impales herself in his footsteps, in a free adaptation that better serves her purposes. As if that weren't sufficient, she tries to upstage him during the curtain calls—to Caruso's obvious irritation, as Schroeter is careful to represent.

Managing to gain admittance to *Ernani* just before the opera's conclusion, Fitzcarraldo witnesses the operatic hero's self-inflicted death, a matter of profoundly misplaced homosocial, hypermasculine honor. On his wedding day, with a masked ball in progress, and at the last possible moment, rival Silva sounds the hunting horn that signals to Ernani that he must kill himself to keep a promise, made in the second act for reasons too foolish to require detailing here. Suffice it to say that Silva blows the horn, and Ernani, true to his word, kills himself as his bride-to-be stands by helplessly (though not, of course, silently).[15]

When Ernani/Caruso dies, he reaches out his hand toward the audience, a stock gesture that Fitzcarraldo, with Molly's help, reads as being directed at him alone: he interprets it as the passing of Ernani's torch to the dream-beguiled Irishman. From that point forward Fitzcarraldo recognizes no worldly impediment to his goal of bringing Caruso to his own personal part of the jungle.

Fitzcarraldo is a man in the middle. He hates the established bourgeois colonizers, if only because he regards them as vulgar. They're interested in rubber for money; he wants rubber for opera—just as he wants opera for the "natives," and the children especially. To bring opera to the Indians, he will colonize them, as it were for their own good. He'll become a rubber baron for art's sake. Fitzcarraldo's quest, driven by opera, is no less absurd than the heroics of *Ernani,* and no less credible than the sonorous passion of the hapless lovers singing their hearts out. It's all mad, *and* it's all perfectly congruent with that which it defines and simultaneously aestheticizes: atavistic romanticism in deep denial of what its own denials of rapacious modernity in turn help to authorize, stabilize, and reproduce. The very Indians who will benefit from Caruso in the wilderness are the ones Fitzcarraldo sarcastically calls "bare asses," picking up the lingo of the colonial Europeans he otherwise despises. The Indians are the laborers who will build his aesthetic pyramid, one that is constructed on what, to all *appearances* at least, is a foundation of cultural kitsch.[16] That is, Schroeter's staging of *Ernani* fundamentally comes off as a good deal less than the high art Fitzcarraldo himself assigns it. In Schroeter's account, it's on a par with music hall—overwrought, and borderline camp—but at the same time utterly sincere in its multiple levels of exaggeration. The point, obviously enough, is that Schroeter and Herzog stage opera as a carnival-mirror reflection of modernity whose truth lies precisely in distortion.[17] Thus, the apparent *lack* of synchronous sound, produced by the consistently bad lipsynching by everyone purporting to sing, produces a yawning gap between image and soundtrack. The discursive indexicality that might emerge from the synchronicity of sound and vision is denied, and obviously so.

The role of technology, as a fundamental constituent of modernity, helps to organize the film's narrative; technology, as a component part of the narrative, accounts in part for the documentary look of *Fitzcarraldo.* Herzog lavishes visual and sonoric attention on equipment and how, by means of equipment, things get done, in particular, of course, the lifting of the boat over the hill, a conceit that becomes literally real, since Herzog eschewed special effects in making this happen. (Herzog has stated that the scene was intended to have the quality of farce, specifically *despite* its actuality. He has referred to the scene as "having the quality of Italian Opera.")[18] However crucial engineering know-how is to the success of Fitzcarraldo's endeavor, the technology of sound recording is, if anything, still greater. As the riverboat, christened *Molly Aida,* steams deeper into country seldom visited by Europeans, the signs of acute danger from hostile Indians increase, culminating in the sounds of mass chanting and drumming—though in fact it's African and not low-land Peruvian drumming that Herzog employs.[19] Fitzcarraldo refuses to answer with the boat's cannon, the usual acoustic certificate of authority and overwhelming power, to silence the unseen Indians' drums and voices, thereby overwhelming them. Instead, he sets up the gramophone on the roof of the pilothouse. Herzog briefly shoots the gramophone in a close-up, stationary and secure, set against the shifting green backdrop of the passing jungle. "Now," Fitzcarraldo says, "it's Caruso's turn"—and the turntable is put in motion. The voice insistently wafts onto the water, and, apparently, penetrates the jungle, spiritlike, reaching the ears of the Indians who, though they can be plainly heard, cannot be seen. The acoustic claim of the Indians is answered by "Il sogno" from Massenet's *Manon*,[20] the second-act aria in which des Grieux relates to Manon a dream he's had of happiness in the country. In the dream he is surrounded by beautiful nature, but his happiness is nonetheless incomplete because Manon herself is absent.

The aria fits the scene. Caruso, as Fitzcarraldo's alter ego, calls out to a Euro-feminized Nature, the woman of the forest and the Indians, which he is prepared to make his own.[21] As Michel Chion once put it, referring to speech, "The presence of a human voice structures the sonic space that contains it."[22] In this instance, the *singing* voice raises the stakes of Chion's insight not least by the illogic of both the look of the gramophone taking the place of the boat's warning whistle, and by the sounds that emanate from it—sounds whose volume Herzog significantly exaggerates. For a few moments, the two musics compete, while Fitzcarraldo stands next to his gramophone, shot from behind as he looks into the green curtain of the jungle. Gradually, however, the sounds of chanting and drumming cease.[23] The mood of Fitzcarraldo, standing next to the revolving turntable, shifts from anxiety to confidence; he puts his hands on his hips in a kind of self-satisfied gloat, while Caruso reaches his melodic, and authoritative, climax. Thus the gramophone, built for and suited to the domestic parlor, merges into the public realm of Eden, with a voice that "speaks" with the authority of the Word made musical. The claim of music—of the Western variety—as the universal "language" plays out here, if only in Fitzcarraldo's lunatic dream, as acoustic conquistador.

Melody and harmony conquer rhythm. Culture, serviced by technology, trumps nature—or so Fitzcarraldo thinks. Caruso silences the Indians, and then pulls them into visibility, out of the jungle and onto the river in their dugouts, in a kind of watery Pied Piper story. (In this regard Fitzcarraldo's gramophone shares a functional relation with the stereo system onboard Kilgore's attack helicopter in *Apocalypse Now*, except that Caruso attracts, whereas the acoustic blasts of *Die Walküre* repel and terrify.) The impact of Caruso is driven by technology, and, indeed, it is impossible in technology's absence. In the modern era, the voice is invariably mediated; it is never "natural"—not even when "live" in the opera house, as I have already suggested. In *Fitzcarraldo*, the social agency of opera is dialectically twinned with the social agency of the machine.

Throughout the narrative, Fitzcarraldo evokes only Caruso's name, despite the fact that the music he plays on his gramophone is for the most part Caruso in ensemble, as is the case in the staged opera scenes that begin and end the film. The other ensemble voice parts are prominently those of women. They don't seem to matter much to Fitzcarraldo; he never once refers to them, though he does of course name his boat after an ancient operatic princess, as well as Molly, a brothel keeper. When all is said and done, he hears only Caruso. Indeed, the women's vocal presence marks the absence of women in the film generally (Molly's rather small supporting role notwithstanding), except to the extent that embodied women serve as iterations of the feminine-nature trope—that is, as the foil that Fitzcarraldo both figuratively and literally penetrates.[24] In short, the feminine is displaced as nature, but as well the feminine is imagined *in* music and *as* music. It is the feminine "voice" of music on which Fitzcarraldo focuses his most urgent desires (the desires he has for Molly, on the other hand, are barely bothered with). The real point is that music, which long played the role of the eternal feminine in European consciousness, makes itself heard through the gender-colonized agency of a man's voice. The singing women are there to fill in the harmonies, or, perhaps better stated, to make things harmonious.

Caruso's voice competes with the background noise common to shellac discs, the effect of which is to remind us of the modern technology upon which latter-day art worship rests, a worship that for Fitzcarraldo otherwise functions as a profound critique of that very modernity for which Caruso acts as antidote. In particular, the singer's muffled voice, the tinny-sounding wind orchestra accompanying him, and the disc noise, not to mention the riverboat's engine (alternately subdued or heightened, as demanded by the context), together emphasize the technological authority brought to bear against mere nature, including the "natural" folk of the jungle. For Fitzcarraldo, that is, Caruso on shellac is His Master's Voice to the Irishman's Nipper; and what's good enough for Nipper will do fine for anyone else within earshot.[25] Whatever Fitzcarraldo introjects will in turn be shared by an uncompromising projection/transference, as it were, on waves of music.

This is to suggest that the cultural hegemony claimed by Caruso on the gramophone in the "wilderness" is overdetermined (if, in the end, oversubscribed by Fitzcarraldo himself). The Indians hear a voice from somewhere, but it is from nowhere they can recognize; the singing voice makes strange claims as it bares its soul in order to colonize theirs. Caruso's singing foretells, with the authority of an untranslated secular scripture, the Indians' future, and whether or not they recognize it matters only insofar as it concerns Fitzcarraldo's immediate instrumental need for their giving him safe passage and, subsequently, their labor.

After the *Molly Aida* is safely back in the water on the other side of the hill, and following a long night's drunken celebration by crew and Indians alike, the Indians cut the mooring lines: the Indians have their own dream, namely, the sacrifice of the riverboat to the gods of the rapids. The boat tumbles helplessly toward disaster, careening through the rock-strewn gorge, while the hungover Fitzcarraldo and the few of his diminished crew on board are thrown about sufficiently to awaken from their stupor—but much too late to do anything but hang on for dear life. In the midst of all this, so we're given to believe, the boat's movement sets the gramophone into motion and it gives us Caruso in the sextet from *Lucia*,[26] with its various commentaries on love and its myriad complications, disillusionments, betrayals, and failures, made gloriously ironic by the interweaving of voices that produce a rampant degree of melodiousness underwritten by the harmonic envelope in which the tunes are wrapped. Even if one knows the language, it's impossible to follow the words, and here in the jungle no one knows Italian, nor likely even the opera's plot, which narrates not only disaster, but also the end of dreams. The unexpected entrance of Edgardo, triggering the sextet, mirrors the cutting of the mooring lines. Nothing will be the same thereafter. A mad scene, and deaths, will follow. Musically, however, the *Lucia* sextet *celebrates* disaster in its immensely pleasurable sonorities. Better said, the sextet "speaks" in its own way of hopeless hope—not through its dystopian text, but in its music, all those splendid thirds, sixths, unisons, and octaves.

As the boat careens through the rapids (figure 6.1), Caruso and his confederates serenade, and the needle never skips. The logically impossible diegetic incongruity—the diegesis confirmed at least at the start by means of a quick close-up of the spinning turntable—sets two sounds in dire conjunction: an operatic ensemble and a riverboat crashing into rocks in a raging rapids, the boat, like the shellac discs, turning in circles, a favorite visual effect found in other Herzog films. Our eyes inform us of disaster and the violent triumph of nature; the soundtrack, however, describes the triumph of culture by means of the harmonies of intertwined voices, never mind the crisis that brought these voices together in song. As if to make the matter clear, Herzog gradually eliminates all sound except that of the sextet. The now-silenced diegesis, visually dramatic, demands acoustics, but hardly opera, except of course in the illusory reality of a film about dreams.[27] The beauty of Donizetti's acoustic wave, undisturbed by the chaos and turbulence surrounding it, is in fact matched by the sublime visual beauty of the

Figure 6.1 *Lucia* in the rapids, in *Fitzcarraldo*.

riverboat rebounding helplessly from one side to the other of the roaring river. The violence of the putatively "real" event, by being completely silenced, reverts to the indexical aesthetics of romanticized nature, the raw energy Goethe fixed on in *Werther*, an unfeeling nature that his psychotic-neurotic and narcissistic young hero at once abhorred and found himself mesmerized by: nature meant nothing, and nature meant more than he could imagine.[28]

Caruso's arias give Fitzcarraldo's ears what his eyes deny him. If the gaze, filmic and otherwise, is intended to penetrate, throughout the film Fitzcarraldo's eyes hit a wall of impenetrable green that acts on him in a way analogous to a blue screen, in front of which he acts out his dream, with the keen assistance of a crucial prop that helps suture him into a narrative that he's trying desperately to write. The narrative is informed by psychic introjection via acoustic displacement. Metaphorically, if hardly literally, the ethereality of music, its ethereality underscored by the reproductive apparatus from which it emanates, drowns out the visually noisy but acoustically "silenced" enemy: nature and the "bare-ass" culture Fitzcarraldo includes under the term. All this notwithstanding, Fitzcarraldo acknowledges nature's agency, but as an amorphous fiend. Caruso, ever at his beck and call, provides him—and not just us—what Adorno and Eisler claimed generally for film music, namely, that it corresponded to the "whistling or singing child in the dark."[29] In short, that is to say, the film's music addresses fear, and is its antidote. Put differently, the sublime visuality of the riverboat in the rapids demands the acoustic hermeneutics of opera for sense to be made of it.

Fitzcarraldo names his boat after two women, Molly and Aida. Aida marks what matters about opera to Herzog. The singing voice makes sensible the utopian desire of perfect expressibility. Opera, as it were, finds the way to name the Name, the imaginary Absolute, the hoped-for Spirit. Aida voluntarily entombs herself so that she can sing to the end (or maybe forever) with her lover. If opera is "about" singing—singing understood to "say" what speaking desperately seeks to convey but can't—then being entombed and ending life in a love duet is not the worst way to go. Indeed, it's possibly the ultimate form of peace (and *"Pace"* is the word that Amneris intones repeatedly in her blessing from outside the sealed chamber). What I'm suggesting is that *Aida* is about its ending, its *sense* of an ending. To die in love is good; to die in love and in song is to accomplish in death that for which life is lived, namely, once and for all time to be able to express love absolutely, exceeding the hopeless inadequacy of mere language.

Aida plays out its final scene in the metaphorical total darkness of a smothering tomb. The eyes can no longer see. Only sound conveys what must be said and before it's too late; those words must be sung—and, to be sure, sung in harmony, a sonoric oneness for all time. *Aida* ends in a dream world; its last scene, in effect if not in staged practice, is a long blackout. All we have is music conveying utterly selfless love. It's there to be heard; seeing it is utterly irrelevant. And just as *Aida* ends, so also does *Fitzcarraldo*. Herzog closes his film with a sustained blackout. The visual sense is denied, while the auditory sense is offered the privilege of a cadence. And this brings me to my own conclusion, via the film's final scene.

Earlier in the film, in a scene involving a conversation with missionaries living in the remote bush and ministering to the Indians, Fitzcarraldo hears a priest's complaint that "We can't seem to cure [the Indians] of the idea that everyday life is only an illusion behind which lies the reality of dreams." Fitzcarraldo replies, simply, "Actually, I'm very interested in these ideas. I specialize in opera myself."

Fitzcarraldo's scheme for a rubber plantation whose proceeds would fund an opera house in Iquitos fails, but in failing he manages a momentary triumph by realizing a substitute dream in the form of live opera on water. He sells the damaged *Molly Aida* and invests the proceeds to hire a small itinerant opera troupe. The absurdity of the mise-en-scène is extreme. Ten small boats pull alongside the riverboat loaded down, variously, with singers in costume, orchestra musicians with instruments in hand and wearing full formal attire—never mind the midday heat and choking humidity—and paltry scenery rather badly representing a castle atop a cliff and a cutaway of battlements. The musicians disembark on shore, welcomed by Fitzcarraldo, and shortly thereafter take their places aboard the riverboat turned opera theater. During this disembarkation, the French horn players acknowledge Fitzcarraldo, however incongruously (and ironically), by playing the horn motif from the opening movement of Beethoven's "Emperor"[30] Concerto (first heard at measures 48–52). Fitzcarraldo, so it seems, is king for a day, as sonically confirmed by the king of all music that really matters (figure 6.2).

Shortly thereafter, the boat approaches Iquitos for the last time, making a grand entrance, in mid-performance, with a staged scene from I Puritani (1835) in progress on its top deck and pilothouse roof.[31] The scene is part of act 1, scene 3, beginning with Arturo's aria "A te, o cara, amor talora," and involves the love duet between Arturo and Elvira, with the chorus performed by mestizo musicians.[32] The Puritan costumes worn by brownskinned people is perhaps visually jarring to our eyes, but no such discomfort is evident among the singers or orchestra. Like opera itself, the hybridization is for them naturalized, indeed comfortable. And all of them seem uncannily happy, even celebratory. Herzog edits the scene to show, alternately, distance and close-up shots of Fitzcarraldo, who, despite the economic ruin facing him, is in a splendid mood. Proud as punch, and smoking what he describes as "the biggest cigar in the world," he takes it all in, and invites us to do the same by means of a grandly sweeping gesture that would fit nicely on any opera stage.

The operatic lovers express their delight and passion with the usual stock moves (figure 6.3). But their happiness is ventriloquized: they lip-synch badly to the playback. The fakery is as obvious as the castle scenery is low budget. Nothing is what it seems, apart from the sublime happiness apparent everywhere, including on the faces of the large crowd on shore hearing opera for the first time. The Puritani lovers recall old torments, now convinced—mistakenly—that joy is at hand (after subsequent trials and tribulations the opera eventually has a happy ending). And then the screen goes black. The music continues for a few seconds, after which the volume is cut quickly to silence at a cadence. We're at a full stop, but not at closure. We have the sense, however momentary, of an ending—indeed, an insistence on it, since the film is literally over at this point, for which reason Herzog placed the credits at the beginning. The reality of the dream meets the alternate reality of the film's end: the house lights return us to the here and now. The dream is kept going only so long as music, which exceeds reality, plays against the perverted rationalities embedded in the film's visual narrative. Herzog sets music in striking dialectical tension with the indexical character of the film image itself, which Herzog constantly inflects with

Figure 6.2 Saluting the "emperor" of opera (*Fitzcarraldo*).

Figure 6.3 The *I Puritani* love duet aboard the *Molly Aida* (*Fitzcarraldo*).

both the resonance and actuality of the documentary. Yet what is documented is at once both more and less than the "reality" available to the eyes. For that matter, the aria and ensemble texts themselves relate *only* fictions. The truth, so to speak, is there nonetheless, but in the sonorous notes, in the evanescent reality of music.

The utopian charge of opera in *Fitzcarraldo* is anchored in the insistence to hear life sung—and notwithstanding the myriad instrumentalities of opera's own material-institutional foundations. This much is acknowledged in repeated shots throughout the film of the gramophone and the shellac discs, which, taken together, visually concentrate the institutionality of opera into the commodity forms associated with mechanical sound repro-duction.[33] In *Fitzcarraldo* music gives life to sight; life musically deter-mined, however, includes nothing of the mundane: recitative is barred. What matters is life heightened in aria form, the acoustic sublime. The re-ality of Fitzcarraldo's dream life is defined by assorted operatic fragments torn from their narrative context. What he chooses to hear, in other words, is a phonograph album of sonic snapshots. His utopian acoustic is consti-tuted from fragile bits of treasured musical detritus inscribed on brittle shel-lac, which with every playing is damaged by the heavy tone arm tipped by a steel needle. Every hearing takes away from what he desires most, bring-ing closer to the foreground what Adorno once named the "hear-stripe" (in reference to radio broadcast interference), and the increasing static of the worn and damaged disc, technology's calling card, the noisy sign of the modernity that Fitzcarraldo at once depends upon and abhors. Each audition of Caruso promises Caruso's ultimate silence. The disc will be destroyed by the love of the writing on its surface.

Fitzcarraldo uses music from a long bygone era and of a sort—opera—that very few people today know or care much about. The musical quotations are likely unrecognizable to most viewers; figuring them out is a game of sorts, since none of the Caruso recordings is identified in the credits. Moreover, the staged opera scenes are made to play off distinctly exaggerated popular clichés about opera, the most characteristically overwrought of all modern art forms. Opera, in short, is now largely strange and estranged. For Herzog, I think, this strangeness constitutes its saving grace in late modernity, for which cinema commonly serves as an aesthetic proponent. In one sense, in other words, in *Fitzcarraldo* Herzog has made a film that functions in acute dialectical tension with the medium through which he speaks. In a film so visually dependent upon turning, and turning in circles, the "visual turn" of modern culture is called into question by the aural, not as supplement of the image, but as the foundation for the insight by which to critique it.

For Herzog, opera foregrounds the ever-widening gap between the mun-dane, perversely hyper-rationalized, and duly fetishized love affair with facts as the sole legitimate index of the real, on the one hand, and the real-ity of the unreal, on the other. Whatever Herzog's complicated relation to nature and to the Others without whom his film would have been impossi-ble, he clearly valorizes the principle of otherness, just as he recognizes the refusal embedded in what Attali, paraphrasing Adorno, called "residual ir-rationality," which for both men was a form of principled alternative to "Mitmachen,"[34] to going with the flow. The old operas, as employed in this film, in spite of everything about them that is otherwise objectionable, still have a truth to tell about the social struggle embedded in the changing hierarchy of human sensing. But to get at this truth we have to look and to hear backwards, so to speak. The film begins with an ending (*Ernani* and death), and it ends with a mirthful beginning (the act 1 scene from *I Puritani*) that, against the odds, celebrates another ending (the collapse of Fitzcarraldo's dream). Herzog thus sets the linearity of narrative historicism akimbo; the usual truths, here of narrative closure and pictorial indexicality, fail in the confusion.

Herzog's point, in a way, is to mark the fallibility of seeing in order to make audible the truths of hearing: hearing music. The advantage of opera is that it accomplishes both tasks at once.[35] All of its fallibilities and, indeed, its absurdities do not overwhelm the truths of the singing voice, the simple fact that people literally *need* to sing. One might say, I suppose, that it's precisely in opera's lie through which its truth is revealed: that truth is at once acoustic, sublime, and in part utopian. Herzog's film, in tension with its own visually determined documentary excess, points to this alternative—and it's there for the hearing.

NOTES

I wish to express my gratitude to Hisham Bizri for his careful reading and thoughtful criticism of an earlier draft of this essay.

1. Manaus is in western Brazil. The first performance in the lavishly decorated Teatro Amazonas took place on New Year's Eve, 1896. The rubber boom lasted from 1880 to 1914. See Lester Caltvedt, "Herzog's *Fitzcarraldo* and the Rubber Era," *Film & History* 18.4 (December 1988), pp. 74–84. According to Richard Collier, *The River That God Forgot: The Story of the Amazon River Rubber Boom* (New York: Dutton, 1968), p. 56, Caruso was in fact invited to sing at the Manaus opera house but never did so; the closest he got was Rio de Janeiro for performances in 1903 and again in 1914. The historical character on whom Herzog loosely based his film was Carlos Fermin Fitzcarrald (1862–97), a rubber baron and merchant. Like Herzog's character, Fitzcarrald brought a boat over a hill—a much higher one than Herzog's—but only by first disassembling it. For the basic biographical details, see Ronald H. Dolkart, "Civilization's Aria: Film as Lore and Opera as Metaphor in Werner Herzog's *Fitzcarraldo*," *Journal of Latin American Lore* 11.2 (1985), p. 129.

2. *Fitzcarraldo* is not the first film to document such a feat. The French documentary *La Croisière jaune* (1934), directed by André Sauvage, a promotional record of an expedition sponsored by Citroën intended to advertise the advanced technology of their automobiles, includes scenes involving the feat of taking the cars across the Himalayas. The vehicles were disassembled and their parts toted by Sher-

pas through the mountain passes. The use of native labor to facilitate the penetration of Western technology into other worlds, a hoary trope, to be sure, is used in both films. See Charles Musser, "Engaging with Reality: Documentary," in *The Oxford History of World Cinema*, ed. Geoffrey Nowell-Smith (Oxford: Oxford University Press, 1996), p. 322. Thanks to Hisham Bizri for telling me about this film.

3. A very brief quotation from another piece of classical instrumental music occurs, this time diegetically, near the film's end; see below.

4. Herzog, in his original story for *Fitzcarraldo*, described his opening shot as follows in his *Fitzcarraldo: The Original Story*, trans. Martje Herzog and Alan Greenberg (San Francisco: Fjord Press, 1982), p. 23:

> As immense as an ocean extending to the edge of the universe, the jungle stretches out, steaming, as on the morning of Creation, still indistinct, full of animal noise. A music swells up, magnificent, breathtaking, and measured, as a hundred million birds awaken far below our feet. The earth lies in wait, calmly and patiently, but the sky begins to quiver as if this were some painful quaking of the heavens, something like the birth throes of heaven.

5. Oscar Hammerstein I held similar views. The following is quoted from an interview in Vincent Sheean, *Oscar Hammerstein I: The Life and Exploits of an Impressario* (New York: Simon and Schuster, 1956), pp. 252–53, as cited by Dolkart, "Civilization's Aria," p. 131:

> Grand opera is, I truly believe, the most elevating influence upon modern society, after religion. . . . I sincerely believe that nothing will make better citizenship than familiarity with grand opera. *It lifts one so out of the sordid affairs of life and makes material things seem so petty, so inconsequential, it places one for the time being, at least, in a higher and better world.* . . . [Opera] will establish a brotherhood of art which knows not race or creed and makes all the civilized world akin; that will erect a shrine of beauty in form, color, and tone, before which all may bend the knee. [emphasis added]

To be sure, Hammerstein seems oblivious of the material reality that makes grand opera possible, and which in turn preserves it as elite entertainment.

6. Opera has long been linked to film, beginning in the silent era. See Joengwon Joe and Rose Theresa, eds., *Between Opera and Cinema* (New York: Routledge, 2002); Jeremy Tambling, *Opera, Ideology and Film* (New York: St. Martin's Press, 1987); and Marcia J. Citron, *Opera on Screen* (New Haven, CT: Yale University Press, 2000).

7. Sarah Bernhardt (1844–1923) was the most famous actress of her age; her career spanned six decades. She toured widely in Europe and the United States, and in 1886 she made one trip to South America, including a visit to Lima, her closest approach to the film's setting. In 1877, Bernhardt had performed in Victor Hugo's *Hernani*, the source for Verdi's opera. Cross-dressed, she played the title role in *Hamlet* in 1899, and she toured across Europe in this role for two years. Interested in modern technology, she recorded her voice and, late in her career, she made eight films, of which five were hits. She also made a number of home movies between 1913 and 1915. Bernhardt starred in several films whose subjects had been used for opera, including *La Tosca* (1908; reprising a stage role she first performed in 1887); *La Dame aux camélias* (1911), the source for *La traviata*; and *Adrienne Lecouvreur*

(1913). At the time of her death at age seventy-eight, she was at work on the film *La Voyante* (The Fortune), completed with a stand-in. Bernhardt, after seeing the final cut of her greatest film hit, the seven-reel *La Reine Elizabeth* (1912), is reputed to have exclaimed, "I am immortal! I am film!" On Bernhardt's film career, see Ruth Brandon, *Being Divine: A Biography of Sarah Bernhardt* (London: Secker & Warburg, 1991), pp. 433–35. In real life, Caruso and Bernhardt only once performed at the same event, though not together, at a war benefit at the Metropolitan Opera House on 17 April 1917, together with Frances Alda. See Francis Robinson, *Caruso: His Life in Pictures* (New York: Studio Publications in association with Thomas Y. Crowell, 1957), pp. 90–91, which reproduces the program.

8. The film's consistent dependence on the displaced singing voice is mirrored in the fact that *Fitzcarraldo* was actually filmed with dialogue spoken in English; the German "original" is dubbed.)

9. Herzog, *Fitzcarraldo: The Original Story*, pp. 11–14, 17–18. Numerous differences exist between Herzog's original story and the finished film.

10. Paul Cronin, ed., *Herzog on Herzog* (London: Faber and Faber, 2002), p. 188. Indeed, for Herzog, it is precisely the plausible within the implausibility of opera that attracts him. "It matters little that most of the libretti are bad or . . . [even] a true catastrophe. In fact, so many of the opera plots are not even within the calculus of probability; it would be like winning the lottery jackpot five consecutive times over. And yet, when the music is playing, the stories do make sense. Their strong inner truths shine through and they seem utterly plausible" (p. 259). Since making *Fitzcarraldo*, Herzog has directed a number of opera productions throughout Europe, as well as in Japan and the United States. For a list, current to 2002, see Beat Presser, ed. and photographer, *Werner Herzog* (Berlin: Jovis Verlag and Arte Edition, 2002), p. 119.

11. The situation is similar to an operatic drag-act performed by Larry, Moe, and Curly in The Three Stooges' short *Micro-Phonies* (1945). The music they attempt to lip-synch is the sextet from *Lucia* or, as they would have it, the sextet from *Lucy*.

12. Theodor W. Adorno, "On the Contemporary Relationship of Philosophy and Music," in *Essays on Music*, ed. Richard Leppert, trans. Susan H. Gillespie (Berkeley and Los Angeles: University of California Press, 2002), p. 136, comments on the Marx Brothers film *A Night at the Opera* (1935), which involves a performance of *Il trovatore*, the scenery for which the boys manage to destroy. Adorno notes the singers' "clumsily grandiloquent, old- fashioned gestures," which contribute to exposing the ridiculousness of opera as an icon of elite art, replete with its affectations and its insistence on the "dignity of music." Even so, Adorno suggests, the comedy reveals a utopian truth about music: "Music that has merely to begin in order to define itself as an exception to normalized life, as a more elevated extreme, places itself, by dint of its always already potential perceptible and nowadays complete integration into the average normalcy of a false life, in contradiction to the claim that its mere sounding inevitably makes." Adorno, in an earlier essay alluding to this same film, compliments his later insight with the following: "Music has become comic in the present phase primarily because something so completely useless is carried on with all the visible signs of the strain of serious work. By being alien to solid

[*tüchtig*] people, music reveals their alienation from one another, and the consciousness of alienation vents itself in laughter." Theodor W. Adorno, "On the Fetish-Character in Music and the Regression of Listening," in *Essays on Music,* p. 314. The "work" of Fitzcarraldo to make opera, involving pulling a riverboat over a small mountain, is—obviously enough—absurdly comic, all the more given the extraordinary seriousness, utterly nonironic, with which he engages in his harebrained scheme. The act is also operatic, a fact not lost on Herzog: "I pulled the ship [sic] over the mountain not for the sake of realism. . . . What you actually see is a very stylized thing. It looks like an operatic event, like a dream-event, and that's what's so strange about it. It's not really a paradox." Quoted by Guido Henkel, "Werner Herzog the Real Fitzcarraldo," *DVD Review* (1 November 1999), online review at http://www.dvdreview.com/html_dvd_Werner_Herzog.shtml.

13. The French actor Jean-Claude Dreyfuss plays the part of Bernhardt, whom he had previously impersonated. (Herzog's commentary accompanying the DVD release of *Fitzcarraldo* refers to the actor as a transvestite.) See further Dolkart, "Civilization's Aria," p. 132; and Presser, ed. *Werner Herzog,* p. 38. For more on Herzog's opera directing, see Cronin, ed., *Herzog on Herzog,* pp. 253–54, 258–60.

14. There are historical antecedents to the cross-dressing, as in an 1865 production of an English burlesque of *Ernani* by William Brough, *Ernani, or, the Horn of a Dilemma,* in which the two male characters, including Ernani himself, were played by women. See Roberta Montemorra Marvin, "Verdian Opera Burlesqued: A Glimpse into Mid-Victorian Theatrical Culture," *Cambridge Opera Journal* 15.1 (March 2003), p. 47. Marvin points out that *Ernani* was the Verdi opera most subjected to burlesquing, though *Il trovatore* and *La traviata* were also popularly mocked. On the extraordinary popularity of *Ernani* in the United States for several decades beginning in 1847, only three years after the opera's premiere, see George Martin, "Verdi Onstage in the United States: *Ernani," Opera Quarterly* 20.2 (Spring 2004): 171–96. In short, there is good historical reason for Herzog's choice of this opera. Not the least sign of *Ernani's* popularity at the time of *Fitzcarraldo's* setting is evident in the fact that the Victor Talking Machine Company by 1912 had released no fewer than forty-five recordings of its arias and choruses (p. 183).

15. See also the discussion of this scene in Roger Hillman, *Unsettling Scores: German Film, Music, and Ideology* (Bloomington: Indiana University Press, 2005), pp. 141–44.

16. Dolkart, "Civilization's Aria," p. 125: "The most significant and enduring lore embraced by elites in Latin America is the division between civilization and barbarism. The separation into two Latin Americas, one civilized, that is positive and progressive, another barbaric, that is negative and regressive, has shaped the foreigner's views, as well as the self-image of the region, as has no other concept." Dolkart explains that opera in particular constituted a sign of civilization among nineteenth-century Latin American elites, concerning which see by the same author, "Elitelore at the Opera: The Teatro Colón of Buenos Aires," *Journal of Latin American Lore* 9.2 (1983), pp. 231–50.

17. Werner Herzog, "The Minnesota Declaration: Truth and Fact in Documentary Cinema," in Cronin, ed., *Herzog on Herzog,* p. 301: "There are deeper strata of

truth in cinema, and there is such a thing as poetic, ecstatic truth. It is mysterious and elusive, and can be reached only through fabrication and imagination and stylization."

18. Herzog, in his commentary to the DVD release of *Fitzcarraldo*.

19. Herzog, in his commentary accompanying the DVD release of *Fitzcarraldo*, indicates that the music is "authentic," but it was recorded in Burundi. Acknowledging that African drumming is "totally different" from the kind of drumming employed by the Indians native to the rain forest, he says he chose it because of what he terms the "certain danger" and "certain menace" he associates with its sound.

20. Caruso recorded the aria in 1904. See J. Freestone and H. J. Drummond, *Enrico Caruso: His Recorded Legacy* (London: Sidgwick and Jackson, 1960), p. 27.

21. Theodor W. Adorno, "The Curves of the Needle," in *Essays on Music*, p. 274: "What the gramophone listener actually wants to hear is himself, and the artist merely offers him a substitute for the sounding image of his own person, which he would like to safeguard as a possession. The only reason that he accords the record such value is because he himself could also be just as well preserved. Most of the time records are virtual photographs of their owners, flattering photographs—ideologies."

22. Michel Chion, *The Voice in Cinema*, ed. and trans. Claudia Gorbman (New York: Columbia University Press, 1999), p. 5. Chion adopts his insight from a remark by Christine Sacco ("The presence of a body structures the space that contains it").

23. Martin Scherzinger, in a private communication:

One reason the Burundi segment synchronizes so easily—too easily—with the photograph's song fragment is because both are hyperbolic indexes of contrasting culture: "Western" music as individualized expressive song, primarily harmonic-melodic in construction (mechanically produced even); non-Western music as functional, primarily rhythmic, collectivist (apparently not mechanically produced, but of course the latter music stops like a recording stops, not like a group of performers stops—an indication that mischief of another sort is afoot). This extreme, almost mannerist, presentation of dualized musical worlds must work well musically because the one fills the obvious inadequacy of the other. This is why the phonograph sounds so isolated when the drumming is switched off.

24. The penetration of the jungle by the riverboat, traveling where no white man has ventured previously, anticipates the resolutely male enterprise of creating the deep gash in the jungle, a literal deflowering, clearing the way for the boat to, as it were, mount the mountain. The scene resonates with the iconography of Watteau's *Embarkation from the Isle of Cythera*, in which a boatload of would-be lovers has penetrated a landmass whose form is analogous to the shape of two legs. At the shoreline stands a small hill, replete with a Venus figure atop the mound. Lutz P. Koepnick, "Colonial Forestry: Sylvan Politics in Werner Herzog's *Aguirre* and *Fitzcarraldo*," *New German Critique* 60 (Fall 1993), especially pp. 133–59, referring to Herzog's "green essentialism" (p. 157), argues that, in the name of filmic authenticity, he clear-cuts forest and levels hills for the land journey of the riverboat. Lutz regards Herzog as "a master in the jargon of authenticity" (p. 158), summing up, "Herzog, in other words, uses the diegetic text of *Fitzcarraldo* to exercise his own

colonial practice, an exercise that cannot but forfeit its alleged aspiration to obliterate the grounds and politics of what I call here colonial forestry" (p. 158). See also John E. Davidson, "Contacting the Other: Traces of Migrational Colonialism and the Imperial Agent in Werner Herzog's Fitzcarraldo," *Film & History* 24, 3–4 (1994), pp. 66–83; and by the same author, "As Others Put Plays upon the Stage: *Aguirre,* Neocolonialism, and the New German Cinema," *New German Critique* 60 (Fall 1993), pp. 101–30. See also Les Blank and James Bogan, eds., *Burden of Dreams: Screenplay, Journals, Reviews, Photographs* (Berkeley: North Atlantic Books, 1984). For Herzog's response, see Cronin, ed., *Herzog on Herzog,* pp. 169–70, 177–84, 188–89.

25. The trademark based on the painting *His Master's Voice* was established in 1902. See Friedrich A. Kittler, *Gramophone, Film, Typewriter,* trans. Geoffrey Winthrop-Young and Michael Wutz (Stanford, CA: Stanford University Press, 1999), p. 69; and Barbara Engh, "After His Master's Voice," *New Formations* 38 (Summer 1999), pp. 54–63. For an illustrated account of the logo, see Leonard Petts, *The Story of "Nipper" and the "His Master's Voice" Picture Painted by Francis Barraud* (Bournemouth, UK: The Talking Machine Review International, 1973/1983).

26. Caruso recorded the sextet three times, in 1908 (with Marcella Sembrich, Antonio Scotti, Marcel Journet, Gina Severina, and Francesco Daddi), 1912 (with Luisa Tetrazzini, Pasquale Amato, Journet, Angelo Bada, and Josephine Jacoby), and 1917 (with Amelita Galli-Curci, Minnie Egener, Journet, Giuseppe De Luca, and Bada). The film seems to use the 1917 recording. See Freestone and Drummond, *Enrico Caruso: His Recorded Legacy,* pp. 40–41, 75, and 104. For a photograph of the ensemble taken the day of the recording session in January 1917, see Robinson, *Caruso: His Life in Pictures,* p. 99. The *Lucia* sextet, performed as an instrumental, was often used to accompany scenes in silent films—in other words, films made at the same time of *Fitzcarraldo's* setting.

27. Michel Chion, *Audio-Vision: Sound on Screen,* ed. and trans. Claudia Gorbman (New York: Columbia University Press, 1994), p. 54: "The cinema is a realist art: but it remains that this realist art has progressed only by means of straining against its own principle, through forceful doses of unrealism." On Herzog's obsession with dreams, dreamers, and dreaming, see also Michael Goodwin, "Up the River with Werner Herzog," in *Burden of Dreams: Screenplay, Journals, Reviews, Photographs,* ed. Les Blank and James Bogan (Berkeley: North Atlantic Books, 1984), pp. 212–34.

28. Johann Wolfgang von Goethe, *The Sorrows of Young Werther, and Selected Writings,* trans. Catherine Hutter (New York: New American Library, 1962), p. 63: "My heart is undermined by the consuming power that lies hidden in the Allness of nature, which has created nothing, formed nothing, which has destroyed neither its neighbor nor itself. Surrounded by the heavens and the earth and the powerful web they weave between them, I reel with dread. I can see nothing but an eternally devouring, eternally regurgitating monster."

29. Theodor W. Adorno, Hanns Eisler, and Theodor W. Adorno, *Composing for the Films* (London: Athlone Press, 1994), p. 75. The text for this monograph was revised for its appearance in a German edition. The somewhat clumsy sentence, as rendered in the original English, cited above, is rearranged and simplified in Adorno's *Gesammelte Schriften,* ed. Rolf Tiedemann et al. (Frankfurt am Main: Suhrkamp

Verlag, 1976), vol. 15, p. 75: "Kinomusik hat den Gestus des Kindes, das im Dunkeln vor sich hinsingt."

30. On the *Molly Aida* riverboat "configured to be suggestive of an opera house," as well as a brief comment concerning the Beethoven citation, see Hillman, *Unsettling Scores*, pp. 144–45.

31. Herzog, *Fitzcarraldo: The Original Story*, pp. 155–59, calls for an unspecified scene from *Die Walküre*.

32. See, on this point, Dolkart, "Civilization's Aria," p. 141. Susan Sontag, "Notes on 'Camp,' " in *Against Interpretation and Other Essays* (New York: Noonday Press / Farrar, Straus & Giroux, 1966), writes, "The essence of Camp is its love of the unnatural: of artifice and exaggeration" (p. 275). Sontag provides a shopping list of canonic camp that includes among its musical artifacts *Swan Lake,* Strauss operas (she cites *Der Rosenkavalier*), and, among the Italian works, *Il trovatore* and "Bellini's operas" (pp. 277, 280, 286).

33. Alexander Kluge, in his 1983 film *The Power of Emotion [Die Macht der Gefühle]*, took on the institutionality of opera in a scathing critique. See also the book with numerous stills by Alexander Kluge, *Die Macht der Gefühle* (Frankfurt am Main: Zweitausendeins, 1984). Caryl Flinn has devoted an excellent essay to this film, "Undoing Act 5: History, Bodies, and Operatic Remains: Kluge's *The Power of Emotion*," in *The New German Cinema: Music, History, and the Matter of Style* (Berkeley and Los Angeles: University of California Press, 2004), pp. 138–69. As she explains, "Kluge turns to [opera] productions, focusing on the material *behind* the fantasies and *underneath* the spectacle, blasting them out in so many directions" (p. 139). For Kluge, she continues, opera "is an industry that capitalizes on human misery, glorifies defeat, and disguises the material aspects of its production. Especially cruel is how tragic opera encourages audiences to buy into its fatalistic worldview, and Kluge aggressively directs his line of fire in that direction" (p. 141).

34. Jacques Attali, *Noise: The Political Economy of Music,* trans. Brian Massumi (Minneapolis: University of Minnesota Press, 1985), p. 6. Attali's insight is indebted to Adorno, whose work he knows well. See Theodor W. Adorno, *Aesthetic Theory,* ed. Gretel Adorno and Rolf Tiedemann, trans. Robert Hullot-Kentor (Minneapolis: University of Minnesota Press, 1997), pp. 53–54 and 228.

35. Holly Rogers, "Fitzcarraldo's Search for Aguirre: Music and Text in the Amazonian Films of Werner Herzog," *Journal of the Royal Musical Association* 129 (2004), p. 98, points out that Fitzcarraldo's operatic music is "supported by the pillars of Western tonality, a music that constantly drives towards closure," which she appropriately contrasts with the acoustic circularity of the music provided by Popol Vuh against which Caruso is heard. And yet such sonic closure is repeatedly set in opposition to the failure textually narrated by the arias and ensembles. In other words, the dream-claims of the operatic excerpts employed in the film are consistently mediated by their own internal dialectics: outright failure (the narrative) and apparent success (musical climax/closure). This fact notwithstanding, opera serves in the film as a protest against the overdetermined inadequacy of modern life.

7 Sight, Sound, and the Temporality of Myth Making in *Koyaanisqatsi*

MITCHELL MORRIS

Since its premiere in 1983, *Koyaanisqatsi,* made by director Godfrey Reggio in collaboration especially with cinematographer Ron Fricke and composer Philip Glass, has acquired a distinctive cult status. A number of early reviews lauded the avant-garde film as overwhelmingly visionary, and it continues to be treasured for its aesthetic dazzle. Moreover, *Koyaanisqatsi* has taken on an additional form of existence as a "live" performance; Philip Glass has frequently performed the score in concert alongside the film, creating a fascinating twist on the practices of silent film accompaniment. What does it mean to suppress a "soundtrack" within the specific apparatus of the film, only to recoup it in the auditorium of a specific occasion? Such a mixed mode of performance suggests, among other things, that there is a commodious, generative "gap" between sight and sound in the film, as if the hyphen in Michel Chion's coinage "audio-vision" were suddenly made manifest in formal terms. But is this a special feature of *Koyaanisqatsi?* Are there other features immanent in the film that enable this kind of performative rearticulation, or is it a permanent possibility for all film?

Perhaps such questions are unanswerable at present. I will certainly not answer them here, for the scholarly study of film music is still relatively young, and many of our perceptions may be insufficiently clouded and uncertain to provide us with good answers to these questions. Rather than offer up unhelpfully clear generalizations, it seems better to wrestle more closely with the refractory object that allows such rearticulation. What are the most distinctive features of the film as first released, of the sonic and visual object that appeared on movie screens in 1983? The complex life of *Koyaanisqatsi* since its release has depended on its unusual shapes and modes of representation. What seems to govern the film's design is a persistent, transverbal symbolic impulse that seems inextricable from its formal characteristics. The impulse has spiritual, political, and aesthetic aspects, all complexly intertwined. In what follows, I will sketch out one important strand of these.

Reggio has said that *Koyaanisqatsi* was designed to communicate "an experience rather than an idea, or information, or a story about a knowable or fictional subject."[1] It is crucial to note the particular refusal of language that undergirds this statement—the assumptions that complexes of attention and feeling that are resistant to or elusive of words are not precisely knowledge (or maybe even thought, as such), but that they may indeed be circumscribed or instantiated in a complex medium such as film. These assumptions may be ordinary, but attempts to work them out so self-consciously are perhaps less so. In the case of *Koyaanisqatsi*, they determine many of the film's most important features.

Consider the overall experience: the audience is presented with a resonant sequence of images that succeed one another at widely (and wildly) varying rates of change, shot through with visual and kinesthetic rhymes and recollections, geometrical alliterations, assonances of color, texture, and density, in complex juxtaposition with features of the score; but most of the standard features of ordinary film are absent. There are no individual characters that act through time; at most, the audience is shown strongly individualized persons for a moment or two, and they are never seen again. There is no dialogue beyond the chanted title word, a few other passages of singing with indiscernible words, and the ambient hum of human voices at a couple of moments in the film's course: dialogue, surely, but totally inaccessible. Without characters and perceivable dialogue, the film is also without a plot other than that which might be discerned in the movement between the larger sections of the film—a trajectory from the "natural world" to the "world of technology" and (briefly) back again. The score, which forgoes any iconic painting of specific affects or gestures, contributes to the film's overall sense of large temporal spans within which smaller motion that seems at once particular and de-individualized takes place. Instead of a human-sized world in which protagonists and antagonists move, or in which the documentarian presents a particular point of view, there is an impersonalized space in which aggregates of things come into being, undergo transformations, and pass out of being.

In such an uncommon context, it's no surprise that the film's score assumes an unusual degree of prominence. This is one of the obvious reasons that Glass has been able to blend live performance with screenings; there are no words present to be hidden, no specific moments that require musical rubrics. But this is also because the film was generated in extraordinarily close collaboration with the composer. Glass would often start with very rough cuts of footage—sometimes only single images—and write a movement of continuous music. Reggio would then often cut the film to match the music, after which the two would adjust the timing and coordination to their mutual satisfaction. The final shape of the film is thus a series of musico-visual movements variously linked together in ways that may seem ritualistic. Contributing to this ceremonial tone is an absence of any moments where it seems that the sound "follows" the image; instead, moments of contact occur in ways that seem to emerge from synchronicity (to use Jung's term) rather than being causal. A descriptor encountered repeatedly in discussions of the film is "meditative."

Part of the idiosyncratic nature of *Koyaanisqatsi* comes from the irregular circumstances of its genesis. Godfrey Reggio is a former Roman Catholic religious who left his order in the 1960s as part of the post–Vatican II wave of clerical social activists. Settled in northern New Mexico, Reggio developed several community organizations and educational initiatives before he turned his attention to matters of public policy through an organization of the political and cultural left called the Institute of Regional Education.[2] In creating a series of public service announcements for the institute about corporate and governmental assaults on the right to privacy, Reggio came into contact with cinematographer Ron Fricke, who became one of the film's primary creative triumvirate. The idea for *Koyaanisqatsi* grew out of a concern for the impact of technology on everyday life and an interest in exploring less verbally bound ways of reflecting on this concern. Describing the central issue of the film, Reggio has observed that

> the main event today is not seen by those of us that live in it. We see the surface of the newspapers, the obviousness of conflict, of social injustice, of the market, welling up of culture, but to me the greatest event, or the most important event of perhaps our entire history, nothing comparable in the past to this event, is fundamentally gone unnoticed, and the event is the following—the transiting from old nature or the natural environment as our host of life, for human habitation, into a technological milieu, into mass technology *as* the environment of life.[3]

The point of the film is not to examine the effect of technology on people's lives, but rather to show how they are always already immersed in it. "It's not that we *use* technology," Reggio states, "we *live* technology."[4] Another way of understanding the cumulative effect of *Koyaanisqatsi* might be to say that it acts as a kind of transverbal myth, a large symbolic form.

WORDS AND THE WORD

When he began to imagine making the film, Reggio had wanted it to be released without any title at all; instead of a title, the film's mark of identity would be a particular image. The practical difficulties of such a choice were too great—and even "untitled" is a particular kind of title—so Reggio settled on a word taken from the Hopi language. Reggio has said that he "felt that their language has no cultural baggage, when you say 'Koyaanisqatsi,' no one knows what that means, it sounds like, perhaps, a Japanese word."[5]

This is an overstatement. Although very few of the film's first audience members would have had any sense of the word's origin or meaning, its inscrutability could not help but incite curiosity. But with that orthography, those phonemes, would we—and here I mean a North American, anglophone "we"—ever really have thought it Japanese? At a subliminal level, at least, we all carry greater or lesser intuitions of linguistic consistency, an aesthetic of speech sounds that, among other things, allows us to recognize different kinds of strangeness and familiarity. An orthographic combination like "Koyaanisqatsi," with its doubled "a" and its "q" appearing without an accompanying "u," unquestionably refers to an Other language; when pronounced, its most plausible rhythms and contours sit strangely in the anglophone mouth.

In a North American context, the question of such linguistic otherness is especially important because it recalls so many recent, troubling historical memories—of genocide and ecological despoliation, for example—and our inability to forget them or remedy them. Take the case of toponyms in the United States, so many of which are derived from Native American languages: Cattaraugas, Pasquotank, Tallahatchie, Kaskaskia, Umpqua—each of these places carries a sonic memory of vanished or subjected otherness. They are scattered across the landscape like broken arrowheads or potsherds, their presence in everyday North American speech a constant though subtle reminder that the reigning language(s) came from elsewhere. They do not mean nothing, but what they mean is often inaccessible, and their difference from one another suggests the enduring specificity of location even while testifying to the vast leveling that has taken place among them in the face of conquest and encroachment.[6]

There can be great moral force in this otherness, in the leverage it provides its deployers, and it has been so used at least since Rousseau. In interviews Reggio has contrasted the "wisdom" of the Hopis with that of "white civilization." *Koyaanisqatsi* is meant as something of a switch, because it reverses the polarity between layperson and exegete, between informant and ethnographer. The ethical trajectory of the film matches this switch, and Reggio's comments have always made this connection between structure and message clear:

> Stripping the film of all that foreground material, we take the background or second unit, and make that the foreground. So, in this case, the building be-comes like an entity, the traffic becomes like an entity, something that has a life of itself. The whole purpose of this film was to try to see the ordinary, that which, let's say, we are basted in. Being marinated in the environment that we live in, it all seems very familiar. And I was trying to show that that very thing that we call familiar is itself a techno-fascistic way of living. So I tried to it from another point of view, I tried to see it as a life-form, albeit a non-organic life-form, that has a life absolutely independent of our own.[7]

But of course this myth of a "non-organic life-form" makes sense only by comparison to the prior organic one: to see the "technological milieu" we must also see "old nature." Their differences are relatively plain: we all rec-ognize how cliffs and apartment buildings are not alike, how the flow of clouds and the flow of strip-mining dust clouds are dissimilar. *Koy-aanisqatsi* pays special attention to how these things are the same. The per-ception of sameness depends on understanding the effect of two related formal and interpretive features, that of repetition, and that of a kind of transitiveness of material objects established by the film's rhymes of direc-tion and velocity.

AGAIN, ALMOST

One of the largest problems posed in the film concerns the nature of what we can call "inexacted repetition." Partial seriation is everywhere in *Koy-aanisqatsi*—in rows of flowers or automobiles, in successions of lunch meat and travelers, in the flow of traffic or the flow of clouds, in scenes human and nonhuman alike. The impact of this seriation changes from scene to scene, especially because the overall motion of the film mostly involves the trans-formation of images of relatively unprocessed or "natural" materials into those that show the products of intensive human activity. To take one pair of scenes as an example, the movement entitled "Pruit Igoe," named after the infamous, disastrous housing project in St. Louis, offers up a series of long shots of condemned buildings.[8] Of course, these shots can be under-stood to display and critique the fundamental hostility to the human scale and functional lifeways that is often attributed to the architectural works of high modernism. To anyone who knows something about public works created for the benefit of urban people of color during the post–World War II era in America, this section might also bring to mind various versions of the history and politics of malign neglect. But the fact remains that there is a kind of aesthetic interest contained in the buildings' rhythmic articulations of space, and furthermore, one that in this context recalls the complexities of the desert rock formations seen earlier in the film. The longish section entitled "The Grid" is the place where the "media sublime," as Robert Fink calls it, is finally achieved. Among the sights in "The Grid" are those unforgettable shots of machines squirting out endless lines of hot dogs and Twinkies. (The inexactedness of the repetition, by the way, requires human beings to remove the occasional defective wiener or snack cake.) This scene evokes the phenomenology of the assembly line, and our attendant sense of overprocessing. Juxtaposed with scenes of commuters rushing up and down escalators, the joke is obvious, though not ineffective. In both cases, inexacted repetition is a necessary part of the film's structures of meaning—but in each context, it means differently.

Particularly in the earliest sections of the film, inexacted repetition helps establish the possibility of assuming a distinctively contemplative frame of mind. The opening of the second musical/filmic movement, labeled "Organic," presents a sequence of panoramic shots of the Four Corners region of the American Southwest. Although the most immediate quality of this landscape might seem to be the absence of human beings—this is "wilderness," if by that term we mean a place where there aren't any people—as the camera continues, what becomes visually important is the remarkable regularity of the vertical fissures of canyons and gullies breaking up the horizontal bands of the sedimentary beds in the rock formations (figure 7.1). (These sights would be largely invisible from the ground; the shots presuppose our awareness of the technologies of airplane and camera. This mediation, plus the concrete distancing, reinforces the contemplative effect.) A marvelous example of what might be called "the poetics of erosion," this corrugated landscape, through the record of its disappearance over extended geological time, embodies the multifarious actions of wind, water, and sun that carve themselves into the stone, even while they reconvert rock back into mud, sand, and dust.

It matters that there is so much repetition. It matters that none of it is identical. The qualities of motion that the camera witnesses more or less directly, as well as the traces of prior motion that it records, carry just enough regularity to feel like complex instantiations of underlying order. What's more, the display of these qualities of motion and traces of prior motion,

Figure 7.1 The poetics of erosion, in *Koyaanisqatsi*.

themselves a product of the film's partial seriations, occurs in so many varieties that the abstract formal patterns that we notice carry enormous authority. What we see are details of the material world, but from them, especially through their pronounced rhythmic character, we can induce the physical laws that shape them. We see, in other words, beneath a particular kind of surface. In the gap between untidy particulars and the schemata that govern them is the space in which a lively irregularity flourishes—and the proliferation of this inexactitude is the source of change.

The slow transformations of pattern in Glass's score take up the question of inexacted repetition in another way by presenting accretions and incremental changes within strongly established patterns of musical flow. Discretely bounded figures may stretch their control of musical space a pitch or a rhythmic unit at a time; layers of figuration may layer themselves one on another; metrical modulations and slow shifts of mode accumulate like sand against a stone. The continuity of Glass's music also works together with the film's other processes of inexact repetition to establish the character of the mutability contained within the frame of physical law.

To a great extent this mutability is a question of alterations in physical matter. In the video documentary "The Essence of Life," Glass makes reference to the old alchemical imagery of the elements, fire, air, earth, and water (we might also add the physical states of solid, liquid, and gas), and

Koyaanisqatsi frequently represents mixtures and transitions between them through mechanisms of inexacted repetition. As Glass's remark suggests, the states of physical matter have, in addition to their nonhuman quiddity, an additional layer of metaphorical significance, but this depends on their specific visual qualities as seen in the camera's eye, plus the synesthetic resonances created by their habitation within the music. Sight and sound together not only define temporal spans of a particular character and the movement between them, but they also delimit possibilities of significance.

PHASES AND STATES

The end of the second musical movement, which Glass entitles "Organic," begins with a series of shots of steam rising, either from hot springs or fumaroles. This is the first time since the film's opening segment that significant motion has been perceptible within the frame. Earlier qualities of motion were all the result of the camera's changes in location, not that of the objects it has demarcated. The music that has come before has been working over the implications of a bass line in the lower strings that allows both E♭ and E♮ above its final of D. (The modal disposition is reinforced by the punctuating woodwind figures in the upper registers; gradually elaborated, they foreground the basic rhythmic structure of the movement while they enrich the sonority.) E♮ is in this passage a destabilizing gesture, always pulled back cadentially to E♭ to restore the music's phrygian character. By the appearance of the steam rising from the earth, the texture thickens and the motion from E♭ to D finds reinforcement in parallel motions from B♭ to A. The music seems to provide part of the impetus for an elaborate choreography of fluid motions. The shots of ascending steam give way to sheets of sand that drift over the slipfaces of dunes, downwards and increasingly leftwards.

These motions all seem to be real time, but the next scene shifts the audience into a different temporal frame. When the camera turns to rough rocks dappled with the shadows of clouds, the apparent motion of the shadows closely matches the apparent direction and speed of the blowing sand that came before. The downwards-and-left direction of the clouds is soon reversed, and as the camera pulls into the mouth of a cave, at a rate that reflects the apparent motion of the time-lapsed clouds just seen, the film's rate returns to real time, confirmed by the movements of the birds in the cave.

The camera surveys the cave's interior while the music settles down onto a long-held A spangled with the faint sounds of the birds.[9] This pitch is the pivot into the next movement, "Resource," and when the mists of the cave give way to clouds in time-lapsed motion, the muted brass chords above the A mark the onset of the new music, and a new set of material transformations. The new musical resources appearing in this next section—the glinting metallicisms of the brass timbres, the increasingly fine subdivisions of musical time, the enriched harmonies—will in turn generate and confirm further enrichments of the visual field.

Within the contemplative frame of mind established by the film's hypnotic recurrences, the frequent transmuted echoes and rhymes suggest the endless mutability of the material world. In the inconceivably *longue durée* of geologic time, everything continually cycles around again. If taken in a more large-scale frame of reference, this also begins to show how the entire world acts as an organism. Lovelock's Gaia is not far away. And yet *Koyaanisqatsi* shows the products of industrial civilization as an integral part of this biomimetic process. One of the best examples of this comes from the lovely time-lapse scenes of traffic streaming through nighttime Los Angeles. Sped up tremendously, the lights of the individual vehicles, red and white, look like slightly oval pools of brightness that smear into one another as they stream forward in rhythmic patterns. The cars, in an endless series (repeatedly used in the film as an example of inexacted repetition), begin to lose themselves in punctuated flow, and they almost seem to shift physical phase from discrete solids to some kind of visual colloid. The scenes of traffic achieve their force in part from the way that in their ambiguous visual state the streams of cars begin to resemble the patterns that we see in footage of the circulation of blood in the human body.

THE MARK OF THE HUMAN

It is important to note that *Koyaanisqatsi* emphasizes the worldliness of the technologies that it wishes to question. This is clear from the opening sequence, which shows "old nature or the natural environment" already inscribed with human action, and the palindromically constructed closing section, which makes explicit some aspects of the film's overall critique. From a black screen a dotted red line disperses horizontally in twenty-three segments. (In an example of inexacted repetition, the short bar at position twenty, read left to right, is separated from the rest by extra black space before and behind.) As the initial pitch of D begins to sound in the bass registers of a pipe organ, recorded with a halo of reverb, the segments of the red line thicken and slowly melt downward. About halfway through the process, the irregular bar at position twenty sprouts small wings at its top, assuming the shape of the "t" in the enigmatic title of the film. The talismanic word takes shape over the bass line's motion—down to B♭, then a leap upward to F♯, a descent down to D, now supported by a quick taste of the fifth degree. By the second occurrence of the ground bass, the resolutely four-by-four metrical structure of the movement begins to become clear. The mode is surely D aeolian, and the antique, ceremonial, vaguely ecclesiastical qualities of the bass line already suggest the film's taste for high rhetoric as well as its seriousness of intent.

At a little less than one minute into the film, the audience has been given two things: a mysterious word, in red on a black background, and an archaizing musical figure. The second occurrence of the ground bass ties the image more closely to the sound: an overdubbed human voice chants "koyaanisqatsi" on a low D as the black screen gives way to an equally mysterious shot of petroglyphs, and the camera pulls back gradually to show abstract human figures painted in black on a bare, cream-colored rock face. The audience does not have to know the specific origin of these figures to know that they are primal, prehistoric. Both the image and the music tell us so.

But what kind of people are these? Ghosts.

The accretionary structure of the music is apparent: first the bass line alone, then ground bass with voices, then the bass line with organ figuration in the middle registers, then voices added, and so on. It is at the return of the chorus that the image of the petroglyphs begins to fade into a roiling slow-motion cloud of smoke and fire. This is perhaps an unsettling moment: although this early in the film it is not clear that causal relationships will tend to be suppressed or ambiguated over the course of the film, it's no great reach to see the juxtaposition of petroglyph and conflagration, seen in figure 7.2, as something eschatological. We can take the petroglyph to be the trace of what the fire has otherwise removed; or we can see the fire as that which follows and erases the petroglyph; or perhaps we somehow retain both possibilities, hovering in some undecidable state not fixable in words.

As the initial roiling orange, white, and black of the fireball subsides, we begin to see a new scene in which unidentifiable debris falls from above onto some kind of industrial equipment. It may take as long as another minute and a half before we realize that what we are seeing is the necessary ekpyrosis that launches a rocket. Despite the positive outcome of the image's development at this point in the film, something of the destruction that gen-

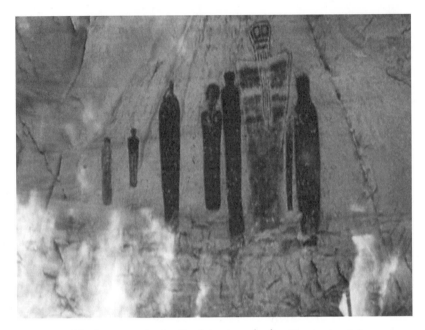

Figure 7.2 The first petroglyphs dissolving into the fire (*Koyaanisqatsi*).

erates the flight remains to disturb the mood. As the conflagration grows to white-hot, and its blankness fills the screen, the music settles onto the initial D of its ground bass, holding it for most of a minute while the camera fades.

Thus do things that we call primitive and things that we call advanced come together. The trace of something that is gone calls up the image of something that, in time, will have also gone. If this is so, then the chant we hear must be one of foretelling as well as one of remembrance. Causality, perhaps because it is so undefined, suddenly seems to work both ways.

The particulars of this opening are important because they give us critical leverage against a common misconception about *Koyaanisqatsi*. One of the most obvious interpretations of the film takes it to be an attempt to critique modernity and late capitalism by juxtaposing scenes of environmental degradation and frenzied modern life with unspoiled vistas from the natural world.[10] Though this summary accurately captures the critical aspect or phase in the film, *Koyaanisqatsi*'s vision of the "natural world" is not so simple. The first image we see is a shot of rock paintings from one of the most celebrated assemblages of the American Southwest.[11] Very little is known from either archaeological or Native traditional sources about the creators of this art. To a significant extent, the petroglyphs take on the character of a ruin; to the degree that their cultural significance has gone missing, their artifactual character, the impress of their making, becomes all the more important.

There is no way of knowing whether the makers of these petroglyphs were ancestors of the Hopi, but it doesn't matter, because the presence of the voices in the music implicitly asserts an ancestral connection. This isn't simply a matter of the coincidence of voice and image. If we suppose, thanks to characteristics of the music, that the aural space evoked has something to do with subterranean matters, as Philip Brophy has suggested, then we're entitled to recall that most important of Hopi ceremonial spaces, the kiva, an underground chamber legendarily modeled on the houses of the ant people, in which our human ancestors found shelter in the three cataclysms that obliterated the three worlds before this one.

The connection with Hopi matters that Reggio has denied becomes central at the end of the film, when the opening music heralds the return of the rocket ship newly launched in the opening sequence. But as it ascends, something goes wrong. There is one glorious explosion, and its shards begin drifting downward. The camera moves to one piece in particular for a shot that begins to seem endless. In fact, this spinning fragment seems to descend against the flat blue of the sky for well over two minutes, the camera very gradually moving closer to it, before the shot shifts to a grainy close-up that slows and freezes as a new set of petroglyphs fades in underneath (figure 7.3).

The music subsides through a minor voice-leading sleight of hand onto an A, and the titles appear, now trailed by definitions. But there's more: an explicitly apocalyptic handful of Hopi sentences, hanging ominously on the screen as the sound of crowd noises fills out the sonic space. This last bit of sound is important because it recalls a haunting moment at the end of the antepenultimate section of the film, "Prophecies" (1:15:02), where a scene of intense commerce is partially faded, "ghosting" the human figures so busily engaged. The music underwriting this spectral scene is a variation on the ground bass of the opening (the music that is soon to return in the next section). These "ghosts" fade into the returning rocket ship in a way that immediately recalls the transition from petroglyph to fireball. But we do not hear the sound of these people at this point; rather, it is left to the end, detached from its makers, a last echo of its vanished makers. The wheel will turn again.

Figure 7.3 The final petroglyphs (*Koyaanisqatsi*).

A WORD FOR MYTH

Reggio had wanted no title for the film, because he regarded contemporary English as damaged, indeed claiming that "our language is in a state of vast humiliation. It no longer describes the world in which we live." The film was to be the equivalent of a single vast word. That he chose to use Hopi rather than Diné, say, or O'Odham or Zuñi, matters a great deal. Though most of the native nations of the American Southwest have become famous in direct proportion to their success at surviving plague and genocide, perhaps no group more than the Hopi has been looked to for critiques of Western modernity. D. H. Lawrence was probably the first person to invest heavily in such an image of the Hopi, but more decisive were surely the writings of American linguist Benjamin Lee Whorf. One of the most luminous products of American anthropology during the 1930s, Whorf is chiefly responsible for the strong theory of linguistic (and cognitive) relativity that usually bears his name.[12] In one of his characteristic formulations, Whorf describes the theory as the principle "that all observers are not led by the same physical evidence to the same picture of the universe, unless their linguistic backgrounds are similar, or can in some way be calibrated."[13] Whorf himself attributed his ideas about the relation of linguistic structure and the perception of reality to his studies of Hopi. To this extent, Whorf's contributions mark an important moment in the campaigns of American anthropology to use the study of so-called primitive peoples to exert humanizing leverage on their own culture.[14] But even more important in Whorf's case was his invention of an especially striking version of neo-primitivist protomysticism. In a famous article entitled "The Punctual and Segmentative Aspects of Verbs in Hopi," Whorf went especially far, claiming that the attitude toward temporality embodied in Hopi verb constructions made the language more scientifically useful than what he often called SAE, or "standard average European," language:

> The Hopi actually have a language better equipped to deal with such vibratile phenomena [i.e. modern particle physics] than is our latest scientific terminology. This is simply because their language establishes a general contrast between two types of experience, which contrast corresponds to a contrast that, as our science has discovered, is all-pervading and fundamental in nature.[15]

Taking Whorf's claim three decades after its publication, and hearing it through the concerns of the 1960s, we could say that Hopi was the perfect language for our new nuclear landscape. A very small step indeed to Reggio's *Koyaanisqatsi*.

It is one of history's little ironies that in fact the Hopi now live in the midst of the first and most important of all nuclear landscapes, between White Sands and Los Alamos on one side and the scattered nuclear test sites and weapons depositories littering the dry lands of Nevada and California on the other. How could *Koyaanisqatsi*, with its desert sensibility, not juxtapose the traces of ancient peoples with the traces of those who will one day be ancient in their turn? And how could it not attend with special care to the multitudinous variations of time as it covers varied the surfaces of the world in such different patterns, at such different rates? In the end, the film aspires to the condition of myth, if myth can somehow be encapsulated in a single, heavily musicalized word. The word is, in effect, the world, at least as seen and heard under one haunting description. The Hopi say that this is the fourth world to be inhabited by humans. Tokpela, the first world, ended in fire. Tokpa, the second, ended in ice. Kuskirza, the third, met its fate in flood. The fate of Tuwaqachi, the fourth world, the "World Complete," is as yet unknown, although it is certain that it will indeed end. Reggio, Fricke, and

Glass left *Koyaanisqatsi* on such a somber note because they had already planned at that point to make two more films—to define two more Hopi words. Those definitions, however, are another story.

NOTES

1. Godfrey Reggio, "Interview: The Essence of Life," *Koyaanisqatsi,* DVD, directed by Godfrey Reggio (MGM, 2002). This transcription and all following ones are mine.

2. Appropriately enough for its aim, the campaign was partially sponsored by the ACLU.

3. Godfrey Reggio, "Interview: The Essence of Life." Would it be mistaken to note that Reggio's language contains more than an echo of the popular works of the French Jesuit Pierre Teilhard de Chardin, whose writings would have been inescapable for someone with Reggio's background?

4. Although the notion may seem perfectly ordinary in the early twenty-first century, the idea that technology and consciousness are mutually intertwined in this way was popularized only in the mid-twentieth century. The most celebrated figure with respect to this notion is surely Marshall McLuhan, whose major works were achieving their greatest celebrity just when Reggio was emerging from the monastery. See McLuhan, *Understanding Media: The Extensions of Man* (New York: McGraw-Hill, 1964).

5. From the documentary feature "Interview," included as special feature on the DVD of *Koyaanisqatsi.*

6. These concerns have frequently been expressed in ecological resistance movements of the last half-century, particularly among those with "deep ecology" or bioregionalist viewpoints. Their appearance in *Koyaanisqatsi,* which is not primarily focused on eco-sensitive critique, arises, however, from the same set of ethical imperatives that shaped environmentalism in the 1960s. For more on Native American languages and ecosensitive composition, see Mitchell Morris, "Ecotopian Sounds: The Music of John Luther Adams and Strong Environmentalism," in *Crosscurrents and Counterpoints: Offering in Honor of Bengt Hambr{ae}us at 70,* ed. Per F. Broman, Nora A. Engebretsen, and Bo Alphonce (Göteborg: University of Göteborg, 1998), pp. 129–41.

7. Sk!, "Interview with Filmmaker Godfrey Reggio," *Green Anarchy* 12 (Spring 2003), available at www.greenanarchy.org/zine/GA12/reggio.php (accessed 15 April 2004).

8. Sections of the DVD are named according to the titles that Glass generated for the movements of the score.

9. Incidentally, this is the second point in the film at which natural ambient sounds—what Michel Chion calls "territory sounds"—enter the aural space of the film.

10. The national origin of the rocket is not labeled, and there are reasons to think that it is not American (it is possibly Soviet). This affects the film's larger ambivalent gaze only in that it allows the celebratory critique to encompass technodolatrous modernity as a whole; but in context, the American landscape, so decisively shaped by industrial capitalism, remains the most cogent situational focus.

11. The film's initial shot, often labeled "The Great Ghost and Attendants," is well known. The "Great Gallery," where these petroglyphs are inscribed, is located in a segment of Horseshoe Canyon, itself part of Canyonlands National Park in southern Utah. The artistic style, known as the "Barrier Canyon" style, is dated between 4,000 and 2,000 years B.C.E.

12. The "Whorf-Sapir hypothesis," as it is usually called, is actually a somewhat open-ended principle, which holds that the conceptual and grammatical resources of a particular language shape the customary perceptions of its users. The notion has been a mainstay of much linguistic philosophy since Herder and Humboldt, and a focus of controversy in twentieth-century linguistics; disputes about this and other issues of linguistic relativism are ongoing. The fullest account of Whorf's work is Peggy Lee, *The Whorf Theory Complex: A Critical Reconstruction* (Amsterdam: John Benjamins, 1996). What matters for *Koyaanisqatsi* is not the degree to which a strong version of the hypothesis can or cannot be held, but rather its "poetic relevance" for the film. And Reggio's comments make clear that he holds to some version of a hypothesis of linguistic relativism.

13. Benjamin Lee Whorf, "Science and Linguistics," *Technology Review* (M.I.T.) 42 (1940), pp. 61–63, 80–83. This article has been widely reprinted, including in John B. Carroll, ed., *Language, Thought, and Reality: Selected Writings of Benjamin Lee Whorf* (Cambridge: M.I.T. Press, 1956), pp. 207–19.

14. The history of American anthropology's use as a resource for self-critique has been studied, but not nearly as widely as it deserves to be. The best introductions are found in Regna Darnell, *And Along Came Boas: Continuity and Revolution in Americanist Anthropology* (Amsterdam: John Benjamins, 1998), and *Invisible Genealogies: A History of Americanist Anthroplogy* (Lincoln: University of Nebraska Press, 2001).

15. Benjamin Lee Whorf, "The Punctual and Segmentative Aspects of Verbs in Hopi," *Language* 12 (1936), pp. 127–31, reprinted in *Language, Thought, and Reality*, pp. 51–56.

8 How Sound Floats on Land

The Suppression and Release of Folk and Indigenous Musics in the Cinematic Terrain

PHILIP BROPHY

. . . IN THE THEATER

You sit in a cinema, facing one way. Suspended above your sightline is a large rectangle of light, formed by a screen onto which are projected moving images. Your peripheral vision—integral to your everyday act of focusing in a three-dimensional reality—has been dislocated. The screen psycho-optically suggests not only a window onto the world but also—and more pertinently—the feeling of being trapped in a black box. You are deprived of even the base power of sight you have when you choose to look idly out a window; your view is controlled, changed, designed beyond your will. All muscular activity, save for the sensation of a certain gravitational pull on an anally oriented posture, has similarly been suspended. Sitting there in isolation, you are subjected to an array of sounds, many of which have no direct relation to that which appears on the screen. Not only do various types of sounds appear gratuitously, illogically, irrationally, they also shift through the black space that engulfs you. They flit at your side, hover at the rear, and dart over your head; sometimes they rumble through your bones, sometimes they sear your temples. You are excited and terrified by that which is beyond the perimeters of the screen, that which is yet to come, that which sounds behind you.

This is the phenomenological meat of the cinematic experience. It is an active removal and suppression of many of our optical and ocular actions combined with a heightening in acoustic and aural activity. When perceived in this way, the cinematic soundtrack is not a slave in service to the image: film sound/music molds a key for realigning our consciousness to form a state of being governed by a nonhierarchical order of the senses. Although we have been conditioned to think that sight is our primary sense for nav-

igating our real world (itself a specious notion considering how acoustic reflections registered by our ears aid our brain in maintaining our equilibrium
as we walk *while* looking), the cinema is a sensorial machine that by design
and default antagonizes how we presume our senses cognitively operate.

Take this further. Accept—at least for the duration of this chapter—that
sound never *matches* anything on the visual screen, and that by ontologi-
cally disruptive yet sensationally enticing ways, sounds were never meant
to synthesize or synergize an amalgam parallel to the screen visuals. Imagine the opposite: sound and silence merely happen during the appearance
and disappearance of visuals. They each can do anything they wish, either
in accordance with or ignoring what the other does. They neither accompany nor accommodate the other: they simply coexist. If one accepts this,
one can feel the absolute index of coincidences that uniquely define the
soundtrack to any single movie. One can forget the conventions, formulas,
rules, and all the professional fundamentalist standards that film industries
worldwide proudly and implicitly promote and celebrate.

There is much to be uncovered by observing how sound and music do *not*
fit the cinematic screen—not by rejecting already limiting synesthetic
ideals, but by realizing the absolute rupture that gapes and throbs at the audiovisual core of cinematic experience. The cinematic experience as outlined
above is often at odds with what much critical orthodoxy and methodology
has used to describe the effects of the cinema. The numerous faults, flaws,
and fictions that have persisted over the preceding two decades of ill-
conceived film sound commentary strongly suggest that not only might our
critical methodologies be severely lacking, but also every categorical breakdown we perform on the soundtrack should be regarded with suspicion. Indeed, the very act of employing categorization as a discursive means of
defining events, sensations, auras, and dimensions that arise from the si-
multaneity of sound-in-space with image-in-motion is a tactic ill-equipped
for assessing the hybrid and polysemous nature of the film soundtrack.

To wit: common and unquestioned binaries like onscreen/offscreen, syn-
chronous/disynchronous, compatible/incompatible, realistic/unrealistic,
and natural/unnatural are rooted in the physicality of theater, and as such
are determined by how time, space, and event are conjoined in a physical location. That is, the palpable physicality of everything that appears within
the proscenium is the base from which these binaries sprout. For example,
someone clapping hands in melodramatic frieze to the timed sound of a
metal sheet clanging offstage suggests a degree of unrealism due to our
knowledge that a mere handclap does not cause such a dynamic sonic event
in everyday life. The theatrical body is always "our" body, defined by phys-

ical limitations we know and share. The cinematic body is only "our" body through acts of supposition, identification, empathy, desire, and dread, and as such it has no stable physical plane to ground and orient those binaries that function within theater. Much critical orthodoxy and methodology in the history of film theory has lackadaisically imported theatrical precepts without giving attention to the phenomenological nature of compound experiences resulting from the fused crafts, languages, technologies, and senses that follow the assignation of the soundtrack to the film strip. This means that a persistent problem with analyzing film sound and film music is the lack of differentiation made between, for example, thunder, the sound of thunder, the recording of the sound of thunder, and the sound effect we call "thunder." Each is perceptually different within the act of listening, yet that very difference is what tends to dissolve once one attempts to address thunder in a movie scene by placing it as a marker, sign, icon, or convention in strict relation to the film screen's placement of the scene.

Now, rather than postulate a laborious and taxonomical blueprint for how we can recategorize the film soundtrack into a new myriad of linguistic types and syntactical forms, I opt not to be cursed by the specter of grammar and suggest a contra-cinematic stratagem. Let us orient our consideration of film sound/music from an awareness of the advanced state of contemporary music and audio art (embracing hip subcultures and academic pursuits). From this perspective, issues of how the performative, the technological, the interactive, the compositional, and the psycho-acoustic network to produce dense and complex comments on how we perceive our own acts of listening are derived from a richly braided flow of modern and postmodern histories of sound and music. Despite a dearth of critical writing to explicate this, our everyday listening experiences have been radically altered over the past half century in terms of distortion, density, grain, spatialization, processing, distillation, transformation, multiplicity, rendering, dispersion, immersion, virtuality, modulation, and appropriation. One should be able to ask where are the soundtrack equivalents of the studio recordings produced by Bohannon, The Breeders, Wendy Carlos, DNA, Duke Ellington, Esquival, Pierre Henri, Led Zepplin, Sergio Mendez, Jeff Mills, Neu, Pauline Oliveros, Optical, Oval, Lee Perry, PiL, Shellac, Karlheinz Stockhausen, Sun Ra, The Velvet Underground, Brian Wilson, and Link Wray? If we can theoretically and musically accept the roles of nonmusicians, studio producers, electronic realizers, and track remixers, could not the film soundtrack critically and sonically support similarly decategorized modules like "uncomposers," "redesigners," and "soundscapers"? In this chapter, my ears will angle toward film soundtracks that do exactly that.

So there you are, still sitting in a cinema, facing one way, looking at the screen. Soon enough you hear something. You presume it somehow comes "from" the screen—yet how do you define the *space* of that "sonic"? Would it be through the characteristics of its original location source, or is there something in the encoding and rendering of that recording that defines its space? Just as the snare crack on Bill Haley's *Rock Around the Clock* is neither that on Martha and the Vandella's *Dancing in the Streets*, The Eagles' *Take It Easy*, Billy Idol's *Rebel Yell*, nor Technohead's *I Wanna Be a Hippy*, so must the space of the sound you hear in the dark of the cinema be as distinctly a product of the processing that creates that "sonic." Following this line of perceptual inquiry, questions more relevant to the conundrum of audiovisuality arise. Is that space imported as an acoustic dome over the screen's visuals? Or is that space a terrain visited by the image? These are simple enough queries, yet ones that effectively bypass the critical orthodoxy that suggests we comprehend soundtrack events via their evaluation through degrees of being onscreen/offscreen, synchronous/disynchronous, compatible/incompatible, realistic/unrealistic, and natural/unnatural. In short, questioning the location and space of a "sonic" is the primary means by which we can accept that 1) the soundtrack is never in service to the visuals, and 2) sound never matches anything on the visual screen.

. . . ON A RUSSIAN BARGE

Europe. World War II. Childhood. Folk music. Cinema. What images come to mind? What memorable films do you fondly and warmly embrace? Maybe you have in mind something along the lines of a particularly uplifting film—something between Ettore Scola's *Le Bal* (1983), Giuseppe Tornatore's *Cinema Paradiso* (1989), and Tony Gatlif's *Latcho Drom* (1993). Discard those pretty postcards and their swelling melodiousness. I give you Vitali Kanevski's *An Independent Life* (1992), the second autobiographical installment of his tremulous telling of childhood, set in an unforgiving, cursed world ruled by the existentialist chasm opened by Stalinist bureaucracy and the amoral survivalism that typified the harsh existence in northern Russia.

I introduce Kanevski's film this way so as to clear the air of the oppressively humanist musicalization that has smeared and marred European folk music in the cinema. For many years now one has only had to project the sound of a distant accordion over a sun-drenched wide shot of fields to evoke the resilience of the peasant, the strength of the extended family, the beauty of the land, the whimsy of life. While such dumbed-down, faux-humble patronizing has proved popular in bourgeois art house cinema, it is time this moldy sack of countrified clichés be thrown down a well. Relevant to our discussion here, *An Independent Life* employs folk music in an entirely radical way. Kanevski does not slop folk music over his images the way restaurants blare The Gypsy Kings through their speakers or television cooking shows plaster Stephan Grappelli over their credits. Instead, Kanevski *follows* folk music. He does not place it anywhere: it preexists in an ever-changing musical landscape, charted only by shifts in wind, temperature, and pressure, and captured as a series of topographical occurrences on top of which his story is told. His music track (a mix of sourced folk performances/recordings and a folk-derived score by Boris Rychkov) is never in the service of his images: his images are the cartographical sheet music to his soundtrack.

The accordion—that gilded musical crown of the art house movie—is beautifully posited as a strange sociocultural machine in *An Independent Life*. Early in the film it wafts onto the soundtrack, unlocatable in source, recalling a melancholic solitary waltz, mixed in with buffets of wind. Set against bleak vistas and icy landscapes, it carries an alien, almost extraterrestrial tone, impossible as it is to imagine how the hearty warmth of dancing music could either survive or take hold in such a harsh environment. But music—both song and instrumental music for dancing—is equally the trigger for memory and its recall to pleasure. When accordion refrains waft across the barren snow, they express both the desire for that warmth and the melancholic cherishing of better times. An earthy erotic device, the accordion, caught in the embrace of its single player, breathes like a living machine, and it sways like the slow-motion twirl of a skirt. The rich, reedy tonality of the accordion mimics orchestral surges, yet is produced by a single player. Conversely, bands—especially in *An Independent Life*—generate an orchestral multiplicity but are tainted by their association with the military. Their sound is designed to bring the individual into line, the metronomic pulse subjecting the listener to scored and conducted control. Bandleaders in this sociocultural domain are Stalinist in the worst sense.

In one scene set in the school, the protagonists Vasiliev (played by Pavel Nazarov) and Valya (Dimara Droukarova) enter a hall. A band is on stage, heaving and wheezing a gasping waltz. Apart from this dirge, the only sounds heard are the feet shuffling on the floorboards as kids dance in pairs like automatons, morbidly entranced by the life-draining, expressionless music. Vasiliev and Valya cut through the crowd and meet some friends.

Vasiliev urges one of them to do a gypsy dance. Suddenly a man with an accordion appears from nowhere to accompany the dancer. All the other dancers stop, as does the band. Everyone gathers around as the dancer enthralls and excites them with his energy, creating a miniature theater for a celebration of music born of nomadic freedom. The climax reached, the band resumes its lethargic recital; the dancers return to their zombie state and circle lifelessly and aimlessly in pairs. Much later in the film another accordion player appears, this time in a tiny radio shack on a wharf. He stops relaying directives from the barge traffic at the port to play his accordion "live" on the air. ("I have a concert to perform," he says.) Again, the accordion is not merely a part of life; it is a means of transcending that life, of shifting from social control to a state of liberation. A solo instrument that sings the sound of a group, the accordion is thus the spirit of the independent life of Kanevski, who battles against the societal forces committed to exorcising that spirit.

True to the figure of the nomadic urchin that Kanevski employs to portray himself as a youth, *An Independent Life* is a carefully composed series of folds—more narrated movements of a musical composition than structured parts of a narrative—that at once create a tapestry of remembered events crisscrossing each other and lay out an undulating landscape of nomadic incidents. The narrative is organized loosely in chronological order and structured in the manner of an oral history. Like a story being told in person, the film demonstrates numerous gaps, breaks, ellipses, and asides that are smoothed together through the performative act of narration. The film opens with an extremely wide shot of pure white over which an unaccompanied voice is heard singing robustly. The voice stops mid-song as a figure approaches in the distance, and yells at the figure to stay back. The film then fast-rewinds until the figure exits the frame. The voice then resumes singing and the scene starts again. The viewer suspects it is the voice of Kanevski himself[1] and quite unabashedly establishes the director as a narrator in control not only of the telling but also of the *staging* of the telling. Less a godly power and more a rambunctious yarn spinner, Kanevski constantly has characters converse in cryptic quotations from bawdy folk song verse. People also continually break out into unmotivated singing, not because of a stylistic narrative conceit, but because folk music and the energy of singing are undoubtedly integral to their social exchange. Yet *An Independent Life* opts not to speciously "document" this musicological milieu and filter it through a softened folksy soundtrack, but to posit folk music in its fundamental sense as the breath of a community's being and the space of their sound. Essentially, folk music in Kanevski's autobiographical texts is never consumed but always *produced,* and he illuminates and celebrates its stratification within the socio-geographical depiction of his life so as to produce a series of "memory maps," tales based on fond remembrances and forgotten moments that are recalled as if hearing a song one has not heard for many years, floating across land on gusts of wind.

The concept of land is deepened by the psychological resonance it holds for those who traverse it. Vasiliev's yearning for independence—to, as he puts it, "be my own man"—is so strong it actually prevents him from championing any ideals or causes in the name of independence. Instead, he is a psychological nomad: restless, transient, disconnected, unstable. Although the film could easily have degenerated into a pithy chauvinistic portrait typical of the "road" mentality that drives many American "wandering minstrel" scenarios, *An Independent Life* is the result of considered reflection on a life *spent.* Kanevski thus captures a precise relationship between his portrayed childhood self (Vasiliev) and the spaces he inhabits (a progressive move toward the remote north of Russia). Many images notably enforce this through the visual presence of fog, smoke, and steam. All are natural manifestations of barometric conditions, and as such project the inhabitable environment as a realm in flux: the fog that sweeps across ice to diffuse sunlight into a glaring and blinding brilliance; the smoke of industry's generation of heat and combustion to forge a sustainable existence in freezing conditions; and the steam that periodically engulfs gatherings as trains leave for isolated zones, either ferrying Japanese prisoners to remote compounds or breaking apart families as relatives depart for what they hope will be a better life in another state. In fact, fog, smoke, and steam often obliterate the visual screen, leaving music, song, and voice to emanate from its visual opacity. Kanevski allows this to occur deliberately. Land is never regarded as something that contains roots, and just as Vasiliev continually slips on the ice he must walk upon, Kanevski's sensibility repels "roots" and the romantic ideologies that govern their establishment. Kanevski represents land as a temporal passage with which his being made contact. When he shows long wide shots of flat ice, he is showing his itch to *leave.* As a grounding for his "memory maps," land is always transitional: the stoking of coals in the metallic cave of a ship's engine room; the skipping with a thick anchor rope on rustic wooden decking of a barge floating on water; the trailing of black smoke across a night sea; the vaporous mist that rolls onto stony inclines at the ocean's edge. Land is never still.

Apart from the ways in which Kanevski allows folk music to live in his film, his most radical approach to the soundtrack lies in the way he frames the landscape for the staging of his oral autobiography. At first, the cinematography of *An Independent Life* appears archetypal of European art house cinema: there are many long shots with little camera movement where nothing much seems to be happening except the ethnographic capture of nature's beauty. But once one notices the way fragments of music waft into the scene, it becomes apparent that music operates as flotsam that floats *into* a scene, thereby determining its placement. Once we are placed "in" the scene, the camera operates like an omnidirectional microphone, mostly moving in response to sounds occurring beyond the frame. A "cinephone" is thereby created whose captured visuals are only part of the total picture, merely a perspectival articulation of the scene courtesy of the angle of the filmic torpedo, the microphone. Instead of a window on the world, this roaming "cinephone" is a statement on the recording of *sound* rather than a conventionally cinematic construct, and thus successfully inverts the paradigmatic sound-image relations we presume so often of the act of "filming."

. . . IN A JAPANESE MINDSCAPE

The opening title and credits sequence to Masaki Kobayashi's *Kwaidan* (1963) instantly throws you into a state of disequilibrium. Delicately, elegantly, sublimely, shots of ink dropping into a swirling expanse of clear water are intercut with full-screen images of written credits. This oscillation between legible, stable inscription (kanji characters) and a liquefaction of the act of inscription (calligraphic brushwork) is of considerable importance. It signifies not simply a collapse or detonation of coded meaning, but a dynamic transformation as contained within the action of slipping between potential meanings. In a perverse play on the Western notion of an aspect of the animation process—"in-betweening"—these cinematographic captures of "in-betweened" calligraphic veins neither destroy meaning nor posit a replacement: they serve as psychic squiggles, phantom doodles, automatic scribbles that refuse to attach themselves to intention, projection, communication. Their beauty is in their deft escape from overt signification through their dynamic presence and the totality of their motion.

If those mesmerizing swirls of inky threads recall the animatic base of cinema's prime mechanical pleasure, the accompanying soundtrack just as effectively exposes what I earlier described as "the absolute rupture that gapes and throbs at the audiovisual core of cinematic experience." *Kwaidan*'s opening title and credits sequence features a score by Toru Takemitsu, a renowned composer who has welcomed, celebrated, and advanced the collapse between sound and music, between sonority and tonality, in film. His score for *Kwaidan* is a landmark in this regard because of its revolutionary means of *discounting* a relationship with nonmusical sound by *becoming sound*. I will explain this notion in full shortly. For now, I make note of its presence during the title credits. The greater part of this sequence unfolds in total silence, into which breaks the occasional sound of small clusters of bells being struck. Each tone is allowed to sustain until it becomes silence, after which there is a measurable pause, as if silence itself is taking a breath. Adjectives like "simple" and "minimalist" (or even "Japanese") do not adequately describe the effect, for just as the spiraling spilled ink achieves a heightened sense of attraction through its simultaneous expansion and diminution, these single strikes of the bell clusters are equally riveting in their purity and clarity. And just as the watery ballet of colored lines suggests the dynamic shaping of an organic life force, so do the bells evoke a sense of performative being—that is, the bells, devoid of any human timing and meter as they are, sound like they are striking *themselves.*

This erasure of human presence and an attenuation to elemental forces is a marvelously apt way of casting the mystical and metaphysical stories of *Kwaidan* (an omnibus of four ghost tales) in an animist light. Obviously it would be difficult for occidental, Judeo-Christian ghost narratives to do this, hamstrung as they are by theological doctrine and fundamentalist indoctrination regarding the relationship between life and death. Pertinent to our inquiry into the "decategorized" soundtrack, *Kwaidan* enacts an Oriental sense of being by rejecting the core of Euclidean physics to which the West clings: synchronism, or the binding of all perceivable form according to a single set of physical laws. The chiming of the bells and the ink patterns conjure their own animist spirits according to their media—respectively, harmonic vibration and decay, and the interplay between color, shape, and movement—yet they operate in *parallel dimensions.* The edits of the visuals seem to refute any temporal relationship with the sonic events of the score. The visuals and the music neither heed nor observe the other: they coexist.

By virtue of their self-contained coexistence, the very concept of synchronism comes into question. Are the veins of ink "in" the water, or does the pressure and density of the water shape those veins? Do the bells rupture the silence, or does the quiet draw out a shape around the bells? The experiential nature of both the visuals' and sounds' dynamics is not fruitfully studied by discussing whether one is in sync or out of sync with the other. Nor is the binary of absence/presence helpful—though perhaps a notion of *pregnancy* is. Just as the calligraphy is in the state of "being in between" and the bells are in the state of "becoming," so might we best understand their relationship through their latent potential to "be delivered." To be sure, the disequilibrium achieved here is engineered by the removal of any base spatiotemporal plane from which we could easily orient an audiovisual model.

Why does *Kwaidan* do this? What is its mysterious purpose in unsettling our desire to interpret its narration? I postulate that *Kwaidan*—specifically, in concert with Takemitsu, and perhaps as an emblem for much audiovisual narration in Japanese cinema—arises from an ephemeral, transitional, and rejuvenescent concept of land. As ecologically terrifying as this sounds, it is worth investigating (there may be key problems in "our" ideal of land as territorial site, cultivated terrain, and exchangeable real estate). *Kwaidan* abounds with images of terra, flora, and aqua, images that often occur in silence. This violent silence to me suggests a refutation of land's holistic embrace as a firm entity. Like the Japanese children's game Junkin Pop (similar to the Western Rock, Paper, Scissors), "the earth" is a meta-cyclical morphing between the elements: oceans house mountains; pools reflect skies; rivers carve plains; trees mirror roots; clouds resemble vistas. All elemental manifestations can thus be viewed as "being in between," "becoming," and "to be delivered." This is a macrocosmological view that strongly informs visual and aural representations of the landscape in Japanese art, especially the cinema. It is a view derived partly from Japan's fragile island status— continually rocked as it is with subsonic shock waves welling up from tectonic plates to subway systems and freeway overpasses—and partly from reincarnation beliefs grounded in a mix of animism, Buddhism, and Confucianism.

Aurally, this has clear ramifications. The instability of the land logically leads to a devaluing of every metaphorical, allusive, and poetic idea of "grounding." The base elements of music—rhythm, melody, harmony—are perceived *sans* the grounding principles of, respectively, tempo, key, and tonality. This is why the many forms of traditional Japanese folk and theater music generate such strange and unsettling listening states. As American producers are often heard to moan when they have to re-dub anime for the Western market, the Japanese put their music "in all the wrong places." I don't need to critique such a shallow understanding of music, but both the appeal and the irritation of Japanese musics lie in their march to a different drum. If we track this breakdown of metaphorical relationships between land and sound/music, we can witness many relational paradigms like foreground/background, above/below, and with/against vanish into thin air.

To take this further, if there is no ground, there can be no earth hum. I use this concept of the conduction, grounding, and looping of electrical current through one's body to the earth as a metaphor for considering that our aural perception is determined by diatonic tonality and binary rhythm patterns in a way that anchors us within a chain of reception. If in Western music and tonality we can feel grounded by the architectonic facets of music's progression, in Japanese music we could be like birds that perch on overhead electrical wires without being electrocuted. By being removed from contact with the earth, we would occupy space and be touched by the earth's energy differently. As it is depicted throughout *Kwaidan*, space is less about how one connects to the ground and its comforting gravitational pull, and more about how we might use our bodies as resonators as we float on land. If the spatial plane of *Kwaidan* has no ground hum, no fundamental tone, and no basis for differentiating interference from that which is being interfered with (as in the opening's water/ink = silence/bells construct), then such an environment must entail a reinvention of architecture. Of course in Japan the stability, solidity, and fixity of architecture as developed in the Greco-Egyptian tradition has little relevance: for a terrain that hums with regular tremors, collapsible paper walls are required. Certainly the notion of building walls *so that they can fall down* seems unworldly to those of us trapped in concrete.

One story in *Kwaidan* ("The Reconciliation," a.k.a. "The Black Hair") is centered on the habitation of a domestic enclosure and renders explicit the body's relation to land, the psyche's occupation of space, and the transfigured laws of spatiotemporal physics that follow in the wake of audiovisual disequilibria. After a samurai (Rentaro Mikuni) leaves his wife (Michiyo Aratama) in order to improve his social standing by marrying into a noted family, he finds he has irrepressible memories of the woman he deserted. Her phantom presence weighs on him so heavily—as demonstrated in numerous scenes in which the sound of her yarn as she weaves obliterates all other sensation—that he eventually returns. Amazingly, he finds her still there, desperate for his touch. He spends the night with her, only to wake up the next morning beside her calcified remains. The realization that he has sexually gratified himself with her dry and shriveled corpse sends him so mad that he, too, withers into a corpse as he is chased by her long black hair, which now takes on a life of its own. The story opens with a slow camera track toward the couple's home. As the camera reaches the large wooden doors to their property, they magically open by themselves. The camera then cranes up and over the doorway's arch, rides into the front gardens, and sweeps across the expanse of long grass toward the front porch of the house. This is a profound gesture toward the relationship between the motion mechanics of the camera as ghostly narrator, and its *disconnection* from the material world that it photographs and captures.

Takemitsu's score for this story almost defies description. It does not even remotely sound like music, with its fractured, spasmodic, unpitched bursts of wood, string, and metal timbres melding into dissonant, ring-modulated sonic splinters. Indeed, it sounds like something is being destroyed rather than recorded, and it is inconceivable that these sounds are being performed. Once again, the decimation of human presence is forceful and consuming, and by discounting even an opposition to sound and literally "becoming sound," Takemitsu's "unmusic" elicits a perplexing response: we actively disrecognize all we hear, just as if we were trying to read those inky swirls in water. While no musical grammar explicates this score, its connotative power is deafening. The score advances an authenticity of texture while foregrounding an aberrant performance: the pressured *shimasen* bowing breathes like the ghost floating through the air of the haunted space of the decrepit house; the destroyed *shakuhachi* bursts augur the accelerated decay of the samurai's corporeal constitution; and the spastic rifling through assorted percussive instruments without playing them suggest a dispassionate, necrophiliac fondling of bones.

The samurai thinks he has returned home to the erotic presence beyond paper walls, the massage of the yarn weaver's wooden rhythm, and the heady fragrance of his first wife's long black hair. Instead, he has returned to a coffin—his own coffin. When he wakes up after breaching sexual taboos, and wakes up to breaking his own promises, his nostalgic space remains, but its tactility is rendered opposite to his original perception. Hysterical, he smashes through the house's now rotting interiors, still believing that he is inside its domain when in fact his world has been turned inside out.[2] His life did not flash before him, but rather his death; his entry into the domain of the dead occurred earlier, before he was unaware of where he was. The splintered soundtrack is the violence of his interiority not merely represented—as if we were in his head—but of his interiority materially *externalized*. Through the psychotic disynchronization engineered by the inversion of spatiotemporal parameters, we experience his sonic hell.

. . . IN CONCLUSION

Folk and indigenous musics have been corrupted by the unnecessary stringent purity that musicological dogma has foisted upon them. Under the most reductionist and restrictive banner of liberalism, they have been aligned with "naturalism," "realism," "truth," and "honesty." Their further cooption by and incorporation into the cinema precedes not only a deafness that impedes sono-musical development of the soundtrack, but also an ignorance that serves to repress the greater power for music to "become sound" in the cinematic terrain. When I see a blonde, ponytailed busker in the street wearing Trotsky/Lennon glasses and strumming songs by Don McLean and Bob Seger, I am incited to intellectual violence. I therefore empathize with the violent release in the soundtracks I have discussed, examples of musical catalysis and sonic dieresis that *never* match anything on the visual screen.

NOTES

This paper is excerpted from the complete version in Philip Brophy, ed., *Cinesonic: Cinema and the Sound of Music* (Sydney: AFTRS Publishing, 2000).

1. The voices throughout *An Independent Life* are a curious mix: documentary sound recording behaving as post-synced dialogue. It sounds like Kanevski delivers dialogue off-camera, dialogue with which on-camera persons converse, but the off-camera voice sounds as if it were closer to the microphone when recorded, while voices on-camera sound farther away, even allowing for boom swinging. This makes it hard to discern whether many of the off-screen voices are post-synced or "live"— though I suspect the latter due to the orchestration of events in continuous long takes. Also, Kanevski is credited at the end of the film as supplying the voice for many of the snatches of folk songs sung throughout.

2. For more on this notion of "inside out" and its psycho-sonic relation to Japanese cinema, see my "Secret History of Film Music Part 3: Violent Silences," *The Wire* 161 (July 1997), pp. 38–39; and "Secret History of Film Music Part 4: Once Upon a Time in the East," *The Wire* 162 (August 1997), pp. 40–41.

9 Auteur Music

CLAUDIA GORBMAN

Auteurism in film studies has led a double life since the 1970s. On one hand, successive waves of theory lapping at the edifice built by the critics at *Cahiers du cinéma* and *Movie* have pronounced the auteur as a locus of value an unacceptably Romantic construct, a fetishized commodity, dead, or irrelevant. On the other hand, auteurist discourses remain remarkably, vigorously resistant. The very film studies departments that teach the death of the film author continue to offer popular courses on directors old and new; and in academic publishing, monographs on directors maintain as strong a presence as ever.

While fully recognizing the ideological construct of the auteur as increasingly commodified and reified, this chapter argues for the consideration of music in the study of some contemporary filmmakers, especially those I will call *mélomanes*. More and more, music-loving directors treat music not as something to farm out to the composer or even to the music supervisor, but rather as a key thematic element and a marker of authorial style.

An illustration: A few years ago, riding on the success of her prizewinning documentary *The Gleaners and I*, the French director Agnès Varda was editing her follow-up film, *The Gleaners and I: Two Years Later*. She invited me to observe a work session with her editor. Before the video screens on the digital console, the editor did his best to keep up with her exacting requests. Among other tasks they performed that afternoon, they laid in some music, all recycled from the first *Gleaners* score, which had been composed by Joanna Bruzdowicz, the Polish-Belgian composer with whom Varda has worked regularly since 1985. For a small group of shots that included a dog peeing on a potted plant, Varda ordered up a particular snippet of music she had in mind. In the space of ten minutes they tried out four versions, snipping frames from images or displacing the music cue with respect to the images until the timing was to Varda's satisfaction. The busy atonal cue made a punch line out of the moment when a flower falls off the plant in response to being peed on. "You see," the septuagenarian commented triumphantly, "digital makes this so simple and fast now."[1] One imagines that scenes like this take place frequently at computer consoles the world over, with people like Joanna Bruzdowicz receiving the music credit, when in reality she had nothing to do with the selection or placement of the music she had written.

Moreover, since she began making films in the 1950s, Varda has filled them with songs, almost all of whose lyrics she wrote herself. These include rap songs in the two *Gleaners* films (2000, 2002), Kurt Weill–like songs in her poetic documentary *l'Opéra-mouffe* (1958), a hilarious pseudo–bel canto tenor serenading the Riviera in the travelogue *Du côté de la côte* (1958), the songs performed in the feminist explorations of *One Sings, the Other Doesn't* (1977), the lyrics to all the songs written with Michel Legrand for *Cléo from 5 to 7* (1961), and many more. Varda coined the term *cinécriture* to describe her cinematic writing, "writing" here referring not only to the screenplay but the whole filmmaking process, thinking in images and sounds that make cinema. Music holds an important place in her *cinécriture*.

The digital revolution has made music ever more accessible and malleable as an increasingly personal means of expression. It has abetted the tendency among auteur *mélomanes* to take more active control of music, an element of filmmaking that previously eluded them as they had to rely on specialists to fabricate it.

MÉLOMANES

Varda does not even rank as an inner-circle *mélomane*.[2] Music, and the passion for music, permeates even more insistently the films of Quentin Tarantino, for example, functioning as an integral aspect of his directorial style. For such directors, songs or scoring are certainly more than something perforce added to the final cut; music participates forcefully in what used to be called, in the simpler days of auteurism, the director's worldview. Auteur melomania is a specific historical phenomenon. Even though the movies have always been filled with music, and although directors such as Ruben Mamoulian, René Clair, John Ford, Jean Vigo, and Alfred Hitchcock integrated music into their films with particular force and efficacy,[3] I prefer to reserve the term *mélomane* for a more recent group. A pantheon of auteur *mélomanes* would begin with Tarantino, Jean-Luc Godard, Stanley Kubrick, Martin Scorsese, Spike Lee, Woody Allen, Alain Resnais, Sally Potter, Jim Jarmusch, Wim Wenders, and Aki Kaurismäki. In the spirit of Andrew Sarris's original auteur pantheon, one could debate and add a good many more.

Significant changes in the post-studio era such as shifts in industry economics, and a new generation of composers schooled not in Vienna but in television and pop culture, resulted in an influx of new musical idioms on one hand, and a vastly more flexible range of ideas concerning the nature, placement, and effects of music in movies on the other. Director-composer collaborations gave consistency to groups of works—those signed by Hitchcock and Bernard Herrmann, Federico Fellini and Nino Rota, Blake Edwards and Henry Mancini, Sergio Leone and Ennio Morricone (and in the same vein, more recently, Steven Spielberg and John Williams, the Coen brothers and Carter Burwell), and so on. With the French New Wave, the Film School generation in the United States, and since, the "auteur director" has placed a premium on asserting control of the texture, rhythm, and tonality of his or her work, and of the social identifications made available through music choices.

To summarize, a confluence of factors has led to the preeminence of auteur music. Over the last twenty years the advent of digital recording and storage of music as well as of digital video editing have made it possible for directors to exert much greater control over the selection and placement of music in their films, and has liberated the music soundtrack from the rarefied province of specialists. The strictures and underlying aesthetic of the classical rules of film music simply no longer hold. Melodies are no longer unheard, song lyrics are perceived to add to rather than detract from audioviewing, and the sky's the limit with respect to the possible relations between music and image and story. The structure of the industry encourages the making of soundtrack CDs as revenue sources, giving filmmakers further incentive to bring music into their films.

The phenomenon of the auteur director involves a film-historical self-consciousness that encourages individuation and even excess, music choices being part and parcel of that individuation. It's a bit like being invited into the living room of an acquaintance who is expressing her cultural identity and communicating her unbridled enthusiasm for music she has discovered and puts on the CD player to share with you. For many filmmakers music is a platform for the idiosyncratic expression of taste, and thus it conveys not only meaning in terms of plot and theme, but meaning as authorial signature itself.

Let us briefly consider Tarantino, Wenders, and Kubrick, three well-known *mélomanes*. From his very first short films, Wenders's works testify to an abiding love for popular music—American blues and rock and roll in an earlier phase, expanded to various ethnic and national traditions in more recent years. In his *Lisbon Story* (1994) the protagonist, played by Rüdiger Vogler, stumbles onto the Portuguese group Madredeus and is haunted by their music and their female lead singer.[4] By the time he directed his much-heralded *Buena Vista Social Club* (1999), Wenders had largely given up the pretense that he needed fictional narrative to house his musical offerings.

Tarantino, for his part, mobilizes music to flesh out narrative worlds laden with cinephilic and pop cultural references. The *Kill Bill* films summon music from samurai, yakuza, and kung-fu films, from spaghetti westerns, and from other odd sources, incorporating everything from the pan flute music of Zamfir to a "Flight of the Bumblebee"–like riff for trumpet (Al Hirt's theme for the television series *The Green Hornet*), to the Japanese surf-music girl band the 5–6–7–8's, all of which contribute to the eccentric hybridity of his female revenge epic. "The whole combination of the right music with the right visual image, I think, is one of the most exciting things you can do in movies. There's a reason why people remember it in my movies. When you do it right, it's memorable."[5] Tarantino freely indulges his own cinephilia and melomania, happiest when audiences participate in his finds and references, like a big club of like-minded collectors and enthusiasts. Often it is on-screen characters who choose a song; Mia and Vincent (Uma Thurman and John Travolta) chat in *Pulp Fiction*, characters discuss "Like a Virgin" at the beginning of *Reservoir Dogs*. In *Jackie Brown* the bail bondsman Max Cherry tenderly acquires and listens to the Delfonics' song "Didn't I Blow Your Mind This Time"[6] after hearing Jackie play it on her living room stereo; from then on "their" song takes on resonance as a repeated theme, a special kind of diegetic resonance involving characters' knowledge or lack of knowledge, and characters' openness (or not) to "hearing" one another.

For Stanley Kubrick, the decisive moment came in 1968 when he mothballed Alex North's original score for *2001: A Space Odyssey* in favor of Aram Khachaturian, Johann Strauss, Richard Strauss, and Györgi Ligeti. Kubrick's deployments of music grew more insistent in his late films. The exactitude of his visual compositions and editing finds an aural equivalent in the music cues. Take his final film, *Eyes Wide Shut* (1999), for which he commissioned some original scoring from contemporary British composer Jocelyn Pook, and otherwise adopted recordings: an orchestral waltz by Dmitry Shostakovich, the second piece from Ligeti's piano suite *Musica Ricercata*, and a number of tunes from the 1930s to the 1990s, as well as brief excerpts from the classical repertoire. Pook reports that she composed all her music for the film "blind"; Kubrick never gave her the opportunity to spot the film. He essentially treated her music as Agnès Varda treated that of Joanna Bruzdowicz—as so much musical material for the auteur to edit into the work.

As for the preexisting pieces, Kubrick deploys them with great precision of both rhythm and meaning. The Khachaturian waltz, which both opens and closes the film, establishes the editing rhythms for the sequences it "accompanies," and thereby makes a kind of operatic whole of the very ordinary opening scene that shows Tom Cruise and Nicole Kidman preparing for a night out.[7] The Ligeti piece has a specific function: it occurs in several scenes during which the very foundations of the ego of the supremely confident Tom Cruise character are undermined. In the middle of this piano piece, which acts as an inordinately long motif, there occurs a sforzando on a single note; on each occasion the film is edited so that the sforzando corresponds with a moment of Cruise's shock and comprehension. And in *Eyes Wide Shut* Kubrick often uses popular songs—rather, their titles or (unstated) lyrics—to provide apt or ironic commentary. A jukebox plays an obscure 1961 rock and roll song in a café as the desperate Cruise, seeking a friend who has disappeared, grills the waitress a few days before Christmas. The song's title? "I Want a Boy for Christmas." During the orgy sequence, Cruise walks through a ballroom populated by anonymous, masked couples, some nude and others clothed; they dance to "Strangers in the Night."

JEAN-LUC GODARD AND TSAI MING-LIANG

Rather than dwell on Wenders, Tarantino, Kubrick, or others whose melomania has already received substantial critical attention, I would like to take up the cases of two particularly idiosyncratic auteurs, the French Jean-Luc Godard and the Taiwanese Tsai Ming-Liang, in order to emphasize the necessity of attending to the deployment of music as a strong authorial marker for a good many directors at work today. To say that music is at the very heart of both directors' work may seem to overstate the claim, for one may read entire books on Godard without encountering any mention of music in his films, and in the case of Tsai, music hardly ever occurs in his work. Nevertheless, both are *mélomanes* of the first order.

As a filmmaker Godard is equal parts romantic and Brechtian, a humanist and a historical materialist; his treatment of music participates fully in the attendant contradictions. His films dismantle the language of cinema, deconstructing conventions of genre, of narrative and character, and, most importantly, of the naturalness of bourgeois ideology. He is perhaps the only director to involve music in what he considers the most powerful attribute of cinema, montage. If we routinely accept the brutality of visual editing, that is, one visual field cutting instantaneously to another, Godard has music participate in that fragmenting and discontinuity also, with the project to problematize and frustrate the viewer's desire for a seamless pseudo-reality on screen. "I try to use music like another picture which isn't a picture, like another element," he has said, "like another sound, but in a different form."[8] At the same time that Godard's films explore this aesthetic territory, however, they also mobilize music's basic emotivity.

Vivre sa vie (1962) is an early Godard film that disrupts the continuity of musical discourse. Royal Brown has documented how Godard commissioned from Michel Legrand a theme and twelve variations but ended up using only one small part of the composition, a barely one-minute-long, classical-style minor-mode piece for a chamber orchestra of strings, two flutes, and a piano. Once Godard selected this brief piece for use in the film, jettisoning the rest of Legrand's score, he then proceeded to cut it up into segments. For each segment, to quote Brown, "Godard ended up with twelve cadenceless measures which, like the film itself, form a kind of closed loop capable of indefinite repetition and manipulation by the director who, working alone, obviously saw himself as the complete *auteur*."[9]

The segments as they appear in the film steadfastly refuse to be coordinated with beginnings or endings of shots or sequences; hence, musical and visual elements are formally independent of one another. As a result, the music is the opposite of "unheard"; since it disregards not only the rules of Hollywood scoring but also the dictates of tonal musical discourse, it calls attention to itself. Music enters into Godard's montage aesthetic in which all filmic signifiers are arbitrary. In the more than forty years since the release of *Vivre sa vie*, however, it has become clear that the music's arbitrary segmentation not only reflects an aesthetic of negation, but it also yields another kind of expressive depth.

An example will illustrate this double-edged effect. Nana (Anna Karina) is unjustly charged with stealing and is arrested. While the police officer interrogates her, to the sound of the typewriter recording her answers, she maintains only a tenuous hold on her autonomy. A cue of several measures of Legrand's stately music begins. It connects one chapter of the film (the scene in the police station) to the next (tracking shots from an automobile showing an empty street), but the film is by no means systematic in using music for scene transitions. The end of the cue is typically robbed of musical resolution, the lack of a cadence felt especially keenly because of how strongly tonal and classical the piece is. When the music first strikes up over a close-up profile of Nana in the police station, it behaves like traditional film music: it washes emotion and sympathy over the character of Nana. The film has just put into her mouth a quote from Rimbaud, adjusted for her gender: *"Je est une autre"* ("I" is someone else). Her social alienation now causes her to turn to prostitution. The film evokes sympathy for her plight, a sympathy of distance rather than identification: along with the Rimbaud reference, Legrand's music carries high-cultural, perhaps religious associations, commenting on a barely literate, provincial young woman. It is the choice of the film's narrating agency, not Nana's kind of music (her taste for sleazy pop is manifested later in a scene where she dances around a billiard room to the jukebox). The second half of the cue accompanies a shot of the street Nana will walk as a prostitute, panning from one side to the other. Does the sad, dignified music underscore the tragedy of her fall into prostitution, or does it simply not convey much of anything, at least in combination with the images of the street? The cut-and-paste strategy of Godard's scoring sometimes lends emotional resonance, and sometimes strikes the audio-viewer as almost haphazard.

Godard continued to commission music from composers, including Georges Delerue and Antoine Duhamel, through the 1960s and '70s. He did not have close dealings with them, preferring to select, fragment, deploy, and mix their music himself. Beginning in the 1960s he also turned to classics: Beethoven as early as 1964, and eventually Mozart, Schubert, Dvořák, Vivaldi, Fauré, Ravel, and Bach. By the 1980s the dead composers had taken precedence over the living ones, although Godard has continued to call upon living musicians and their music—the Rolling Stones, Les Rita Mitsouko, Tom Waits, David Darling, and many others. In any case, as Michel Chion writes,

> Whether he commissions a score and then deploys it in segments, or borrows classical pieces only to cut them up, it comes to the same thing. The "audio signature" of Godard's works in terms of his use of music is nothing other than this way of bringing it into a system of reciprocal and constant ruptures and interruptions, which brings into play all the film's elements. With other directors, music is the sole element spared, but not with Godard.[10]

We may see the extent to which Godard's musical fragmentation and montage aesthetic developed by considering his 1983 retelling of Mérimée's and Bizet's *Carmen, Prénom Carmen*. Although one may hear the habanera from Bizet's opera whistled a couple of times in the film, it is mainly

Beethoven's late quartets, of all things, that punctuate the soundtrack. The diegesis, if such a term can still be applied to a film such as this, is frequently interspersed with Beethoven's music that is apparently nondiegetic, but the execution of the latter music is sometimes seen on-screen, in the form of a string quartet playing it in rehearsal. As Godard's vision of the Carmen story unfolds, with Carmen as a bank robber seducing a handsome police-man who becomes her accomplice and lover, and repairing to a hideout by the sea, the segments of Beethoven become increasingly, irresistibly asso-ciated with images of the sea, renaturalized into the Romantic function of music.[11]

The fragmentary and semiotically multilayered quality of music, how-ever, predominates for most of the film. Early on, for example, Carmen goes to her uncle Jean (a washed-up film director living in a mental hospital—played by Godard) to ask to borrow his ocean-side house. She lies to him about her motives, and insistently manipulates and pressures him in her re-quest. Uncle Jean listens to Carmen distractedly, at the same time uttering non sequiturs and listening to his boom box, which he refers to as his "cam-era that makes music." It plays a radically reshuffled piano rendition of *Au clair de la lune*—in which the notes of the simple melody alternate between very high and very low registers—and seems to stand metonymically for the audio, or audiovisual, apparatus of cinema.

In addition, *Au clair de la lune* becomes mixed on Godard's soundtrack apparatus with sounds of dive-bombing airplanes. It is tempting to consider the warplanes as underscoring the battle of the sexes, the manipulative as-sault by Carmen on her uncle, who in turn paws her too familiarly, over the superficial familial innocence of *Au clair de la lune*. At any rate, the meta-phor this sound-camera proposes, in place of or in addition to Alexandre As-truc's *caméra-stylo* (camera as pen), is a *caméra-magnéto* (camera as tape recorder), so much more appropriate for its appeal to the audio as well as the visual, and for the now sonic montage that it implicitly suggests. The auteur can write in cinema, using sound as well as the camera.

Prénom Carmen is structured in three parallel realities. There is the main space-time continuum of Carmen, her uncle and her accomplices in crime, and her seduction of Joseph, the police officer. Second, there are scenes of the string quartet (a real quartet, the Prat) rehearsing Beethoven. Third, there are shots of the sea. The images and sounds of all three series inter-mix freely, and eventually a narrative connection occurs between them: the young woman violinist becomes part of the main story when it turns out that Carmen plans to kidnap a rich industrialist who happens to be the vi-olinist's father. When Beethoven is heard over the images of Carmen's story, then, the music is another element in the crisscrossing series. The Beethoven sometimes seems to comment on the Carmen story, but despite our desire for musical syntax and affect, the music is interrupted more often than not, splintered, yielding to silence or noise or dialogue or mixed with them to the edge of incoherence.

In a scene late in the film, the string quartet pauses during their play to discuss the music. When the male violinist comments about the violence of the musical passage at hand, our impulse is to interpret: we link that musical violence with the physical violence of the bank robbery scene with which it is interwoven. At other moments during the robbery, the music on the soundtrack is interrupted by gunshots and is silenced momentarily, as if in shocked response to the gunshots. But Godard constantly reminds us that the aleatory effects of his audiovisual editing are just as important: there is musical silence, too, and there is the comic artifice of the scene as some bank patrons sit around and read, oblivious to the "dangerous" shootout unfolding around them. Even as the film tells its story or stories, it continues to proclaim that making sense of editing takes place in the viewer's head.

Godard's films constantly quote other works, and musical quotations can create knots of meaning. In *Eloge de l'amour* (2001) the protagonist Edgar, having walked along the Seine with a young woman, stands with her under a footbridge to look across at the shuttered Renault factory at Billancourt. Over shots of the river, one of Maurice Jaubert's theme songs from *L'Atalante* (Vigo, 1934) is heard in its original form. How does this citation work? The song instantly evokes life on the Seine, the working-class milieu of *L'Atalante,* and the very nostalgia itself evoked by a classic of French cinema. Inserted into the new setting of a Seine with a big rusting automobile plant, the song poignantly plays into *Eloge de l'amour*'s thematics of *histoire* and *l'Histoire,* of (love) stories and History, and of the state that is incapable of love. The past politicizes the present and vice versa, enriching a scene where the characters both serve as mouthpieces for ideas, and delicately suggesting the potential for a relationship. As Douglas Morrey writes, "*Eloge de l'amour* implies . . . that we have to *work* at history, and the complex montage of Godard's film, which requires the spectator to work to reconstruct a narrative, seeks to demonstrate this sense of history as an active *process*. . . . *Eloge de l'amour* implies that we can learn not only from the history of resistance, but also from the *resistance of history,* its fundamental incompatibility with easy solutions and the difficulty of its appropriation."[12]

In conventional cinema, music's syntax is surely secondary to narrative syntax. The arc and timing of music is normally subordinated to the demands of the scene, but a set of long-established rules "softens" the way the narrative flow determines the length of music cues—making music elastic to fit the form of the scene, fading music up or down rather than cutting it off abruptly, and so on. For Godard, music is a montage element, subject to radical disruption and placed in dialectical relationships with the image and other soundtrack elements. On one level, Godard's music foregrounds the arbitrariness of all film elements; it is difficult to experience it as "invisibly" reinforcing the mood of narrative scenes. On another level, music carries cultural meaning, as part of the vast reservoir of references from which Godard draws. His characters speak lines from poets and philosophers, images from European painting and cinema are recontextualized, and even characters' names borrow from literary and cultural texts. Finally, although Godard may truncate music cues, he does not murder them; music retains its evocative and emotive force.

Melomania may be at work even in the films of directors who hardly use music at all. The Taiwanese director Tsai Ming-Liang sets his stories in the contemporary, crowded, alienating technological landscape of Taipei. His films convey a world of water-soaked apartments, anonymous sexual encounters, fractured nuclear families, and desperate loneliness. Dark as they are, they hold out the slim possibility of redemption and human communion, and amid their sadness they are comical. The films deploy music very sparingly, since they are so concretely rooted in the absurd prison of the present; sound effects predominate, and dialogue is sparse. But when music does appear, it conveys a flood of memory, or it suggests an escape to a more bearable world of fantasy for the characters.

In an otherwise musicless story, for example, there is a transcendent moment in Tsai's 2001 film *What Time Is It There?* The protagonist (Lee Kang-Sheng) becomes fixated on a girl who has gone off to Paris. He rents a French movie, Truffaut's *Les Quatre cents coups* (1959), in order to feel nearer to her. The segments of *The 400 Blows* we see from Lee's repetitive viewings comment on his own anomie. Both films' young protagonists are lost souls in modern urban society, yearning for escape. A wisp of the Georges Delerue score is heard as Lee watches a scene on his VCR, and as the only music cue in the entire film, it takes on considerable weight. Though it functions primarily to develop Lee's character as obsessed with the girl (the Paris connection), and to draw thematic parallels between the two films, it is also Tsai's personal ode to Truffaut. Just as Jean-Pierre Léaud was Truffaut's screen alter ego, so is Lee for Tsai Ming-Liang. The poignant scene in *The 400 Blows* where Antoine (young Léaud), alienated from his parents and trying to survive in the city at night, steals milk resonates strongly against Tsai's lonely young protagonist seeking nourishment with the New Wave on his VCR. Like Proust's madeleine, the Delerue fragment powerfully calls up the past: 1958 Paris, Truffaut-the-Father, and, as we know from interviews, Tsai's own early *coup de foudre* for the cinema of the New Wave.

Tsai most overtly exhibits his melomania in *The Hole*, his 1998 science-fiction existential melodrama. In Taipei on the cusp of the millennium, a mysterious virus has taken over parts of the city, and whole neighborhoods have been evacuated. The virus starts innocently with cold-like symptoms, but then fatally turns people into photophobic human cockroaches. Two characters remain in a dilapidated apartment building despite the dire health warnings; He (Lee) lives above Her (Yang), and a never-finished plumbing repair has left a hole in his floor / her ceiling. The atmosphere is palpable: it is muggy, and constantly and loudly raining, as the two characters, each in isolation, mechanically perform their various bodily functions in a perpetual state of waiting.

Late in the film, the woman downstairs lies in her bath and suddenly sneezes—an ominous symptom. The sneeze motivates the "Achoo Cha-Cha," an extravagant musical number in Cantonese whose mise-en-scène and mood could hardly differ more from the relentlessly damp main story; from the characters' drab, existential monotony the film moves to campy, colorful glamour and music. In the musical number Yang slinks down a staircase, like the Marilyn Monroe of "Diamonds Are a Girl's Best Friend," in a pink sequined minidress with a fuchsia feather stole and white gloves, lip-synching to Grace Chang's 1950s cha-cha song, while a phalanx of four tuxedoed men dance around her. The high point of each verse of the song comes with the "Ah-choo!" followed by her alluring "Gesundheit!" to the camera, in a hilarious concoction of campy surrealism. Amid the stylized glamour of the dancers, costumes, and lighting, the shot foregrounds the cracked and chipped gray concrete of the staircase of a food market that has been seen in the film's story.

The Hole has five musical numbers, each one motivated by a detail or gesture in the story. For example, at one point Yang sprays malodorous insecticide through the hole in her ceiling to get back at Lee for peering down through it at her. He reels back, tries to fan away the stench, and covers the hole with a garbage can lid. Suddenly the musical number begins, in the hallway and then continuing in the stairwell, with Yang in a brilliantly colorful rose-patterned dress, shoulder-length hair with a hair band, and long red gloves. Accompanied by three chorines, she lip-synchs an appropriately passive-aggressive song, "Go away, don't come back / Come on now, take a hike."

Are we to understand that the musical numbers inhabit an ideal world of which the characters dream? Possibly. But the numbers act in a more Godardian or Akermanian way, too, their tenuous relationship to the story providing reminders of the arbitrary conventions of musicals. The contrast between the characters' depressing isolation and the energetic style of the musical numbers takes one off guard: muted colors contrast with Technicolor-style high-key lighting; the costumes, movement, and other aspects of the mise-en-scène vary sharply; and of course, the world of human silence made deafening by the sound of endless rain contrasts with the brassy, reverb-filled, happy pop music. The sets for the musical numbers, however, remain closely tied to the story's locales—the drab hallways, the market stairway—though a bit of window dressing (hundreds of small starry lights in the elevator for "Calypso," gauzy white streamers atop the stairway in the cha-cha number) pays lip service to fantasy. Tsai's decision to locate even these ostensibly escapist musical numbers in the apartment block has the effect of amplifying the film's *huis clos,* its sense of doom condemning its characters, and it suggests that the promise of redemption at the end is false (the girl has, after all, contracted the fatal virus).

The brassy songs for all five numbers in *The Hole* consist of recordings by the singer and actress Grace Chang or Ge Lan, who was a wildly popular star of Hong Kong movies in the 1950s and '60s. In her Western musical style and costumes and her self-assured seductiveness, she represents a transgressive female sexuality. Sympathetic vibrations resonate between Chang's performances and Tsai's queer surrealist sensibility. In addition to more standard pop tunes, Chang recorded specialty numbers, such as Chinese pop adaptations of operatic arias (including, indeed, the habanera from *Carmen*), Latin mambos, and the like. The first Chang number in *The Hole* is called "Calypso," to which Yang lip-synchs and gyrates inside an elevator in the apartment building, wearing a modified Carmen Miranda outfit, complete with a tall red headdress.

Two ideas animate *The Hole*: the existential comedy-drama of the two characters in their vertically stacked apartments, increasingly united by desire through the hole with all its symbolic associations, and the dialectical tension between the diegetic events and the Grace Chang numbers. It may well be that the songs themselves inspired the story, and that the inclusion of the "Achoo Cha-cha" necessitated concocting the whole plot about the virus. But whether or not this is the case, the music clearly figured early in the plans for the film. Tsai makes his nostalgic admiration for Grace Chang quite explicit in interviews, and a postscript to *The Hole* in the end credits reads, "In the year 2000 we are grateful that we still have Grace Chang's songs to comfort us." Thus, more sparingly than Tarantino to be sure, Tsai works from and through melomania, transporting it intact into the new millennium.[13]

NOTES

1. This session occurred in March 2002. As it happens, the finished version of *Two Years Later* does not include the cue they used that day, but yet another by Bruzdowicz.

2. *Mélomane* is the French term for "music lover" or "music-loving." Containing the Greek roots for music *(melo)* and passion or madness *(mania)*, it implies a more excessive, even irrational love for music than its English equivalent. I use this French term to make reference and pay homage to English-language film critics' adoption of the French word *auteur* in the early 1960s: its very lack (or rather multiplicity) of definitions fostered fruitfully contentious debate over who was an *auteur* and why.

3. Elisabeth Weis wrote the best study of the functions of music in the works of an older-generation auteur; see the chapter "Music and Murder" in her book *The Silent Scream: Alfred Hitchcock's Soundtrack* (Rutherford, NJ: Fairleigh Dickinson University Press, 1982), pp. 87–106.

4. "I knew the music of the band before I started working on this film. . . . I wanted to make a film in and about their city, and from the beginning I thought there should be a band in my story. The musicians should play the music of the film, hopefully also compose it, and they could appear in the film as well. But I had no script yet, so my ideas were rather vague." Wim Wenders, "There are a few things I want to say about the music of Madredeus," *Lisbon Pages*, http://lisboa.kpn qwest.pt/i/ouvir/madredeus/madredeus.html#wimwenders.

5. *Kill Bill: Volume 1*, DVD bonus interview with Quentin Tarantino.

6. Ken Garner, "Would You Like to Hear Some Music? Music In-and-out-of Control in the Films of Quentin Tarantino," in *Film Music: Critical Approaches*, ed. K. J. Donnelly (New York: Continuum, 2001), pp. 188–205.

7. Claudia Gorbman, "Ears Wide Open: Kubrick's Music," in *Changing Tunes: The Use of Pre-existing Music in Films*, ed. Phil Powrie and Robynn Stilwell (London: Ashgate Press, 2006), pp. 3–18. See especially pp. 7–9.

8. Interview-montage with Abraham Segal, *Image et son* 215 (March 1980),

quoted in Miriam Sheer, "The Godard/Beethoven Connection: On the Use of Beethoven's Quartets in Godard's Films," *Journal of Musicology*, 18.1 (Winter 2001), p. 170.

9. Royal Brown, *Overtones and Undertones: Reading Film Music* (Berkeley and Los Angeles: University of California Press, 1994), p. 191.

10. Michel Chion, *La Musique au cinéma* (Paris: Fayard, 1995), p. 331 (translation mine).

11. In a wonderful essay on Godard's uses of Beethoven, Miriam Sheer notes the remarkable fact that all the Beethoven insistently heard through *Prénom Carmen* maintains the quartets' original order of composition intact, running from Op. 59 through Op. 135. "His freedom consists in skipping certain quartets or movements and varying the cited length of his numerous immediate repeats as he did in previous films" ("The Godard/Beethoven Connection," p. 172).

12. Douglas Morrey, "History of Resistance / Resistance of History: Godard's *Eloge de l'amour* (2001)," *Studies in French Cinema* 3.2 (2003), pp. 123–24.

13. Tsai's 2002 short film *The Skywalk Is Gone* is unavailable in the United States as of this writing, but it, too, includes Grace Chang's music. *Goodbye, Dragon Inn* (2003) has no music, although of all Tsai's films to date it is perhaps the most patently nostalgic for the popular culture of an earlier era.

10 Transport and Transportation in Audiovisual Memory

BERTHOLD HOECKNER

I

Try to picture this television commercial for United Airlines, which was produced by the advertising agency Leo Burnett in the mid-1990s. The ad was presented in two parts.

Part one opens with a shot of the Art Institute of Chicago, a cadential flourish from Gershwin's *Rhapsody in Blue,* and a voice-over: "Not many things are more Chicago than United." An amusing montage follows with still shots of paintings from the Art Institute depicting musical performances, for example, Renoir's *Woman at the Piano* and Picasso's *The Old Guitarist.* The instruments depicted (including a trombone, two recorders, and a trumpet) appear to play Gershwin's tune, resulting in a funny medley of quickly changing timbres. The finale of part one of the ad returns to full orchestra and piano, which match a shot of a Boeing 747. The voice-over states: "United, proud to fly more Chicagoans than any other airline. Come fly Chicago's hometown airline." In a coda, a museum guard inspects the Renoir as if he had heard something. The moment he turns away the camera zooms back onto the painting and we hear a glissando on the piano. This sound makes the guard turn a second time, while the voice-over concludes: "Come fly the friendly skies."

Part two of the commercial begins at once with the montage of painted instruments "playing" Gershwin's tune, while the voice-over states: "The great masters: they defined civilization in Europe for centuries. . . . Now where do you find civilization on the way there?" In response, the orchestral *Rhapsody* returns, accompanied by shots of a popping champagne cork, the bottle's contents being poured into a glass, a passenger closing his eyes and reclining comfortably in his seat, and a Boeing 747 cruising toward the horizon. As the music reaches a high point, the voice-over pronounces: "United Airlines' renowned international service to fifteen cities all across Europe. . . . Come fly the airline that united the world. Come fly the friendly skies." The ad ends pointedly on a high note "sung" by Edgar Degas's *Café Singer*.

The ads establish good connections between the Old and New Worlds that figure through the connection between music and images. European paintings "perform" a signature piece of American music, Gershwin's *Rhapsody in Blue*, itself a hybrid of modern jazz and classical concerto form. The promotional ploy of the advertisement is evident. Although it is critical for commercials to catch our attention, though not our critical attention, here the sophisticated frequent flyer is not just meant to enjoy the witty disjunction between, for instance, the "baroque" timbre of the two recorders and their "blue" tune, but to realize that the music miraculously issued from these paintings is as real as the magic of the commodity it sells. Hence the *second* turn of the puzzled museum guard after "hearing" the piano glissando from the Renoir. The clever audiovisual montage creates a miracle and reveals it as a created one. Miraculous connections *are* possible. The ending of the second part of the commercial drives that point home, when the passenger leans back with closed eyes, his plane flies into the friendly skies, and we hear a climax from Gershwin's *Rhapsody*.

The plane and the music are carriers in a double sense. They are not only a means of transportation, but also a means of transport, which, according to the *Oxford English Dictionary*, is the "state of being 'carried out of oneself,' i.e. out of one's normal mental condition, through a vehement emotion of a pleasurable kind, leading to exaltation, rapture, ecstasy." The commercial suggests that United offers not only transportation between different continents, but also transport that elevates the airline's customers into a different world—the world of luxury and refined culture. Music is a carrier in a double sense, too. The *Rhapsody in Blue* is a jingle, a musical reminder of a particular product. Its tune carries the commodity. That is *musical* transportation. But the music also gives us a lift into a realm of heightened experience. A rhapsody, according to the *New Grove Dictionary of Music and Musicians*, is an "exalted expression of sentiment or feeling." That is *musical* transport. In short, the commercial insinuates the equivalence between transportation and transport on two different planes: the aircraft and the aesthetic.

II

I will now suggest that transportation can be associated with the musical production and remembrance of images, and transport with their destruction and forgetting. A passage from Nietzsche's fragment "On Music and Words" will serve as a point of departure:

> Music can generate images. . . . [b]ut how should the image, the representation . . . be capable of generating music? . . . While it is certain that a bridge leads from the mysterious castle of the musician into the free country of images . . . it is impossible to proceed in the opposite direction. . . . Populate the air with the imagination of a Raphael and contemplate, as he did, how St. Cecilia is listening, enraptured, to the harmonies of angelic choirs: no sound issues from this world though it seems to be lost in music. But if we imagined that this harmony did actually acquire sound by virtue of a miracle, where would St. Cecilia, Paul, and Magdalen and the singing angels suddenly disappear? We would immediately cease to be Raphael, and even as the instruments of this world lie broken on the ground in this painting, our painter's vision, conquered by something higher, would pale and vanish like shadows.[1]

Of course, in light of so much music that has been inspired by images, Nietzsche's suggestion seems plainly wrong. But we need to consider the "Fragment on Music and Words" in the context of Nietzsche's *The Birth of Tragedy from the Spirit of Music,* which sought to explain Wagner's music drama as a modern version of the ancient dialectic between Apollonian and Dionysian forces (or the powers of sight and of sound). As a result, Nietzsche makes two contradictory claims. First, he asserts that the relationship between music and image is a one-way street: music brings forth images, but not vice versa. Second, however, images that do actually make music will self-destruct or disappear. Nietzsche explained this paradox—that music can create and destroy images—in terms of music's ability to make us remember and to make us forget. As a vehicle of images music jogs our memory; but in the moment of transport it makes us forget, perhaps even ourselves.

Let us look at transport first. Transport is Saint Cecilia's visionary moment in Raphael's painting (figure 10.1). For Nietzsche, the saint's gaze at the choir of angels suggests that the purity of their heavenly singing has undone the musical instruments of this earth, which fall to the ground like the little hand organ that slips from the saint's hand. Although it seems bizarre to claim that divine music actually sounding from the painting would make the painting vanish, Nietzsche asserts later in the "Fragment"

Figure 10.1 Raphael, *St. Cecilia* (1514, Pinacoteca Nazionale, Bologna). Reproduced by permission of Scala/Art Resource, NY.

that such spellbinding music as Beethoven's "Ode to Joy" "blinds us totally to images and words and we *simply do not hear anything of Schiller's poem*"[2]; and that, in the opera house, where the power of "pure, self-sufficient, entirely Dionysian music . . . strikes the listener like lightning, the eyes that behold the action and were absorbed in the individuals appearing before us become moist, and the listener *forgets* the drama and wakes up again for it only after the Dionysian spell is broken."[3] It is this kind of forgetting that Nietzsche has in mind when he speaks of the disappearance of Raphael's vision, that is, his painting, before music. While Nietzsche's *Birth of Tragedy out of the Spirit of Music* was a justification of music drama, the "Fragment on Music and Words" (written at the same time) challenged Wagner's assertion, made throughout the Zurich writings, that words had to justify musical meaning.[4] Nietzsche was on his way to becoming perhaps the most radical advocate of absolute music, but he does have a point: powerful music can impair our perception and make us forget what we see around us. That is musical transport.

How does musical transportation differ? Nietzsche asked, "what kind of music is it that may *not* exert any Dionysian power over the listener?"[5] He listed two possibilities. First, this music is possible "*as purely conventional symbolism* from which convention has sucked all natural force—a music that has been weakened to the point where it is no more than mnemonic devices." Such music is "to remind the spectator of something that he must not miss while watching the drama if he wants to understand it, as a trumpet signal is for a horse a command to trot." And second, it is "*music that aims at excitement* as a stimulant for jaded or exhausted nerves." What kind of music is merely a "reminder" and a "stimulant"? In film, it would be music that is replete with clichés and redundant with the action. Such music is merely a vehicle for fixed associations and meanings. Musical excitement may reinforce the drama, but it does not transcend it. In his remarks on film music, Siegfried Kracauer noted that "scores arranged from melodies with fixed meanings are apt to produce a blinding effect." Since popular tunes "call forth stereotyped reactions to them," a classic such as Mendelssohn's "Wedding March" chosen to accompany a wedding will remove from the spectator's consciousness "all visual data which do not directly bear on that ceremony."[6] In other words, musical clichés restrict the frame of reference and produce a maximum of redundancy with the image. By narrowing the focus on the image, they limit our imagination.

The blinding effect through the transportation of musical clichés is of course different than the blindness created through musical transport. Music that is not attached to a fixed association spurs our imagination.

There is a difference between having ordinary vision and being a visionary, like Saint Cecilia seeing angels in the sky. Musical transport, in that sense, destroys real images by replacing them with imaginary ones. This is why Nietzsche didn't want music to be tied to a common place or enslaved to merely carrying the dramatic situation. He wanted music to be free—free to "choose" images as a metaphorical expression of itself, which is another way of saying that it controls the creation of images, or "image sparks" *(Bilderfunken)*, as he puts it elsewhere in a formulation evocative of the silver screen.[7] In film this choice is often made for music, which is usually adapted to the image. But once music is attached to the image, the image becomes attached to the music, which turns into a mnemonic device. While images wither, music remains evergreen.[8] The aesthetic premise and commercial promise of the soundtrack is to keep images fresh and deliver them alive. This is musical transportation.

The relationship between musical transport and transportation is not a strict opposition, however. Although Nietzsche conceived of them as contradictory forces, it would be misleading to conclude that they are mutually exclusive. Music has both elements of transport and of transportation, just as it is both expressive and illustrative, a mixture of both affect and effect. Let us recall that *Rhapsody in Blue* functions as a carrier for United Airlines and produces a feeling of exaltation. The relationship between transport and transportation helps us understand better the dynamic relationship between music and image. Music is not just bound to carrying specific images, but it may at the same time fire up the imagination. Put differently, music may call up memories, but it may also create new ones at the same time. Given this double disposition, I will now explore how musical transport and transportation influence the relationship between music and image in several examples from three films in which audiovisual memory is a central theme.

III

Casablanca was certainly not the first film to exploit audiovisual memory, but as a Hollywood classic it offers two paradigmatic scenes in this respect. Recall from the plot that Ilsa Lund Laszlo (Ingrid Bergman) has arrived in Casablanca in 1942 with her husband, a leader of the anti-Nazi resistance, hoping to secure an exit visa to Lisbon and eventual safe passage to the United States. Much of the wheeling and dealing in Casablanca is done in Rick's American Café, which Rick (Humphrey Bogart) runs with a black pianist, Sam (Dooley Wilson). Surprised to see Sam, Ilsa inquires about Rick.

When Sam replies with some evasive answers, she asks him to play "some of the old songs." His reluctance to do so prompts her famous request:

ILSA: Play it once, Sam, for old time's sake.

SAM: I don't know what you mean, Miss Ilsa.

ILSA: Play it, Sam. Play "As Time Goes By."

SAM: Oh, I can't remember it, Miss Ilsa. I'm a little rusty on it.

> *Of course he can. He doesn't want to play it. He seems even more scared now.*

ILSA: I'll hum it for you.

> ILSA *starts to hum.* SAM *begins to play it very softly.*

ILSA: Sing it, Sam.

> And SAM sings.

SAM: You must remember this,

A kiss is just a kiss,

A sigh is just a sigh,

The fundamental things apply,

As time goes by.

> *The door to the gambling room opens.* RICK *comes swinging out. He's heard the music and he's livid.*

SAM: And when two lovers woo,

They both say I love you,

On that you can rely,

No matter what the future brings,

As time goes by.

> RICK *walks briskly up to the piano.*

RICK: Sam, I thought I told you never to play . . .

> *As he sees* ILSA *he stops short.* SAM *stops playing.*

> *Two close-ups reveal* ILSA *and* RICK *seeing each other.* RICK *appears shocked. For a moment he just looks at her.* SAM *prepares to move the piano away.*[9]

The exchange initiates the gradual discovery of Ilsa's and Rick's past. Once Ilsa presses Sam to sing, the generic text of the song points to the secret it holds: an old romance. The music makes Ilsa see, but as we see her, we cannot see what she is seeing. We know that the song is a carrier, but we don't know the cargo. In a brilliant stroke, this lack is compensated by showing the music's effect on Ilsa—perhaps the most beautiful shot of a woman's face ever. As Martin Marks puts it, "Most of the time while he sings, we are shown Ilsa, listening, and it is the triple counterpoint of words, music, and photography—the soft lighting that perfectly captures the gleams of her hair and jewelry, her beautiful face a frozen, introspective mask—that makes for such a powerful effect."[10] Ilsa's face, we should add, is not entirely frozen: there are gleams of tears in her eyes. In other words, while we cannot see the transportation, we can still see the transport.

The very moment Rick looks at Elsa after entering the room, the music moves from the diegetic to the nondiegetic. A minor variant of the melodic phrase for "you must remember this" in the oboe prolongs the effect of a dissonant stinger chord that resounds the moment the former lovers recognize each other.[11] Compared with the distant suaveness of the song, the music now mimics and expresses the jolt the lovers experience as they see each other. As Ilsa returns to the present, her emotional transport is transferred to the underscoring. It lingers there through the following painful conversation that reveals more details about Rick's and Ilsa's past, and particularly the last time they met, in the café La Belle Aurore on "the day the Germans marched into Paris." But it is only later that night—when Rick is sitting alone in his bar with a bottle of gin—that we will actually see what happened:

> *Suddenly he* [RICK] *pounds the table and buries his head in his arms. Then he raises his head, trying to regain control.*
>
> RICK: Of all the gin joints in all the towns in all the world, she walks into mine.
>
> *He holds his head in his hands.*
>
> RICK: What's that you're playing?
>
> SAM: Just a little something of my own.
>
> RICK: Well, stop it. You know what I want to hear.
>
> SAM: No, I don't.
>
> RICK: You played it for her and you can play it for me.
>
> SAM: Well, I don't think I can remember it.
>
> RICK: If she can stand it, I can. Play it!
>
> SAM: Yes, boss.
>
> > SAM *starts to play "As Time Goes By."*
> >
> > RICK *just stares ahead as orchestra* MUSIC *slowly joins Sam's playing.*
> >
> > *Dissolve to montage—Paris in the spring*
> >
> > *A) The Arc de Triomphe from a distance*
> >
> > *B)* RICK *drives a small, open car slowly along the boulevard.*

He puts his arm around ILSA. *The background scenery changes to a country road as she snuggles close to him and puts her head on his shoulder.*

C) An excursion boat on the Seine. RICK *and* ILSA *stand at the rail of the boat. They seem to be transported by each other as* ILSA *laughs.*[12]

Although Rick had banned the music, he, like Ilsa, presses Sam into service, saying, "You played it for her and you can play it for me." But what follows is musically and visually very different from the previous scene. Now we see in an extended flashback what the music makes Rick see and made Ilsa see before. Toward the end of the flashback the very song that initiates the flashback is also embedded in it, when Rick and Ilsa meet at La Belle Aurore to plot their escape from Paris. Sam's playing of "As Time Goes By" in the café stands for the formation of the audiovisual memory. The music attaches itself not just to a feeling or an event, but to an entire period of time, for which the song becomes what Rousseau called a "memorative sign."[13] Moreover, the lyrics do not just comment on the dramatic situation; they also communicate the essence of the film: "It's still the same old story, a fight for love and glory, a case of do or die."[14] Although Ilsa enters the past through the song alone but is then brought to the present abruptly, for Rick the transformation is seamless. As the flashback ends with a visual and a musical dissolve, one can hear the changing timbre as the agent of the visual transformation. Now there is no fissure and the function is inverted. We no longer see Rick, but see what he is seeing. In other words, we no longer see the transport, but the transportation.

By breaking the taboo on musical memory, Rick's flashback also conveniently fills in the backstory, which helps the viewer understand why Rick and Ilsa must, and why they now can, confront the past. In the two strands of the story—romance and war—Rick begins to work through his loss of Ilsa and changes his passive cynicism into heroic action. The voluntary recall of repressed memories enables him to transform first a traumatic memory into a nostalgic one, and then the nostalgic memory into a memory without loss and pain. "We'll always have Paris," says Rick when seeing Ilsa off at the airport. "We didn't have, we'd lost it, until you came to Casablanca. We got it back last night." And when Ilsa objects, saying "And I said I would never leave you," Rick replies, "And you never will." Rick's heroic renunciation rescues Paris from the past and promises to preserve it for the future. Music's mnemonic power is part of this promise. Even as time will go by, the former lovers can rely on "As Time Goes By."

IV

The predicament of Woody Allen's *Radio Days*—a nostalgic film about the golden days of radio—is a paradox that confronts the apparent visual lack of the radio with the seeming visual surplus of film. I say "apparent" because the radio's visual lack is compensated by becoming a source of imagination, which the film seeks to flesh out. Making visible, in retrospective, the world of production, *Radio Days* defuses the paradox by demystifying the radio as the perfect *acousmêtre,* an unseen source of sound.[15] The film does so by telling two parallel stories about the two worlds on either side of the transmitter. On one side there is little Joe (Allen's youthful alter ego), who is growing up as part of an extended Jewish family in Rockaway Beach. On the other side there is the cigarette girl Sally (Mia Farrow), who eventually succeeds in the world of entertainment by becoming the host of a radio show. From the detached vantage point of hindsight, the narrator's voice-over and the sounds of the radio suture the two narrative strands, as well as the distance between past and present.

Despite the faithful creation of a period sound and ambience, and despite Allen's penchant for humorous episodes, the retrospective of *Radio Days* remains encased in a melancholic frame. When Allen remembers his old neighborhood with a shot of Rockaway Beach on a stormy and rain-swept day—"because that was it at its most beautiful"—he underscores the image with a solo piano playing Kurt Weill and Maxwell Anderson's *September,* whose unsung text adds poignancy to the subdued tone of the music. The line "And the days dwindle down" resonates deeply with Allen's remark, at the end of the film, that his memories have become "dimmer" as time went on. Although the text recalls a romance in spring, the musical affect is of fall. Of the two components of the neo-Greek term nostalgia—*nostos* (return) and *algia* (sorrow)—Weill's music emphasizes loss and forgetting.[16] As an emotional frame for the film, therefore, Allen cites the music not for transporting a memory, but for the transport of remembrance—not as uplift, but as sadness and sorrow. At the same time the line that speaks of "songs" as the only worthy "goods" of spring seems to give Allen a raison d'être for filling the frame with the *nostos* of nostalgia, with the return home through reminiscence.[17] According to Allen, the inspiration for the film was "to make a memory for each important song from my childhood. . . . And when I started to write the memories of the sounds, I got inspiration for other scenes and sequences, which could strengthen and support these memories. If I had done *Radio Days* faithfully, I would have done about 25 different songs and described what comes into my mind when I hear them."[18] While the film is full of wonderful tunes from the last years of the Depression and the beginning of World War II, only once does Allen stick to his creative premise in a literal way. In an extraordinary sequence—labeled in the DVD release as "Memorable Music" (chapter 8)—he presents the film's poetics of audiovisual memory through seven songs, explaining in the voice-over that "to this day there are certain songs that, no matter where I am, the minute I hear them I get instant memory flashes." The songs, of course, become a Proustian trigger for musical transportation.

RADIO DAYS: MEMORABLE MUSIC

Introduction. "The Donkey Serenade," by Bob Wright, Chet Forrest, Rudolf Friml, and Herbert Stohart
Joe's Aunt Bea sits on the front steps listening to the radio as Joe runs down the stairs with his friends.

1. "You and I," words and music by Meredith Willson (instrumental version)
Joe has a crush on Evelyn Goorwitz, overcoming her reluctance to take a few kisses from him.

2. "I Am Gonna Buy a Paper Doll," by Johnny S. Black, performed by the Mills Brothers
Joe witnesses the only time his parents kiss, as his father presents his mother with a new coat on their wedding anniversary.

3. "Pistol Packin' Mama," by Al Dexter, performed by the Andrews Sisters
Little Joe and his friend build a snowman in front of his school, placing a carrot in the bottom third of the body. An outraged teacher comes outside, takes away the carrot—and takes a bite.

4. "South American Way," by Al Dubin and Jimmy McHugh, performed by Carmen Miranda
Cousin Ruthie dances and mimes Miranda's radio performance, while Joe's father and uncle look on.

5. "Mairzy Doats," by Jerry Livingston, Milton Drake, and Al Hoffman
Joe's neighbor, Mr. Zipsky, has a nervous breakdown, running amok in his underwear waving a cleaver about.

6. "You Are but a Dream," by Moe Jaffe, Jack Fulton, and Nat Bonx, sung by Frank Sinatra

> Joe goes with Aunt Bea and her "then-boyfriend," Chester, to
> Radio City Music Hall to see *The Philadelphia Story.*

Despite the narrator's claim that the songs create "instant memory flashes,"
the images are carefully composed to the music, which is not unusual for
preexistent music in film, but serves here to underscore the precision of audiovisual memory. Faster music for funnier incidents alternates with suave
crooning for touching moments. A few slapstick source sounds added to the
former give way to music alone in the latter. Although the potpourri form
suggests that memories attach themselves to music by accident, the song
texts provide humorous or ironic commentary on the narrative. In the
episode with the snowman, for instance, the line "Lay that pistol down" really suggests "Lay that carrot down," while the carrot's pointed placement
suggests that it is a pistol of a different sort. If "Paper Doll" calls up the kiss
of Joe's parents, the text gives this "wonderful" memory a bittersweet tinge.
As the song speaks of replacing lost love with a paper doll that "other fel-
lows cannot steal," it hints at deeper domestic dilemmas that surface elsewhere in the film.

But Allen's choice of music also goes beyond narrative concerns, opening up a broader perspective on music-image relationships. In the last song,
little Joe associates Frank Sinatra's "If You Are But a Dream" with his first
visit to Radio City Music Hall, which he experienced as "entering heaven."[19]
Although the other selections use only fragments, this song is heard in full.
The first and final verses will suffice us here:

> If you are but a dream
> I hope I never waken,
> It's more than I could bear
> To find that I'm forsaken.
>
> . . .
>
> So darling,
> If our romance would break up,
> I hope I never wake up,
> If you are but a dream.

At first, of course, the text comments on one of the narrative threads of
Radio Days: Aunt Bea's bad luck with men and her unfulfilled romantic
dreams, which make the emotional pitch of the song more poignant. Going
to the movies with her "then-boyfriend" and with little Joe she appears as
the mother of a happy nuclear family (like the many other families shown
on their way to the auditorium). But that appearance turns out to be an illusion. A second meaning emerges from the close alignment of the text with

the sound and image tracks. As the music builds up along with the song's goal-oriented syntax, the camera follows the would-be family climbing the stairs and walking through a long corridor, as they enter the Parnassus of entertainment. When they open the door of the auditorium, shot from the dark interior, the music arrives at the climactic chord before the last line, "If you are but a dream." Strikingly, the phrase "a dream" coincides with a reverse shot of the silver screen—the moment in *The Philadelphia Story* when Jimmy Stewart and Katharine Hepburn kiss passionately. This is the one instance in *Radio Days* where the film faces film as the other. It advances the song as an allegory of cinematic experience. The romance with fantasy becomes a figure for cinema's precarious love affair with images. It reflects, as Peter Bailey puts it, as "conflicted [an] attitude toward the consolations of film's illusions" as Allen has ever presented."[20] Like the chimera of true love, film is a product of the dream factory, whose images will invariably vanish. Touching the screen would be a transgression. It would reveal that the projected pictures last no longer than the passion sealed by the forbidden kiss in *The Philadelphia Story*.

Momentarily, at least, "If you are but a dream" holds out the hope that music can hold on to the images it evokes. As the summation of the musical memory sequence, the song creates a critical conjunction of musical transportation and musical transport. Clearly, this has been music as transportation—a vehicle for text that comments on the story and a vehicle for a memory that materializes in the images. And clearly, the music—especially in the last song—is also a moment of transport, taking the young Joe (and the old Allen) from Rockaway reality into Hollywood heaven. Music is not only a carrier of memories, but also a catalyst of their rapturous return. And yet, despite the hope that music can recall the images, the hope to keep them beyond the sound is dashed, for the song inevitably ends and the dream vanishes. With the music's final flourishes, the camera turns back from the screen toward the door of the movie theater, shutting its eye as the door closes, leaving us behind in the dark.

V

"Music," writes the British director Terence Davies, "plays a crucial part in all my films. I was brought up in a house that was filled with music—on the radio, on records and people singing. And, of course, the musical comedy films of the period were part of this. . . . If the music in my films represents my emotional autobiography, the stories represent my actual autobiography."[21] Davies's autobiographical films include *Trilogy* (1984), *Distant Voices, Still Lives* (1988), and *The Long Day Closes* (1992), and it is the second one from which I chose two examples. Davies notes that *Distant Voices, Still Lives* "dealt with things that I had learned second-hand from my mother and my two eldest sisters and my brother," whose stories about their father became "so vivid to me that their memories became mine."[22] Since the subject was memory, Davies realized that the form of the film "should be cyclical not linear. . . . The film constantly turns back on itself, like the ripples in a pool when a stone is thrown into it. The ripples are the memory." The cyclical nature of *Distant Voices, Still Lives* is evident in frequent and potentially disorienting flashbacks, when scenes from childhood and adolescence unexpectedly cut away from the present, which is itself organized not in a linear narrative but in a string of episodes.

The sound advance is the fingerprint of Davies's technique. Sound calls— or calls back—the image, and vice versa. In the opening shots of *Distant Voices, Still Lives* and *The Long Day Closes*, the distant voices over an empty staircase summon the distant bodies of the protagonists who will populate the film. According to Phil Powrie, the symbolism of the threshold pertains to liminal events in the family—funerals, weddings, and baptisms, as well as changing schools, Christmas, and New Year's—which become a point of departure for the passage into the past. [23] If the threshold is the line, one might say, the staircase is the lane. One must cross the former in order to travel down the latter. Davies's narrative rhythm emerges between pausing and passing, between steady images and long tracking shots or slow pans. "If music is movement and rhythm in time," Davies writes, "then film is both movement and rhythm in space *and* time."[24] In her recent study of Davies's cinema, Wendy Everett has pointed out that his "films are, to a large extent, even structured by music, which also dictates their internal pace and rhythms, while their underlying meanings are, to a considerable degree, actually dictated by its presence or absence from the soundtrack."[25]

Two examples from *Distant Voices, Still Lives* showcase this twofold rhythm in space and time and exemplify the shifting threshold, as it were, between musical transport and transportation in the service of audiovisual memory. On one hand, Davies has a penchant for recalling the ethnographic immediacy of unadorned and unaccompanied singing at family gatherings or community festivities at home, in a pub, on the street, or even in a bomb shelter. On the other, he combines his memory of preexistent music from a range of styles and sources with camera movements across imaginary spaces and temporal distances, often evoking the surreal or the symbolic.

The first example constitutes a clearly structured unit, as determined by the music and camera movement (see table 10.1). It can be divided into five sections, which are framed by two static shots (sections 1 and 5). In the opening section 1, Davies's just-married sister Eileen and her husband pose behind the wedding cake for a photo. In the closing section 5, Eileen is seen as a child sitting at the Christmas dinner table with her sister Maisie, her brother Tony, and their father, all waiting for the mother. Although the stillness of these images is thus motivated by the narrative, it corresponds to the musical silence that frames the composition of the entire unit.

The two types of music we hear in this sequence appear to initiate the movement of the camera, indicated by the arrows in the table. After the photo op at the wedding, the camera tracks slowly from left to right across the wedding guests in section 2. The camera thereby follows the sound advance of the guests singing "If You Knew Suzie" by Eddie Cantor, made popular by Frank Sinatra and Gene Kelly in the 1945 musical *Anchors Aweigh* and suggesting tongue-in-cheek commentary on the bride. The tracking comes to a halt in section 3 when the camera focuses on the bride's sister Maisie, who sings "My Yiddishe mama—I miss her more than ever now / My Yiddishe mama—I long to kiss her wrinkled brow / I long to hold her hand once more as in days gone by / And ask her to forgive me for things I did that made her cry." As Maisie continues her song we cut outside to her brother with Eileen, crying loudly, "I want me dad." Holding steady, the camera allows the song to reflect on the different relationships of the two sisters with their parents. While Eileen was the father's favorite daughter, Maisie had been traumatized by his violence against her and their mother, to whom her song is a heartfelt tribute. Paradoxically, the tribute to the mother triggers the memory of the father, embedded in the most cherished memory from childhood—Christmas. Again, in section 4, the music—an ethereal a cappella rendition of Harold Darke's "In the Bleak Midwinter," with the first stanza sung solo—seems to set into motion the camera, now tracking very slowly from right to left.

This retrospective move in the opposite direction creates an inversion in the visual composition of this segment, pitting the present against the past. Passing windows illuminated in the dark, the camera traverses an imaginary space and time to arrive at Christmastime during Eileen's childhood. The tracking finally stops at a window behind which the father is decorating the Christmas tree. A cut inside leads to two brief narrative elaborations (section X), showing his tender side in two bedtime rituals. All the time, the carol—nondiegetic—rings out through all four stanzas, connecting personal and collective memory, for "In the Bleak Midwinter" is a staple of the Festival of Nine Lessons and

Table 10.1 *Distant Voices, Still Lives*: Wedding-Christmas Sequence

Section of Montage	1	2	3	4	X	5
Movement	Stasis	Left to right	Stasis	Right to left	Flexible	Stasis
Action/setting	Wedding photo	Wedding celebration in pub	Eileen crying	Illuminated windows; family praying, Christmas preparations	Christmas preparations inside the house	Christmas family dinner
	(present) ————————→			(past) ————————→		
Soundtrack/music	Silence	"If I Knew Suzie"	"My Yiddishe Momma"	"In the Bleak Midwinter"	"In the Bleak Midwinter" continues	Silence
		(wedding guests: diegetic)	(Maisie: diegetic)	(choir: nondiegetic) ————→		

Carols, which has been broadcast from King's College, Cambridge, every Christmas Eve since 1928. The final chord coincides with the shot of the family waiting silently at the dinner table for the mother, but this silence is unexpectedly shattered by the father's violent outburst in section 5 when he pulls the tablecloth, screaming at the top of his lungs, "Nellie! Clean it up!" While the friendly explosion of the popping flash light at the wedding had kicked off the celebration in the present, here the terrible outburst of the impatient father effectively ends another one in the past. To articulate the end of this formal unit Davies abruptly cuts to the father on his deathbed.

To read this sequence in terms of transport and transportation, recall Nietzsche's view of Raphael's Saint Cecilia as standing on the threshold between the real and the imaginary. As the camera moves left to right through real space, the singing of the wedding guests would stand for the music of this world: earthy and embodied. As the camera moves right to left through imaginary space, the singing of the choir would stand for the music of angels: disembodied and divine. In both cases, the camera searches, as it were, for the source of the sounds. In the first case, it locates the bodies of the singers; in the second case, it conjures up the spirit of Christmas. But if music either reinforces the sense of reality or the experience of ideality, it also undercuts these tendencies. Although the mother is present, "My Yiddishe Momma" imagines the mother's loss in the future through the pain of forgetting (the *algia* component of nostalgia). Although the father is dead, the carol calls up his image through happy childhood memories (the *nostos* component of nostalgia). The grainy texture of the sentimental song creates its own moment of emotional transport, while the ethereal sound of the boys' choir produces its own moment of mnemonic transportation. The changing relation between musical transport and transportation articulates the shifting relationship between music and image, from a reality where memory is merely imagined, to an imaginary where memory is actually realized.

These inversions between actual image and imagined image emerge in my final example as a self-conscious commentary on film as a medium of audiovisual memory. Again, Davies exercises strong control of form through spatiotemporal movement, creating another five-part structure (see table 10.2) that is both symmetrical and linear. Between an outer frame of heavy rain without music (sections 1 and 5), two complementary movements up and down (indicated by the arrows in sections 2 and 4) enclose an inner moment of relative visual stasis (section 3). From the shot of a crowd of umbrellas waiting in front of the movie theater, the camera slowly cranes up without a cut into the auditorium, focusing on Davies's sisters who sob over the tragic ending of Henry King's 1955 tearjerker *Love Is a Many-*

Table 10.2 *Distant Voices, Still Lives*: Movie Theater Sequence

Section of Montage	1	2	3	4	5
Movement	Stasis	Up	Zoom in	Down	Flexible
Action/setting	Crowd waiting outside movie theater	Crane up along the wall of the movie theater	Maisie and Eileen crying in the movie theater over ending of *Love Is a Many-Splendored Thing*	Tony and George fall from a scaffolding	Maisie runs to George's sickbed
Sound/music	Rain	Orchestra (*Love Is a Many-Splendored Thing*) ⟶			Rain

Splendored Thing (a poster of the film is shown on the way up). The story of an ill-fated romance between a Eurasian doctor (Jennifer Jones) and an American journalist (William Holden) who is killed in the Korean War, the film picked up both music Oscars for Alfred Newman's score and the title song by Sammy Fain and Paul Francis Webster, whose closing lines point to the moments of the movie that create the deepest impressions, shot in a park overlooking Hong Kong:

> Once on a high and windy hill
> In the morning mist
> Two lovers kissed and the world stood still
> And your fingers touched my silent heart
> And taught it how to sing
> Yes, true love's a many splendored thing.

While a chorus tops off with a final burst of Dionysian force the final scene, where Jennifer Jones revisits the hill in search of her memories, Davies chose for his sequence the instrumental version of the melody, so that its climax coincides with the shot of the sisters in tears. The result is a miraculous moment of audiovisual remembrance. By depriving us of the words, Davies trusts that the listeners who know the song may recall its words; and by depriving us of the images, he trusts that viewers who know the film will see in their minds that final scene—perhaps searching themselves not just for their own memories of the film, but also recalling the circumstances they saw it for the first time. In other words, trusting that the music will do the transportation, Davies can also show the transport. Thus the music does more than jog the viewers' visual recollection. As a place for memories, music doubles up its function in the film not shown: namely, to harbor true love. Davies refigures that love as the love not just for this film, but for this kind of film. For those who never heard or saw *Love Is a Many-Splendored Thing*, hearing its music and seeing its effect on the two sisters is enough to fancy a cathartic moment of melodrama. On the level of collective memory, therefore, Davies's montage is not merely about recovering a specific image, but also about remembrance as an ongoing process of cultural imagination. It is a process that is both precious and precarious.

The third part of his montage drives this point home by showing how Davies's audiovisual memory refuses to separate nostalgia from trauma and reconstruction from destruction. In a perfect match of the melody's plaintive *Abgesang*, predictably played by the celli and the oboe, we see Maisie's brother Tony and her husband George fall from a scaffolding through a glass roof in surreal slow motion. By substituting the originally planned low-angle shot looking straight up with a shot of the tumbling men from a high angle, the initial crane up into the movie theater is countered by a fateful fall—utopian uplift undone by a real letdown.[26] Apart from the obvious juxtaposition of imagined and actual tragedy, the scene is also an allegory of Nietzsche's paradoxical claim that music generates images and destroys them. The inverted shots resemble two points of view in Raphael's painting. While the disembodied music guides our glance up toward the heaven of Hollywood, the falling bodies crash through the glass as if they were shattering its screen.

NOTES

1. Friedrich Nietzsche, "On Music and Words," in Carl Dahlhaus, *Between Romanticism and Modernism: Four Studies in the Music of the Later Nineteenth Century* (Berkeley and Los Angeles: University of California Press, 1980), pp. 109–10. Nietzsche goes on, asking: "But how could such a miracle occur? How could the Apollinian world of the eye, wholly absorbed in visual contemplation, be able to generate a tone, which after all symbolizes a sphere that is excluded and overcome by the Apollinian abandonment to mere appearance? The delight in mere appearance cannot generate out of itself the delight in non-appearance. The delight of seeing is a delight only because nothing reminds us of a sphere in which individuation is broken and annulled."

2. Ibid., p. 113 (original emphasis).

3. Ibid., pp. 118–19 (original emphasis).

4. On 11 February 1872, Cosima noted in her diaries: "Of *Opera and Drama,* which he is correcting, he says: I know what Nietzsche didn't like in it—it is the same thing . . . that set Schopenhauer against me: what I said about words. At the same time I didn't dare to say that music produced drama, although inside myself I knew it." *Cosima Wagner's Diaries,* ed. Martin Gregor-Dellin and Dietrich Mack, trans. Geoffrey Skelton, 2 vols. (New York: Harcourt Brace Jovanovich, 1978–80), vol. 1, p. 457.

5. This and the next three quotations are from Nietzsche, "On Music and Words," p. 118 (original emphases).

6. Siegfried Kracauer, *Theory of Film: the Redemption of Physical Reality* (New York: Oxford University Press, 1960), p. 141.

7. Nietzsche, "On Music and Words," p. 112, notes in the context of a composer setting a poem a reversal of the generative process, originating not with the text but with music: "A musical excitement that comes from altogether different regions *chooses* the text of this song as a metaphorical expression of itself." On "image sparks," see Friedrich Nietzsche, *The Birth of Tragedy,* trans. Walter Kaufmann (New York: Vintage Books, 1967), pp. 50 and 53.

8. In German, "oldies" are called "evergreens."

9. Cited from "A synthesis of extant versions of the shooting script, the conti-

nuity script, and a close analysis of the finished film," available at http://www.geocities.com/classicmoviescripts/, pp. 43–44.

10. Martin Marks, "Music, Drama, Warner Brothers: The Cases of *Casablanca* and *The Maltese Falcon*," in *Music and Cinema*, ed. James Buhler, Caryl Flinn, and David Neumeyer (Hanover, NH: University Press of New England, 2000), p. 174.

11. See ibid., pp. 174–75, and David Neumeyer and James Buhler, "Analytical and Interpretive Approaches to Film Music (I): Analyzing the Music," in *Film Music: Critical Approaches*, ed Kevin J. Donnelly (New York: Continuum, 2001), pp. 21–22. Needless to say that my reading here is not meant to do justice to the rich resonances of the song throughout the film; nor can I do justice to the many cultural and racial implications of music making, from ethnic stereotyping to racial discrimination.

12. See note 9, pp. 51–52.

13. Jean Jacques Rousseau, *Dictionary of Music*, trans. William Waring, reprint of the 1779 edition (New York: AMS Press, 1975), p. 267. According to Jean Starobinski, "The Idea of Nostalgia," *Diogenes* 54 (1966), pp. 92–93, Rousseau helped to advance an "an 'acoustical' theory of nostalgia."

14. See Marks, "Music, Drama, Warner Brothers," p. 176.

15. See Michel Chion, *The Voice in Cinema*, trans. Claudia Gorbman (New York: Columbia University Press, 1999), pp. 16–29.

16. Starobinski, "The Idea of Nostalgia," p. 85.

17. "When you meet with the young man early in Spring, / They court you in song and rhyme / They woo you with words and a clover ring, / But if you examine the goods they bring / They have little to offer but the songs they sing, / And a plentiful waste of time of day / A plentiful waste of time." See Carol Goodson, "Song as Subtext: The Virtual Reality of Lyrics in the Films of Woody Allen," in *Woody Allen: A Casebook*, ed. Kimball King (New York: Routledge, 2001), pp. 2–3.

18. Woody Allen and Stig Björkman, *Woody Allen about Woody Allen* (New York: Grove Press, 1995), p. 164; see also p. 158.

19. See ibid., p. 166.

20. Peter J. Bailey, *The Reluctant Film Art of Woody Allen* (Lexington: University Press of Kentucky, 2001), p. 66.

21. Terence Davies, *A Modest Pageant: Children, Madonna and Child, Death and Transfiguration, Distant Voices, Still Lives and The Long Day Closes: Six Screenplays with an Introduction* (London: Faber and Faber, 1992), p. x.

22. Ibid.

23. Phil Powrie, "On the Threshold between Past and Present: 'Alternative Heritage'," in *British Cinema, Past and Present*, ed. Justine Ashby and Andrew Higson (London: Routledge, 2000), pp. 316–26.

24. Davies, *A Modest Pageant*, p. x.

25. Wendy Everett, "Music and Time: A New Dimension," in *Terence Davies* (Manchester: Manchester University Press, 2004), p. 172. See also Everett's essay "Songlines: Alternative Journeys in Contemporary European Cinema," in *Music and Cinema*, ed. James Buhler, Caryl Flinn, and David Neumeyer (Hanover, NH: University Press of New England, 2000), 99–117.

26. See ibid., p. 179, and Davies, *A Modest Pageant*, p. 128.

11 The Fantastical Gap between Diegetic and Nondiegetic

ROBYNN J. STILWELL

It is one of the most basic distinctions in film music: diegetic or nondiegetic? It is a simple, technical matter—is the music part of the film's story world or an element of the cinematic apparatus that represents that world? It is one of the easiest things to teach students about film music—to comprehend, if not to spell (it's getting to the point where I see "diagetic" so often, it's starting to seem right to me). Even on the first night of a film music course, college students can recognize moments that challenge their sense of that boundary even before they have a name for it. Yet recently the issue has been the subject of a great deal of discussion, formal and informal, in film music circles. It is repeatedly pointed out that there are quite a lot of cases that do not seem so easy to label as diegetic or nondiegetic.

The attitude toward these cases ranges from curiosity to dissatisfaction; the response has largely been at the extremes. Some have responded with a taxonomic approach, breaking down various stages or states between diegetic and nondiegetic, while others have responded with dismissal—if this border is being crossed so often, then the distinction doesn't mean anything. One thing both of these reactions have in common is a need to "freeze" the border crossing at a point: either, like a specimen for an old-fashioned electron microscope, it has to be killed in order to be examined; or the border itself evaporates so the point becomes invisible.

These reactions seem unsatisfactory for some basic experiential reasons. My objection to the latter is simple: because the border between diegetic and nondiegetic is crossed so often does not invalidate the separation. If anything, it calls attention to the act of crossing and therefore reinforces difference. My problem with the former is more the stop-motion aspect: the border crossing is not so much an event as a process, not simply a crossing, or even passing through distinct intermediary states, but a trajectory, a vector, a gesture. It unfolds through time, like film, like music. Even when the transition is acknowledged, it is often suspiciously cast as "transgression"— which it can be, but isn't always.

Why are we coming to this questioning of a basic concept just as the relatively new field of film music studies is beginning to reach a coherent and critical mass? I suspect that the state of film music studies is, in fact, the reason for the investigation. Foundations have been laid, basic parameters mapped. We have a sense of where we are, and now we are moving into an area of greater refinement, more focused inquiry. We are also moving beyond a repertoire of classical Hollywood films, European avant-gardes, and documentaries with scores by famous concert hall composers. The terrain is shifting, and productive analysis will move with it.

In Noël Carroll's terms, it is a move from Theory, a proper noun with a capital T, an overarching construct into which a text is fitted, to theorizing, an activity that engages with the text on much more limited, specific terms in order to understand better how the film or films work.[1] We might consider it a shift from casting to sculpture. Although Carroll was speaking specifically about the field of *film* studies, his wariness about the effectiveness of a single Theory that presumes to explain everything is salutary to any field (even physics, the field of inquiry in which the unified field theory is still the holy grail and which has struggled for nigh on a century with a full reconciliation of Newtonian, Einsteinian, and quantum principles); theorizing breaks this massive undertaking into bite-sized chunks, not only easily digestible but nourishing:

> Film theorizing . . . should be piecemeal. But it should also be diversified. Insofar as theorists approach film from many different angles, from different levels of abstraction and generality, they will have to avail themselves of multidisciplinary frameworks. Some questions about film may send the researcher toward economics, while others require a look into perceptual psychology. In other instances, sociology, political science, anthropology, communications theory, linguistics, artificial intelligence, biology, or narrative theory may provide the initial research tools which the film theorist requires in order to begin to evolve theories of this or that aspect of film.[2]

Carroll does not specifically mention music as a source of enlightenment (demonstrating yet again the dominance of the visual/verbal in film studies), but music is perhaps particularly well placed to throw new light from its outsider position—something that Carroll unintentionally suggests:

> In opposition to the essentialist theorist who might disparage explorations in other disciplines as fatally alloyed, it is my claim that anxieties about theoretical purity are impediments to theoretical discovery. Film theorizing

should be interdisciplinary. It should be pursued without the expectation of discovering a unified theory, cinematic or otherwise. That is, it should be catholic about the methodological frameworks it explores.

Perhaps at this historical juncture it seems strange to urge that film theory be multidisciplinary, since it might be asserted that the Theory—that assemblage of Althusser, Lacan, Barthes, et al.—is patently interdisciplinary, given that Althusser was a philosopher, Lacan a psychoanalyst, and Barthes a literary critic. And yet, I wonder about the interdisciplinary pretensions of Theory since Theory, as it is practiced in film departments—and neighboring literature departments—is really a body of canonical texts or authors, which body of authors serves rather like the paradigm of a *single discipline* in the making.[3]

In the past couple of decades, musicology has been converging with this "unified field" itself, but it still has a unique language and analytical practice that allows that outside perspective, a different angle of approach, and other models of understanding. The specific shapes, structures, and dynamics of music and of film are individually challenging—and the element of unfolding over time is perhaps too often "frozen" into a spatial metaphor for ease of analysis, or sliced into discrete moments; the combination of film and music merely complicates matters.

The trajectory of music between diegetic and nondiegetic highlights a gap in our understanding, a place of destabilization and ambiguity. The diegetic and nondiegetic are conceived as separate realms, almost like two adjacent bubbles, and there seems to be little possibility of moving from one to the other without piercing the skin that explodes the two "universes," which certainly is one reason for the reliance on the language of "transgression." But perhaps it is a failure of metaphor. It seems a perfect candidate for theorizing.

When that boundary between diegetic and nondiegetic is traversed, it does always *mean*. It is also hardly ever a single moment—one moment we're in the diegetic realm and in the blink of an eye, like walking through Alice's mirror, we are in the nondiegetic looking-glass world. The thickness of the glass, as it were, like any liminal space, is a space of power and transformation, of inversion and the uncanny, of making strange in order to make sense.[4] That these transitions are *sometimes* transgressions only heightens that liminality.

On a film music roundtable for *The Velvet Light Trap*,[5] this ambiguity of diegetic and nondiegetic came up, and between us, Jim Buhler and I built up the term "fantastical gap."

JIM: Likewise, a film such as *King Kong* plays with the distinction to productive effect. The music on the island, for instance, is neither diegetic nor nondiegetic. I would locate the fantastic in fact in the gap between what we hear and what we see. But without some sort of distinction between D/ND sound, such a gap isn't even really audible.

ROBYNN: re Jim & *King-Kong,* yes, that "fantastical gap" is exactly what I was pointing to. . . . I think the "geography of the soundscape" is far more complex and flexible than we have begun to chart.

The phrase "fantastical gap" seemed particularly apt for this liminal space because it captured both its magic and its danger, the sense of unreality that always obtains as we leap from one solid edge toward another at some unknown distance and some uncertain stability—and sometimes we're in the air before we know we've left the ground. "Fantastical" can literally mean fantasy (cinematically, a musical number, dream, or flashback), and in fact this is one implication of the change of state that has begun to be explored by scholars like Rick Altman[6] and David Neumeyer;[7] but it can also mean, musically, an improvisation, the free play of possibility.

The Heisenberg principle of physics tells us that observing a particle or wave[8] alters its state, causing it to change from a superposition of all possibilities to a singular position. The observer may hypothesize but not predict the final position, and the ambiguity of that superposition is analogous to the destabilization and multiplicity of possibility that occurs during the transition between one diegetic/nondiegetic state to the other. In the spirit of theorizing, we will look at several examples of transition, not in order to reduce the process to a single trajectory, but to start to map the geography of the soundscape and contemplate some of the axes[9] along which we can negotiate that gap.

GEOGRAPHY OF THE SOUNDSCAPE

Although cinema is normally assumed to be a distinct medium, it has an obvious historical antecedent in theater. The frame of the screen becomes the proscenium arch; the incidental music rises from the orchestra in the pit below and in front of the stage—the musicians are heard but not seen by the audience. The conductor can see the stage and respond to the action and mood, but the characters on the stage do not acknowledge the presence of the musicians at their feet, even if they perform with them during a musical number (only the actors may do so at the end of the play, or by break-ing the fourth wall and interrupting the illusion on stage). The term "un-derscore" has several interlocking meanings, including the delineation of emotional or narrative content by musical accompaniment, or the more lit-eral meaning of score running *under* the dialogue and/or action. This last meaning also shades over into a geographical meaning, of music emanating from a physical space underneath the stage.

Cinema changes almost none of this construct, musically. It is the "stage" itself that is collapsed into two dimensions. However, it also throws into re-lief the difference between diegetic and nondiegetic; silent cinema in par-ticular highlights the divergent existence of black-and-white two-dimensional images, and living, breathing, blowing, bowing musicians in the theater. The two may converge, for instance, in a ballroom scene, where the live music is pretending to be that of the musicians seen or presumed on screen, but the physical separation is plain to anyone in the audience.[10]

The arrival of sound caused a crisis of conceptualization. Some film mak-ers, notably René Clair in France and the Soviets, found novel solutions, but the ways in which the music related to the diegesis were often explicitly ar-tificial—the unsynched dialogue in *Sous les Toits de Paris,* for example, or the more abstract composition of Eisensteinian montage. The Hollywood model from the beginning strove toward a putative "realism" (in quotes, heavy irony)—not reality as lived experience, but rather reality as based on theater, leading to the well-known early proliferation of backstage musicals and nightclub-centered gangster films to allow the quasi-realistic insertion of music. In fact, one could argue that the visuals of your basic Busby Berke-ley extravaganza are far more "nondiegetic" than the music: the extraordi-nary rail yard through which Dick Powell carries Ruby Keeler at the end of "I Only Have Eyes for You" in *Dames* (1934) is an example of a space that could never exist in a theater as depicted, while the numerous optical trans-formations of objects into formations of women and vice versa are manip-ulations beyond physical reality. The nondiegetic becomes a space of fan-tasy, at least in part because of anxiety over its "impossibility."

As late as 1944, Hitchcock famously still asked, "But where is the or-chestra?" about a proposed underscore for *Lifeboat.* Apocryphal or not, the question is illuminating. It wasn't the *function* that concerned Hitchcock in *Lifeboat,* but the extra-diegetic location of the musicians.[11] Perhaps the question never was the *absence* of the musicians, but the *uncertainty* of where they might be. Unidentifiable, unlocatable sound is disturbing be-cause we (potential prey) are alerted to potential threat; it makes us uneasy; we look around for visual grounding.

Max Steiner exploited this anxiety—which had suppressed nondiegetic scores in other films—when he created the score to *King Kong* in 1933. The film is both fantasy and horror, so Steiner could take advantage of what may have been in other contexts disadvantages, or at least distractions. After the pit-orchestra overture and a watery dissolve into the diegesis, the scenes in gritty, realistic New York are unscored, as are the initial scenes on the ship. Music rolls in with the fog, a visual metaphor for the fantastical gap. It is not yet the elsewhere of Skull Island, but an amorphous border that extends around it, blurring its edges. If we watch the sequence carefully, it is not very difficult to classify the various elements: the comments of those on board the ship pin down the drums as diegetic; the harp-arpeggio music of the sea (a music already established by the opening scenes of the New York harbor) is retrospectively confirmed as nondiegetic because no one is talking about it. Yet there are moments of slippage. More intriguing and more complex is the elision between the water music and the drums; those on board the ship are speaking about the drums over the nondiegetic water music before we can clearly hear them, and then when the scene changes to Skull Island, the drums remain heard but not seen for several minutes, creating an acousmatic underscore for the film crew's search for the source.[12] There is a play here not only between diegetic and nondiegetic, but also between foreground and background. While these may seem to be synonymous at first blush, they are not: diegetic and nondiegetic are a matter of technical placement; foreground and background are a matter of perception, conditioned by a complex of factors, including dialogue, postures of attentiveness from the actors, and aural perspective. The fairly primitive sound production of 1933 results in a flat aural perspective; we must rely more heavily on the visual and verbal cues to help us locate the music.

We can also be misled by this same constellation of factors. A moment complementary to the approach to Skull Island occurs at the end of *The Winter Guest*, a story that takes place at the edge of the frozen Scottish sea, in a tiny clutch of houses, shrouded in fog. As the intertwining stories of generational transition resolve, the reconciled mother and daughter walk toward home, arm in arm. The daughter, Frances, speaks of plans for her house for the spring, and her mother realizes that Frances's plans to move away to Australia have been shelved. Frances looks into the distance, tilts her head, and smiles. At first her gesture seems to be inspired by her recognition that the decision has been made and the pleasure she takes in it, but then she utters a quiet, astonishing observation: "Listen. That's a boy playing that." Although our recognition of that fact occurs almost instantaneously when Frances says these words, the realization then unfurls backward for the entire length of the film, recontextualizing all the solo piano underscore we have heard to this point as diegetic, as the two little boys who had contemplated oncoming adolescence by the shore race hopefully out onto the ice, into the fog, to almost certain death.

We can certainly make the argument that the music was always diegetic. But the ability to retroactively classify the entire score of *The Winter Guest* as diegetic—or, similarly, when we are able, in hindsight, to differentiate the diegetic and nondiegetic on the approach to Skull Island—does not defuse the destabilizing effect of *experiencing* the shift of perception. The fullness and pervasiveness of the music in the soundscape of *The Winter Guest* leads us to understand it as nondiegetic. Of course, careful consideration would suggest that it is impossible for the piano in one house to sound equally loud in a neighboring house, the high street, and down on the beach, but the acknowledgment by a character of the music is so powerful that it can override the immediate rational response, particularly as the music seems to rise in a warm, concluding gesture as a benediction on all the stories that have come to peaceful resolutions. Frances's invocation of the acousmatic piano takes the foreground as we are returned to one boy on the ice, a kitten tucked into his jacket, turning in a circle, searching for the way to go. The beach or the open sea? All is obscured by the fog, but finally he turns away from the camera, and, underneath the music, we hear his call to his friend, "Tom! Wait for me!" as he disappears into the fog. The conflict between the hopeful music and the impending disaster for these children—perhaps Tom is already drowned—is almost subsumed by the startling shift from nondiegetic to diegetic.[13] The disjunction of that shift vaults the music from background to foreground, and from empathetic underscore to anempathetic source music.

THE EMOTIONAL TERRAIN

The alliance of empathy with the underscore and anempathy with source music is certainly prevalent in the classical Hollywood aesthetic, and it is still a dominant mode of scoring. Still, it is only an alliance, not an unbreakable bond. One has only to think of Rick wallowing in diegetic nostalgia in *Casablanca* to realize that just as diegetic and nondiegetic, foreground and background are neighboring but not parallel axes, so are empathy and anempathy and their close neighbors, subjectivity and objectivity.

It is true that nondiegetic scores tend toward subjectivity and source music to a kind of realistic "objectivity," which would seem to make them synonymous with empathy and anempathy, but they diverge from a single point, the point-of-view/audition/feeling of a character in the diegesis. Empathy/anempathy is the relationship that the audience,[14] presumably conditioned by the gestures in the music, has with the character: they recognize and identify with the feelings that the character is experiencing, and may feel them, though in an attenuated form. When we talk about subjectivity in film and film music, the connection between character and audience is more intense and more enveloping. Anempathy can be "objective," an observation and even understanding of a character's feeling, but it can also be a rejection or abjection of those feelings—neither closer to nor further from the character's feelings (on the objective/subjective axis), but rather perpendicular to them.

In an infamous scene from *The Silence of the Lambs,* we are presented with an unusually stratified, and thus clarifying, projection of objectivity, subjectivity, empathy, and an anempathy that at least invites abjection. The murderous cannibal Hannibal Lecter is confined to an iron-barred cage. Overhead lighting does not dispel the gothic shadows of the formal room in which the cage is located. The framing is essentially objective, if somewhat voyeuristic, the camera moving slowly over the tape recorder chained to the table and Lecter's sketch of Clarice with a lamb, finally coming to rest on Lecter, half hidden behind a semisheer curtain, apparently on a toilet. The cassette is playing Bach's "Goldberg" Variations. Medium-close-up and full-body shots of the guards bringing him his requested second dinner of rare lamb chops, and of Lecter through the bars, alternate with close-ups of Lecter's face. His impassivity, not to mention his well-established malevolence, do not invite empathy, although at one point, he is seen humming along with the Bach, seemingly enveloped in the music even as he is clearly plotting his escape. We may glimpse his subjectivity, but only in an objective fashion. Despite his calm demeanor, Lecter unleashes a vicious attack on the guards, violence we see in a flurry of medium close shots, many of them half-obscured and accompanied by low, fairly generic nondiegetic horror music that swamps the Bach, filling the foreground of the soundscape as the sequence ends with a point-of-view shot, from the perspective of the guard being bludgeoned by a nightstick. In the aftermath, we are given an overhead shot, echoing the opening shot,[15] looking over the carnage as the nondiegetic music fades and the Bach reasserts itself. The camera pulls back and up as we see a blood-spattered Lecter standing over the tape recorder conducting the Bach, the steadiness of his hand highlighting his lack of concern.

The basic structure is not complicated: source music is continuous throughout the sequence (although the real time elapsed during the attack is elided by a gap in the Variations), while a nondiegetic score is layered over it (a somewhat unusual inversion). But questions of objectivity and subjectivity, empathy and anempathy are complicated. The Bach is objectively playing and is anempathetic to the violence Lecter perpetrates. Lecter's involvement with the music, however, is framed by intimate close-ups and his physical interaction with the music, which are techniques of creating empathy and identification. We can observe his deeply subjective communion with the music, and, if we are so inclined, even join in his reveling in the music. The nondiegetic underscore loosely mickey-mouses the violence (is the underscore "objective," a rhythmic approximation of the onscreen action?), but with its low, rumbling orchestral booms and mid-range brass blasts, we are likely to perceive it primarily as "powerful." This could make it empathetic with Lecter, as it matches the measured pace of his swift but unhurried attack, his utter control of the situation. The combination of the powerful music and the sudden, violent images might, however, be read as "scary" because the audience finds itself in a position submissive to Lecter. Is the music empathetic with the guards, or does it in fact act directly on the viewer, who becomes one with the beating victim because of the POV camera? The subjectivity of the guard is an understood term in the identity equation, but the music, like the shrieking violins in *Psycho* or the heart-pounding bass semitones in *Jaws*, mimics a kinesiological response in the audience. And then the horror music fades, like an adrenaline rush, and the near-POV shot of Lecter serenely communing with Bach returns.

Does it matter at which position exactly the audience perceives itself at any one instant during this scene? Not really. The point is that the position is constantly shifting, that we are sliding along these various axes at different speeds and in different directions, and in our disorientation we are more susceptible to the effects along the way. Is it worse to be sharing the subjectivity of the guard being beaten or of the madman who can kill so suddenly and remorselessly? This latter possibility invites abjection—a recognition, even an identification with, a character's emotional state, but a rejection of those feelings out of revulsion. The dizzying shifts may, in the end, hold us at a distance by centrifugal force.

This is an extreme, and rare, example. Filmmakers rarely aim for rejection of their characters—and indeed, the paradoxical appeal of Hannibal Lecter and other charismatic villains is in part achieved by a push-pull of empathy and abjection. The more common strategy is the drawing of the audience to a character by using a trajectory through the fantastical gap between diegetic and nondiegetic, along multiple axes including empathy/anempathy, objectivity/subjectivity, and aural perspective (there/here).

Michael Powell and Emeric Pressburger's *I Know Where I'm Going!* is a disquisition on border crossing: from working class to upper class, whether via money or marriage; from England to Scotland; and from reality to fantasy (although which is which is up for debate), symbolized by that final border that Joan is unable to cross, from highland to island, a fantastical gap on whose beach she is stranded. As she waits, she is taken to visit an old woman who is a friend of the industrialist Joan is about to marry, even as she begins to fall in love with Torquil, who is the impoverished hereditary laird of the island that Joan's fiancé rents.

Old Rebecca Crozier hosts a tea for Joan, Torquil, and a nouveau riche family. She mentions that her gardener, Campbell, is going to be holding a ceilidh to celebrate his sixtieth wedding anniversary, and she begins to reminisce about balls from her own youth. Highland pipes sound softly, distantly, as she recounts the details to Joan, and, as the music gradually increases in volume and fullness, creating a sense of drawing closer, the image dissolves from the dining room to the croft, where the ceilidh is in full swing—and where Torquil and Joan watch from a ladder outside, becoming an audience within the frame.

This scene is especially dense with crossings—the working-class dance underscores the memory of an aristocratic one; the impoverished aristocracy graciously acts as servant and landlord to the obnoxious nouveau riche; Joan's social-climbing marriage is juxtaposed with the Campbell's lifelong bond—and soon we will get to know to the teenaged lovers Kenny and Bridey, who provide the model for true love for Joan and Torquil. The unstable placement of the music opens up the fantastical gap in which these crossings can play.

This is a simple moment in terms of cinematic technique, but ambiguous in its meaning. The music could, after all, be simply diegetic; we have been told that the ceilidh is eminent, but this narrative cue and the musical cue are set far enough apart that the audience is more likely to connect the music with Rebecca Crozier's description of a highland dance, particularly because it sounds "distant." After the fact, we can recast this distance as geographical, but only because of its diegetic status; as long as we assume that it is nondiegetic, that faraway sound tends to suggest that the distance is temporal. It is a technique that often leads to a flashback, though here it is a moment that flows both backward and forward in time—literally forward as we jump to Torquil and Joan at the ceilidh, but backward not only in memory but to a utopian simpler time, where love wins out over money.

Although there is no completely rational way to understand the placement of the music (if we take it as purely diegetic, the uninterrupted musical phrasing is untenable), in the experience of this moment we are most likely to hear the distant pipes as an underscore to Rebecca Crozier's memory, and therefore what Claudia Gorbman has called "metadiegetic" ("pertaining to narration by a secondary narrator").[16] Her example of metadiegetic music seems to have been written with this scene in mind: "the scene's conversation seems to trigger X's memory of the romance and the song that went with it; wordlessly, he 'takes over' part of the film's narration and we are privileged to read his musical thoughts."[17] Putting this a slightly different way, the nondiegetic music places us inside a character's head, within that character's subjectivity.

The trajectory between diegetic music and nondiegetic music that might more precisely be called metadiegetic is not an uncommon trope in modern movies, and is often used as a way of drawing the audience into the subjectivity of a character. It happens twice in *The Killing Fields*, for instance, the first time as Sydney Schanberg puts "Nessun dorma" on his stereo as a backdrop for news footage from Cambodia. As he fast-forwards through the videotape, the atrocities are intercut with Schanberg's increasingly horrified expression. The accelerating tempo of the images is a visual analog to the swelling of the music that comes to envelop the soundtrack and the audience, wrapping them up in a sonic embrace that empathetically mimics Schanberg's feelings, though the interposition of the television between him and us may block a full entry into his subjectivity (figure 11.1). At the end of the film, John Lennon's "Imagine" plays on the loudspeaker as Schanberg and Dith Pran are reunited, and the music expands from tinny and realistic to the all-encompassing sound we normally hear as nondiegetic as the two men embrace. The utopian promise of the song is realized for just a moment in their reunion, yet is also deeply ironic given where and when they are.

This technique is employed more subtly in *The Insider*. If the division between diegetic and nondiegetic still has a kind of experiential reality derived from theater, the difference between nondiegetic and metadiegetic is much more subtle, often measured by the distance between "empathetic" and "subjective." In the scene in which tobacco company whistle-blower Jeffrey Wigand decides to testify against his former employers, a minimalist mandolin underscore emphasizes his jitteriness with its repetitive fluttering. His decision made, he is bundled into a car for the trip to the courthouse in a motorcade. The line of cars, the flashing patrol car lights, and the motorcycle escort would normally elicit a resolute, decisive action cue, reflecting the import and busyness of the moment. Instead, all diegetic sound fades and the

Figure 11.1 Entering Schanberg's subjectivity, in *The Killing Fields.*

delicate mandolin cue rises in volume and fullness to encompass the sound-scape, underscoring camera shots from Wigand's point of view as one lawyer looks at him with concern, and an over-the-shoulder shot as Wigand gazes out the car window at rows of gravestones flashing by. The combina-tion of visual and aural puts us in Wigand's emotional shoes, concerned not about the moment but about its consequences. As the cemetery the motor-cade passes symbolizes, he has chosen a dangerous path. What makes this scene unusual is that the music is *always* nondiegetic, but it has clearly also traversed a gap into interiority with the suppression of the diegetic and the foregrounding of an instrument as soft as a mandolin, an aural perspective of great intimacy. When Wigand steps outside the car, the music drops out as the diegetic sound of the reporters crowding around the car door over-whelms both Wigand and the audience.

The difference between the memory of Rebecca Crozier and the medita-tion of Jeffrey Wigand might prompt us to refine our conception of "metadiegetic," to consider making new distinctions between a literal form, which is probably best exemplified by the composition scenes in *Amadeus,* where we hear the notes as Mozart conceives them, and the more common forms, exemplified by Rebecca Crozier's memory of the dances of her youth (quite often, such a sound advance leads into a flashback, carrying the music across the gap between nondiegetic and diegetic) or a foregrounded nondiegetic pop song, the lyrics of which express feelings that we can identify as those of the character onscreen. The mandolin score in this scene in *The Insider* could be perceived as an even more abstracted form of metadiegetic sound, the subjective/empathetic underscore to unarticulated emotions, leaving the audience to traverse yet another gap. We could consider this as either closer to a traditional nondiegetic underscore or as even further removed into the metadiegetic, depending upon our views of the literal and the subjective.

Although fine distinctions may be fascinating to explore, they also risk recapitulating the stratifying or branching taxonomic approach. To preserve the sensation of motion through a field rather than create more discrete boundaries between states (and attendant terminology), we might refine the concept of the metadiegetic as a kind of represented subjectivity, music clearly (through framing, dialogue, acting, lighting, sound design, or other cinematic process) situated in a character who forms a particularly strong point of identification/location for the audience. The character becomes the bridging mechanism between the audience and the diegesis as we enter into his or her subjectivity. This is a space beyond empathy; its location with regard to the diegesis does, however, reach out and engage us in a way that starts to tear at the fabric of the usual conception of diegetic/nondiegetic—or, it acknowledges a relationship between audience and film that diegetic/nondiegetic has displaced by concentrating on the construction of the text within its own boundaries.

Diegetic/nondiegetic is a distinction that takes place "behind" the screen. The diegetic is firmly rooted in the depicted world; that is, of course, its very definition. The diegesis can become sound-permeable at its boundaries, and music may osmose through that boundary,[18] but the nondiegetic is usually conceived as a space behind/beneath the diegetic (our background music or underscore / pit orchestra). There is, however, another nondiegetic space, usually reserved for the voice, and that is "over." "Over" is a foregrounded space, under the control of a character/narrator who is usually to some degree controlling our responses, through omniscience, knowledge gained through time, or language. It might be possible to think of the metadiegetic as music existing in or around "over," rising up into the foreground and into the expression of a particular point of view. But within that space, we can also range along the axis of objectivity/subjectivity. Captain Kirk narrating a series of events into his log or Mozart composing is fairly objective. Rebecca Crozier's memories of dances past or the adult Scout recalling the events of her youth in *To Kill a Mockingbird* are more gently subjective. Ardent feelings can produce a subjective overlap or fusion of the over/metadiegetic space: one could suggest that in *The Wizard of Oz*, Dorothy's singing is not strictly diegetic, but that her voice meets the nondiegetic orchestra in a metadiegetic space of longing for a happy place far away, "Somewhere Over the Rainbow").[19] In intense emotional subjectivity, the metadiegetic can even carry us to a place beyond verbal articulation—Mildred Pierce's contemplation of suicide, or Jeffrey Wigand's anguish over his decision to blow the whistle. If we were to follow the Romantic idealistic line of philosophy, music could surpass the voice/verbal into a sort of metadiegetic sublime soaring above the diegesis.

This theoretical positioning might seem tenuous, subjective, but then that would also resonate with the emotional impact produced by that positioning. When the music takes the foreground, it can, literally and metaphorically, seem to spill out over/from behind the screen and envelop the audience, creating a particularly intense connection. Although film studies may still be debating the precise psychological effect of "subjectivity," and whether it creates a real form of identification between a character and the individual audience members, whether empathy is assumed or genuinely felt, we do not generally debate those fine distinctions while experiencing a film. We are more likely to feel that the connection is weak or strong, and music is one of the most powerful forces forging that connection. The metadiegetic might be conceived as a kind of musical "direct address," threatening to breach the fourth wall that is the screen.

DIEGETIC MUSIC, SUBJECTIVE SPACE

A simple, extended sound advance, a transition from nondiegetic to diegetic, over the opening credits of Jane Campion's *Holy Smoke* is technically unexceptional. Many films begin with credit music that is full sounding and apparently nondiegetic but "shrinks" to the diegetic space of the first post-credit scene. A closer look, however, reveals that, contrary to most practice, we move from relative objectivity in the nondiegetic to relative subjectivity in the diegetic.

A young Australian woman, Ruth, is visiting India with a friend. It is established with diegetic sound overlaying the apparently nondiegetic music that the blonde, fair-skinned Ruth initially feels somewhat exotic and out of place; but while her friend is happy to do touristy things, Ruth is looking for a more authentic experience. Her attention is caught by a happy group of young, mostly European women in Indian dress, and she follows them to a multistoried building that houses the cult into which Ruth will be drawn.

Neil Diamond's "Holly Holy" is, on one level, a fairly obvious choice, in part because of its cryptic lyrics, because whatever it means, it is clearly about a search for meaning and redemption, reflecting Ruth's search for "the real stuff" in India. The music has a strong, steady ostinato (piano bass octaves sound out a tonic on the downbeat of a slow 4-beat measure, with the fourth and the fifth on beats 3 and 4), and the texture is very spare, with a strummed guitar over the piano. The voice begins calmly and gradually increases in intensity and volume and rises in range throughout the song. The effect is vaguely non-Western. Rather unusual for a preexisting pop song in a film, the recording is not the album version but a live version, which lends an urgency and immediacy to the music and further widens the fantastical gap as the sequence ends in performance.

The combination of the camera technique and the hypnotically building music draws Ruth, and us, into this liminal space where she will become transformed. As she enters the house where the Baba's followers reside, there is a vertiginous, spinning quasi-point-of-view shot up the atrium as the music shifts to the incantatory bridge, which builds and rises (shifting from strong beats on 1 and 3 to steady eighth notes, the voice moving higher and creating extended syncopations)[20] as Ruth rises into this new state.

Although the sound quality never really changes, the transition from nondiegetic to diegetic takes place slowly, in an almost dreamlike fashion, with different camera speeds, as Ruth emerges onto the roof where the Baba's followers are eating, conversing, and dancing. We lose a sense of time, though we are clearly experiencing a time dilation, moving from afternoon to evening.

It is only at the peak of the music, the drive to the recapitulation of the chorus from the bridge, that the visuals—people dancing and singing— and the music coincide, confirming that it is indeed, or has become, diegetic. This creates a sense of arrival, of the completion that Ruth will find here. The music creates the through-line—even the story takes a little hitch backward as we see Ruth leaving her friend and entering the building alone at the end of the song. It is as if the music overrides diegetic time, and the visuals become the nondiegetic accompaniment to the real narrative in the music.

A final example, from Michael Mann's 1986 thriller *Manhunter*, takes this inversion of expectation to an extreme. The music is explicitly diegetic the entire way, yet the overwhelming effect is that of being drawn into subjectivity—doubly so, as the central character, FBI investigator Will Graham, is drawn into the disturbed mind of the man he is profiling. The music is a way of claiming space and power; it is an assault from the moment the serial killer Francis Dollarhyde slips the eight-track into the player. The volume and power of the music flatten his prospective victim against the windows of his house, isolated in a misty Florida swamp.

Dollarhyde's control is only amplified by Mann's choice of "In-A-Gadda-Da-Vida" by Iron Butterfly, a notoriously dark, proto–heavy metal anthem that was the obsession of a real-life serial killer whom Mann had studied. The twelve-minute climax sequence of the film uses a trimmed version of the seventeen-minute original, but nonetheless seems to play out in real time. Its diegetic nature is emphasized by the cross-cutting between the investigators closing in and Dollarhyde's intended murder. The music belongs *only* to the killer's space, and its representation of his subjectivity is increased by the gradually ever more dancelike quality of his actions, responding to the rhythm and line of the music.

But this movie is about Will Graham and the process by which he gets into the mind of the killer, almost losing himself, and this psychological dynamic is played out in this sequence. As he draws closer to the killer's house (like Skull Island, it is surrounded by a fantastical gap filled with fog and music), the song has reached the solo section, with its agonizingly extended prolongation at the end of the bridge/development section. Despite its undeniably diegetic state, complete with quasi-realistic aural perspective, the music is symbolically metadiegetic, forming a miasmic connection between Dollarhyde and Graham, while musically it is functioning like nondiegetic underscore, building tension toward the long-delayed return to the tonic bass riff, the exact moment when Graham literally bursts through the glass wall between nondiegetic and diegetic, into the red dragon's metadiegetic lair (figure 11.2).

Mann shot the final confrontation in real time with multiple cameras at different speeds, building the scene in the edit bay, so—as with *Holy Smoke* or an old Busby Berkeley number—the putatively diegetic music holds together a fantasia of fragmented images. This figure-ground reversal is appropriate to another one in which the physical violence is an outward manifestation of a psychological battle: Will Graham is submerged into Dollarhyde's subjectivity as he is physically overwhelmed by the loud music.

The distinction between diegetic and nondiegetic seems to easy to make, but often the most basic aspects of an issue are rarely explored because they simply seem to be a given, even when they are in fact part of the construct. The background radio noise that interferes with detailed galactic mapping turns out to be the distant echo of the Big Bang; but it is the close examination of how matter forms strings and clumps that gives us deeper insight

Figure 11.2 Bursting the barrier into the metadiegetic, in *Manhunter.*

into how the universe works—in movement, in action. It is a natural instinct to want to control unruly information, to put it in order and give it a name, but taxonomy also has the unpleasant side effect of mummifying that which is observed. After all, the Greek root *taxis*, to arrange, is shared by both taxonomy and taxidermy.

Diegetic or nondiegetic may be a simple distinction, but it need not be a simplistic one. The fact that the boundary is crossed so often should not invalidate the integrity of the distinction; indeed, the manner in which the meaning in the distinction multiplies and magnifies in the crossing is indicative of its power. The border region—the fantastical gap—is a transformative space, a superposition, a transition between stable states. Although that geography may be abstract and even sterile when we are talking about photons, when we are talking about movement through the gap between diegetic and nondiegetic, that trajectory takes on great narrative and experiential import. These moments do not take place randomly; they are important moments of revelation, of symbolism, and of emotional engagement within the film and without. The movies have taught us how to construct our phenomenological geography, and when we are set adrift, we are not only uneasy, we are open to being guided in any number of directions. It is the multiplicity of possibilities that make the gap both observable and fantastical—fantastical because it changes the state, not only of the filmic moment, but also of the observer's relationship to it.

We have looked at only a few axes that traverse the fantastical gap. They are perhaps the most basic ones, but they are certainly not the only ones—and maybe not even the most important ones—just the ones most closely adjacent to our current models. The distinctions sometimes cut very fine, but then so do our perceptions, and subtle fluctuations can *mean* so much.

It is doubtful that any single taxonomy or Theory with a capital T would be able to neatly encompass the examples discussed here without leaving out what makes them unique, what makes them work. By exploring the nuance of individual instances, however, we do gain insight into how film and films work, and we also become more alert and agile analysts. It behooves us, in more ways than one, to mind the gap.

NOTES

1. Carroll is not completely resistant to the idea of overarching theory, but simply suggests that we are not there yet: "As compelling answers are developed to small-scale, delimited questions, we may be in a position to think about whether these answers can be unified in a more comprehensive theoretical framework." "Prospects for Film Theory: A Personal Assessment," in *Post-Theory: Reconstructing Film Studies*, ed. David Bordwell and Noël Carroll (Madison: University of Wisconsin Press, 1996), p. 58.

2. Ibid., p. 40.

3. Ibid.

4. For a discussion of liminality and transformational ritual, see particularly Victor Witter Turner, *From Ritual to Theatre: The Human Seriousness of Play* (New York: Performing Arts Journals, 1982).

5. James Buhler, Anahid Kassabian, David Neumeyer, and Robynn Stilwell, "Roundtable on Film Music," *Velvet Light Trap* 51 (Spring 2003), pp. 73–91.

6. See, for instance, Rick Altman, *The American Film Musical* (Bloomington: Indiana University Press, 1987).

7. David Neumeyer, "Source Music, Background Music, Fantasy and Reality in Early Sound Film," *College Music Symposium* 37 (1997), pp. 13–20.

8. I will, for the moment at least, refrain from commenting on quantum packets or string theory.

9. I am using axes rather than vectors in this discussion because the transition can occur in multiple directions.

10. Ironically, perhaps, it is not Al Jolson's musical performance in *The Jazz Singer* (1927) that creates the sensation of sound film—there had been synchronized music and sound effects before—but the breaking of the fourth wall, the suddenly improvised speaking to the diegetic audience, which extends and blends with the real audience in the cinema. The "there" of the cinema screen becomes "here," a potentially disconcerting, and exciting, change of space and engagement.

11. Composer David Raksin's response, "Where's the camera?" or, alternatively, "Behind the camera," depending upon the version of the tale you hear, highlights both the greater willingness to suspend disbelief in the visual realm and the positioning of the "background" music. The placement of music "behind" the screen is an option that cinema presents, although it is still an inferior and "covered" position, so in that sense, not far removed from "underscore."

12. We are never given, however, a visual anchor for the horns, though we may accept them without much questioning as part of the general aural ethos of the scene.

13. The film's ending is more ambiguous than that of the stage version, which clearly sends the boys out onto the ice, but the implication remains that they are headed toward the ice and nearly certain death, in part because of the movement away from the camera. The same sorts of perceptual assumptions that lead us to understand the music throughout as nondiegetic will tend to lead us to think that the camera is placed on the beach.

14. The implications of the terminology for those on the receiving end of a film are tendentious. The typical film studies terms "spectator" and "viewer" demonstrate an obvious visual bias. "Audience" has lost most much of its original connotation of hearing, but because the trace remains and the term also tends to suggest the plural, I prefer using it.

15. It is distinctly possible to misread this as a point-of-view shot from Lecter's position at the beginning, increasing the sense of subjectivity.

16. Claudia Gorbman, *Unheard Melodies: Narrative Film Music* (Bloomington: Indiana University Press, 1987), p. 22.

17. Ibid., p. 23. This "wordless narration" brings us close to another crossing that can happen within the nondiegetic: the moment a human voice is introduced, even in a wordless vocalise, the music pops from its inferior position (geographically speaking) position of "underscore" or "background" to the superior position of "voice-over" and "foreground." As Michel Chion has noted, "Il y a les voix, et tout le reste . . . la présence d'une voix humaine hiérarchise la perception autour d'elle" (*Le Voix au Cinéma* [Paris: Cahiers du cinéma, 1982], p. 18).

18. A sound effect would probably, without a great deal of cinematic encouragement, register as "off" rather than nondiegetic.

19. This would bring us into the realm of Rick Altman's description of "audio-dissolve" in the musical number, in *The American Film Musical* (Indiana University Press, 1987). Since musical numbers often function to signal time dilation and narrate a particular emotional state (Don Lockwood's celebration of being in love in "Singin' in the Rain," for instance), the leap of the diegetic into the metadiegetic would also be crossing a gap from the everyday into the fantastic. See also Heather Laing's "Emotion by the Numbers," in *The Musical: Hollywood and Beyond*, eds. Bill Marshall and Robynn Stilwell (Exeter, UK: Intellect Press, 2000), pp. 5–13.

20. A verse of the song before the bridge in which the bass ostinato is absorbed into fuller orchestration is excised, disturbing the slow, pyramidal building of volume, pitch, and texture, as a sensitive musical listener will feel. At the presentation of this paper at the Beyond the Soundtrack conference at the University of Minnesota in April 2004, Martin Scherzinger asked me during a break what had happened to the bass line in that sequence; he felt something was wrong, even though he did not know the song.

PART III

Musical Identity

12 Early Film Themes

Roxy, Adorno, and the Problem of Cultural Capital

RICK ALTMAN

For decades, analyses of the musical accompaniment for sound films—and especially Hollywood films—have been heavily driven by attention to themes and leitmotifs. By and large, thematic analysis has been treated as a convenient analytical tool, whose history has appropriately been considered beside the point. The rare paragraphs that film music specialists have devoted to the history of themes and leitmotifs typically share two strategies, nicely summarized by Roy Prendergast. "The Wagnerian device of the leitmotiv," affirms Prendergast, "fell naturally into use in the composition of scores for Hollywood films."[1] Hollywood music thus not only borrows Wagnerian technique, but it does so "naturally." Everything we need to know can be explained by this twin appeal to the odd couple formed by a long-dead composer and Mother Nature. Instead of simply invoking a vague Wagnerian tradition and a timeless Nature, this chapter attempts to locate the thematic approach historically. Because the thematic approach has never received proper historical treatment, its investments and its meaning have never been made fully clear. Not surprisingly, a thoroughgoing historical treatment of the thematic approach to film music produces theoretical as well as historical results.

With few exceptions, silent film sound has been treated as a single practice, unaltered over two or three decades. Critics have systematically treated silent film accompaniment as if it had no history. According to Kathryn Kalinak, for example, "it was Wagnerian opera with its continuous musical expression, its linkage of music to drama, and its use of the leitmotif to unify its structure which provided the most direct model for the silent film accompanist."[2] This use of the singular to describe silent film accompaniment practices is encountered repeatedly throughout the literature. The facts do not support the notion that thematic accompaniment was continuously practiced from the 1900s through the 1920s, however. Careful inspection of musical suggestions, musical programs, and cue sheets reveals that a substantial change took place in accompaniment style around 1915, as demonstrated by the following representative examples.

In September 1909, the Edison *Kinetogram* began issuing suggestions for incidental music to accompany Edison pictures. The very first installment recommended the following numbers to accompany *The Ordeal,* an Edison version of a portion of the first volume of Victor Hugo's *Les Misérables:*

SCENE

1—An andante.

2—An allegro changing to plaintive at end.

3—Plaintive.

4—Adagio or march changing at end to allegro strongly marked.

5—Andante to plaintive, changing to march movement at end.

6—Lively, changing to plaintive at Fantine's arrest.

7—March with accents to accompany scene finishing with andante.

8—Andante.

9—Allegro, to march at arrest.

10—March, changing to andante at end.

11—Slow march, p.p. [pianissimo]

12—Andante p.p. hurry at action of putting passport, etc., in fire.

13—March p., changing to f.f. [fortissimo] at the entrance of Jean Valjean, the Mayor.

14—Andante to Javert's entrance, then a hurry till the Mayor tears off the piece of iron from the bed. Adagio to end.[3]

In keeping with period practice, the *Kinetogram* typically designated music not by title but by type, with the clear goal of achieving an appropriate match between narrative and musical characteristics.

The *Kinetogram's* incidental music suggestions lasted only nine months, but by 1911 *Moving Picture World* began to publish actual musical programs submitted by readers, such as this November 1911 West Hoboken, New Jersey, accompaniment for Thanhouser's *David Copperfield:*

FIRST REEL

1. "Song of Comfort," by Charles Davidson (McKinley Publishing Co.).

2. "Charme d'Amour," by Edward F. Kendal (Witmark).

3. "Temptation Waltzes," by Henry Bauer (Bauer Music Company).

4. "Heather Rose," by G. Lange, op. 78, No. 8 (McKinley Pub. Co.).

5. "Alcyone Waltz," by Gertrude Buck (Thompson Music Co.)

SECOND REEL

1. "Good-Bye," by F. Paolo Tosti (McKinley Pub. Co.).

2. "I Adore Thee," by E. Van Alstyne (McKinley Pub. Co.).

3. "Dear Eyes, Dear Heart," by Paul B. Armstrong (McKinley Pub. Co.).

4. "Sweet Remembrance," by W. A. Pratt (McKinley Pub. Co.).

5. "Juanita," by T. G. May (McKinley Pub. Co.).

6. "Anchored," by Mitchell Watson (Pub. by McKinley Pub. Company).

THIRD REEL

1. "My Lady's Bower," by Hope Temple (McKinley Pub. Company).

2. "Golden Butterfly," by Reginald DeKoven (J. H. Remick).

3. "Queen of my Heart," by Alfred Cellier (McKinley Pub. Company).

4. "Moonlight Fancies," by T. H. Collinson (Oliver Ditson).

5. "No Blossoms," by Abbie A. Ford (McKinley Pub. Company).

6. "My Lady Laughter," by Charlotte Blake (J. H. Remick). Arr. by J. B. Lampe.

7. "Only Once More," Frank L. Moir (McKinley Pub. Company).[4]

Though this time the specific compositions are identified, the accompaniment strategy continues to operate one scene at a time. Compositions are chosen scene by scene to match the narrative situation, with nary a repetition.

The following year Ernst Luz would begin to provide what he called "musical plots" in *Moving Picture News*. For several years he provided suggestions like these simple recommendations for Vitagraph's *Two Battles*:

SET-UP

No. 1. Slow waltz (very legato).

No. 2. Dramatic (battle music, lengthy).

No. 3. Military March (any Von Blon march appropriate).

No. 4. Dramatic (battle music, short).

No. 5. Dirge or Funeral Chant (Funeral Chant by Hauptmann appropriate and effective).

No. 6. Sentimental (Traumerei [sic] or similar).

No. 7. Waltz (slow).

CUES

Play No. 1 until leader "In Africa"

Play No. 2 until Leader "Two Letters"

Play No. 3 until soldiers go to the front

Play No. 4 until Gordon walks among dead on battle field

Play No. 5 until Gordon covers body of friend with flag

Play No. 6 until Army Club scene, crescendo while fiancee plays piano

Play No. 7 until end. Crescendo as they embrace[5]

Once again, each segment of the film is treated separately, with no musical connection between the segments.

Starting in 1911 and continuing for several years, Vitagraph regularly provided musical suggestions for all its films in its *Vitagraph Bulletin of Life Portrayals*. Here is a typical musical program, as recommended by the October 1913 *Vitagraph Bulletin*:

> THE WAR-MAKERS. Two-Part Drama. (Diplomatic Story.) Opening smoothly with "When I Dream of You" (Chorus only. Shapiro)—continue with "Fernande" (Feist) as Russian ambassador appears—becoming dramatic with "Simple Aveu" (Haviland)—with "Overture From Wilhelm Tell" for kidnapping scenes—until banquet scene—then "The Priest's March" (Haviland) or "Serenata" (by Moszkowski) (Suspense effects) with "Miserere" (P) until end of Part One. Part Two. Continue tension with "Melody in F" (Rubinstein, Century)—quickening to "La Rumba" (Stern) as title "Secret Service men" appears—until Rosa books passage—then

(Accel.) "Brazilian Dreams" (Penn)—continuing with "Over the Waves" (Feist)—until title "The Third night"—then (Mysterioso) "The Barcarole" (by Offenbach)—until title "A Collision with a Derelict"—then "The Storm" (Weber, Century)—until title "Her Shoes"—then "Meditation from Thaïs" (Schirmer), concluding with "It Takes a Little Rain" (Shapiro) or "You're My Girl."[6]

Like virtually all other early musical suggestions of the 1910s, Vitagraph's selections are systematically chosen from a fairly narrow range of well-known melodies by such favorites as Massenet, Mendelssohn, Moszkowski, Offenbach, Rossini, Rubinstein, Schutt, Thomé, and Weber. Unlike most other contemporary sources, however, Vitagraph liberally mixes popular songs with its light classical offerings, often signifying a happy ending by concluding with an up-tempo popular number.

When H. S. Fuld took over the "Music and the Picture" column formerly penned by Luz for *Moving Picture News,* he continued the widespread tradition of offering musical programs built around discrete light classical numbers, once again resorting to compositions by Grieg, MacDowell, Nevin, Rossini, Suppé, and Thomé. Here, for example, are his suggestions for Biograph's *Judith of Bethulia,* directed by D. W. Griffith:

1. Open with "Maritana" (by Wallace) until Judith in prayer.

2. Then "The Rosary" (by Nevin) until she leaves woman with child.

3. Then back to "Maritana" until "The Army."

4. Then "William Tell" (by Rossini) the last movement. Play this to end of reel.

5. Then "Pique Dame" overture (Suppé) all through.

6. Then "Poet and Peasant" overture (Suppé) until "Water and Food Famine."

7. Then "Simple Aveu" (Thomé) until "The King."

8. Then "Peer Gynt," Suite II, opus 55 (Grieg), until Judith has vision.

9. Then "Woodland Sketches 1 and 2" (McDowell) until she puts on fine clothes.

10. Then "Lament of Roses" (Sounakolb) until "The King."

11. Then "Peer Gynt"—Suite II, opus 55, until end of reel.[7]

Throughout the early teens, similar suggestions could be found in the film music features of several important trade publications, including columns by Clyde Martin in *Film Index*, Clarence E. Sinn in *Moving Picture World*, Ernst Luz and H. S. Fuld in *Moving Picture News*, and, starting in 1915, Frank A. Edson in *The Metronome*. When he first began to publish suggestions for musical accompaniment, even the self-proclaimed father of the cue sheet, Max Winkler, produced nothing more than lists of familiar musical compositions, each matched to a single shot or scene, with neither theme nor leitmotif in view.[8]

Given the staunchly themeless similarity of pre-1915 musical suggestions, it is altogether surprising to witness the total turnaround that took place in late 1915. During the late fall of 1915, the Photoplay Department of New York music publisher G. Schirmer began to prepare "Musical Suggestion Cue Sheets" for films by several different studios. In December 1915, S. M. Berg, the Schirmer employee primarily responsible for producing these musical programs, joined Clarence E. Sinn as author of the *Moving Picture World*'s "Music for the Picture" column. Henceforth, a musical setting prepared by Berg would be featured in each issue of the journal. Unlike previous musical suggestions, Berg's cue sheets always began by designating an existing number as "theme." At first, as in the 25 December 1915 suggestions for accompanying Metro's *Rosemary*,[9] both the title of the number chosen as theme and a parenthetical reminder that it is the theme were provided each time the theme was called for. Soon, however, reader familiarity with the thematic approach made it possible to simplify the process. Instead of constantly repeating the title of the selection chosen as the theme, the scene-by-scene listing of appropriate accompaniment music simply notes "Repeat: THEME" throughout, as in the 11 November 1916 musical setting for Metro's *The Brand of Cowardice* (figure 12.1).[10] Typically, Berg calls for the theme to be repeated five to seven times out of twenty to thirty total cues, for a thematic incidence hovering around 20 to 25 percent.

By 1917, the thematic approach to musical accompaniment pioneered by Schirmer, Berg, and *Moving Picture World* would be broadly accepted throughout the industry. Whereas thematically inflected musical suggestions had first been introduced like their nonthematic predecessors in the pages of trade journals, the new thematic cue sheets were rapidly promoted to standalone items, regularly distributed by film exchanges. Once cue sheets became easily available through film distributors, they were replaced in the trade press by short synopses, like the following examples from the

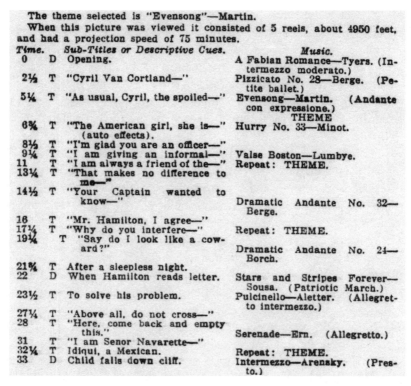

The theme selected is "Evensong"—Martin.
When this picture was viewed it consisted of 5 reels, about 4950 feet, and had a projection speed of 75 minutes.

Time.		Sub-Titles or Descriptive Cues.	Music.
0	D	Opening.	A Fabian Romance—Tyers. (Intermezzo moderato.)
2½	T	"Cyril Van Cortland—"	Pizzicato No. 28—Berge. (Petite ballet.)
5¼	T	"As usual, Cyril, the spoiled—"	Evensong—Martin. (Andante con expressione.) THEME
6¾	T	"The American girl, she is—" (auto effects).	Hurry No. 33—Minot.
8½	T	"I'm glad you are an officer—"	
9¼	T	"I am giving an informal—"	Valse Boston—Lumbye.
11	T	"I am always a friend of the—"	Repeat: THEME.
13¼	T	"That makes no difference to me—"	
14½	T	"Your Captain wanted to know—"	Dramatic Andante No. 32—Berge.
16	T	"Mr. Hamilton, I agree—"	
17¼	T	"Why do you interfere—"	Repeat: THEME.
19¼	T	"Say do I look like a coward?"	Dramatic Andante No. 24—Borch.
21¾	T	After a sleepless night.	
22	D	When Hamilton reads letter.	Stars and Stripes Forever—Sousa. (Patriotic March.)
23½	T	To solve his problem.	Pulcinello—Aletter. (Allegretto intermezzo.)
27¼	T	"Above all, do not cross—"	
28	T	"Here, come back and empty this."	Serenade—Ern. (Allegretto.)
31	T	"I am Senor Navarette—"	
32¼	T	Idiqui, a Mexican.	Repeat: THEME.
33	D	Child falls down cliff.	Intermezzo—Arensky. (Presto.)

Figure 12.1 S. M. Berg's musical setting for Metro's *The Brand of Cowardice,* as published in Berg's *Moving Picture World* "Music for the Picture" column.

"Music Suggestion Synopsis" section of George W. Beynon's *Moving Picture World* column:

MOTHER'S SIN, A (Vitagraph)—Theme for the Heroine—Moderato. Suggest "Barcarole" (Offenbach), or "Bowl of Pansies," Reynard. This is a society drama requiring a few Valse Lentos, some heavy stuff, and two misteriosos. In the last reel use some hunting scene selection. Close with the Theme. Cue sheet can be obtained from the Vitagraph Exchange.[11]

JACK SPURLOCK, PRODIGAL (Fox—5 reels).—Theme for hero—Fox Trot. Suggest "Bedouin Girl," Romberg; "Free and Easy," Berger, or "Hi Ho Hum," Isel. This is a five-reel comedy requiring light music. Many One-Steps and Fox Trots are necessary. A Valse Lento can be used in reel three, and a light "Hurry" in reel five. Close with the THEME. Cue sheets can be obtained from the Fox exchanges.[12]

By the end of the 1910s, a standard cue-sheet protocol had been established. For a full decade, companies under contract to the film studios would produce a stand-alone "musical synopsis" for each release. With its "thematic music cue sheets," M. J. Mintz's Cameo Music Service took the lead in this domain. Throughout the 1920s cue sheets remained strikingly similar, regularly mentioning the publisher of each recommended number, offering both taxable and free selections, and transcribing a few bars of each selection's melody. At the beginning of each cue sheet, a main theme is typically identified by the title of an existing piece. Though these cue sheets were compiled by composers and conductors, the themes that they offer are most often not original. Introduced as early as the film permits, the theme is repeated several times and systematically played as the final number. In some cases, like the 1922 musical synopsis for *A Doll's House* (figure 12.2),[13] the presentation is spare. In others, like the 1924 cue sheet for *The Sixth Commandment* (figure 12.3),[14] a musical incipit accompanies each selection. With the exception of the mid-'20s tendency to introduce multiple themes, little changes between Berg's 1915 musical suggestions and the cue sheets of the late '20s.

Why, after half a decade of resolutely unthematic trade press musical suggestions, did the industry so suddenly and completely adopt the thematic approach starting in 1915? The prime instigator of this new technique was without a doubt Samuel L. Rothapfel, the fabled impresario and exhibitor better known as Roxy. As early as 1911, while still at the Minneapolis Lyric Theater, Roxy began to stress the importance of a main theme in moving picture settings.[15] After taking over the New York Regent in 1913, and especially after moving downtown to the Strand in 1914, Roxy and his methods garnered an extraordinary level of national attention. Trade papers competed to explain Roxy's exhibition philosophy. In November 1913, *Moving Picture World* explained that Roxy uses "distinct 'motifs' to stir and intensify the emotions of the audience . . . a thought based on the philosophy of Wagner's music."[16] According to Roxy's explanation to *Metronome*, "I admire every class of good music, with Richard Wagner as my favorite. . . . In arranging my music for a film, I go as far as I think best to have some individual strain, some *leit-motif*, connected with the picture."[17] As H. S. Fuld affirms in *Motion Picture News*, Roxy was the first to apply the thematic approach to full orchestral accompaniment.[18]

Thanks to his constant scrutiny, we have a record of several early musical settings selected by Roxy himself. For Kleine's *Last Days of Pompeii*, as *Motion Picture News* reported in December 1913, Roxy achieved dramatic

Musical Synopsis *for*

NAZIMOVA *in* "A DOLL'S HOUSE"

By JAMES C. BRADFORD

Nora Theme	"Chanson D'Amour"	Suk
No. Min. (T)itle or (D)escription	Tempo	Selections

MUSICAL PROGRAMME

1	1½	At	Screening	4-4 Andante	....	Melody of Peace—Martin
2	4	T	Torvald Helmer Had Been Married......	6-8 Andantino	....	Pleading—Wood
3	2½	T	The House of Krogstad....................	3-4 Lamentoso	....	Borghild's Dream—Grieg
4	2½	T	And a Few Days Later....................	4-4 Adagio non troppo	......	NORA THEME
5	4¾	T	Six Years Pass..........................	3-4 Allegretto Scherzando	..	Butterfly—Densmore
6	2½	T	You Don't Recognize Me.................	6-4 Allegretto von moto	....	To Spring—Grieg
7	1	T	I Saved Torvald's Life...................	2-4 Allegretto	....	Rosamunde Ballet—(2) Schubert
8	4½	D	Nora Handed Card.......................	3-4 Lamentoso	....	Borghild's Dream—Grieg
9	2	D	Krogstad Leaves	4-4 Allegretto	....	Puck—Grieg
10	4½	D	Krogstad Returns and Enters Room......	4-4 Andante	....	Intermezzo—Hadley (Atonement of Pan)
11	6	D	Letter Dropped in Box..................	9-8 Appassionato	....	Notturno—Grieg
12	2	T	Dr. Rank You Know.....................	3-4 Moderato	....	I Love You—Grieg
13	2	T	Keep Him as Long as You Can..........	12-8 Appassionato	....	In the Silence of the Night—Rachmaninoff
14	2	D	Nora Starts to Rehearse Dance..........	6-8 Allegro	....	Tarentella—Bohm (Piano accompaniment)
15	2½	T	Nearing the End of the Masquerade......	2-4 Allegro con fucco	......	Russiska March—Olson
16	2	D	Krogstad Enters Room, Sees Former Sweetheart	2-4 Andantino	....	Evening Song—Martin
17	1	D	Krogstad Kisses Girl's Hand.............	6-8 Allegro	....	Tarentella—Bohm
18	2	D	Nora Laid on Sofa......................	4-4 Adagio non troppo	......	NORA THEME
19	2½	D	Torvald Rests Hand on Letter Box.......	6-8 Andantino	....	Poem—Fibich
20	4	D	Torvald Reads Letter...................	3-4 Adagio	....	Adagio Pathetique—Godard
21	3¾	T	I Am Saved ..,.........................	4-8 Andantino	....	Erotik—Grieg
22	4½	T	Am Leaving You, Torvald................	3-4 Adagio Lamentoso	.....	Adagio Lamentoso—Tschaikowsky (Pathetique)
23	1¾	D	Nora Leaves Room......................	4-4 Adagio non troppo	......	NORA THEME

THE END

The timing is based on a speed of 12 minutes per reel of 1,000 ft.

Figure 12.2 A typically spare early 1920s cue sheet: the 1922 musical synopsis for *A Doll's House.*

unity through repeated use of "the soft, beautiful song from *Aïda*, symbolic of the gentle blind girl and her hopeless love for the Athenian, Glaucus."[19] For the 1914 Famous Players production of *Such a Little Queen,* as we learn from the second installment of W. Stephen Bush's six-part study of Roxy's "Art of Exhibition," Roxy chose "a little waltz from *Sari*" to accompany leading lady Mary Pickford. "It had a note of pathos alternating with brilliancy," asserted Roxy, "and I thought it typical of the character of the

Figure 12.3 A typical mid-1920s cue sheet, with musical incipits: the 1924 cue sheet for *The Sixth Commandment*.

queen." Similar logic became the rule for musical directors: select an existing number that matches the personality of the film's dominant character, with both the character and the music conceived as invariable. "I had the original waltz played as the little queen was coming down the stairs, and it interpreted in a flash the characteristics of the leading character," Roxy noted, thereby underscoring the ideal of a clear music-to-character correspondence that came to dominate film accompaniment.[20]

Roxy's musical programs at the Strand rapidly became a model for theaters around the country.[21] As George W. Beynon put it, "live exhibitors everywhere began to pattern their amusement palaces after the Strand model."[22] By the fall of 1915, Roxy's musical practices had attracted the attention of exhibitors across the nation. Thanks to Roxy's national visibility, theaters around the country began to increase the size of their orchestras, upgrade the quality of their music, and adopt a thematic approach to film accompaniment. The theme-oriented cue sheets produced by S. M. Berg and others are a direct reflection of Roxy's methods. Repeatedly attributing their techniques to Wagner, Roxy and his followers must take responsibility for the confusion that has reigned ever since in film music circles, where the terms "theme" and "leitmotif" are often used interchangeably and regularly applied to an approach that has little to do with Wagner. One of Roxy's own themes provides a convenient example. When Lasky's 1914 *Rose of the Rancho* played the Strand, Roxy chose as the theme the "Serenade" from Ricardo Drigo's *Les Millions d'Arlequin*.[23] Like many contemporary theme selections, this number was too well known to audiences to be perpetually varied like an original motif. Whereas contemporary organists were exhorted to modify motifs to match evolving narrative situations, the thematic approach introduced by Roxy and adopted by the entire industry involved instead the deployment of complete numbers. "When themes are used they should be memorized numbers," insists Ernst Luz, thereby assuring rote repetition and depriving the thematic approach of any possible development.[24] For a decade and a half the standard approach to film accompaniment thus involved the simple repetition of stock pieces, with only tempo, dynamics, and instrumentation varied.

Once the film music establishment opted for the economy and simplicity of compiling musical settings from existing numbers, any chance of a truly Wagnerian approach to moving picture accompaniment disappeared. As J. Harold Weisel insisted in the *American Organist:*

> I become impatient when someone tries to justify the "theming" idea by arguing that it is the application of the principle Wagner introduced in opera. Misapplication would be the correct term. It is indeed a far cry from Wagnerian Leitmotiv and the way it is handled in that genius's scores, to the bare unadorned sixteen-bar melody that develops nothing but monotony and nausea when repeated at every appearance of the character for which it was intended.[25]

Regular repetition of sixteen-bar melodies did indeed become the order of the day, as we know from regular protests regarding the use of existing compositions as oft-repeated themes.

As early as 1915, Ernst Luz was already bemoaning the abuse of themes.

> To illustrate, we will say that the female lead is a love-sick maiden and we se-
> lect Mendelssohn's "Spring Song" as her theme, and knowing that such a lead
> is on the screen fifty per cent of the time we might well say "The Fates pre-
> serve Mendelssohn's 'Spring Song.' "
>
> We might call Schumann's "Traumerei" [*sic*] a number with a positive pa-
> thetic appeal, and use it at all times when screen action is of a pathetic char-
> acter, could we hope that the audience would enjoy its third or fourth repeti-
> tion in one hour?[26]

For a full decade, similar critiques pervaded the trade press. George W. Beynon did not mince words about the problems of the current vogue for thematic accompaniment:

> It may be that you, too, have suffered. It may have happened that you entered
> a theater to see Mary Pickford or Doug. Fairbanks earn their paltry stipend.
> It is possible that after you had enjoyed the Comedy and Review, the feature
> you came to see was thrown upon the screen and you settled back in your
> seat, for an hour and a quarter of unadulterated joy. The orchestra opens the
> picture with a beautiful number as Miss Mary is introduced. The music
> changes. In a few minutes the first selection is played again. It's a nice num-
> ber. Two or three short numbers intervene and you hear it again. It's a fair
> number. An agitato follows, it is repeated and becomes a monotonous num-
> ber. The third reel is being shown, and again you hear it. You cannot under-
> stand why they play it so much. It palls. As the music continues, this poor
> little number is dragged in by the heels whenever Mary appears in the fore-
> ground, until your soul rebels and you hate that music forever. This innocent
> little musical piece that has caused you so much irritation is called the
> THEME.[27]

Themes were constantly abused. In February 1922, a pair of *American Organist* articles panned their misuse. In the aptly titled "Repeat Theme—" Aaron Burr reiterates Debussy's famous castigation of Wagner's leitmotifs as musical calling cards, while Roy L. Medcalfe notes that "It would be just as proper for the leading lady to wear the same gown in every scene as for the organist to gush forth 'Love Me and the World Is Mine' every time she makes an appearance."[28] Initially praised, Louis Silvers's and William F. Peters's setting for Griffith's 1920 *Way Down East* was later criticized for thematic abuses. According to Tim Crawford, the accompaniment was composed of "nothing *but themes* (about 12 of them and practically no other music in the score)"—a good example, as he put it, of "*theme-ing* an audience to death."[29] Even average accompaniments devoted substantial time to the theme. A survey of 1920s cue sheets reveals that themes represented approximately one-sixth of all cues, rarely dropping below 10 percent and sometimes climbing above 25 percent. The average feature film would thus dwell on the theme for at least fifteen minutes.

Why, in the face of repeated scathing criticism, did the moving picture music establishment stick to the thematic approach? One reason may be discovered in the newfound stability that film music enjoyed throughout the 1920s. The thematic approach was part of an interlocking structure that served all participants well. Themes simplified cue sheet compilation, reducing by a substantial percentage the number of selections required for the average setting. Themes also successfully publicized photoplay music. Orchestras and organists welcomed thematic repetition because it simplified execution and fostered repertory expansion. As well, the use of a main theme was facilitated by the physical composition of orchestras, which increasingly doubled instruments, thus permitting musicians to pull out the music for the theme while their stand partners finished the previous number.[30] No attempt to explain the popularity of thematic accompaniment would be complete, however, without close attention to spectator investment in the repetition and recognition of musical themes.

From the very beginning of film music, efforts were made to balance the twin requirements of novelty and familiarity. Like turn-of-the-century bandleaders and orchestra conductors, film musicians made ample use of old favorites. Moving picture pianists and orchestras found grist for their mill in folk tunes, familiar ballads, Irish ditties, and the compositions of Stephen Foster. These songs worked so well because they were the repository of a cultural memory that exhibitors knew they could bank on. In the same way, the classical pieces most often used by early twentieth-century piano teachers were pressed into service in theaters in the early 1910s. Rubinstein's "Melody in F," Schumann's "Träumerei," and Massenet's "Elegy" were chosen not just because the musicians knew them, but also because they were well known to audiences, who took pleasure in rediscovering their favorites. The arbiters of musical taste soon discovered, however, that the musical capital constituted by audience knowledge is far from infinite. Like any other form of capital, spectator familiarity with existing tunes is quickly depleted by overspending. For a time this dilemma was solved by reliance on the popular music industry. Every week, nickelodeon pianists would choose from a new set of tunes already popularized by the sheet music and phonograph industries. Thanks to a constantly renewed supply of illustrated songs and latest hits, storefront audiences regularly enjoyed the reassuring pleasure of rediscovering something familiar. The nickelodeon's orientation toward popular song was perhaps welcome in the early days, when the film industry could not meet exhibitors' needs, but once the film industry solved its own supply problems and settled patent litigation, the days of popular songs were numbered. The illustrated song slides that had so effectively supported the industry's taste for popular songs ended their bright but brief career in 1913.

To compound the difficulties of locating a permanent supply of new music, in the mid-1910s trade press writers began to insist that familiar pieces like Tosti's "Good-bye," Moszkowski's "Serenata," and the overtures to Suppé's *Light Cavalry*, Rossini's *William Tell*, and Wagner's *Rienzi* had worn out their welcome. By 1921, George W. Beynon would have these disparaging words for the very numbers that had carried the industry through the 1910s:

> Hackneyed "has beens" like the "Trio from *Faust*," "Quartet from *Rigoletto*," and "Sextet from *Lucia*," should find the light of day only when that day is so wet and dreary that the patronage has completely crippled the cash box. Aside from the fact that these "Hurdy-Gurdy" favorites have traditional associations which forever bar them from depicting new ideas, no one wants to sit through a picture which he has paid to see and be regaled with music which he has frequently paid to be rid of. . . . You may not have played the *Faust* trio for some months, yet the organ-grinder that very morning chose it as his *pièce de résistance* for the neighborhood.[31]

Standing as something of a memorial to the industry's need to renew its repertory is Roxy's 1921 revival of Griffith's *Birth of a Nation*. Far from recycling Joseph Carl Breil's celebrated score, which was partially original and partially compiled from the warhorses of the mid-1910s, Roxy instead offered an entirely new musical program. Here is how he explained this decision:

> The art of the musical presentation has progressed so markedly during the seven years since *The Birth of a Nation* was first produced, that different standards and methods of adaptation have educated the public to new musical values. In the original adaptation such selections as "Rienzi," "Freischütz," "Ride of the Walkyrie," and "Light Cavalry" were used. The movie going public has since then become familiar through the medium of the motion picture theater and popular opera with these operas and the stories of these works, and their usage today in the accompaniment to *Birth of a Nation* would have seemed inadequate and misrepresentative.[32]

What we might term the "wear factor" was a constant concern for musical directors. During the 1928 presidential campaign, for example, the chief editor of *Musical Courier* offered several "planks with which any candidate can win our own vote for the Presidency," the very first of which was "Less use of Tschaikowsky's Pathetique in moving pictures."[33]

Musical directors' first reaction to the wear factor was to turn to new photoplay compositions and to expand the range of classical choices. This move solved the novelty problem, but it neglected the requirement of familiarity. While the majority of 1910 filmgoers could be expected to recognize "Melody in F" or "Traumerei" (as it was then spelled and pronounced), the same could not be said a decade later of new compositions by M. L. Lake, Ernst Luz, and Otto Langey, or about little-known pieces by Delibes, Liszt, or Mussorgsky. Audience recognition of this new repertory was aided by repeated renditions in moving picture theaters, but the number of new pieces was so large, and the need to vary accompaniment so great, that this process was too slow to solve the problem by itself.

The adoption of the thematic approach offered a creative escape from this quandary. Well-applied, thematic construction of film accompaniments delivered novelty and familiarity in the same compact package. When first played near the beginning of a film, the love theme might be unknown to the audience, but spectators were used to dealing with the unknown at the outset of a narrative. By the time the film reached its climax, with the young couple huddling together to keep out of harm's way, the audience needed the security provided by familiarity. By now, the repeated theme had entered into every spectator's subconscious and was thus available to serve as a refuge for audience emotions. Instead of depending on cultural capital to assure familiarity, each individual film would, as a stand-alone object, take on the challenge of creating—and expending—the necessary musical capital. Instead of continued dependence on hackneyed numbers, musical directors were thus liberated to select their themes from a wide spectrum of musical traditions.

> Predictably, the resultant thematic repetition was anathema to Theodor Adorno. His comments on Wagner's leitmotif approach are typically acerbic: Every element of the present sounds as if it were a reminiscence. The expression of sweet nostalgia merges with the allure of the familiar, the promise of security at home, together with the feeling, "When was I here before?", and the archetypes of the bourgeois find themselves invested with the nimbus of what is long since past. . . . Each listener has the feeling that [the work] belongs to him alone, that it is a communication from his long-forgotten child-

hood, and from this shared *déjà vu* the phantasmagoria of the collective is constructed.[34]

Characteristically, Adorno sees the seeding of individual operas with pseudo-reminiscences as a way of preparing the listener for "the amorphous bliss of a pre-individual condition," and thus as a dangerous failure to grapple with the complexities of the present. In the late 1910s and 1920s, film music columnists, cue sheet compilers, and musical directors instead saw this appeal as a clever way to create an alternative public sphere. However factitious the "collective" constructed by the thematic approach, it had the benefit of offering audiences ever-new experiences of recognition and recovery. When rock concert audiences hear the first bars of a former top-ten tune they roar in approval, even before the singer can open her mouth, thereby rediscovering their own past and sharing a moment of communion with other audience members. By the same sleight of hand, Roxy's followers succeeded in creating a new sense of community through a savvy reiteration of musical themes.

This lesson was not lost on the economic establishment spawned by silent film music. It was not long before the cultural capital created by thematic repetition generated its own product. If audiences can derive special pleasure from listening to a composition at the end of a film that they had never heard before the start, then wouldn't they continue to derive pleasure from that number after the film is over? In short, why not just package the theme as a separate product? The drive to profit economically from film themes fully realized Adorno's fears about Wagner. "Among the functions of the leitmotiv can be found," he insists, "a commodity-function, rather like that of an advertisement: anticipating the universal practice of mass culture later on, the music is designed to be remembered, it is intended for the forgetful."[35] Once a portion of Breil's *Birth of a Nation* score had been separately published as "The Perfect Song," a pathway was opened from film themes, which gain meaning from their participation in a complex audiovisual narrative structure, to theme songs, which function as reminiscences of a borrowed past. In many ways, theme songs were an ideal fit with contemporary practices. Even when all other accompaniment selections were borrowed from the classics or the photoplay repertory, an original main theme made it easier to vary repetitions while avoiding possible copyright problems.

Starting in 1917, copyright became an active issue for motion picture exhibitors. Until the mid-1910s, standard practice had allowed so-called "incidental" use of copyrighted music in restaurants, hotels, vaudeville venues, and moving picture theaters. In 1914, however, the American Society of Composers, Authors, and Publishers was organized to protect against widespread copyright violation, and in 1915 Victor Herbert brought suit against Shanley's Broadway Restaurant for unlicensed performance of "Sweethearts," the title song of a recent Herbert operetta. On 22 January 1917, the Supreme Court reversed a lower court decision in the case of Herbert v. Shanley Co., once and for all guaranteeing composers and their publishers protection against unauthorized performances of copyrighted music.[36] While some theaters agreed to pay ASCAP's "music tax" of ten cents per seat per annum, others chose an alternative path. Increasingly, theaters would build their accompaniments around two categories of music that escaped the copyright problem. Many used European light classical numbers that were not covered under American copyright law (or to which music publishers like Schirmers allowed free access). Larger theaters soon discovered the benefits of selecting a theme composed by an in-house musician. By tapping into the lucrative sheet music and phonograph record markets, enterprising music directors could actually turn a well-confected original theme into a moneymaking proposition.

Starting with "Mickey" (music by Neil Moret, lyrics by Harry Williams), Mabel Normand's theme from Mack Sennett's 1918 film of the same name, theme songs became serious moneymakers. Throughout the early 1920s, photoplay composers and cue sheet compilers regularly transformed main themes into freestanding theme songs, like Ernst Luz's "I Have a Rendezvous with You," published by the Photo Play Music Company and labeled "As Introduced in the Musical Interpretation to *The Four Horsemen of the Apocalypse*," a 1921 Metro film directed by Rex Ingram. Only modestly successful in the early 1920s, theme songs became big business after the spectacular success of Erno Rapee's "Charmaine," the theme song from Fox's 1926 *What Price Glory?* When Rapee's next theme song— "Diane" from Fox's 1927 *Seventh Heaven*—also sold a million sheet music copies, the theme music craze could not be stopped. "Ramona" and "Laugh Clown Laugh" (from movies of the same name) were Feist's best sellers ever.[37] The industry's conversion to sound reinforced theme song mania. Soon a single theme song was insufficient. "As a general thing, there is only one theme song published from the specially composed scores for superpictures," asserted *Metronome* in 1928. "*Abie's Irish Rose*, however, which opened at the Forty-Fourth Street Theatre, New York, recently, has the unusual. That is, two important theme songs, 'Rosemary' and 'Little Irish Rose.' The music, of course, is by J. S. Zamecnik."[38] The most successful film of 1928, Warner's *Singing Fool*, also boasted two million-selling Jolson titles, "There's a Rainbow 'Round My Shoulder" and "Sonny Boy," which had the distinction of selling both a million records and a million sheet music copies.[39] Had the vogue for theme music not reached its height just as Hollywood was experimenting with sound, the industry would certainly have viewed possible conversion quite differently.[40]

Two important conclusions may be drawn from this analysis. First, our habit of equating themes and leitmotifs does not stand the test of historical research. Though he consistently attributed his approach to Wagner, Roxy's use of complete numbers as themes has little to do with leitmotif technique. Whether our topic is silent or sound cinema, we would do well to recognize the substantial differences between these two practices. Second, the use of repeated themes has almost always been treated as a narrative device whose main importance lies in story construction. As we have seen, at least two other major functions are played by themes and theme songs. On the one hand they serve to replenish a depleted repertory, thus restoring some of the cultural capital expended through the repeated use of compilation scores. On the other hand, they offer viewers an experience of recognition and return that fulfills an anchoring function essential to American cinema.

NOTES

1. Roy M. Prendergast, *Film Music: A Neglected Art. A Critical Study of Music in Films* (New York: Norton, 1992), p. 73.

2. Kathryn Kalinak, *Settling the Score: Music and the Classical Hollywood Film* (Madison: University of Wisconsin Press, 1992), p. 61.

3. "Incidental Music for Edison Pictures," *Kinetogram* (15 September 1909), p. 13.

4. "Colonial Theater, West Hoboken, N. J.," *Moving Picture World* (18 November 1911), p. 560.

5. Ernst Luz, "The Musician and the Picture," *Moving Picture News* (12 October 1912), p. 20.

6. "Music Suggestions," *Vitagraph Bulletin of Life Portrayals* (October 1913), p. 14.

7. H. S. Fuld, "Music and the Picture," *Moving Picture News* (10 April 1915), p. 114.

8. For Winkler's early programs, see summer 1915 issues of the *Universal Weekly;* also see Clarence E. Sinn's "Music for the Picture" columns in the *Moving Picture World*, starting in July 1915.

9. S. M. Berg, "Music for the Picture," *Moving Picture World* (25 December 1915), p. 2367.

10. S. M. Berg, "Music for the Picture," *Moving Picture World* (11 November 1916), p. 856.

11. George W. Beynon, "Music for the Picture," *Moving Picture World* (2 March 1918), p. 1242.

12. George W. Beynon, "Music for the Picture," *Moving Picture World* (9 March 1918), p. 1374.

13. Cue sheet for *A Doll's House,* in *Cinema Pressbooks from the Original Studio Collections* (Woodbridge, CT: Research Publications, 1988), n.p.

14. Cue sheet for *The Sixth Commandment,* Balaban & Katz Collection, Chicago Public Library.

15. James S. McQuade, "The Belasco of Motion Picture Presentations," *Moving Picture World* (9 December 1911), p. 796.

16. W. Stephen Bush, "The Theatre of Realization," *Moving Picture World* (15 November 1913), p. 714.

17. Frank A. Edson, "Samuel L. Rothapfel: The Belasco of the Moving Picture World," *Metronome* (August 1915), p. 18.

18. H. S. Fuld, "Using the Resources of an Orchestra to Interpret a Photoplay," *Motion Picture News* (12 December 1914), p. 114.

19. "A De Luxe Presentation," *Motion Picture News* (6 December 1913), p. 16.

20. W. Stephen Bush, "The Art of Exhibition II," *Moving Picture World* (31 October 1914), p. 627. *Sari* is a 1914 musical play with music by Emmerich Kalman and lyrics by C. C. S. Cushing and E. P. Heath. Published separately as "Love's Own Sweet Song," the waltz from *Sari* achieved substantial success.

21. On the details of the Strand's construction and operation, see W. Stephen Bush, "Opening of the Strand," *Moving Picture World* (18 April 1914), p. 371.

22. George W. Beynon, *Musical Presentation of Motion Pictures* (New York: Schirmer, 1921), p. 13.

23. Fuld, "Using the Resources," p. 114.

24. Ernst Luz, "Theme Playing as Used and Abused," *Motion Picture World* (14 August 1915), p. 130.

25. J. Harold Weisel, "Cue Sheets: Two Dimensions," in *American Organist* (July 1922), p. 290.

26. Luz, "Theme Playing," p. 130.

27. George W. Beynon, "Proper Presentation of Pictures Musically. The Theme," *Moving Picture World* (23 February 1918), p. 1093.

28. Aaron Burr, "Repeat Theme—," and Roy L. Medcalfe, "Themes," *American Organist* (February 1922), pp. 67–68.

29. Frank Stewart Adams, "*Way Down East* and the Future," *American Organist,* (January 1921), pp. 23–27; Tim Crawford, "The Use and Misuse of Themes," *Metronome* (1 May 1927), p. 24. See also Joseph O'Sullivan, "Adaptation of Music to Motion Pictures," *Metronome* (July 1917), p. 58.

30. This connection between themes and doubled stand partners is regularly mentioned in the trade press, e.g., by Beynon, "Proper Presentation," p. 1093.

31. Beynon, *Musical Presentation of Motion Pictures,* p. 69.

32. Samuel L. Rothapfel, quoted in May Johnson, "Musical Comedy—Drama—

Motion Pictures," *Musical Courier* (2 June 1921), p. 64. On the new score for *Birth* see also Johnson's *Musical Courier* columns on 12 May 1921, p. 69; and 19 May 1921, p. 65.

33. "Variations, by the Editor-in-Chief," *Musical Courier* (14 June 1928), p. 33.

34. Theodor Adorno, *In Search of Wagner,* trans. Rodney Livingstone (London: NLB, 1981), p. 120. Adorno is here explicitly discussing *Die Meistersinger,* but his remarks are clearly aimed at Wagner's leitmotif technique in general.

35. Ibid., p. 31.

36. For the legal details of this and related cases, see Louis D. Frohlich and Charles Schwartz, *The Law of Motion Pictures, Including the Law of the Theatre, Treating of the Various Rights of the Author, Actor, Professional Scenario Writer, Director, Producer, Distributor, Exhibitor and the Public, with Chapters on Unfair Competition, and Copyright Protection in the United States, Great Britain and her Colonial Possessions* (New York, Baker, Voorhis and Company, 1918). Relevant texts are in Section 184 ("Music in theatres"), which starts on p. 649.

37. Russell Sanjek, *American Popular Music and Its Business: The First Four Hundred Years* (New York: Oxford University Press, 1988), vol. 3, p. 106. Uncharacteristically, Sanjek mistakenly attributes "Charmaine" to *The Big Parade* instead of *What Price Glory?*

38. "Music to Fit the Picture," *Metronome* (June 1928), p. 32.

39. Sanjek, *American Popular Music,* vol. 3, pp. 106–7.

40. On theme songs, see also "Theme Songs Help Good Pictures," *Exhibitors' Herald* (5 January 1929), pp. 45–46; David Mendoza, "The Theme Song," *American Hebrew* (15 March 1929), p. 124; and Maurice Fenton, "The Birth of the Theme Song," *Photoplay* (November 1929), pp. 66–136.

Before *Willie*

Reconsidering Music and the
Animated Cartoon of the 1920s

DANIEL GOLDMARK

Some months before the "Beyond the Soundtrack" conference I took a long look at the conference rationale (described in the Introduction to this volume). What stood out to me, especially as I considered the role music plays in animated cartoons of all stripes, were the phrases "the ways in which film conceptualizes music" and "how films position music and musicality as parts of . . . a fictional world." I've argued elsewhere that dichotomizing cartoon music into diegetic and nondiegetic or source and underscore perpetuates a fundamental misunderstanding of how music functions in cartoons.[1] I therefore saw in this chapter a chance to make my case for hearing and listening to cartoon music differently.

My interest in music has usually involved what I feel are simple questions. In almost every case, the questions concern the evolution of generalized concepts of musical types or sounds. Phrases such as "cartoon music," "cowboy music," or "porn music" quickly bring to mind notions—stereotypical or archetypal in nature—of what such music sounds like, yet these notions are far from singular entities or sounds, but rather remarkably heterogeneous concepts. In the case of my present concern, Hollywood cartoon scores typically consist of a mixture of mood music, idiosyncratic original cues, and pop songs.

I am not just questioning where our everyday ideas of musical genres or styles come from; I'm trying to tease out and make more visible the roots that make up composite musical styles. Of course, it's not enough to identify the ingredients; we must also look at the social and cultural circumstances that would have brought these sounds into such proximity that they would stick well to such an idiosyncratic form of media, one that continually defies easy critical compartmentalization. The technology of cartoon music and cartooning itself has certainly evolved over time, but the approach and mentality of the music seem to have largely stayed in place. In this chapter I therefore question where our notions of what cartoon music is meant to do come from and, in turn, how we are meant to interpret the codes being delivered in cartoons. To explore such ideas we must go back to the understood beginning of synchronized sound cartoons—Walt Disney's cartoon *Steamboat Willie*—and reconsider some fundamental ideas about music's purpose and role in cartoons.

At the very least, we know one thing for certain: *Steamboat Willie*, Walt Disney's first foray into animation with synchronized sound, premiered at the Colony Theatre in New York on Sunday, 18 November 1928.[2] The lead character, Mickey, who bore a striking resemblance to Krazy Kat, Oswald the Lucky Rabbit, and numerous other characters derived from the ubiquitous feline Felix, ably set himself apart from his duotone brethren through his ability to whistle, sigh, yell, and musick on barnyard animals with great skill (and without a hint of self-awareness that he himself was just another animal). Mickey reacts not only visually but also audibly to each new direction taken in the narrative. Likewise, we can hear as well as see his musical exploits. Contemporaneous reviews indicate that the film appealed to critics not because the film had sound (it wasn't the first, as I will discuss), but rather because of its singular use of synchronized music and effects. One review reproduced on a Disney promotional sheet, produced in late 1928 and compiling several newspaper reviews from *Willie's* premiere, said "The union [of cartoon and sound effects] brought forth laughs galore. . . . It's a peach of a synchronization job all the way, bright, snappy and fitting the situation perfectly." The film succeeded precisely where its predecessors had failed: it established a concrete connection between the animation and the musical score. Disney specifically wanted a *sound* cartoon, not a silent cartoon with an added soundtrack.[3] That is, the music, sound effects, and (albeit limited) dialogue had to form an integral part of the story, working *with* the narrative to shape the overall plot, rather than simply mimicking the story (not forgetting the irony that musical mimicry of on-screen action would soon be pejoratively referred to in live-action circles as "mickey-mousing").[4]

While this much may be canonic in film and animation history, scholars have mostly been unaware of attempts to bring music and animation together prior to 1928 due to a lack of interest and a deficit of material support. This combination has continually bolstered the notion that little, if any, music existed for use with animated cartoons before *Steamboat Willie*.

But a reexamination of accompanying guides, collections of photoplay music, and promotional materials for cartoons and theaters reveals a great deal of useful information regarding exhibition practices for cartoons.[5] By questioning various assumptions concerning music's presence (or lack thereof) in early cartoons, the interrelationships between cartoons and their bigger, more widely scrutinized live-action, feature-length cousins become more clear, thus compelling us to reevaluate our notions of the development of the sound of music for cartoons, music's role in the sonic revolution of the late 1920s, and the subsequent model early cartoon music provided for cartoons to follow for years to come.

MUSICALS, SHEET MUSIC, AND NOVELTIES

Presound interactions between cartoons and music certainly occurred, and involved characters that first found fame as newspaper attractions. Stage musicals based on comic strips date back to the beginning of the century: a vaudeville loosely based on the antics of "The Katzenjammer Kids" premiered in 1900; Victor Herbert created a hugely popular musical in 1908 based on the dreamy adventures of Nemo, as drawn by the pioneer animator (and cartoonist) Winsor McCay in his weekly strip, "Little Nemo in Slumberland"; and in 1911 the first of several shows based on "Mutt and Jeff" began to circulate in New York, around the same time the first of more than a half-dozen different spectacles inspired by "Bringing Up Father" also appeared.[6] Another of Winsor McCay's strips, "Dream of the Rarebit Fiend," inspired in 1906 a highly successful film by Edwin S. Porter (already renowned as the director of *The Great Train Robbery* [1903]), some fifteen years before an animated version of the same strip first appeared. A piece for a midsized band (eighteen to twenty pieces), possibly inspired by the film, or perhaps even meant to accompany it, was released in the same year, with music by T. W. Thurban.[7] This song was recorded several times, including on cylinders distributed by Columbia Phonograph in 1907 and 1910.

Another approach to the cartoon musical (or musical cartoon) appeared in the early 1920s. Chicago-based composer John Alden Carpenter melded two popular cultural icons—Krazy Kat and jazz—in his "Jazz Pantomime for Orchestra" simply entitled *Krazy Kat*, which premiered at New York's Town Hall on 20 January 1922. Unlike the artists responsible for the comics on which the musicals mentioned above were based, who had tangential involvement, if any, with the creation of the cartoons, Krazy Kat creator and illustrator George Herrimann developed the scenario for Carpenter's work, as well as provided illustrations for the score and created a moving background that was used for the piece's first performances.[8] *Krazy Kat*, the first such piece to use the term "jazz" in its title, drew largely from early forms of jazz circulating in Chicago, where Carpenter lived when he composed it and where dozens of jazz musicians from New Orleans and other points south migrated in the early 1920s. Carpenter's score did not seek to create a sound for cartoons; rather, he sought to devise a musical portrait of a world-famous cultural figure, one that had been confined until that time to two silent dimensions, either in the newspaper or in animated cartoons. His choice to use the sounds of jazz he experienced in Chicago, as well as modernist sounds similar to Stravinsky, Grofé, and Gershwin, attests to this.

None of these stage musicals had any role defining the "sound" that became associated with cartoons in the late 1920s. The Broadway-style musicals had no reason to break new musical ground and simply followed conventional styles of songwriting and storytelling used in other shows. Indeed, the very style of these revue-type shows (like "Mutt and Jeff" or "Bringing up Father") was to give audiences plenty of good songs and comedy, and not much by way of great drama or challenging music. As for Carpenter's work, *Krazy Kat* excelled as a ballet, but the popularity of the Krazy Kat strip compelled critics to say that the piece missed the spirit of the drawn story. Widespread admiration combined with a lack of understanding of early jazz also led many critics to condemn the music as either indulgent of jazz or too polished. Some suggested that Irving Berlin or Deems Taylor might have done better (ironically enough, as all of the men, critics and composer, were white, and their implicit criticism was that the music wasn't black enough!).[9]

The song factories of Tin Pan Alley also found cartoon characters an effective catalyst for selling sheet music. Numerous publishers capitalized on the fame of different animated characters; songs can be found about Aesop's Fables, Krazy Kat, Ko-Ko the Clown, and, of course, Felix the Cat. Naturally, far more pieces associated with print or newspaper cartoons existed. Just as the comic strip industry had seen many of its characters adapted into animated avatars, an even greater number had songs written about them, many by well-known songwriters. Several sheets were published in which characters like Happy Hooligan, Barney Google, Skeezix, and Jiggs from *Bringing Up Father* would give us some musical insight into their personalities, something they could not do in the newspaper. Based as they were on the Tin Pan Alley model of popular songs, these music-comic interactions had little to do with early animated cartoons other than the trademarked imagery. Likewise, Rube Goldberg's series of music sheets about cartoons bore the collective title "Cartoons in Tunes," yet they too had no noticeable impact on cartoon music.

One possible connection exists, however, as we cannot rule out the possibility that an industrious conductor and/or accompanist might have drawn on the published theme (1923) for Ko-Ko the Clown when accompanying an "Out of the Inkwell" short, or played the chorus from "Felix Kept on Walking" (1923) during a Felix cartoon. For example: among the holdings in the Carl W. Stalling Papers at the University of Wyoming is the sheet music to "Felix the Cat," the 1928 theme song published by Sam Fox. This song's presence just might indicate that Stalling, a film accompanist and theater organist at the time of the song's publication, knew and used the song when accompanying Felix cartoons.[10]

EARLY ACCOMPANYING GUIDES

Looking back at extant criticism from the 1910s and 1920s confirms that many writers considered animation less important than traditional live-action films. The existing evidence regarding film music prior to the development of synchronized sound indicates that far less attention was paid to scoring cartoons than features. Only in special circumstances would a studio commission a completely original score for a film. Cue sheets, a list of musical suggestions that a theater's music director could choose to use or ignore, also accompanied a certain caliber of film. Such musical documentation simply does not exist for cartoons of the period. Why? One possible explanation lies in the opinion accompanists had of cartoons. George Tootell's handbook from the 1920s, *How to Play the Cinema Organ,* had this to say:

> In this category we also include "Cartoon" comedies, such as those of the famous Felix, though in these more opportunity is offered for the exercise of the musician's wit. The organist is recommended to extemporise accompaniments to cartoon comedies, which are always short and concise, and offer scope for witty extemporisation; it is not too much to say that a skillfully accompanied cartoon can often be the most popular item in the programme.[11]

Rather than spending any time discussing the possible techniques for using music to establish mood or define character, the author simply states that cartoons are a good place for composers to be "witty" and perhaps show off their musical abilities.

Edith Lang and George West's *Musical Accompaniment of Moving Pictures* offers similar advice to Tootell's, providing an entire chapter (albeit a short one) on music for comedies and animated cartoons. A good accompa-

nist must have a sense of humor for, as they put it, "Nothing is more calami-
tous than to see 'Mutt and Jeff' disport themselves in their inimitable antics and to have a 'Brother Gloom' at the organ who gives vent to his perennial grouch in sadly sentimental or funereal strains." No indication of
original music fills out the authors' description of appropriate music; rather,
they emphasize the use of popular songs, as "this part of the show is ad-
mirably adapted to the introduction of all sorts of popular songs and
dances."[12] By focusing on existing music, whether Tin Pan Alley songs or
nineteenth-century mood pieces (the authors specifically mention
Gounod's "Funeral March for a Marionette"), Lang and West equate the
role of music in comedies to that in larger (and more substantial) narratives;
their instructions involve the use of a wide variety of preexisting music.[13]

This connection between cartoons and live-action comedies was borne
out a half-decade later in Erno Rapée's *Encyclopedia of Music for Pictures*
(1925). Containing lists of songs appropriate for use in hundreds of situations, the *Encyclopedia* has a separate entry for "Aesop's Fables," which
refers the reader to the more general category of "Comedy Pictures." The
fact that "Aesop's Fables" received its own category suggests that those cartoons, and others like them, were a strong enough presence in theaters to
receive Rapée's attention (yet not strong enough to warrant original
music—at least not yet).

Two years before Rapée's book appeared we find a reference to an early
original musical arrangement for a cartoon. The *Motion Picture News*
printed the following on June 2, 1923:

JAZZ AND "AESOP'S FILM FABLES" GOOD MIXERS

Jazz music goes well with "Aesop's Film Fables." That's the conclusion reached
after a number of tests, and consequently hereafter Pathe, the distributor of
these subjects, will furnish musical effect sheets to each distributor booking
one of these cartoons, declares a statement from the Pathe home-office. At the
New York Capitol this week "Spooks" was presented with a musical jazz accompaniment, and at the Strand "The Mouse Catcher" was similarly presented.[14]

Exactly what the reviewer means by "jazz" is far from clear, and the review
leaves us with little stylistic information regarding the music used. Rag-
time, early ensemble Dixieland jazz in the style of the Original Dixieland
Jazz Band or King Oliver, stride piano as played by Fats Waller or James P.
Johnson—any or all of these styles might work and could have been used.
The music of the Original Dixieland Jazz Band actually seems the most
likely choice, particularly from the use of the term "musical effects sheets,"

as many of the ODJB's earliest recordings (as well as those of other very early jazz groups) made extensive use of instrumental sound effects, imitating the sound of animals and executing other crowd-pleasing gimmicks.[15]

Tangible examples of cartoon-appropriate music also exist in collections of descriptive cues—often called photoplay music—released by various publishers in the late 1910s and throughout the 1920s. Photoplay music's usefulness comes from a generalized specificity; that is, each piece belongs to a certain descriptive category ("Western," "Indian," "Hurry," "Funeral," and the like), and thus is both specific enough to characterize certain scenes common to most narrative films yet relies on a common, almost archetypal melody that allows it to be used in any film without the danger of the audience knowing the music and associating it with another production. The *PianOrgan Film Books of Incidental Music, Extracted from the World Famous "Berg" and "Cinema" Incidental Series*, which comprised seven volumes in the 1920s, included five pieces under the heading "Animated Cartoonix." The collection of mood cues or "film themes" published by Carl Fischer in the 1920s included a piece copyrighted in 1924 entitled "Children's Party—Animated Cartoons (General Merriment)."[16] Two years later we find the *Loose Leaf Collection of Ring-Hager Novelties for Orchestra* from Sam Fox, a music publisher based in Cleveland. The second of ten pieces in the collection, "Funny Faces," was listed as "A Comedy Sketch (For Animated Cartoons, Eccentric and Acrobatic Dancing, Etc.)." These same pieces would be listed in Sam Fox's classified catalogue three years later, while a four-volume collection of music from the same company in 1931 bore the title *Incidental Music for Newsreels, Cartoons, Pictorial Reviews, Scenics, Travelogues, etc.*, with works by various composers (including J. S. Zamecnik, a very prolific composer who wrote, among his several thousand compositions, numerous books of photoplay music for Sam Fox). As with all photoplay music, however, the songs listed as appropriate for cartoons are little more than mood cues, short pieces that can be trotted out at a moment's notice to create the proper sense of atmosphere.[17] Nothing about the cue is "cartoony" per se; practically every cue for upbeat or comic situations in photoplay collections has similar musical characteristics: short, catchy tunes, up-tempo rhythms, major key, and so on.

One photoplay collection that focuses exclusively on music for cartoons has (very recently) come to light: "Komedy Kartoons Theatre Organ Series," which was "Sketched for the Organ by Emil Velazco" and published by Irving Berlin Standard Music Corporation in 1928.[18] The five songs included in the folio are "Aesop's Fables," "Noah's Ark," "Monkey Biznezz," "Green Giraffe," and "Ignatz Mouse." Aside from the titles, nothing in the music indicates when these pieces are appropriate for use, either for specific cartoons or for particular moments or moods during an unspecified short. The "Composer's Note" on the inside front page concerns the performer's choice of organ manuals (keyboards) for various pieces. As we might expect, the five pieces are all in upbeat-sounding major keys, and are all to be played "fast" or "lively."

One telling detail, however, is on the inside back cover, which carries an advertisement for all four folios in Velazco's series, headed with the proclamation "Acclaimed!! by THEATER ORGANISTS." The collections are "Komedy Kartoons," "Novelty Intermezzos," "Scenics," and "Organettes." The note for the "Komedy Kartoons" series reads: "These excellent 'Komedy Kartoons,' supply the long felt need of original grotesque compositions. 'INDE-SPENSIBLE FOR COMEDIES.'" The labels "grotesque" and "cartoon" are seemingly synonymous in the parlance of film accompaniment.[19] Like the other photoplay pieces, Velazco's music seems to conform to the common stereotype for comedies of any style, animated or not: it consists of peppy, happy, and frenetic-sounding pieces meant to accompany and amplify the on-screen antics of an Arbuckle or an Ignatz.

Whether or not Velazco's music ever accompanied an animated cartoon is not known. The year of publication would suggest that these pieces had a limited shelf life, as they appeared the same year that *Steamboat Willie* began animation's move toward synchronized sound in earnest. We do know, however, that these pieces were heard in concert. At the Warner Bros. theater in Hollywood, Harry Q. Mills performed a program for the Los Angeles Theatre Organists' Club on September 18, 1928, concluding his recital with "Green Giraffe," "Ignatz Mouse," and "Noah's Ark." The program does not indicate that any films were shown and, judging by the other pieces on the program, it seems likely that the performance was for organ sans visual accompaniment.[20] Photoplay music clearly was not written exclusively for film accompaniment but could also function as mood pieces for organ or orchestra, much like the characteristic, descriptive works for piano written at the turn of the twentieth century by such composers as Edward Mac-Dowell, Charles Griffes, William Grant Still, Nathaniel Dett, and E. T. Paull.[21]

BIRTH OF THE BOUNCING BALL

The ultimate merging of sound and image did not come as an epiphany to an inspired animator but, supposedly, to a pioneer of American musical entrepreneurship, Charles K. Harris, who in 1892 wrote and published one of the most famous songs of the time, "After the Ball." He quickly started his own publishing company in order to cash in on both ends of music production: writing and publishing. Later in his career, in the mid-1920s, just as recordings and movies were giving Tin Pan Alley new and lucrative outlets for inspiring, marketing, licensing, and promoting songs, Harris visited the Fleischer animation studio in New York with an idea: could audiences be made to sing with a cartoon?[22]

Theater sing-alongs were nothing new at the time. Musical audience-participation events date back to vaudeville practices, which included sing-alongs led from the stage and illustrated song slides. This latter style involved a series of glass slides of photographs, paintings, drawings, or a combination of the three, all chosen specifically to illustrate the words to a popular Tin Pan Alley song. Each slide would be projected to the front of the theater, where a singer or bandleader would lead the verse; everyone would join to sing the chorus. By the turn of the century hundreds of song slide sets were produced yearly. By the late 1910s, however, the practice had slowly begun to wane, possibly from the combination of vaudeville's slow demise and the contemporaneous rise of more spectator-driven approaches to entertainment, typified by the ever-growing popularity of narrative film.[23]

Clearly there was still an interest in the sing-along in the 1920s, and the Fleischer series of Song Car-Tunes gave the medium a new lease on life, with only subtle changes to the form at first. Stylistically, only an animated "bouncing ball" leading the audience through each syllable of the on-screen lyrics differentiated the screen song from the slide song. The first in the series, *Oh, Mabel,* appeared in 1924, and was followed by dozens of others for the next decade.[24]

By 1926, the bouncing-ball series was two years old and more than a dozen titles had been produced. That year, the Fleischers collaborated with Lee de Forest, a technologist and inventor who was trying to bring greater popular acclaim to his Phonofilms, a series of short films that used synchronized sound—still a novelty of sorts. Warner Bros.' *Don Juan* had premiered with an orchestral score in 1925, using Vitaphone's approach to synchronized sound, so the presence of a synchronized score was not foreign to audiences, although it was still far from the standard.[25] The nature of the *Don Juan* soundtrack—purely orchestral music, containing no dialogue at all—simply did not convince audiences of its usefulness. Nevertheless, de Forest continued to promote his own sound film process, convinced that showing films of differing types and genres (including animation) would demonstrate sound's potential. The first of the cartoons created from the Fleischer–de Forest collaboration was *My Old Kentucky Home* in 1926; several others followed the same year. As with *Don Juan*, audiences did not seem thrilled about the animated sound-image combination, perhaps because the cartoon did nothing particularly innovative with the music.[26] While the selling point of the bouncing-ball cartoon was singing, having prerecorded voices of performers lead the audience may not have been enough of a difference to sell the idea. The fact that most theaters did not have the technology necessary to play the soundtracks for these films robbed the films completely of their novelty. It would take the aural/visual combination *and* a compelling star for another studio (Disney) to make their mark with the form.

HAS ANYBODY HERE SEEN KELLY?

One of the Fleischer–de Forest films was based on the song "Has Anybody Here Seen Kelly?" "Kelly" is both a comic ethnic song and a spelling song, in the vein of other such tunes as "M-O-T-H-E-R (A Word That Means the World to Me.)"[27] The song, by C. W. Murphy and Will Letters, was first popularized in England by Emma Carus. It initially faltered in the United States, possibly because its lyrics made several humorous references to British culture. When William J. McKenna adapted it for the Lew Fields–produced show *The Jolly Bachelors* in 1909, it became a hit, no doubt in part because it was sung by superstar Nora Bayes, who also popularized "Shine On, Harvest Moon" and "Over There."[28] Like other Tin Pan Alley tunes that achieved a certain degree of popularity, "Kelly" spawned several sequels, all of which focus on the ethnic angle of the song, including "Kelly's Gone to Kingdom Come" (1910), "I'm the Man They're Looking For; Kelly, That's My Name" (1910), and "If I Knock the 'L' Out of Kelly" (1912).[29] Its success also led it to be recorded several times—a particular sign of popularity in the earliest days of popular music recordings. Its ongoing popularity and cultural currency made it a natural choice for an animated treatment, even seventeen years after it first hit Broadway (see figure 13.1).[30]

The song's lyrics are as follows:

> Michael Kelly with his sweetheart came from County Cork,
> And bent upon a holiday, they landed in New York.
> They strolled around to see the sights alas, it's sad to say,
> Poor Kelly lost his little girl upon the Great White Way.

Figure 13.1 Sheet music for the 1909 version of "Has Anybody Here Seen Kelly?"

She walked uptown from Herald Square to Forty-second Street,
The traffic stopped as she cried to the copper on the beat.

[chorus]
Has anybody here seen Kelly?
K. E. double L. Y.,
Anybody here seen Kelly?
Have y'seen him smile?
His hair is red, his eyes are blue,
He is Irish through and through,
Anybody here seen Kelly?
Kelly from the Emerald Isle.

Over on Fifth Avenue, a band began to play,
Ten thousand men were marching for it was Saint Patrick's Day.
The "Wearing of the Green" rang out upon the morning air,
'Twas Kelly's fav'rite song, so Mary said, "I'll find him there."

She climbed upon the grand stand in hopes her Mike she'd see,
Five hundred Kelly's left the ranks in answer to her plea.[31]
[repeat chorus]

The cartoon itself focuses almost entirely on the song. The little animation in the short consists of the introduction, when Ko-Ko jumps from the
inkwell and invites his four friends (the Ko-Ko Kwartet) to join him on
stage (a stock opening used for many of the Song Car-Tunes), where he
writes the following on a chalkboard (see figure 13.2):

The Ko-Ko Kwartet
Will now execute
That old familiar
Song we sang in
Our boyhood days—
"Has Anybody Here Seen Kelly?"
If you remember it
Join in!

Conceptually, the film *Kelly* does not differ significantly from its immediate predecessors. Each line of the verse and chorus appears on screen separately, with a different, nonmoving matte image in the background (as with
song slides) illustrating the words of the particular line, with the bouncing
ball moving along, syllable by syllable. The only other animation in the cartoon occurs during the refrain, when "Kelly's" chorus appears, one line at a
time, and a little dancing man hops, leaps, or jumps from word to word in
proper time to lead the audience in song.[32] The words of the chorus appear
slowly on the screen, four lines at a time; the third and last time the chorus
is sung, however, a line drawing of Kelly himself (a stereotypical Irishman
with beard and pipe and, as the lyrics in the cartoon describe, a green necktie) slowly begins to fill the screen from top down as the words continue to
appear along the bottom of the screen.

While *Kelly*'s visual makeup is typical of the Song Car-Tunes, the score
created to accompany it is not. There are numerous revealing features in
this artifact. While the cover illustration is signed by Fleischer animator Doc
Crandall, no name is provided for the composer of the unique arrangement
of "Kelly" (nor are the names of the original composers and lyricists mentioned anywhere on the score). In all probability the arrangement was created by Lou Fleischer, one of the Fleischer brothers who had been a theater
pianist and a published arranger of popular songs, and who eventually took
charge of the musical affairs at the studio.

There is also no indication on the score of a publisher, although the Fleis-

Figure 13.2 Frames from *Has Anybody Here Seen Kelly?*

chers' corporate identity, Red Seal Pictures Corporation, is listed as the distributor, suggesting that the Fleischers created this score exclusively for use
with this cartoon.[33] One member of the Red Seal Pictures partnership was
Hugo Riesenfeld, also the conductor of the orchestra at the Rivoli Theatre,
just down the street from the Fleischer studio on Broadway.[34] Like Lou
Fleischer, Riesenfeld had a background in film music, which makes him a
possible creator of the score. We might also surmise that the studio published and distributed the music itself, providing a copy of the score with
each copy of the film sent out to theaters, a practice typical for companies
distributing special scores with feature films. The music's inside cover
strengthens this assumption, where the text reads (in part):

> THE RED SEAL PICTURES CORPORATION PLACES A HIGH VALUE ON THESE SCORES
> AND IT IS UNDERSTOOD THAT NOT ONLY ARE THEY TO BE HANDLED CAREFULLY
> DURING THEIR USE WHILE SHOWING ONE OF THE "KO-KO SONG CARTOONS" BUT
> ARE TO BE RETURNED IMMEDIATELY UPON THE COMPLETION OF THE ENGAGEMENT
> OF THE FILM.

The music itself is arranged for keyboard with the melody of "Kelly"
written in small notes throughout the treble line, a notational device typical for keyboard parts (organ or piano), as the musician playing was expected to lead the rest of the band from his or her instrument, if not playing solo. The melody's notation, and the numerous instructions to the
"musical director" of the theater, suggests that the score is part of the phalanx of band arrangements of popular songs made available to theater organists and conductors of the time. This theory is strengthened by the message printed on the back cover, which reads: "Ko-Ko Song Car-Tunes are
issued with full orchestration, including Special Piano and Organ Parts."
While these arrangements were a standard part of any conductor's library
(the collection from which this score comes includes hundreds of such

arrangements), the score is unique in that it was meant to be used with a specific film, rather than simply used as material during the course of a show. Nothing on the score itself indicates that *Kelly* has a soundtrack, or that *Kelly* is unlike any other Song Car-Tune, from which we might surmise that the score was intended for those theaters that could not technically realize *Kelly's* soundtrack, although, as Rick Altman has demonstrated, performance practices varied so drastically from theater to theater that any such assumptions would be unwise.[35]

The score is divided into three sections: the opening music for when Ko-Ko takes the screen and prepares the audience to sing, the verse, and the chorus. The verse and chorus are simplified versions of the original "Kelly" keyboard part. A comparison of "Kelly"'s original sheet music and the Fleischer version shows that the original keyboard part doubled the singer's melody throughout in the right hand; the Fleischer version eliminates this melodic/rhythmic doubling (presumably another instrument in the arrangement would play this part), reducing the keyboard line significantly. The music for the opening section—which is a vamp, or a sequence that can be repeated as needed until the actual song begins—is not the music for "Kelly" but rather the chords to "Auld Lang Syne," a sly reference to "Kelly"'s theme of separation, especially with the line "Should auld acquaintance be forgot . . . ." (Ironically, "Auld Lang Syne" is Scottish in origin.)[36] The score also provides three performance notes; that is, it indicates three moments in the score to which the keyboardist or musical director can synchronize the performance to the cartoon.

The performance guide gives us much more than just the music for *Kelly;* we also get numerous performance hints and suggestions, such as this helpful idea:

> SPECIAL NOTE TO MUSICAL DIRECTOR: It has been found after experimentation that the most satisfactory method of playing the Ko-Ko Song Car-Tunes is to have the orchestra led by a single instrument such as the violin or cornet, the player of which carries the melody, and *follows it by watching the screen.* [Emphasis in original.]

These notes also give us some information about the performance history of the cartoon. One note states:

> These orchestral settings are the real tunes, and in no instance has any liberty been taken with the originals. THEY WERE USED BY THE CAPITOL THEATRE GRAND ORCHESTRA OF EIGHTY PIECES IN NEW YORK AND ARE JUST AS ADAPTABLE TO SMALLER ENSEMBLES, OR ORGAN.

While the presence of one score for these cartoons is exciting enough, the inside cover indicates the possibility that scores were created for as many as five of these original sound cartoons. The back page bears the title "Striking Prologues with 'Ko-Ko Song Car-Tunes' " and provides performance instructions for the shorts.

> Exhibitors will find that the songs lend themselves ideally to prologues. By opening the act with singers in costumes appropriate to the song, the stage number can be blended into the film and the audience will unconsciously be drawn into the sprit of participating in the songs.

Finally, while *Kelly*'s score and soundtrack make it singular sonically, it also had an unusual appearance: the entire film was tinted green. This would make *Kelly* doubly unique. Tinted films were nothing new, but the combination of color and sound might have made for an especially novel experience for viewers; as the score points out, the color gives the film "added comedy value." And in a well-conceived bit of color coordination, the cover of the document is a shade of "Kelly" green.[37]

Kelly's entire purpose, as that of its bouncing-ball brethren, is a performance; whether the audience sings or not is inconsequential. We might assume that audience participation is the goal here, but really, if we believe Charles K. Harris, the cartoons existed to sell the music through whatever means necessary. The viewer takes in the song by reading the words, saying or singing the words, and hearing the words sung by his or her neighbors (and possibly the soundtrack)—or a combination of all three. The success of these cartoons did more than just create a new act or number in the daily theater line-up. The idea of music and performance (especially popular songs) became much more closely integrated with the animated cartoon.

STEAMBOAT WILLIE, REVISITED

As we return inexorably toward the turning point of 1928 and *Steamboat Willie,* we lack any evidence of a "special score," a musical score composed specifically to accompany a cartoon. Such a score could close the conceptual gap between the mood pieces I discussed earlier, the popular songs used in the bouncing-ball cartoons, and the music composed for the first sound cartoons. One possible candidate has not survived: Paul Hindemith's player piano roll for the 1927 film *Felix at the Circus.* Even if this film did still exist, we could not tell if the music was improvised or written and then performed.[38] With years of sound experiments and silent cartoon accompaniment behind them, many of the early cartoon composers spent the first years of the sound era groping for a style that made sense. For someone like Carl Stalling, who eventually was to define the sound of cartoon music through his work for Disney, Iwerks, and Warner Bros., such a transition was natural: "I just imagined myself playing for a cartoon in the theater, improvising, and it came easier."[39] Stalling suggests the possibility that cartoons prior to 1928 were improvised and not scored in advance, which might explain the lack of scores from this time.

While *Kelly* and its cohorts give us a unique view of possible performance practices, they remain an outgrowth of Tin Pan Alley marketing tactics, especially if the anecdote about Charles K. Harris is true. The success of the bouncing-ball series tell us several things, however. First, audience participation acts in 1920s theaters were far from dead. Second, as animation was in a mid-decade creative lull, the song-image union gave audiences an entirely new perspective on cartoons, one that made animation more than just short novelties. This is a film form that had a remarkable amount of social currency and power; consider McCay's *Sinking of the Lusitania* or the Fleischers' *The Einstein Theory of Relativity,* to give just two examples. Perhaps most important, however, is the notion that audiences were apparently willing to accept the conceptual union of popular music and animation. By relying entirely on pop songs, the bouncing-ball cartoons fused animation and song together, so much so, in fact, that Hollywood theatrical cartoons would be *permanently* joined to the idea of some form of popular music for forty years.

Conventional wisdom tells us that *Steamboat Willie* made obvious sound's possibilities when harnessed to animated films, yet we can see now that *Willie* neither gave birth to the sound age nor did it kill the silent form. I mentioned earlier that *Willie*'s appeal came partly from the ability to see as well as hear Mickey's exploits, particularly those involving the performance of music. Disney's vision of using sound thus came, in part, from seeing poor applications of sound in his competitors' work. Disney himself saw a Paul Terry Aesop's Fables short (possibly *Dinner Time*) in September 1928; the short included a rudimentary soundtrack or, as Disney himself put it, "a lot of racket and nothing else . . . it merely had an orchestra playing and adding some noises." If nothing else, the cartoon showed Disney precisely what role he did *not* want music to play in his shorts: a veneer added on at the end with little consideration for the story. The very next month, Disney saw the Fleischer short *The Sidewalks of New York*, which he preferred over the Terry film, particularly for how the animation and music seemed to interact and respond to each other. By this time, however, *Steamboat Willie* had already been recorded.[40]

Disney executed his ideas for sound cartoons in a remarkably short time. His fondness for the Fleischer over the Terry sound shorts might indicate both his admiration for the Fleischers' construction of a short around a song, as well as their integration of sound as a key element to the narrative. When we look closely at *Steamboat Willie*, it quickly becomes apparent that the only compositional technique that we might consider remotely "cartoonish" in nature is the pervasive use of mickey-mousing, a term that most likely dates from the early 1930s. In 1928, when *Steamboat Willie* was created, mickey-mousing could have been considered exciting and innovative, instead of being seen as a shortcut, a crutch, as many composers would look at it from the 1930s onward. (Then again, those composers were not cartoon composers, but composers for live-action film, where such techniques drew undue attention to the music.)

The arrival of synchronized sound did not revolutionize the industry overnight; it took years for most studios to adapt both technologically and conceptually to the idea of deliberately using sound, in all its forms, as part of the larger filmic space. One genre that could adapt quickly was the cartoon.[41] The Fleischer bouncing-ball cartoon, in all its forms, prolonged and therefore continued to concretize the association between music making and animated cartoons, so that when widespread acceptance of synchronized sound finally occurred, the connection between the two seemed logical, a natural continuation of the scoring practice used for cartoons in the pre-sound days, amplified by the fortuitous relationship created with the bouncing ball, in addition to, of course, the use of pop songs in other short subjects. The musical predilections of the earliest sound cartoons are already well known; Disney's Silly Symphonies purported to let the music give rise to the narrative, as opposed to the score simply being added on as an afterthought. Likewise, Hugh Harman and Rudy Ising produced two series of cartoons for Warner Bros., the Looney Tunes and Merrie Melodies, which began appearing in theaters in 1930 and 1931, respectively, with a contractual obligation to feature a Warner-owned song in the latter series. Both pre- and postsound cartoons rely on pop songs to drive and underscore the action. What differs is that, in the sound era, the cartoon's musical director deliberately synchronized the music to the action to bolster the music-image connection, to give an extra sense of rhythm to all the action on screen, and perhaps to impart a sense of life to those drawn images that never lived themselves.

NOTES

Thanks to Michael Barrier, Jerry Beck, Greg Breed, Jeremy Butler, Mark Kausler, Mark Langer, Louis Niebur, Ray Pointer, and the University of Alabama's Interdisciplinary and Interpretive Studies Group for their advice, criticism, information, and encouragement on this essay.

1. See my "Introduction: Why Cartoon Music?" in *Tunes for 'Toons: Music in Hollywood Cartoons* (Berkeley: University of California Press, 2005).

2. Michael Barrier, *Hollywood Cartoons: American Animation in Its Golden Age* (New York: Oxford University Press, 1999), p. 55.

3. The limitations of sound production in early cartoons has been discussed by Scott Curtis, "The Sound of the Early Warner Bros. Cartoons," *Sound Theory, Sound Practice*, ed. Rick Altman (New York: Routledge, 1992), pp. 191–203.

4. One anecdote about the coining of this term can be found in Elisabeth Weis and John Belton, *Film Sound: Theory and Practice* (New York: Columbia University Press, 1985), pp. 409–10.

5. Rick Altman and Tim Anderson, among others, have recently compelled scholars to reconsider assumptions made about music's role in movie exhibition practices prior to the invention and popularization of synchronized sound in the late 1920s, most commonly associated with the premiere of *The Jazz Singer* in 1927. See Rick Altman, "The Silence of the Silents," *Musical Quarterly* 80.4 (1997), pp. 648–718, and *Silent Film Sound* (New York: Columbia University Press, 2004); and Tim Anderson, "Reforming 'Jackass Music': The Problematic Aesthetics of Early American Film Music Accompaniment," *Cinema Journal* 37.1 (Fall 1997), pp. 3–22.

6. Gerald Bordman, *American Musical Theatre: A Chronicle*, 2nd ed. (New York: Oxford University Press, 1992), pp. 246, 272, 399, 745. McCay did not have any active part in the creation of *Little Nemo*, although he did manage to advertise it in his comic strip. Donald Crafton, *Before Mickey: The Animated Film 1898–1928* (Chicago: University of Chicago Press, 1993), p. 98.

7. A copy of this piece can be found in the files of the Carl W. Stalling Papers at the American Heritage Center at the University of Wyoming.

8. A thorough stylistic and historical explication of this work can be found in Howard Pollack, *Skyscraper Lullaby: The Life and Music of John Alden Carpenter* (Washington and London: Smithsonian Institution Press, 1995), pp. 190–209.

9. Ibid., pp. 203–4.

10. Carl W. Stalling Papers, American Heritage Center, University of Wyoming.

11. George Tootell, *How to Play the Cinema Organ: A Practical Book By a Practical Player* (London: W. Paxton & Co., n.d.), p. 84.

12. Edith Lang and George West, *Musical Accompaniment of Moving Pictures* (Boston: Boston Music Company, 1920), p. 35.

13. This entire section from Lang and West has been reprinted in Daniel Goldmark and Yuval Taylor, eds., *The Cartoon Music Book* (Chicago: A Cappella Books, 2001), pp. 17–19.

14. *Motion Picture News* (June 2, 1923), p. 2651. Michael Barrier refers to this short article in *Hollywood Cartoons*, p. 51.

15. Such songs by the Original Dixieland Jazz Band include "Livery Stable Blues" and "Barnyard Blues."

16. Thanks to Greg Breed for bringing this cue to my attention.

17. Rodney Sauer, "Photoplay Music: A Reusable Repertory for Silent Film Scoring, 1914–1929," *American Music Research Center Journal* 8/9 (1998–99), pp. 69–70.

18. Thanks to Jerry Beck for bringing this collection to my attention. An earlier piece for solo organ by Velazco, published by Jack Mills Inc. in 1927, bears the title "Krazy Kat" and is very similar in affect and style to those described above, but it is not included in the "Komedy Kartoons" folio.

19. Under the heading "Grotesque," Rapée's *Encyclopedia* has no music listed, only a cross-listing with "Comedy Pictures"—exactly like the heading for "Aesop's Fables" mentioned earlier. Erno Rapée, *Encyclopedia of Music for Motion Pictures* (New York: Belwin, 1925), p. 237.

20. "Fine Demonstration," *The Overture* 8.6 (October 1928), p. 22. Other works on the program included MacDowell's "Witches Dance," Debussy's "Clare de Lune" [*sic*], and "Lento" by Cyril Scott, as well as selections from Rudolf Friml's music for *The Three Musketeers* and John Alden Carpenter's "Tango Américaine," both played by Emil Baffa.

21. Several of these composers wrote works that not only had descriptive elements, but even included epigrams instructing listeners as to what they should be thinking.

22. Ray Pointer related this anecdote to me; it also appears in Leslie Cabarga, *The Fleischer Story,* 2nd ed. (New York: Da Capo Press, 1988). Charles K. Harris mentions the Fleischers in his autobiography, but only that the studio had taken three songs owned by Harris's publishing house and turned them into "Out of the Inkwell" bouncing ball cartoons: "Mother, Mother, Mother Pin a Rose on Me," "Come Take a Trip in My Airship," and "Goodbye, My Lady Love." Charles K. Harris, *After the Ball* (New York: Frank-Maurice, 1926), p. 365.

23. Richard Abel, "That Most American of Attractions, the Illustrated Song," in *The Sounds of Early Cinema,* ed. Richard Abel and Rick Altman (Bloomington: Indiana University Press, 2001), p. 144–55.

24. Mark Langer, "Max and Dave Fleischer," *Film Comment* 11.1 (January–February 1975), pp. 49–50.

25. The Vitaphone "sound-on-disc" process involved recording the sound on separate discs and playing the discs with each reel of the film. This would eventually be passed over as the primary sound system for the "sound-on-film" process.

26. The Fleischers seemed determined to make a mark on cartoon music history. Not only did they experiment with synchronized sound before their competitors,

they were also the first studio to have sheet music inspired by one of their own characters: "Out of the Inkwell," featuring Ko-Ko, was published in 1923.

27. The proclivity of Tin Pan Alley songwriters to focus on ethnicity has been extensively noted elsewhere; as the pseudo-Gaelic elements of "Kelly" do not figure into this discussion, I will not engage with that discourse here. See William H. A. Williams, 'Twas Only an Irishman's Dream: The Image of Ireland and the Irish in American Popular Song Lyrics, 1800–1920 (Urbana: University of Illinois Press, 1996); Charles Garrett, "Chinatown, Whose Chinatown? Defining America's Borders with Musical Orientalism," Journal of the American Musicological Society 57.1 (Spring 2004), pp. 119–73; and Jeffrey Magee, "Irving Berlin's 'Blue Skies': Ethnic Affiliations and Musical Transformations," Musical Quarterly 84.4 (Winter 2000), pp. 537–80.

28. Sigmund Spaeth, Read 'em and Weep: The Songs You Forgot to Remember (New York: Halcyon House, 1939), p. 258. Spaeth also points out that the verse to the tremendously successful song "It's a Long, Long Way to Tipperary" (1912) is adapted largely from much of the music for its verse from the verse to "Kelly."

29. Williams, 'Twas Only an Irishman's Dream, pp. 194–95.

30. "Kelly" 's cultural currency recently rose with the film Catch Me If You Can (2002). At one point in the film Frank Abagnale, played by Leonardo DiCaprio, is living with a family in Georgia who watch the 1960s variety show Sing Along with Mitch, hosted by producer/musician Mitch Miller. The show featured sing-along segments that used a bouncing ball so that audiences could indeed "sing along with Mitch." The song the family sings in the scene is "Has Anybody Here Seen Kelly?" which, not surprisingly, awakens feelings of homesickness, and possibly guilt, in Abagnale, a fugitive who is shown throughout the film longing for his parents and home life.

31. The lyrics used in the cartoon vary slightly from those in the original sheet music to "Kelly." The word "has" is often added to the line "Anybody here seen Kelly?" in the cartoon, particularly in the second and third choruses. Also in those choruses the last line is changed to from "Kelly from the Emerald Isle" to "Kelly with the green necktie."

32. The bouncing ball appeared to move with lifelike accuracy because, by 1926, it was not animated, but actually a ball painted white and affixed to a stick, which Lou Fleischer would move over the words in time while a camera filmed the action.

33. The song's American copyright of 1909 meant that "Kelly" was not yet in the public domain when the cartoon was produced, which would strengthen the notion that this music was distributed exclusively for use with the film and not meant to be sold, as sales of the song, even as a score to accompany a film, would be a clear infringement of copyright.

34. Thanks to Mark Lagner for this information.

35. Altman, "Silence of the Silents," passim.

36. Also interesting is that, on the de Forest soundtrack for Kelly, the opening music heard is not "Auld Lang Syne," but an original piece that lightly underscores Ko-Ko's actions on screen. The printed score therefore enabled one particular per-

formance of *Kelly,* while the soundtrack, for those who had the technology, provided another.

37. Langer, "Max and Dave Fleischer," p. 51.

38. Daniel Goldmark, "Classical Music and the Hollywood Cartoon," in Daniel Goldmark and Yuval Taylor, eds., *The Cartoon Music Book* (Chicago: A Cappella Books, 2002), p. 113.

39. Michael Barrier, Milton Gray, and Bill Spicer, "An Interview with Carl Stalling," *Funnyworld* 13 (Spring 1971): 26.

40. Barrier, *Hollywood Cartoons,* p. 55.

41. Hank Sartin, "From Vaudeville to Hollywood, From Silence to Sound," *Reading the Rabbit,* edited by Kevin S. Sandler (New Brunswick, NJ: Rutgers University Press, 1998), p. 78.

14 Side by Side

Nino Rota, Music, and Film

RICHARD DYER

Music is everywhere in film, in documentary and the avant-gardes just as much as in feature fiction films, and this has been true ever since there has been film, not just since the so-called coming of sound. Yet as Luigi Pelliz-zoni (1996) puts it, in the title of the lead article to a collection entitled *Cinema's Music (La music del cinema)*, music and cinema constitute "a 'difficult' relationship."[1] In what follows I want to examine some of the familiar reasons for saying this and to glance at a couple of the standard ways the difficulty has been resolved, before looking at a practice, that of Nino Rota, that runs not so much counter to as alongside these solutions. In the process, I shall suggest that the author's examination may make us modify our assumptions about music and film narrative, and about film narrative *tout court*.

Music's omnipresence in film poses a number of problems for analysis. First, outside its occurrence in the world depicted or documented by a film, music has no business being there. There is no Rachmaninoff playing in the provincial train station in *Brief Encounter*, nor Johann Strauss in outer space in *2001: A Space Odyssey*. The characters are oblivious to music that is heard all around them; similarly, animals do not seem to mind that they carry on their business to music in nature documentaries. At the same time, we are so completely used to all this that we do not customarily note the oddness of the presence of music. This very general problem has been addressed by Claudia Gorbman in *Unheard Melodies*,[2] which both traces the multiple determinants on the historical development of music-with-film and outlines the conventions by which the presence of music is concealed from notice. Gorbman thus shows how the convention of there being music with film developed to the point that it is taken for granted and the craft is left unquestioned.

A second problem is that music has its own structural and temporal agendas that do not coincide unproblematically with those of film narration. Music's patterns of repetition and development—the architecture of, for instance, the sonata form or the blues, the infectiousness of a good tune or the insistence of a great beat—may all be at variance with the shifts and tempi of enacted narrative.

In the model of classical cinema, all such elements have to be made to fit, subordinated (in the ways that Gorbman and others have demonstrated) to the needs of telling the story effectively and unobtrusively. Yet this second problem may continue to be registered in many different ways. When Nino Rota was discussing the music for *Senso* (1954), he dissuaded the director, Luciano Visconti, from using the first theme of the third movement of Brahms's Third Symphony, suggesting Bruckner instead:

> He wanted to use Brahms; but at a certain point it changes, the second subject comes in.
>
> "Yes," he said, "it's fine up to here, but then we'll have to lengthen this theme."
>
> "Listen, my friend, I can do this job, but I can't add something to Brahms. . . . You can't manipulate it."
>
> So we used one of Bruckner's symphonies, and I found a way of "manipulating" it without manipulating it.[3]

The Brahms theme is immediately graspable and memorable, with a relatively short span, and it uses a repeated melodic figure and very clear-cut instrumentation. The Bruckner, on the other hand, is a very long melody whose contours are hard to grasp and even harder to reproduce even after several hearings, in part because of the thickly textured orchestration. It's hard to miss the Brahms melody and thus hard to break it up, to elongate or shorten it, to fit the film's narrative requirements without drawing attention to what you are doing. The Bruckner, on the other hand, is not really damaged by some nips and tucks here and some dragging out there. In fact, Rota manipulates the piece quite dramatically, as Roberto Calabretto notes in detail,[4] but he does so imperceptibly: the manipulation is not evident to any but the most perceptive ear.

It is, however, characteristic of Rota, as we shall see, that his "manipulation" is much less drastic than that performed by the classic Hollywood composers on their own material, where melodies are broken up into smaller phrases and subject to endless variations in tempo and instrumentation to fit the narrative very precisely. Bruckner is to be respected (not least in the context of *Senso* so that it retains the considerable symbolic significance of its Austrianness), but the musical vocabulary of Hollywood drew on the postclassical Western symphonic tradition (to which Bruckner belongs) precisely because its long melodies and range of orchestral coloring lent themselves to doing the work of narrative underscoring. It has proved much more difficult to adapt jazz, with its flow of a musically based logic of improvisation and underlying repetition,[5] or rock, where the maintenance of the beat remains paramount, to the narrative film's need for variations, and changes in tempo, on the basis of story and character. In standard cinematic practice, jazz and rock have generally had to be incorporated into the wider language of postclassical symphonism or else confined to sequences emphasizing mood (jazz), action (rock), or sex (both).

The third problem that music poses for film analysis is the perennial one of determining what music expresses. Perhaps I may be allowed to polarize the debate over this within musicology[6] as a disagreement between those who argue that music essentially expresses emotions—sadness, joy, hope, anger, and so on—and those for whom music is the formal organization of sounds, such that if it expresses anything it is itself; if it conveys emotion it is purely musical emotion. Both positions seem problematic. It is clear that whatever feelings music expresses, they go beyond those that can be labeled; the feelings in music so often fall through the gaps in our crude vocabulary for describing emotions.[7] On the other hand, formulations about music expressing itself do not really get at why it moves us so: why on earth should we be moved by something that is "only" the arrangement of sounds?

It seems most plausible that music has something to do with feelings of the kind we have in real life, yet attempts to specify these tend to founder. Music does, for instance, express a broad range of feelings. It would be aberrant to consider Stravinsky's *The Rite of Spring* an evocation of a calm and light-hearted day in the country. In song and in narrative forms, including film, music is anchored to emotions, and thus the piano accompaniment in Schubert lieder is commonly held to echo, or even to express, the hope or despair of the words, while there are well-developed codes in movie music for suspense, excitement, love, and distress. Yet deprived of their verbal or narrative context, such musical elements are not necessarily so categorically expressive: the parameters of feeling are more open in music that does not have a verbal or narrative anchor, and so are the possibilities of echoing words or situations and of developing narrative-feeling conventions. All these phenomena imply that music is affective yet also indicate that the way in which it is cannot be reduced to the kinds of emotion that words and narratives most readily and commonly deal with.

It seems to me valuable to revisit Suzanne Langer's suggestion that one conceptualize the feeling level of music—what I shall, following her, hereafter refer to as the affective level—in terms of its embodiment of the whole shifting range of feelings, responses, instincts, and senses that are a constitutive part of the lived texture of sentience (a term that valuably combines physiological and intuitive sense, cognition, consciousness, and unconsciousness). In her classic statement:

> The tonal structures we call "music" bear a close logical similarity to the forms of human feeling—forms of growth and of attenuation, flowing and stowing, conflict and resolution, speed, arrest, terrific excitement, calm, or subtle activation and dreamy lapses—not joy and sorrow perhaps, but the poignancy of either or both—the greatness and brevity and eternal passing of everything vitally felt. Such is the pattern, or logical form, of sentience; and the pattern of music is that same form worked out in pure, measured sound and silence. Music is a tonal analogue of emotive life.[8]

Langer's formulation has well-known problems. Philosophers and musicologists have suggested various qualifications and refinements to it,[9] and from a cultural materialist viewpoint, there is in it little sense of cultural and historical specificity or of music as something that is made (rather than just being an analogous emanation). However, as a description of the nature of musical feeling it also has many advantages, not least for a consideration of music and film. It finds a way between a purely formalist account of music that cannot account for why music moves us and those formulations that reduce affect to nameable emotions. In drawing attention to what may be termed the extra-semiotic or amodal dimension of music (in the sense of that which is not available to be readily codified emotionally or spoken of in terms of meaning), it does not suffer from either of the common misunderstandings of this dimension. That is, it does not assume that because we cannot name or categorize affects they are either ineffable and mysterious or else dangerous and inchoate. Both of these qualities are products of the intellectual's simultaneous investment in and frustration with the limitations of linguistically rendered ideas, which produces the sense—or rather the furious desire—that what is beyond language must either be transcendent or transgressive. Langer's formulation rescues us from these delusions. It allows us to treat musical affect as related to ordinary and familiar, albeit generally unarticulated, aspects of sentient life, to the eddies of unprompted mood that constantly accompany us, to the differing intensities of our experience of the nameable emotions, and to the way we feel what we feel.[10]

The above may be said of all the nonrepresentational aspects of film (and all other arts), including color, lighting, the dynamics of editing, the management of sound, aspects of performance and bodily appearance, and so on. However, it perhaps most insistently true of music. Music can only ever be representational in a limited sense.[11] The nonrepresentational, semiotic, amodal, affective level is its primary and often only level. In film, this is reinforced by the sense that it has its own internal aesthetic agenda, and that most of it has no diegetic business being there.

The relationship between film and music has long been discussed as a tension between possibilities of synchronism and counterpoint, implying a degree of autonomy and even incommensurability between the two forms. That is, because of their profound essential differences, they have to either be made to (seem to) fit, or else played off against each other. Writing in the context of considering combinations of media, including music and film, Rudolf Arnheim argued for a complementary approach, a "double track"[12] that will make sense only if the components do not simply convey the same thing. They must complete each other in the sense of dealing differently with the same subject. Each medium must treat the subject in its own way, and the resulting differences must be in accordance with those that exist between the media.

Theodor Adorno and Hanns Eisler in *Composing for the Films* (1947)[13] draw a celebrated contrast between Hollywood practice, in which music is disciplined to the needs of narrative, notably through the crass use of the leitmotif and direct musical mimicry ("mickey-mousing") of what's on screen, and their preferred practice, which emphasizes disjuncture between filmic and musical agendas to create (in principle) counterpoint between film and music. A third formulation is that proposed by Max Steiner, where he speaks of two schools of composition:

> "Mickey Mouse" and "over-all" scoring. The "Mickey Mouse" scoring (my way of scoring) . . . fits a picture like a glove. In other words, if I want to underline a love scene in a parlour and we were to cut away to a boat on the water, I would try and write my music so that the love theme would modulate into some kind of water music or what have you, as naturally the love theme would have nothing to do with the boat as the locale would be changed and probably would indicate time elapse. The "over-all" school . . . would keep right on playing regardless what happens.[14]

Considering the work of Nino Rota, I want to suggest that the "overall" school can be more interesting than Steiner makes out, producing work that may not be contrapuntal in the Adorno-Eisler sense but is often somewhat complementary in Arnheim's sense. Rota himself saw it as his practice "to produce music for film that keeps itself apart as music, which runs alongside the film and doesn't submit itself to it, only adapts itself materially."[15] Elsewhere he speaks, in the context of working with Fellini, Visconti, and Zeffirelli, of music that "expresses above all the spirit of the film rather than the materiality of the succession of images."[16]

Rota's practice, like any other, is a product of circumstances. On the one hand, sound, including dialogue and ambient elements, was until very recently always postsynchronized in Italian cinema. The sense, then, of sound not quite emanating from the image and the possibility of it being thought through after filming make a slightly less conjoined conception of sound-image relations possible. On the other hand, Nino Rota's habit was to write the score after the film was made, often without reading the script or being on set, let alone watching the finished cut. He was extremely busy: in addition to writing 157 film scores, he composed 74 concert works and 28 works for theater, opera, ballet, and television, and he conscientiously filled a full-time post as director of the Bari Conservatory of Music. He did all his film work in a hurry, often on the train. Stories abound of him chattering away at lunch when someone would remind him that he had a score to record that afternoon. He would then realize he had not even composed it yet and throw it together in a couple of hours. No wonder that the scores took an "overall' approach. What interests me is how effective this approach can be.

Commonly, Rota's music carries on alongside the narrative, broadly in tune with it but not underscoring every minute action, gesture, or shift of emotion à la Steiner. His generic scores—for comedies, melodramas, and even the odd epic (*La regina di Saba* [The Queen of Sheba], 1952) or war film (*Sotto dieci bandiere* [Under Ten Flags], 1960)—set an appropriate tone, occasionally modified according to the particular emphasis of a sequence. They only occasionally (as in the Macario comedy *L'eroe della strada* [The Hero of the Way], 1948) adapted the music more precisely to what was happening in the story.[17] In *Plein soleil* (1960), the first adaptation of Patricia Highsmith's *The Talented Mr. Ripley,* a burbling theme redolent of pre-pop contemporary nightlife music for the early sequences in Rome and then a coy *meridionale* theme on mandolins for the sequences in the Southern port-cum-resort of Mongibello run alongside, but do not precisely respond to, the complex ins and outs of the story, reflecting the lazy, amoral hedonism of the characters. There is a similar effect in *La dolce vita* (1960), although here the Roman-ness of the music comes across as less touristy and the main thematic elements carry more sinister or threatening orchestration; by the end, the untroubled repetition of thematic material during the final party is remorseless, infernally trivial, as Guido descends inexorably into perdition. Yet in neither *Plein soleil* nor *La dolce vita* does the music by any precise coordination with the image underline the detail of the ins and outs of the road to perdition.

I want to look at two rather more particular aspects of Rota's practice (not unique to him, but especially characteristic of him).[18] One has to do with the question of musical and narrative agendas, the other with a kind of disjuncture that I want to characterize as ironic attachment.

Especially in his early films, Rota often composed scores that have their own internal structural logic. The score for *Un americano in vacanza* (An American on Holiday, 1945), for instance, is in two halves, with the second recapitulating the material from the first half, working variations on it but moderating it only slightly to fit the length of the scenes and only once introducing one entirely new musical element, an old-fashioned waltz. This is, of course, not done with total disregard for the rest of the film. The dividing point between the two musical halves occurs with the break that is even today standard for screenings in Italy, forcing an interval between a *primo* and *secondo tempo*. Moreover, the boy-and-girl narrative of the second half pretty well repeats that of the first: postwar contextualization, pursuit, misunderstanding, falling in love, the intervention of religion, and regretful parting. This, however, is submerged in the visual patina of (neo)realist convention, whereas Rota's score tends to suggest the formal structures of the narrative peripeteia. It also plays on the potential for both comedy and pathos in repetition itself, although the introduction of the new element—a very Rota-ish sweetly melancholic waltz—perhaps finally inflects the recapitulation more toward gentle pathos.

More commonly, Rota's early scores are organized on the principle of theme and variations. This has affinities with the use of leitmotifs more widely in film, but not only are Rota's themes less tied to characters than in some other versions,[19] but their elaboration constitutes true musical variations not just changes in instrumentation. This is especially clear when familiar musical material is used as a point of departure (for example, a music hall song in *Mio figlio professore* [My Son the Professor, 1946], Negro spirituals in *Senza pietà* [Pitiless, 1947], and the 1941 hit "Mattinata fiorentina" in *È primavera . . .* [Spring Is Here, 1949]). In *Molti sogni per le strade* (Many Dreams along the Way, 1948), a love tune established in the credits (over the names of the two stars, Massimo Girotti and Anna Magnani) keeps being hinted at by snatches and phrases but only gets a full statement toward the end; this fits the development of the narrative (an out-of-sorts married couple who finally rekindle their love), but it also has a musical logic, the final delivery of a promise of melodic fulfillment that has been repeatedly deferred.

An especially complex example is provided by *Campane a martello* (Alarm Bells, 1948). A number of original themes are gradually introduced, themes that we might characterize as a descending melancholic/tragic melody, a *meridionale* tune, a love theme, and comic material. These are then variously combined, sometimes with new melodic material (for example, the descending theme with a theme reminiscent of the second subject of the second movement of Dvořák's Ninth Symphony, acting in *Campane a martello*, as in the symphony, as a quickening offsetting of the solemnity of the first theme), sometimes using only already established material (for example, the descending theme punctuated by the comic material). The last six minutes of the film interweave all the elements, although all take their tone from the descending theme, thus bringing the score to a conclusion on a note of harmonic resolution. While the score of *Campane a martello* would probably not stand alone as a concert piece, it can be described, as I have just tried to show, in purely musical terms. All the above is relevant to the story of two reformed prostitutes (Gina Lollobrigida and Yvonne Sanson), obliged to return to the former's native Ischia, much to the pleasure of her abandoned fiancé but the disapproval of the local dignitaries. However, the score is neither subordinate to the actions and details of the narrative nor is it in dialectical counterpoint to it; rather, it provides a set of colors, flavors, or tones to the film. If in *Campane a martello* stars, plot situations, character types, and conventions of entering and identifying within the diegesis all pull us toward direct emotional engagement, the music offers a perspective on it (plaintive but not downcast) that is no less engaging or affective. It is a kind of irony, but one that encourages attachment rather than detachment.

The affective keys provided for *Un americano in vacanza, Molti sogni per le strade*, and *Campane a martello*, if not very precisely synchronized to the plots, are in tune with their basic directions. However, Rota's practice can be more disjunctive (though never, I think, disruptive).

Probably the most famous instance of this is the main theme[20] in the *Godfather* films. This is a waltz, often nostalgic in its instrumentation (blowsy trumpet or mandolins), with a tendency toward melancholy in the way each phrase ends on a dying fall, but also sometimes sweet to the point of comic when the $3/4$ time is brought to the fore, and in any case always ostensibly at odds with the cold violence and eventual bleakness of the narrative. The most vivid example is perhaps the arrangement of this theme for quiet trumpet and music box over the horse's-head-in-the-bed scene. Such procedures have become commonplace since *The Godfather* (for example, the use of Samuel Barber's Adagio for Strings in *Platoon*, and the scores of John Ottman for *The Usual Suspects* and Christopher Young for *Copycat*), but they were seen as innovative at the time of the first *Godfather* film. They often suggest a sensuous or sentimental relationship to cruelty and carnage, that is, another kind of ironic attachment, both able to see how terrible the events are and yet understanding, too, their emotional appeal, something characteristic of Coppola's work.[21]

The violent context of *The Godfather* was unusual for Rota, but there is a similar disjunctive relationship in much of his work. Sometimes a precise narrative point may be made, but it is done so unobtrusively. There is a scene in *Rocco e i suoi fratelli* (Rocco and His Brothers, 1960), in which Rocco (Alain Delon) is called into the office of the boxing trainer, Cecchi (Paolo Stoppa), to discuss the progress of his brother Simone (Renato Salvatori). Rocco and Simone are migrants from Southern Italy; Simone, the elder of the two, has become a successful boxer but is ruining his career by smoking, drinking, and womanizing; Rocco hates boxing, though he has a gift for it. When Simone goes tragically and criminally downhill, Rocco has to become a boxer to save his brother financially and avenge the family's honor. In other words, in terms of the film's thematic schema, Rocco acts out of old, Southern, feudal values of familial loyalty and in the process destroys the possibility that he might adapt to modern, Northern ways. In the scene concerned, Rocco and Cecchi speak about the problem of Simone, and at one point one of the film's leitmotivic themes comes in barely perceptibly on the soundtrack, its entry hidden in the sound event of the word "Rocco" and the music played very quietly, without insistence that it be noticed. The motif "Paese mio," which has been established in the credits, is a folksong (nevertheless written by Rota) from Puglia, the heel of Italy, which sings of longing to return home. Its entrance in the scene with Cecchi, in which there is no talk of home or Puglia, and in which nothing in the rather desultory dialogue calls it forth, nonetheless signals the association of Rocco's emotional attachment to the South with his self-destroying decision to become a boxer. It adds an overtone of emotional understanding, a hint of foreboding (but not at all expressed as ominous premonition), through which to chart, if you want, the onset of Rocco's tragedy.

I want to end with a scene from a much less familiar film, *Vita da cani* (A Dog's Life, 1950), which seems to me perhaps the most exquisite expression of this kind of procedure. The film tells of a number of young women who join a variety show. One, Franca (Tamara Lees), is at the start of the film engaged to be married to a garage mechanic, Carlo (Marcello Mastroianni). The young couple visit the flat they are to move into after they marry. Franca looks around balefully at the sparsely furnished rooms, the dust, and the beetles; Carlo talks eagerly of his new invention to improve petrol consumption. She is indifferent, but to his surprise ("You always said we should wait"), she invites him to join her on the bed. The scene ends.

The scene is in its subject matter typical of that strand in neorealism dealing with ordinary people in ordinary settings without particular sociopolitical significance (see also *Molti sogni per le strade, Una domenica d'agosto* [A Sunday in August, 1950], and *Cronache di poveri amanti* [Chronicles of Poor Lovers], 1954). However, three things give it a very particular feeling. One is the casting of Tamara Lees. Mastroianni was already established as a minor star, playing to perfection, as here, the classic *ragazzo per bene* (nice young man), but Lees, with only a couple of movies behind her, suggested something much less familiar. Displaying considerable but distinctly Nordic beauty (she was, in fact, of English and Russian parentage), she, with her almond shaped eyes and slim figure, suggests a melancholy and refinement at odds with the earthily Italian beauties such as Gina Lollobrigida, Sophia Loren, Silvana Mangano, and Franca Marzi that were so much part of postwar and quasi-neorealist culture.[22] Secondly, the cinematography, by Mario Bava, creates evidently crafted and slightly mysterious patterns of clearly delineated chiaroscuro. Thirdly, there is the nondiegetic music, a delicate waltz. These three elements—Lees, the lighting, and the waltz—create a disjunction between the banality and relative cheerfulness of the scene and the elements' affective qualities: melancholy, mystery, delicacy.

The use of a waltz was already an anachronistic choice in 1949. The melody has basically an AABA structure, but each of the A parts is subtly different so that it might more properly be rendered as $A_1A_2BA_3$. The basic line of each A mounts up and down in a series of little spiraling phrases. A_1 is on violins; A_2 uses woodwinds and both goes higher and ends lower; A_3 uses lower strings, predominantly cellos, and goes even higher but is slower, with a clear rallentando at the end. Each A ends with more separated notes, emphasizing the waltz rhythm. Thus the melody repeatedly soars a little and sinks back, but not back into the stillness or calm of sadness but rather to the charm of the gently suggested underlying rhythm. This offsetting of upward against sinking phrases and both against an endearing rhythm suggests an affective register that encompasses yearning rather than keen longing, aspiration rather than ambition, melancholy rather than tragedy, ruefulness rather than self-pity. All of this is very different from the dull, drab apartment and Carlo's banal conversation.

The music occupies the length of the scene and is dovetailed to its beginning and end. In the previous scene, Carlo picks up Franca on his bicycle from outside the factory where she works; the first spiraling phrase accompanies the movement of the bicycle off screen, the movement of music and the bicycle alike seeming to be at the same pace. At the end of the scene, the music slows down as Carlo moves toward Franca on the bed and fades as they start to kiss. Yet despite this care over the beginning and end, in between the music does not follow Carlo and Franca's movements about the flat or the shifts in feeling between them.

It would be possible to interpret the music as expressing her feelings. Her dissatisfaction with the prospect of a safe marriage to a nice young man on the outskirts of Milan has been indicated in the previous scene, and the romantic tenor of the music could be taken to express what she is feeling in the face of the dreary prospect of living with poor old Carlo in this characterless flat. Later in the film, the theme is reprised. Franca has had a brief career in the variety show and entered a loveless marriage to a rich man; Carlo has become a successful engineer who works for Franca's husband; Franca meets Carlo the day after her wedding; realizing her love for him and the emptiness of the choices she has made, she kills herself. In both sequences you could take the music as expressing what she is feeling, but the music seems to me too ironic and melancholic, not wholehearted or passionate enough, for that. Instead it points to aspects of her character—sympathetic, feeling, affectionate—while also suggesting the limitations of her dreams, their anachronistic prettiness and melancholy undertow.

Though the film's music is consummately handled and especially interestingly developed by Rota, this approach to film music is not unique to him. It points more broadly to the way the affective qualities of music do not so much express or underscore a film's explicit narrative material as suggest or explore affective relationships—not what the characters feel, but what filmmakers propose spectators may feel about what they feel. This may in turn suggest two avenues of thought in relation to film and narrative.

First, it suggests a different way of thinking about spectatorship and character than that proposed by much psychoanalytic film theory. Rather than treating characters as objects of projection and identification, we may instead relate to them much more as we do with people in reality: with interest, sympathy, affection, adoration, or even frustration and despair, but not often actually imagining ourselves as them.

Second, it is also suggestive in relation to the basic paradox of feeling and film, and indeed art generally. When we attend or respond to the extra-semiotic, amodal dimension of an artwork, we are never entirely within extra-semiotic or amodal reality precisely because we are in art and discourse, we are in what is already only analogous to affect, what is always already worked, historical, contingent. Art can never quite get affect, partly because it can never actually *be* affect, only its formal and conventionalized objectification. I believe everyone knows this intuitively; everyone knows that art falls short of the real. Yet still we respond, still we are moved. The complexity of music's role in film, especially when flexed toward parallelism and disjunction, makes evident the complexity of our relationship with narrative involvement in film. We are at once within and without it, longing for it yet also knowing we can never quite fully inhabit it; we are ironically attached. It may tell us something not just about how music can work in film, but also why we care at all.

NOTES

1. Luigi Pellizzoni, "Musica e cinema un rapporto 'difficile'," in Enzo Kermol and Mariselda Tessarolo, eds., *La music del cinema* (Rome: Bulzoni, 1996), p. 25.

2. Claudia Gorbman, *Unheard Melodies: Narrative Film Music* (Bloomington: Indiana University Press, 1987).

3. From "Colloquio con Nino Rota," in Sergio Miceli, *Musica e cinema nella cultura del Novecento* (Florence: Sansoni, 2000); quoted here from Roberto Calabretto, "Luchino Visconti: *Senso*, musica di Nino Rota," in *L'undicesima musa. Nino Rota e i suoi media*, ed. Veniero Rizzardi (Rome: RAI–ERI, 2001), pp. 75–76.

4. Ibid., pp. 75–135.

5. This difficulty pertaining to jazz music was illustrated at the Beyond the Soundtrack conference by Krin Gabbard, whose paper discusses the eclipse of Miles Davis's famous jazz score for *Ascenseur pour l'échafaud* (Elevator to the Gallows, Louis Malle, France 1958) whenever dialogue or narrative events became of paramount importance.

6. I am drawing especially on Stephen Davies, *Musical Meaning and Expression* (Ithaca, NY: Cornell University Press, 1994); Kathleen Marie Higgins, *The Music of Our Lives* (Philadelphia: Temple University Press, 1991); Peter Kivy, *The Corded Shell: Reflections on Musical Expression* (Princeton, NJ: Princeton University Press, 1980); Susan McClary, *Conventional Wisdom: The Content of Musical Form* (Berkeley and Los Angeles: University of California Press, 2000); Leonard B. Meyer, *Emotion and Meaning in Music* (Chicago: University of Chicago Press, 1956); and Jenefer Robinson, ed., *Music and Meaning* (Ithaca, NY: Cornell University Press, 1997). Specifically in relation to film, music, and expression, see also Cristina Cano

and Giorgio Cremonini, *Cinema e musica. Il racconto per sovrapposizioni* (Florence: Vallecchi, 1990); Kay Dickinson, ed., *Movie Music: The Film Reader* (London: Routledge, 2003); Gorbman, *Unheard Melodies*; Kathryn Kalinak, *Settling the Score: Music and the Classical Hollywood Film* (Madison: University of Wisconsin Press, 1992); and Peter Kivy, "Music in the Movies: A Philosophical Enquiry," in *Film Theory and Philosophy*, ed. Richard Allen and Murray Smith (Oxford: Oxford University Press, 1997), pp. 308–28.

7. Nonetheless, Kivy, *The Corded Shell*, and Anthony Newcomb, "Sound and Feeling," *Critical Inquiry* 10 (1980), pp. 623–41, for instance argue that music can express particular emotions.

8. Suzanne Langer, *Feeling and Form* (New York: Scribner's, 1953), p. 27.

9. For example, Davies, *Musical Meaning and Expression*; and Higgins, *The Music of Our Lives*.

10. Kivy, "Music in the Movies," proposes, in the context of a discussion of music and film, an interesting way of considering this in terms of the emotions that leak out despite the management of emotion in both everyday life and actorly performance. Music, he suggests, works with this dynamic, and it does so especially valuably in relation to character and performance in film.

11. Cf., for instance, Davies, *Musical Meaning and Expression*; Jo Urmson, "Representation in Music," *Royal Institute of Philosophy Lectures* 6 (1973), pp. 132–46; Howard Vernon, "On Representational Music," *Noûs* 6 (1972), pp. 41–54; and Kendall Walton, "Listening with Imagination: Is Music Representational?" in Robinson, ed., *Music and Meaning*, pp. 57–82.

12. From the essay "A New Laocoön: Artistic Composites and the Talking Film," first published in 1938 but taken here from Rudolf Arnheim, *Film as Art* (London: Faber and Faber, 1958).

13. Theodor W. Adorno and Hanns Eisler, *Composing for the Films* (London: Athlone Press, 1994). Among the many discussions of this text, see Gorbman, *Unheard Melodies*, pp. 99–109; and Philip Rosen, "Adorno and Film Music: Theoretical Notes on *Composing for the Films*," *Yale French Studies* 60 (1980), pp. 157–82.

14. Interoffice memo, March 1940; quoted in the introduction to James Buhler, Caryl Flynn, and David Neumeyer, eds., *Music and Cinema* (Hanover, NH: Wesleyan University Press, 2000), p. 15.

15. "Nei film di fare una musica . . . che sia a sé stante come musica, che si affianchi al film, non che si sottometta, che vi si adegui solo materialement." From an unpublished interview with Guido Vergani, quoted in Pier Marco De Santi, *Nino Rota. Le immagini e la musica* (Florence: Giunti, 1992), p. 46.

16. "Esprima sopratutto lo spirito del film più che la materialità della successione delle immagini." In an interview with Giorgio Saponaro for the Pugliese edition of *Il Tempo* (5 November 1967), p. 4; reprinted in Dinko Fabris, ed., *Nino Rota compositore del nostro tempo* (Bari: Orchestra Sinfonica di Bari, 1987), pp. 31–32.

17. Macario plays a demobilized, unemployed conscript in postwar Italy who takes on whatever jobs turn up, each new direction wittily echoed in appropriate, lightly parodic music. At one point he gets a job from a political party painting wall slogans; as different people pass by Macario nervously alters the slogan to fit what

he takes to be their affiliation, each alteration accompanied by squawky, perky versions of, among other pieces, "The Internationale," "Deutschland über alles," a Sousa march, and an operetta tune. Here—and, with Rota, more often in comedy than elsewhere—each twist in the music underscores one on the screen.

18. Rota of course worked in conjunction with directors and producers, but I have here for the sake of brevity mainly written as if he made the decisions about the form and use of music in the films. It is the case that he was remarkably adaptable to circumstances, and yet there is also a consistency of practice across all his film music output.

19. Cf. the discussion of Rota's work with Fellini by Claudia Gorbman, "Music as Salvation: Notes on Fellini and Rota," *Film Quarterly* 28.2 (Winter 1974/1975), pp. 17–25.

20. The main theme discussed here is not be confused with the love theme that, as "Speak Softly Love," became a hit song when recorded by Andy Williams, Johnny Mathis, and others. This was the theme that Rota—as was his wont—had recycled from an earlier film (*Fortunella,* 1957), which cost him the Oscar for best original score, the Academy of Motion Picture Awards deeming that the score was, after all, not original. Rota's endless autoplagiarism, as well as his propensity for pastiche and allusion, are further aspects of a practice that is less ineluctably tied to the material proposed by narrative and image.

21. Rota had not wanted to write the music for *The Godfather;* he was busy, as usual, did not write music for mafia movies, and did not know who Coppola was (quite reasonably—Coppola only became famous with *The Godfather*). He didn't answer letters and calls and eventually demanded that unreasonable conditions be met, such as that he would not have to come to the United States to compose or oversee the recording of the score, which he hoped would put Coppola off. Coppola prevailed over him and also over Paramount (who wanted Henry Mancini). One feels that Coppola must have sensed the affinity between his procedures and Rota's.

22. On neorealism and such women stars, see Alberto Farassino, "Il cinema come premio," in Alberto Farassino, ed., *Neorealismo. Cinema italiano 1945–1949* (Turin: E. D. T. P., 1989), pp. 140–41.

15 White Face, Black Noise

Miles Davis and the Soundtrack

KRIN GABBARD

Although Miles Davis died at the age of sixty-five in 1991, he is more prominent then ever in American culture. Like Oprah Winfrey, James Earl Jones, and very few other black Americans, Davis no longer raises associations with African American culture in the minds of most white Americans. *Kind of Blue*, his album from 1959, is the best-selling jazz record in history and is itself the subject of two books. Numerous movies have put Davis's music on the soundtrack, both before and after his death and with and without his cooperation. At least two novels, a fiction film, and several television documentaries have been devoted to him, not to mention at least five biographies.

As the twentieth century gave way to the twenty-first, Davis's image as well as the sound of his trumpet took on a life of their own. He is, for example, a startling presence in a television commercial for Mercedes-Benz that received wide distribution in the summer of 2001. An announcer asks, "If you were loading the Ark today, what would you bring?" After animals walk up the gangplank two by two, a line of people follow them carrying van Gogh's *Sunflowers*, Michelangelo's *David*, piano scores of Bach and Mozart, and a grand piano. They also carry artifacts that do not belong to high culture such as an Apple computer and a small refrigerator full of expensive ice cream. As the camera cuts quickly from one item to another, we see a pair of hands carrying a stack of LPs with Miles Davis's *Birth of the Cool* prominently displayed on top. The commercial ends as two silver E-Class Mercedes drive up the gangplank and the rain begins.

This commercial reflects a trend that was especially prominent just before and after the year 2000. It may have culminated with Ken Burns's eighteen-hour celebration of jazz on public television in 2001. Jazz (or at least older jazz—the *Birth of the Cool* sessions were recorded more than fifty years ago) has become the peer of high art. Perhaps the man in the commercial with his stack of old jazz LPs is meant to be associated with the ice cream and the computer, but I doubt it. The camera deliberately focuses tightly on the LPs, *not* on the person carrying them, just as the camera had focused on the names of Bach and Mozart on the books of scores. Jazz, especially when it's packaged with the iconic image of the ultra-cool Miles Davis on the cover, can symbolize affluence and elegance in the same way as Michelangelo's *David*, van Gogh's *Sunflowers*, and the music of Mozart. And it is significant that the old photograph of Miles Davis makes him the only black person whose work is being carried onto the Ark. In a commercial for a product aimed squarely at upper-middle-class Americans, the blackness and "jazzness" of Miles Davis have made him a valuable icon for a company trying to sell status symbols.

While Mercedes-Benz has made Davis the peer of Mozart, van Gogh, and Michelangelo, the cable channel VH1 has placed him in the august company of the Beatles, Bob Dylan, and the Beach Boys. In the early 1990s, the pop culture specialists at VH1 made up their list of the "100 Greatest Artists of Rock 'n' Roll." In that list, Miles Davis is ranked No. 39, between Elvis Costello (38) and Michael Jackson (40). Then, in another of VH1's blandly provocative lists, the "100 Greatest Albums of Rock 'n' Roll," Miles Davis is represented by not one but two items: *Bitches Brew* comes in at No. 64, and *Kind of Blue* is 66.

No other figure from popular culture is represented in the Mercedes-Benz ad, and unless we wish to argue that Steely Dan, Stevie Wonder, and Joni Mitchell play jazz, no other jazz artist appears in either of VH1's rock and roll lists. Just as Davis becomes the peer of Mozart, Michelangelo, and van Gogh in the Mercedes-Benz ad, he is in the same league with Janis Joplin, Kurt Cobain, and Crosby Stills and Nash, all of whom he outranks in the VH1 list of the Greatest Artists of Rock 'n' Roll. The image of no other artist is as omnipresent in the popular imagination. This may be at least in part because Davis worked very hard at managing how people saw him. Thanks in part to the interventions of Debbie Ishlom, a resourceful publicist at Columbia who helped construct an image for Davis in the 1950s, the trumpeter was as much involved with controlling his own visual identity as he was with controlling his music.

Toward the end of his life, however, Davis was less concerned about his image, even if he complained loudly about the photograph on the back cover of his autobiography—he said that he was smiling too broadly. But Davis also began appearing in television commercials (in Japan), and took acting jobs in an episode of the television program *Miami Vice* and in *Dingo*, an Australian movie that appeared in theaters in 1992, a year after his death.

He also appeared in the 1988 film *Scrooged*, briefly joining several other musicians in a delicately hip version of "We Three Kings of Orient Are." The song was appropriate for a film that takes place on Christmas Eve, but Davis seems out of place performing on a street corner in Manhattan. As the soon-to-be-transformed miser based on Charles Dickens's Scrooge, Bill Murray ridicules the musicians, even shouting, "Great! Rip off the hicks, why dontcha? Did you learn that song yesterday?" With Davis are David Sanborn, Paul Shaffer, and Larry Carlton. The camera reveals a hand-lettered sign in Davis's trumpet case: "Help the starving musicians."

Since almost everyone recognizes Davis and his trumpet and probably the three other musicians as well, few are likely to misunderstand the scene in *Scrooged*. The joke is on the self-involved philistine played by Bill Murray as well as on the extremely successful musicians who, unlike many jazz artists, are certainly not starving. But meanings are not always so clear in the other films in which the trumpet of Miles Davis can be heard. There are major differences among (1) films in which Davis was in control of the music, (2) films for which he recorded music without knowing how the music would function, and (3) films in which someone else put an old recording by Davis on the soundtrack. It makes a great deal of difference, for example, when black musicians invisibly provide background for a film about white people, especially when the film may conceal a racial agenda of its own. Many American films have appropriated the music of the African American Davis while sidestepping any overt engagement with the racial issues that are essential to understanding Davis's history. Although it is possible to accept or even celebrate the film industry's lack of concern about the color of the musicians playing on movie soundtracks, the constant use of black music in films about whites needs to be questioned if only because it is so seldom mentioned by film critics and others from the American film industry.

A touchstone film for assessing Davis's movie music, however, comes from France: *Ascenseur pour l'échafaud*, usually translated as *Elevator to the Gallows* (British title: *Lift to the Scaffold;* alternate American title: *Frantic*). When the young French director Louis Malle invited Davis to improvise music for the film, the trumpeter went into a Paris studio with three French musicians (René Urtreger, piano; Barney Wilen, tenor saxophone; and Pierre Michelot, bass), as well as the American expatriate drummer Kenny Clarke. This group, with which Davis had been touring Europe for several months, was afforded the same privileges as almost every film composer in mainstream movies since the 1930s: they were given a complete copy of the film and allowed to put their own music where they thought it worked best. The musicians actually improvised as they watched the film. The CD of the music for *Elevator to the Gallows*, reissued in 1988 with several alternate takes, reveals how many times Davis and his sidepeople went through the exercise until they knew they had it right. And in many ways they succeeded. Thanks largely to the music, the film won the prestigious Prix Louis Delluc in 1957.

Elevator to the Gallows, however, contains a stern lesson for anyone seeking the perfect marriage of jazz and cinema. In only one scene does the music really transform the images on the screen, specifically the moment when the film's female protagonist, Florence (Jeanne Moreau), slowly walks through the Paris night while Davis and his quintet read her mind with their improvisations. Florence has conspired with her lover Julien (Maurice Ronet) to kill her husband, a wealthy industrialist. After Julien has carried out the carefully planned murder in the victim's own office, he prepares to drive away to meet Florence. But once he has arrived at his car, he looks up at the office building where the dead body remains undiscovered and sees that the rope he used for surreptitious entry can still be seen from the street. Leaving the motor of his car running, he reenters the building and is immediately trapped in the elevator when the custodian shuts down the power as the workday comes to an end. The young florist who works across the street and her petty thief boyfriend take the car for a joyride while Julien is desperately looking for a way out of the elevator. A few blocks down the street, Florence sees the pair driving off in Julien's car, but she sees only the young woman in the passenger seat. She suspects that the driver is Julien, but she cannot be certain.

The director has written a scene for Florence that perfectly accommodates the improvisations of a jazz group. (Louis Malle did not know that Davis would consent to provide the music until after the film was almost finished.) There is no dialogue while the camera follows Florence for several minutes through the streets of Paris, only a series of shots of the face and body of Florence. As she wonders if her husband is dead, if Julien has betrayed her, and if she will ever see her lover again, Davis solos on his trumpet. Many critics have pointed out how jazz instrumentalists—especially African American jazz instrumentalists—make their instruments sound like the human voice. At one point as Davis plays for Florence, Davis's trumpet sounds almost as if it's singing in French. We could argue that Davis is engaging in a dialogue with the character, trying to find a musical means for expressing what she is feeling. Florence utters only one word of dialogue in this scene, when she sees a car that looks like Julien's. She calls out his name, only to see that the car is being driven by a man she does not know. At this point Davis lays low, holding a long note as the man gets out of the car and the audience has a moment to sort out whether or not Florence has found her lover. Davis returns to his agitated but soulful improvisation when the heroine realizes that the driver is not Julien and continues her slow walk through the city. Davis obviously knew that music must not get in the way when the audience expects a crucial plot point.

But this is the problem with jazz in the cinema. If it's too good—if we actually find ourselves listening to the music—it's no good. Film theorists know this as well as the composers of movie music. Since the early days of cinema, film scores have been carefully relegated to the background, only swelling up for a moment or two when the audience is meant to feel what the characters are feeling. But even on these occasions, composers have prevented the music from calling attention to itself by making it sound like other movie music. The codes for film music were established early in the 1930s by a small group of composers, almost all of them schooled in the European music of the late romantic period. Max Steiner, Miklós Rózsa, and Erich Korngold transformed Mahler, Wagner, Richard Strauss, and Borodin for the cinema.[1]A large part of the film audience already knew this music from radio and from the piano in the parlor—they knew when the music was telling then to be sad, to feel happy, or to fear the worst. With these codes in place, audiences did not need to think long about what they were hearing, especially when the codes were completely consistent with what was happening on the screen. Claudia Gorbman has described the standard film score as invisible and "inaudible."[2] In other words, the music is meant to be felt and not really listened to.

Many who went to *Elevator to the Gallows* expecting to see a suspense story about two attractive people hoping to get away with murder may have sat through Jeanne Moreau's night walk without paying attention to the music. On one level, the music that Davis created for the film gestures toward the codes that were already well established in the history of film music. Few in the audience were likely baffled, wondering what the music was doing there behind the action. On the other hand, the music is completely faithful to a jazz idiom. Those who know the music can hear the improvised solos and the group interactions that only Miles Davis could create. But the sequence with Florence on the streets of Paris is the only scene in the film in which the band plays for more than a few minutes. It is practically an anomaly. Virtually every other musical moment in *Ascenseur* is brief and unremarkable. We can celebrate a few nearly perfect minutes when jazz and the cinema elegantly complement each other, but we cannot expect it to work for more than those few minutes.

Ashley Kahn has suggested that the music for *Elevator to the Gallows* has the modal feel that Davis used again two years later in recordings such as "Flamenco Sketches" on the *Kind of Blue* album.[3] I would argue that the practice of supplying music for specific moments in a film teaches the artist to avoid conventional gestures of beginning, middle, and end that go with the standard chord structure of a popular song. Working in films may have been partially responsible for Davis's idea of creating improvisations free of conventional song structures at the *Kind of Blue* session. I would also argue, contra the standard wisdom of the jazz purist, that the music for *Elevator to the Gallows* is best understood as part of a movie and not as stand-alone music. Davis was creating specific sounds to go with specific images. As an African American jazz artist, he is somewhat stereotypically associated with urban nightlife in the French film, but the filmmakers granted a great deal of control to Miles Davis, and the result is something much more than a racial stereotype. It is the unique statement of a black artist working well outside the boundaries that usually contain African American jazz musicians.

Thirty years after *Elevator to the Gallows,* Davis was again making music for a movie, but with much less involvement in the process. Working with keyboardist Robert Irving III on *Street Smart,* directed by Jerry Schatzberg in 1987, Davis simply laid down a number of tracks in the studio and left it to Irving and the music supervisor to put the music into the film. As a result, the music often seems extraneous, entirely unlike what is heard in *Elevator to the Gallows.* In one scene, Davis's music simply stops and gives way to a familiar recording by Aretha Franklin. Christopher Reeve, playing a newspaper reporter, is interviewing a prostitute played by Kathy Baker. Although it is not the reporter's intention, he ends up having sex with her as Franklin's "You Make Me Feel Like a Natural Woman" swells on the soundtrack, overwhelming the dialogue and Davis's doodling, which was already very much in the background.

The introduction of the Franklin song at a crucial romantic moment in *Street Smart* is an excellent example of how the music of black Americans is recruited to sexualize the lives of white Americans in Hollywood films. Think of the voice of Johnny Hartman enhancing the love scenes between Clint Eastwood and Meryl Streep in *The Bridges of Madison County* (1995) or Ray Charles and choir performing "You Don't Know Me" while Bill

Murray and Andie McDowell fall in love in *Groundhog Day* (1993). (See my book *Black Magic* for many other examples.) Although it would not be the case a few years later, in *Street Smart* a recording by Davis is considered inadequate for a love scene. Davis's work was therefore replaced by the more accessible music of Aretha Franklin when Kathy Baker begins making love to Christopher Reeve.

In 1990, working with composer Jack Nitzsche, Davis provided music for Dennis Hopper's *The Hot Spot*. Dennis Hopper met Jack Nitzsche in 1969 when Hopper directed *Easy Rider*, with its brief appearance by Phil Spector. Nitzsche and Spector were producing rock and roll artists at the time, but Nitzsche went on to provide some of the most compelling music ever created for American films. In *One Flew Over the Cuckoo's Nest, Blue Collar, Cutter's Way, Cannery Row, The Indian Runner*, and many others, Nitzsche found unusual ways to transform the action through music. A few months before he died in 2000, Nitzsche spoke to Philip Brophy about working with Davis. He recalled Davis with genuine affection. At one point he exclaimed, "I loved Miles. God, I miss him."

In the liner notes for the soundtrack CD of *The Hot Spot*, Dennis Hopper claims that Davis had once punched out Hopper's heroin dealer and then told Hopper that he would kill him if he ever did drugs again. It was Hopper's idea to create music for *The Hot Spot* by matching Davis's trumpet with the blues guitar and vocals of John Lee Hooker. Eventually Hopper and Nitzsche brought in another blues singer and guitarist, Taj Mahal. Although Nitzsche did not think that Davis would agree to work on Hopper's film, let alone with straight blues artists, Nitzsche dutifully asked Davis if he wanted the job. To his surprise, Davis said yes. John Lee Hooker showed up a day ahead of Davis, and when he was laying down some tracks in the studio with Nitzsche, it became clear that John Lee Hooker, like many blues musicians, could only play three chords. In his conversation with Philip Brophy, Nitzsche said that he then called Davis in despair, saying, "Miles, John Lee Hooker only knows three chords. What are we going to do?" Nitzsche said that Davis replied, "Am I in your movie? How can that be bad?"[4]

For *The Hot Spot*, Davis was once again uninterested in watching the film while he made music as he had with *Elevator to the Gallows*, but he was working with Jack Nitzsche, who had a print of the film and knew exactly what should go where. One of the moments when the music is most noticeable is comparable to the scene when Jeanne Moreau wanders through the night in the earlier film. Don Johnson plays Harry, a drifter who has arrived in a small Texas town for reasons that the film never bothers to establish. Although he has become involved with two women, one pure and innocent, the other a femme fatale, Harry still has time left over to rob the local bank. His plan is to set fire to a building across the street in order to create a distraction while he empties the cash drawers. As in *Elevator to the Gallows*, Davis and the other musicians jam demurely during a long, dialogue-free sequence while Harry carries out the bank job. Thanks to Nitzsche's editing, Davis's piquant solo suddenly stops when an elderly blind African American man wanders into the bank. Taj Mahal croons a cappella while we wonder what the blind man is going to do. After Johnson tiptoes around the man and out of the bank with the stolen money, Davis's trumpet and Hooker's guitar kick in again. It is especially intriguing that the blind man is black. In fact, he's the only black person in the entire film. I associate his blindness with the invisibility of black musicians in so many American films about white people. The blindness of the audience toward blacks on the soundtrack is displaced onto the black man.

The Talented Mr. Ripley (1999) finds complex strains of eroticism in Davis's music. Directed by Anthony Minghella, the film absents black people almost completely even as it borrows liberally from African American culture. In the 1950s, Tom Ripley (Matt Damon) meets the wealthy parents of Dickie Greenleaf (Jude Law) at a party on a terrace overlooking New York's Central Park. Although he is employed as an attendant in a washroom and never attended college, Tom is an accomplished classical pianist. To accompany a singer at the party, he has borrowed a blazer with the insignia of Princeton University. When the Greenleafs ask him if he knew their son while he was at Princeton, Tom leaps at the opportunity to pose as an aristocrat. He soon accepts a thousand dollars from Greenleaf Senior to bring his son back from Italy, where Dickie lives in a seaside village with his girlfriend Marge (Gwyneth Paltrow). Instead of participating in his father's shipping business, Dickie enjoys playing jazz on his saxophone as well as sailing, swimming, and dallying with at least one of the attractive local women.

In order to enter Dickie's affluent world, Tom must, paradoxically, put aside his passion for classical music and learn jazz, the music that Dickie loves but that the elder Greenleaf calls "insolent noise." In early scenes Tom clings to conventional 1950s hierarchies of taste, practically holding his nose as he learns to recognize the playing styles of Charlie Parker, Dizzy Gillespie, Chet Baker, and others. In a comment that resonates with the homoerotic role that Baker's music plays later in the film, Tom says, "I can't tell if it's a man or a woman," as he listens to Baker singing "My Funny Valentine." Indeed, throughout much of the film, jazz marks Tom and Dickie almost as strongly in terms of race as in terms of sexuality. The play with race and sexuality is immediately apparent when Tom first encounters Dickie and Marge on the beach near their house. When he approaches them in his bathing suit as they lounge in their beach chairs, the contrast between the perfectly tanned flesh of Dickie and Marge and the pale skin of Tom is so obvious that Dickie says, "You're so white!" Then to Marge, "Did you ever see a guy so white?" Tom makes the most of the situation, smilingly insisting that his color is just "primer" and an "undercoat," as if his whiteness were only temporary.

But like the pale-skinned protagonists in African American passing novels such as *The Autobiography of an Ex-Colored Man*,[5] *Plum Bun*,[6] and *Passing*,[7] as well as films such as *Pinky* (1949), *Show Boat* (1936 and 1951), and *Imitation of Life* (1934 and 1959), Tom does not change color so easily. Later he is suspected of being an imposter by Freddie Miles (Philip Seymour Hoffman), who senses immediately that Tom is not a member of the moneyed classes and certainly not someone with the contempt for upper-class decorum that Dickie exhibits in his bohemian passion for jazz. If *The Talented Mr. Ripley* borrows the passing narrative from African American culture, it relies even more heavily on black music to develop the character of Dickie. On several occasions Dickie plays boppish solos on his saxophone, and after the local woman with whom he had been having an affair becomes pregnant and drowns herself, he consoles himself by playing "You Don't Know What Love Is," a favored song among African American vocalists and musicians. The film endows Dickie with natural grace and a talent for expressing himself through music, qualities that many Americans associate with black people.

As the film progresses it becomes clear that Tom is not just an aspiring aristocrat posing as a white Negro in order to get close to Dickie Greenleaf; he is also a gay man passing as a heterosexual. *The Talented Mr. Ripley* is based on Patricia Highsmith's novel of the same title. Published in 1955, the novel includes a brief suggestion that Tom's interest in Dickie might be more than friendly when Marge asks Dickie if he thinks Tom is gay. Highsmith herself was a lesbian, and several of her novels directly addressed the homosexuality of her characters.

Minghella has enlarged the novel's gay subtext in subtle as well as obvious ways. Among the less overt references to gayness is the film's fascination with jazz trumpeter/vocalist Chet Baker and the Richard Rodgers / Lorenz Hart song, "My Funny Valentine," that Baker recorded and performed throughout his career. In the 1950s Baker won the hearts and minds of an audience that was large even by non-jazz standards. Some responded to his youthful beauty (he was regularly compared to James Dean); some heard depths of emotion and sensitivity in his understated singing and trumpet playing (his music epitomized the West Coast or "cool" school of postwar jazz); and, sadly, some cast him as jazz's Great White Hope, the anointed heir of Bix Beiderbecke and a paragon of the more sedate, less threatening strains of the jazz trumpet that have always coexisted alongside the more intense music associated with African Americans.

A charming sociopath who was accustomed to having everything his own way, Baker suggests a comparison with Jude Law's Dickie Greenleaf in the film version of *The Talented Mr. Ripley*. Like Baker, Dickie possesses youthful beauty and natural grace and unself-consciously carries great appeal for men as well as for women. Also like Baker, Dickie is accustomed to being adored and does little to repay the love he receives. In order to make an early, positive impression on Dickie, Tom pretends that several jazz LPs, including a copy of *Chet Baker Sings*, have accidentally dropped out of his briefcase. When Dickie picks up the Chet Baker LP, he says, "This is the best." Minghella may or may not have known Baker's biography well enough to see how much he shares with the Dickie of his film. Regardless, "My Funny Valentine" is an especially appropriate choice for Minghella's version of *The Talented Mr. Ripley*, if only because the lyrics are by Lorenz "Larry" Hart, a gay man who is clearly suggesting that heterosexual romance is a joke. When Tom uses his prodigious abilities as a mimic and sings in a Bakeresque voice ("You can't tell if it's a man or a woman") while Dickie and a group of male musicians accompany him, he enjoys the homoerotic thrill of sharing an intense moment with Dickie.

Although Tom reaches a pinnacle of sorts when Dickie's saxophone embroiders his appropriately androgynous performance of "My Funny Valentine," Miles Davis helps provide an even more significant jazz moment in the sexual tension between the two men. In a deeply homoerotic scene, full of tight close-ups and pregnant pauses, Tom and Dickie play chess while Dickie sits nude in the bathtub. The music is "Nature Boy," recorded by Charles Mingus in 1955 for his own Debut label and featuring the trumpet of Miles Davis. Still in his shirt and trousers, Tom runs his fingers through the warm bath water and says, "I'm cold, can I get in?" Slightly uncertain but not afraid to let a note of teasing into his response, Dickie says no. He then gets out of the tub, exposing his nude body to Tom as he walks away to pick up a towel. He looks over his shoulder to see that Tom is watching him in the mirror. Tom quickly turns away.

This is the turning point in Tom's erotic fortunes. For Dickie, Tom has become a burden, as much because of his emotional vulnerability as because of his need to keep Dickie on his own timetable. Moments after the scene with the bathtub and "Nature Boy," Tom is shut out of Dickie's life when Freddie Miles arrives and almost completely steals Dickie's attentions. When Freddie pulls up at the outdoor café in Rome where Dickie sits chatting with Tom, the music of a jazz saxophone seems to be coming out of his car radio. The music, however, continues uninterrupted into the next scene at a record store where Freddie seals himself into a listening booth with Dickie so that they can share a set of headphones. Tom is on the outside looking in, devastated that Dickie is much more in his element with Freddie. The music is "Tenor Madness," featuring the tenor saxophones of Sonny Rollins and John Coltrane, both African Americans. Freddie adopts an almost ghoulish posture as he slowly gyrates to the music and fixes his gaze on Tom, clearly aware that he is looking at a parvenu upstart. At this point, Dickie only wants to lose himself in the music and cares little about his schedule for the rest of the day. Nevertheless, Tom taps on the window of the listening booth to announce the departure time of the train they had planned to take back to Mongibello, clearly hoping that Dickie will join him. Freddie shakes his head and snorts with derisive laughter at Tom's joyless, compulsive behavior.

The switch from Davis's "Nature Boy" to "Tenor Madness" is as striking as the arrival of Freddie, played with immense confidence by Hoffman. Minghella has exploited all of the eroticism, yearning, and tension in the slow version of "Nature Boy" as well as the more boisterous, agonistic spirit of "Tenor Madness." In Mingus's "Nature Boy," Davis's trumpet, elegantly softened by the stemless harmon mute that was so often in its bell, plays over the delicate chimes of Teddy Charles's vibraphone, the subtle brush work of drummer Elvin Jones, and the steady heartbeat of Charles Mingus's bass. At this stage in his career, Davis was developing an intimate, even introverted approach to improvisation that was completely unlike the style of the extroverts who preceded him in the roster of great jazz trumpeters. And like Chet Baker at this same time, Davis was learning not to leave a song's melody behind for the sake of elaborate improvisation. Both trumpeters took the melodies seriously, as if they were singing rather than playing the songs. The album on which Mingus and Davis perform "Nature Boy" was released as *Blue Moods*. Listening to their collaboration today, one does not hear much tension between the bassist/leader and the trumpeter, but according to John Szwed, Davis would not walk the two blocks to the *Blue Moods* recording session because he had been promised a ride. "And once he got the ride, he told the driver, 'I hope I won't have to hit Mingus in the mouth.' "[8] The choice of the recording of "Nature Boy" from the *Blue Moods* session, with its looming tension between two men sharing a moment charged with musical eroticism, was especially appropriate for the scene in which Tom approaches Dickie in the bathtub. It even anticipates the additional tension of Freddie's arrival.

The unheard lyrics to "Nature Boy" contain the phrase, "The greatest thing you'll ever know, is just to love and be loved." Although Davis and Mingus were at odds when they recorded "Nature Boy," the song and its words have little in common with "Tenor Madness," taped one year later. "Tenor Madness" is the happy result of John Coltrane's decision to tag along with the rhythm section that Sonny Rollins took into the studio for a recording date on May 24, 1956. "Tenor Madness" consists of muscular, up-tempo blowing by Rollins and Coltrane, two larger-than-life tenor saxophonists who only recorded together on this one occasion and only on this one cut on the LP. If "Nature Boy" features one hornman speaking clearly about love while Tom tries to move closer to Dickie, "Tenor Madness" is the hot-blooded confrontation between two masters of the horn while Freddie barges in and snatches Dickie away from Tom. In each case, African American musicians are as essential to the film's meanings as are the passions for jazz exhibited by Dickie and Freddie.

In spite of his low tolerance of jazz, and despite the later scene in which Tom sheds tears at a performance of Tchaikovsky's *Eugene Onegin* after he has killed Dickie, the recording of "Nature Boy" seems to be entirely consistent with Tom's emotional yearnings. And yet the film never acknowledges the extent to which it allows music by Davis and other African American artists to work its magic on the characters. Even with all their passion for jazz, Dickie and Freddie have only the most superficial interactions with black people, a truth about two bohemian rich kids that the film also neglects to acknowledge.

An even more perversely color-blind use of Davis's music is in Gary Ross's *Pleasantville* (1998). The film has no African American actors whatsoever, and yet the white inhabitants of a 1950s TV sitcom are allowed to have a civil rights revolution of sorts. The premise of *Pleasantville* is that two teenagers from the present (Tobey Maguire and Reese Witherspoon) are magically transported into the black-and-white world of an old TV sitcom, "Pleasantville," clearly based on "Father Knows Best," which had successful runs on three different television networks between 1954 and 1963. While the nerdy David (Maguire) is out of place among his peers, Jennifer

(Witherspoon) leads a group of postmodern teenage girls and has no trouble attracting boys. Jennifer is appalled to be "stuck in Nerdville" when she and her brother arrive in Pleasantville, but when she sees the blandly attractive Skip drive by in his car, she quickly begins to find the town more interesting. To David's horror, she starts bringing color to the lives of the black-and-white people, at first by introducing them to sex. According to the logic of Ross's film, the people in Pleasantville only know as much about life as was shown on TV in the 1950s. Since they do not have sex, for example, they have never seen a double bed. And since no one ever reads a novel in the TV show, the books in the library have blank pages, and so on. As Ross is at pains to point out in his commentary on the DVD release of the film, the residents of Pleasantville turn colorful whenever they have some kind of transformative experience. Since young people are most open to change, and since sexuality makes for fast and fundamental transformations, the town's teenagers are the first to earn their colors. Later on, characters change color because they have become angry or highly emotional. After Jennifer hustles Skip off to Lover's Lane for his first sexual encounter, he sees a vivid red rose on a bush as he drives home. As Jennifer the sexual adventuress begins to influence behavior throughout the high school, color suddenly appears as a pink bubble of gum emerging from a girl's mouth and as a red taillight on a car from which hang the suggestively swaying limbs of young lovers. Everything else in these early scenes remains in black and white.

The film sets up a musical hierarchy as it works its way toward the most profound transformative moment. When Jennifer first begins seducing Skip exclusively in black and white, the audiences hears the "wholesome" voice of the white Pat Boone singing the pop ballad "Mr. Blue." Later, when the first traces of color begin to appear, audiences hear Gene Vincent, who might be called a "white black singer," hiccuping his way through "Be-Bop-a-Lula." As more people turn colorful, we hear the African American Lloyd Price shouting a grittier example of rock and roll, "Lawdy Miss Clawdy." Later on, as the young people in Pleasantville begin to realize that David knows much more about life than they do, they congregate in the soda shop where he works. Previously a brightly lit diner where teens listened to a jukebox and consumed ice cream sodas, the shop has become darker, with light filtered through Venetian blinds, giving the scene a film noir effect. As Ross points out, the place has been made to resemble a coffee shop where beatniks would have assembled back when the sitcom was first shown on television. Consistent with the soda shop's new ambience, the audience hears the Dave Brubeck Quartet playing "Take Five" as David arrives for work.

As Brubeck's quirky anthem of white hipness continues to play in the background, the young people in the shop ask David questions about what is outside Pleasantville. While the pop rock of Gene Vincent and Lloyd Price played behind scenes of sexual discovery, the film now associates jazz with thinking rather than with feeling. David soon discovers that one of the teens in the shop has been reading *Huckleberry Finn,* thanks to a halting attempt by Jennifer to tell the boy what ought to be inside a book with blank pages. Since she only read up until "the part about the raft," only the first pages of the book have, according to the film's logic, filled themselves in. David, however, has been more conscientious about his homework. The wide-eyed congregation of teenagers is suddenly obsessed with what happens to Huck and Jim.

The camera closes in on the face of the perky blonde cheerleader, Margaret (Marley Shelton), as she asks David to tell them what happens in the novel. As David begins to talk about Huck Finn and watches while all the remaining pages in the book are dutifully filled in, Brubeck's music gives way to a new recording. We then hear what is surely the most elegant music in the film and unquestionably one of the most important recordings in the history of American music, the Miles Davis Sextet's 1959 recording of "So What." *Pleasantville* disposes of the introductory duet between bassist Paul Chambers and pianist Bill Evans, the only white member of Davis's group at the time. The music starts abruptly with the second statement of the tune's sketchy melody as the three black hornmen (Davis, John Coltrane, and Cannonball Adderley on alto sax) answer the questions posed musically by the bassist with the two-note phrase that suggests the title, "So What." Ultimately, the audience only hears the solo of Davis, and even that has been edited down to roughly half its length, but Davis's solo occupies almost a full minute of *Pleasantville*'s soundtrack while a great deal happens on the screen. The elegant but vernacular sounds of Davis's trumpet accompany the discovery by the town's young people of a literature that is about as radical as the timid liberalism of the film is prepared to endorse. Even though David's interpretation of *Huckleberry Finn* is basically a conservative one, the film uses Davis's music to impart a sense of wonder and experimentation as David tells the town's teenagers about Huck.

In laying out the plot of the novel, David refers to Nigger Jim simply as "the slave." As the innocents sitting in the soda shop listen in wide-eyed anticipation, David explains that as Huck and Jim try "to get free, they see that they're free already." The film is telling us that freedom is internal and not about the daily conditions in which people actually live their lives. In his commentary, Ross says that *Huckleberry Finn* is a "picaresque adventure" about getting knowledge, an important theme he claims for his film. He also mentions the many times that the book has been banned, but he neglects to mention that the book is banned not because of politics or scatology but because of its repeated use of the word "nigger." In the 1950s there were no national movements to ban the book. Only after black students began making demands in the 1960s did the book begin to disappear from libraries and reading lists. The other book that David introduces to the curious young people, *Catcher in the Rye,* was in fact banned from school libraries in the 1950s, specifically for the explicit language used by the teenaged narrator. For Ross, however, the two controversial books are an appropriate pair to drive home his theme that knowledge—especially knowledge that is controversial or threatening—has the power to change people.

As the youthful residents of Pleasantville rapidly acquire color and line up at the library, the black-and-white city fathers attempt to control the transformations, even putting a "No Colored" sign in a shop window. Ultimately, David is arrested and put on trial in a courtroom scene that is clearly designed to recall a moment in *To Kill a Mockingbird* (1962) when the townspeople are strictly segregated: "colored" people sit in the courthouse balcony while white people—or, in the case of *Pleasantville,* black-and-white people—sit below on the ground floor. Taking the stand, David successfully provokes all the black-and-white characters into experiencing some strong emotion, thus turning all of them colored.

Pleasantville works hard at connecting political oppression and the anxieties about sex and race that have always been a part of American culture. At one point the black-and-white citizens of the town declare that the only permissible music is Johnny Mathis, Perry Como, Jack Jones, John Philip Sousa, and the "Star Spangled Banner." In the logic of the film, civil rights is about popular entertainment rather than the fundamental restructuring of American society. And in terms of the white appropriation of blackness, that's as far as it has to go. When David brings color to the town's more conservative citizens, he says, "It's in you, and you can't stop something that's inside you." Just as David suggested that the freedom sought by Nigger Jim was always already there inside him, he now reveals that everyone in Pleasantville was already colored. All strife ends when everyone discovers this truth. But *Pleasantville* disingenuously sidesteps any substantive issues by presenting everyone as *also* the same on the outside. Thanks to the magic of the movies, we're all colored. The allusions to civil rights, an unstated part of the film's dynamic from the outset, no longer matter. *Pleasantville* suggests the civil rights revolution of the 1950s and '60s has become so much a part of the American story that it belongs to all of us and can be just as valid when everyone is white. And as long as Miles Davis and his sidepeople remain invisible throughout the film, audience members can respond to their own feelings about the music rather than to the music itself.

There are several ways of thinking about these films. With *Elevator to the Gallows, Street Smart,* and *The Hot Spot,* we could recapitulate the familiar narrative of Davis's decline: he takes great pains making the music for *Elevator to the Gallows,* but thirty years later, he is simply providing generic doodling for films like *Street Smart* and *The Hot Spot.* I'd rather not buy into that narrative completely. Although jazz purists will tell you that Davis sold out in the late 1960s and continued to record conventional, throwaway pop music for the rest of his career, there are many other ways of responding to the music he made in those final decades. For one thing, Davis did not wish to repeat himself. He makes the definitive jazz soundtrack for a film in 1957, and then moves on. Been there, done that. Later he tries other approaches to the art form, for example taking the unique opportunity to record with folk blues musicians like John Lee Hooker and Taj Mahal in *The Hot Spot.* We could even argue that Davis's flamboyant concert appearances of the 1970s and '80s were his own dramas with music and that he was less interested in Hollywood's dramas with music. By playing with blues musicians for a film score, or in concert with musicians from India, Africa, and Latin America, Davis was continuing what Gary Tomlinson has called his "cultural dialogics."[9] These dialogues with people from other cultures first became vital when he worked with French filmmakers and French musicians in creating music for *Elevator to the Gallows.*

We can also make different cases about the role that Davis's music plays in the white Hollywood cinema of today. On the one hand, films like *The Talented Mr. Ripley* and *Pleasantville* deny personhood to African Americans and keep them off screen at the same time that the films use black music to give depth and romance to their white characters. White filmmakers have claimed the great achievements of black Americans—including jazz and the civil rights movement—for their white characters without acknowledging any obligation to African American people. On the other hand, in the case of Miles Davis, we have a music that long ago transcended its historical and personal moment and has provided a universe of compelling musical signification for filmmakers as well as for the rest of us.

NOTES

1. Kathryn Kalinak, *Settling the Score: Music and the Classical Hollywood Film* (Madison: University of Wisconsin Press, 1992).

2. Claudia Gorbman, *Unheard Melodies: Narrative Film Music* (Bloomington: Indiana University Press, 1987).

3. Ashley Kahn, *Kind of Blue: The Making of the Miles Davis Masterpiece* (New York: Da Capo Press, 2000).

4. Philip Brophy, "Revolutionizing the Cinema: Or, How I Put Rock 'n' Roll in the Movies. Jack Nitzsche in conversation with Philip Brophy," in *Cinesonic: Experiencing the Soundtrack* (North Ryde, Australia: Australian Film Television and Radio School, 2001), p. 10.

5. James Weldon Johnson, *The Autobiography of an Ex-Colored Man* [1912] (New York: Penguin, 1990).

6. Jessie Redmon Fauset, *Plum Bun* [1928] (Boston: Beacon, 1990).

7. Nella Larsen, *Passing* [1929] (New York: Penguin, 1997).

8. John Szwed, *So What: The Life of Miles Davis* (New York: Simon and Schuster, 2002), p. 117.

9. Gary Tomlinson, "Cultural Dialogics and Jazz: A White Historian Signifies," *Black Music Research Journal* 11.2 (1991), pp. 229–64.

16 Men at the Keyboard

Liminal Spaces and the Heterotopian Function of Music

GARY C. THOMAS

Multimedia spectacle, as Richard Wagner presciently theorized, would be the mass theater of the future. Films especially, whether projected on public screens or on home computers (and one should include here the entire spectrum of post-celluloid media technology) remain one of the few and dwindling sites of public pedagogy. People read less and less—we stand, in any case, at the end of the era of the book—and few engage in public debate, attend lectures, visit avant-garde film houses, or participate in the uncommodified music scenes. And despite its productive pleasures, most perform very little in the way of political reflection and cultural analysis. But we *all* go to the movies. And, thus, what we see and hear on those screens—and how we see and hear it—matters more than ever. My interest here is twofold: first, in a perhaps unlikely conjunction of images, sounds, and narrative found on the commercial screen—storylines featuring men playing music on a keyboard—and, second, in another, rather more overarching conjunction, that of oedipal-capital, my shorthand for the cultural processes of psychic subjection in the service of political-economic exploitation, the analysis of which constitutes one of the urgent projects of critical cultural studies.[1]

If most of my materials are historical (older film, older music, even some older theory), this is deliberate, as they are part of an effort to counter what I see as a danger in the ahistorical strain of some of our current theorizing—let me call it uncommitted postmodernist presentism. It is dangerous in the sense that it is inadequate to address, among other things, the massive regression attending the current neo-con political turn in the United States with its concomitant cultural recidivism, neocolonialism, and homophobia. One might say that history, including key moments in critical theory of the past, now matters more than ever as well.

THEATER

Before keyboards appeared in twentieth-century cinema they had a long history of semiotic appropriation. Since early modernity pipe organs, harpsichords, and pianos have featured prominently as painted objects, as works of art in themselves, and as incidental props or narrative centerpieces in novels and, since the invention of the medium, in film as well. In short, they signify. Inevitably gendered, but also marked in terms of class and race, such representations, starkly ideological, articulate relations of social hierarchy, power, and desire. The pipe organ, for example, appears as an emblem of early modern technological prowess and control, a vast mechanical apparatus—its massive consoles prefiguring airplane cockpits and computer control centers—that generated at the time the most powerful musical sounds ever heard. A more fitting superstructural analogue to the penetrating expansionist power of a new capitalist economy and its exploitative, colonizing reach can scarcely be imagined. This techno-musical counterpart to Descartes's triumphant autonomous man, poised to make himself "master and possessor of nature,"[2] would resurface in the crepuscular obsessions of the nineteenth-century gothic and its progeny, only to be trivialized in kids' cartoons and the Broadway musical *(Phantom of the Opera)* in the twentieth.

If the piano takes center stage in the bourgeois era, the reasons are not far to seek.[3] First, playing the piano, like playing the organ, is an inherently singular—monadic, if you will—experience. Pianos may be played against an orchestra, but they don't normally become a part of one. The piano, like cognate cultural forms such as the sonata and the *Bildungsroman,* thus participates in the bourgeois ideology of the individual and his home or "castle" as the Archimedean center of things. Second, the piano offers a seemingly self-contained plenitude of sounds, from high to low, and, as its original name "forte-piano" indicates, a range of expressive possibilities from very loud to very soft; in short, a world—one, moreover, that can be brought into the home and owned as a possession. Also salient is the two-handedness of the play, which enables both melody and accompaniment to be performed but may also entail dramatic tension between the two. Most significant in this regard, the piano affords access to the all-important codes of Western harmony and the various possibilities of relation between grounding harmonic structure ("langue") and solo-individual melody ("parole"), as well as improvisatory explorations beyond or outside it.

Unlike the pipe organ, however, with its baggage of masculinist power fantasy, the piano registers from the start a distinct gender ambivalence.[4] Played in public, for money or show, it's been mostly a manly affair; played in private, for pleasure or its sublimation, a decidedly feminine, even emasculating one, often appearing, as in later Hollywood westerns, as the very icon of "feminine" interiority or of domestic middle-class stability.[5]

The piano may thus be understood as a site of multiple, cross-cutting ambivalence and tension—high/low, loud/soft, male/female, public/private, and control/freedom, for example—and its representation in film as a theater that stages, in microcosm, the historical play of such tensions and antinomies as they work to produce the conditions of possibility, emancipatory as well as enslaving, of the modern subject. Such a reading—of pianos, music, and subjects enmeshed in the grid of material history—presupposes, indeed demands, a willingness to approach its object, film, precisely *as* theater, understood as performance but also, in perfect consonance with its etymon, as stagings and projections of *theory*, that is, as *potentia* (power, possibility). The familiar objection that films are frozen in time, and thus lack the ever-changing performative nature of, say, a play or an opera, tends unduly to reify them as culture industry commodities. To this one must object, first, that films aren't nearly as "frozen" in time as one might think—or hope[6]—and, second, that films do change over time, and constantly, as they are continually reread, in a sense rewritten—in the form, among other things, of "constructive descriptions"[7]—by active spectators themselves. What Adorno wrote in his remarkable late essay, "Wagner's Relevance for Today," is certainly relevant here:

> As spiritual entities, works of art are not complete in themselves. They create a magnetic field of all possible intentions and forces, of inner tendencies and countervailing ones, of successful and necessarily unsuccessful elements. Objectively, new layers are constantly detaching themselves, emerging from within; others grow irrelevant and die off. One relates to a work of art not merely, as is often said, by adapting it to fit a new situation, but rather by deciphering within it things to which one has a historically different reaction.[8]

The dialogical and dialectical activity of educated, committed reading—reading *for*—is not only constructive. It is also performative in that it inevitably renders all texts mobile, freeing them to become what they in fact always already are: allegories (to use Jamesonian language) of a political unconscious that participate, willy-nilly, in the complex processes, vicissitudes, and flow of history, contest, and struggle—over meaning and the political stakes of meaning.

EDGE

> The margins may be the only place where the center becomes visible.
> LEO BERSANI

My specific focus is the male subject's encounter with music and the piano in a kind of liminal experience. By liminal I understand a space at or beyond the borders and boundaries of the normal, of the familiar, the *heimlich*, that is, the already thought and comfortably settled. The liminal is a subjunctive space and time—of instability, of the in-between, of the queer *unheim-lich*[9]—of process and change itself. It is thus associated with movement, transitions, margins, and, as the root indicates, thresholds. A kind of epistemological process (as opposed to ontological identity)[10] where one comes to *know* differently, the liminal experience may point to a corresponding ontological space—that of the *heterotopia*—where one may imagine *being* differently or, again as the word suggests, in an "other" way. In his well-known essay "Of Other Spaces," sometimes translated as "Different Spaces," Michel Foucault outlines some diverse types and sites of the heterotopia such as the garden, the bathhouse (brothel), the colony, and especially the ship, which he names the "heterotopia par excellence." Liminal spaces, one might say, put as at sea—the sea and water metaphors are important here—that is, put us at risk, and bring us into the open-ended possibilities of experimentation, improvisation, and play, the heterotopian life possibilities that then emerge into view. Unlike a utopia—a "no place," often a nostalgic wish-fulfillment dream—the heterotopia is real, or potentially so. Where utopias render passive and docile, heterotopias incite agency.

For much of its studied life music has been relegated to the utopian, and with disastrous effects, mainly that of disenfranchising it, in a gendered and infantilizing sort of way, from participation and agency in the material affairs of the world.[11] But precisely those qualities that have served to marginalize it—its fabled semantic indeterminacy, its existence as temporality, movement, affect, and bodily gesture; in short, its very "otherness"—render it, on the contrary, a mode of unruly knowing and powerful interference. That is, music may offer for the hearing and feeling not a dreamy utopia, but a way out.

The cultural relations I alluded to at the beginning are the two by which modern male psyches and bodies—finally, all psyches and bodies—are produced as subjects to serve in oedipal and capitalist social structures. Breaking down into myriad local mechanisms or nodes of power, as Foucault would have it, these two always function in tandem; both are relations of domination. Moreover, they are always cloaked by the mechanisms of their intended naturalization, and hence their smooth and successful totalizing operation. To paraphrase Adorno, any analysis of the individual returns us to the social reality that produced it; any discussion of social structure returns us to consideration of the psychology that *re*-produces it.[12]

I have chosen for a provisional reading along these lines two films, Alfred Hitchcock's *Rope* (1948) and Bob Rafelson's *Five Easy Pieces* (1970), both of which feature men at the piano and which, I believe, stage moments of liminality, where the psychic and social wounds of modernity—contradictions and alienations of the twin-headed oedipal-capital machine—are rent open and, as it were, made public.

ACID

> The thing that is still most likely to help us is to force what is false, flawed, antinomical out into the open, rather than glossing over it and generating a kind of harmony.   THEODOR W. ADORNO

Before turning to these films I want briefly to visit two texts, neither of which features a keyboard of any kind, but that will, I hope, serve to clarify the broader parameters of my argument.

The first, the locus classicus of the encounter of the male subject with its cultural, in this case feminized, Other, is Wagner's *Tristan und Isolde*. Here, the elements of the drama of the oedipal subject—the threat of its undoing, as well as its panicked policing—emerge with striking and paradigmatic clarity. The key moment, one of the most famous in all theater, and a moment of liminality par excellence, comes at the end of the second-act love duet. It is a scene of intense passion, of eroticism unheard of at the time; of the massive destabilization of discursive categories, of the gendered subject itself, and a full frontal assault on bourgeois notions of decency, restraint, control, and propriety. Such intensities are endowed with new and ironic life in the happily controversial 1999 production from the Munich Bayerische Staatsoper.[13] In the scene in question the illicit lovers have stripped off their outer clothes and Tristan stuffs a kitschily flowered, Marge Simpson–esque pillow into his now shed armor. Just as Tristan is overcome to the point of dehiscence, his ego, name, and identity dissolving in the surging acid bath of Wagnerian chromaticism, the scene is violently interrupted—by some of the clunkiest, most deliberately vulgar music Wagner ever wrote, and, in this production, by the simultaneous throwing on of all the house lights, as Kurwenal screams the ambivalent and panicked line: "Rette dich, Tristan!"

(Save yourself, Tristan!) But from what? The answer to this question is in many ways the whole point of the opera.

I'd like to articulate this briefly with a second scene, this one from the film *American Beauty* (1999). Here, the virulent homophobe "Colonel Frank Fitts, United States Marine Corps," having failed to oedipally castrate his nongay but comic-queer son, undergoes a radical shattering of the male-fascist ego armor the likes of which, to my mind, have rarely been projected on a mainstream cinematic screen. He appears here in the rain—another water bath, a symbolic acid rain, as it were—stripped and dripping in his wet T-shirt as he walks away from his oedipal destiny into the liminal zone of Freud's narcissistic, socially repudiated space of the anal, the garage-turned-heterotopia set up by the already comically de-oedipalized subject, Lester Burnham (figure 16.1). What has been massively repressed as the price of masculine autonomy and symbolic sphincter control returns here in the form of the sublime anal-feminine: the dread homosexual kiss.

BOX

You're very fond of that little tune, aren't you?
RUPERT (JIMMY STEWART), *ROPE*

Subjectivity is a box.   THEODOR W. ADORNO

The role of the panicking king in *Tristan* and the shattered colonel in *American Beauty* (who, rebuffed, returns with his gun to annihilate the object of his desire) shows up in *Rope* in the figure of Rupert Cadell (Jimmy Stewart), a teacher turned detective. Read as a straight murder mystery, *Rope* narrates the discovery and punishment of a crime and the consequent restoration of the law. But, as I will suggest momentarily, this restoration is so precarious and troubled as to require for its stabilization the herculean intervention of the nondiegetic orchestra that we hear over the film's final credits.

What makes *Rope* a great and enduringly interesting film, however, is precisely the ways it refuses such an easy read. This is evident from the outset in the techniques Hitchcock employs, notably single-shot filming in a single-set location, the rectangular box that is Philip and Brandon's apartment—where homosexuality is unacknowledged but everywhere present—but also, and especially, in the devices that give the film the look, not of film, but of theater: the backdrop with its giant cyclorama with clouds of spun glass and miniatures of the New York City skyline, the symbolic steam

Figure 16.1 Fitts in the liminal zone, in *American Beauty.*

vent (a favorite device of.Hitchcock's, found in *Rear Window* and elsewhere as well), and so forth. Also, two objects in the symbolic form of, as Freud decoded them, "anal" boxes,[14] dominate this stage: the piano, and the wooden chest, which conceals the body of Brandon and Philip's murdered classmate.

The narrative takes the form of a macabre party, which, for Rupert, turns into the search for his missing former student. Once he has finally solved the mystery and goes to open the chest, Brandon jeers, "I hope you like what you see." But it is precisely what the box contains that the film leaves open to question, and not inadvertently. On the surface there is a dead body, to be sure, but only the box's twin image—the piano, its music and its playing—holds the key to the final answer.

Philip plays the piano on a few occasions in the film, but always the same tune, the first of three pieces by Francis Poulenc titled *Mouvements perpétuels.* Published in 1919 when Poulenc was twenty, these perpetual motions were composed on the piano in a local elementary school in Saint-Martin-sur-le-Pré for the children of that school. The piece is built, in the absence of a key signature, on the opposition between an unchanging ostinato in the left hand, which oscillates ("perpetually moves") between B♭ and F, or its own tonic and dominant. Above this, in the right hand, Poulenc gives us clear little melodic fragments, also repeated but in opposition to the ostinato, the first one falling pentatonically, the second undulating like a scale in the key of C, and so forth. Interjected into this happily regressive childlike world of repetition and nondirectional, nonconclusional motion, however, is a jarringly dissonant version of the opening melody in G♭, which, so to speak, thumbs its queer nose at the original and which it ornaments with some playful Stravinsky-esque details. All the music is recapitulated, "sans nuance," as Poulenc specifies in the score (or "deadpan," as I read it), and comes to its inauspicious inconclusion with a short coda. (This strange and "deviant" classical music is provided with a commodified and familiar counterpart, a mainstream romantic pop tune by the Three Suns played on a radio in the background.) In the film, as Scott Paulin has noted,[15] Philip never plays the Poulenc all the way to the end, but rather continually goes back to the beginning, starting and stopping at random moments. A key scene, one that unlocks this reading of the film, comes when detective/mentor Rupert stands in an imperious, effeminizing gesture over Philip, subjecting—in every sense of the word—both Philip and Poulenc's music to the rigors of the metronome (figure 16.2).

To cut to the end: Rupert is far from happy with what he sees. His final speech, disavowing his own role in the drama and the distortion of his own words by Brandon and Philip, as he claims, is as panicky as it is unconvincing: "They don't mean that, and you can't make them mean that." Thus, Rupert goes over and reshuts the box, and with it all ambivalence, all meaning, all heterotopian otherness. Similarly, the piano, the player, and the music are stilled, Philip left poking out a few notes (with his now symbolically wounded and bleeding finger); Poulenc, as it were, "peters out." And now, having been already reduced, amid blaring police sirens, to the point of silence, Poulenc's queer and disturbing "little tune" is massively recuperated. To put it in the terms of this chapter, it is re-oedipalized and pressed into the service and interests of capital, a happy end for profit. This is accomplished by the penetrating Wagnerian orchestra—the world's first amplifier[16]—the symphonic machine that has been waiting like a sonoric deus ex machina in the wings to, so to speak, resolve all contradictions by fiat.

Poulenc is here radically hijacked by the full force of the Hollywood soundtrack apparatus; the music's harmonies are straightened out and its deviant tune is corrected and brought to a "rightful," hetero-lawful, tonic conclusion: the way, as it were, God intended.

SCHIZO

> Two souls, alas, abide within my breast, each seeking riddance from the other. GOETHE, *FAUST*

> We have become at once more mobile and more privatized.
> RAYMOND WILLIAMS

For their April 5, 1999, issue, the editors of *The Nation* asked a number of prominent figures to write a short paragraph on what they considered the

Figure 16.2 Rupert wields the metronome, in *Rope*.

most significant film in their experience. As his choice, Edward Said named *Five Easy Pieces*, ending his brief remarks by saying, "At the core of the film is a terrifying emptiness. I think it's a work of genius."

The film is structured around a male protagonist, the Jack Nicholson character, here again in largely oedipal terms, replete with rebellion from and return to the father. In this it of course stands as one among innumerable instances of that persistent and quintessentially American genre, the "road picture," as a simulacrum of modernity. But most road pictures don't feature schizophrenic classical-pianists-turned-oil-rig-workers, or structure their anti-oedipal narrative around the conflicted and degraded state of music in relation to advanced capitalism.

Such contradictions, however, lie at the heart of *Five Easy Pieces*—and, arguably, of the noir film *Detour* (1945)[17]—which limns in turn the ruptures and disconnects, in short, the alienation, that lies at the heart of Western modernity. The narrative reproduces the implacable restlessness of the vaunted individual, and the emptiness and terror that shadows it. Moreover, it rejects all reconciliation along with every nostalgia, committing its hero, Robert "Eroica" Dupea, to cold and musicless oblivion.

The narrative is framed within a series of oppositions that are maintained throughout: between the parched Southern California oilfields and the verdant Pacific Northwest; between the sights and sounds of the public working class (in the south) and those of the private aristocratic bourgeoisie (in the north—the home being literally isolated, that is, on an island); the incompatible world of physical labor and the carefree pursuit of art; between the alliterating names Robert Dupea and Rayette DiPesto; and also between two musics—Rayette's mass-mediated country-western (which she listens to on records but also reproduces in her own singing) and the privatized and privileged cultivation of the classical canon.

Between these worlds stands, or rather incessantly moves, the schizophrenic character of Bobby/Robert Dupea. The stock narrative of the progress of the adventuresome son and rebel—*sans foi, ni loi*—to upstanding husband, father, and good bourgeois citizen is here rejected, the film staging instead of a kind of Faust myth in reverse. Like many road films featuring a rebellious protagonist, this one is counter-oedipal as well: Bobby returns to his mute father—appearing here as an amalgam of Brahms, Nietzsche, and God—but only in order to refuse him. Rather than the archetypal transgressor who, seeing the error of his ways, is brought back to his "natural" role as castrated, ready to play Daddy's natural and hetero-lawful successor, Bobby remains the misfit and outsider. No reconciliation, comic or tragic, is possible here.[18]

A key moment, perhaps the pivotal point of the entire film, comes about a third of the way through, when Bobby, caught with his co-worker Elton in rush-hour traffic, leaves his car, jumps onto a mover's truck just ahead of him, takes the cover off an out-of-tune piano, and launches into one of the dramatic sections of Chopin's F-Minor Fantasy, op. 49 (figure 16.3). The scene is highly ambivalent. On the one hand it reveals Bobby's "hidden" past; his classical musicianship is thus a link to the alienation from and disavowal of his pre-scripted journey. The pounding on the piano also connects, by structural homology, with two other scenes: the violent pounding of the steering wheel of his car when he attempts to leave Rayette at home on his trip north, and the famous and also violent "clearing of the table" scene in the roadside restaurant (his, like Faust's, is a tortured soul). But it is more than that. The scene constitutes the film's one heterotopian moment, and in two senses. First, it stages the only moment of integration for Bobby, in which the music, the piano, and the pleasure of spontaneous play are fused, where music has been neither commercially and ideologically commodified nor anesthetically entombed in a refuge for the privileged. Second, it functions precisely to open onto a critique of those conditions by reintroducing, in this powerful synecdoche, the historical-material basis of class privilege

Figure 16.3 Bobby playing Chopin, in *Five Easy Pieces.*

itself: the piano and the music are set literally upon the ground of their material conditions of possibility. Put differently, what is entirely suppressed in the scenes on the verdant island—the colonialist ravaging of an indigenous population, the ubiquitous but hidden presence of money in the form of inherited wealth—emerges here for the seeing and hearing. Chopin untuned amid a cacophony of car horns, yelling drivers, and yapping dogs aptly points to the dialectical reality that beauty feeds well on material subjection.

But, by God, it is still Chopin. Among the few commentators on this film—curiously, it seems to have defied much in the way of critical attention[19]—few identify the piece correctly. Said recalls Bach, possibly because Tita ("Partita" Dupea) plays the Bach Chromatic Fantasy later in a recording studio; Ivan Raykoff names Liszt's Hungarian Rhapsody No. 2.[20] The detail might not seem to matter since, after all, what we are meant to hear is "classical piano music." But in fact it does matter, and, like the full names of the characters Robert Eroica, Carl Fidelio, and Partita Dupea, the piece is duly listed in the end credits. Chopin's Fantasy seems well chosen. The fantasy form is itself fragmented and in some respects oedipally regressive. It has the feel of improvisation and, despite the tyranny of notated editions, probably was, or was meant to be, played differently every time.[21] Akin in some respects to film scores *avant la lettre*, perhaps even to Freud's notion of the psychic "film," Chopin's musical fantasias—this one begins in one key and ends in another, constantly disavowing its signature F-minor-ness in favor its relative A♭ major—ebb and flow, move often non-teleologically in and out of affective spaces, and employ a vocabulary of sonoric gestures that gives them the feel of the open-ended and unbounded.

DEATH

"Tod denn alles—alles tod." (Now all—all is dead.)
WAGNER, *TRISTAN UND ISOLDE*

Resist psychic death. BIKINI KILL

I began with a call to view films as performative theater, as allegories of a political unconscious. Jameson's felicitous yoking of the material-political with the unconscious has lost none of its hermeneutic reach, indicating as it does two things: first, that the political, especially in American culture, *is* unconscious, which is to say ubiquitously repressed or censored (we're always "Americans," never "capitalists"); and, second, that the cultural processes that either structure the unruly desires of the psychic unconscious into regimes of discourse (psychoanalysis, for example) or, on the contrary, that tap into them as modes of resistance, are themselves also deeply and inevitably political. The concepts of liminality and heterotopia will, I hope, be similarly productive as hermeneutic metaphors that allow us to dialogically revivify and reanimate the films and other cultural objects we engage.[22]

Taking my cue from Foucault, I have suggested mobilizing the metaphor of the piano as ship (Foucault's heterotopia par excellence) that takes us out to sea, as it were, and into music (arguably the site of liminality par excellence), danger, and risk. As it appears in at least some films, the piano does perform this heterotopian function, transporting us to a space beyond both the commodified norm and the psychic familiar—or, as in *Rope*, beyond the soundtrack. In this, a hermeneutics of the liminal-heterotopian will ally itself with other critically aggressive, corrosive counter-discourses that function in the mode of *interference*, whether parodistic, ironic, or dialogical-carnivalesque.

The alternative, to stay in the realm of metaphor (but not only), is nothing less than death—of "perpetual movement," growth and mobility,[23] fantasy,[24] power, and possibility *(potentia)*.[25] This, finally, is what our political allegories have offered us for the seeing and hearing: that failure to accede to oedipal-capital will end in death *(Tristan, American Beauty)*, arrest by the police *(Rope, also Detour)*, or relegation to the outer cold, the "terrifying loneliness" of oblivion and unbelonging *(Five Easy Pieces)*. But in their liminal ruptures they also point to heterotopian beyonds. It must be our business to seek these out, wherever they may be, and then go there.

NOTES

This chapter is dedicated to the memory of Philip Brett, musicologist and queer theorist extraordinaire.

1. On the convergence of the two, see Donald Morton, *The Material Queer: A LesBiGay Cultural Studies Reader* (Boulder, CO: Westview Press, 1996), especially pp. xv–xviii, "A Note on Cultural Studies."

2. René Descartes, *Discourse on Method* (1637), trans. Laurence J. Lafleur (Indianapolis: Bobbs-Merrill, 1950), p. 40.

3. Of the considerable literature on the piano, see especially James Parakilas et al., *Piano Roles: Three Hundred Years of Life with the Piano* (New Haven, CT: Yale University Press, 1999).

4. On the nexus of piano and "feminine" domestic space, see various chapters in Richard Leppert, *The Sight of Sound: Music, Representation, and the History of the Body* (Berkeley and Los Angeles: University of California Press: 1993).

5. To this roster of gendered piano roles should be added that of the pianist as virtuoso spectacle (Liszt) and camp queer (Liberace and, on the organ, Virgil Fox). See Richard Leppert, "Cultural Contradiction, Idolatry, and the Piano Virtuoso: Franz Liszt," in James Parakilas et al., *Piano Roles*, pp. 252–81. The ambivalence of the piano exceeds all simple binarism, however: for every Franz Liszt, Liberace, or Little Richard one can cite the likes of Jerry Lee Lewis, Billy Joel, or Ben Folds as counterexamples.

6. I refer here not only to the availability of "director's cut" versions and ancillary materials such as trailers and production discussions on DVD versions, but also to the current and disturbing vogue for censoring, altering, and otherwise "sanitizing" films in the interests of fundamentalist ideology.

7. See Lawrence Kramer's argument concerning the necessity, the inevitability, of the reading (hearing, viewing) subject's recourse to meaning as verbal discourse ("constructive description") in "Subjectivity Rampant! Music, Hermeneutics, and History," in *The Cultural Study of Music: A Critical Introduction*, ed. Martin Clayton, Trevor Herbert, and Richard Middleton (New York: Routledge, 2003), pp. 124–35.

8. Theodor W. Adorno, "Wagner's Relevance for Today," in *Essays on Music*, ed. Richard Leppert, trans. Susan Gillespie (Berkeley and Los Angeles: University of California Press, 2003), pp. 586–87. Leppert's commentary on this passage: "Hearing itself is historical; history determines a way of hearing. As a result, any of the myriad qualities immanent to a work either emerge or recede in relation to historical change," p. 535.

9. Literally: the un-homely, outside the home and family, "unfamiliar."

10. See Susan Buck-Morss, *Thinking Past Terror: Islamism and Critical Theory on the Left* (London and New York: Verso, 2003), pp. 64–67.

11. This is one of the overarching themes of Caryl Flinn's *Strains of Utopia: Gender, Nostalgia, and Hollywood Film Music* (Princeton, NJ: Princeton University Press, 1992).

12. Susan Buck-Morss, *The Origin of Negative Dialectics: Theodor W. Adorno, Walter Benjamin, and the Frankfurt Institute* (New York: Free Press, 1977), p. 185.

13. Which Adorno might have appreciated, as he did the "latest parodistic and aggressive" interpretation of the second act of *Die Meistersinger* he (presumably) had seen in Bayreuth. Adorno, "Wagner's Relevance for Today," p. 600. In light of the many new and controversial stagings of Wagner operas in our time, those scornfully dismissed by their detractors as "Euro-trash," Adorno's remarks on the need for critical-creative license in the case of Wagner are more pertinent than ever: "Only experimental solutions are justified today; only what injures the Wagner orthodoxy is true. The defenders of the Grail shouldn't get so worked up about it; Wagner's precise instructions exist and will continue to be handed down for historians. But the rage that is unleashed by such interventions proves that they strike a nerve, precisely that layer where the question of Wagner's relevance for today is decided" (p. 600).

14. Here I should invoke the by now (in)famous essay by D. A. Miller, "Anal Rope," in *Inside/Out: Lesbian Theories, Gay Theories*, ed. Diana Fuss (New York and London: Routledge, 1991), pp. 119–41.

15. Scott D. Paulin, "Unheard Sexualities?: Queer Theory and the Soundtrack," *Spectator* 17.2 (1997), pp. 36–49. I wish to signal the indebtedness of my reading of *Rope* to this insightful and little-known article.

16. See Friedrich Kittler, "World-Breath: On Wagner's Media Technology," in *Opera Through Other Eyes*, ed. David J. Levin (Stanford, CA: Stanford University Press, 1993), p. 224. Cf. Kittler's summary (p. 233) of Wagnerian music-drama: "The text is fed into the throat of a singer, the output of this throat is fed into an amplifier named orchestra, the output of this orchestra is fed into a light show, and the whole thing, finally, is fed into the nervous system of the audience."

17. This section may be read in dialogue with Flinn's analysis of Edgar G. Ulmer's B cult classic in Flinn, *Strains of Utopia*, pp. 118–33.

18. On this same issue in *Detour* see Tania Modleski, "Film Theory's Detour," *Screen* 23.5 (1982), pp. 72–79.

19. But see David Brackett, "Banjos, Biopics, and Compilation Scores: The Movies Go Country," *American Music* 19.3 (Autumn 2001), pp. 247–90.

20. Ivan Raykoff, "Hollywood's Embattled Icon," in James Parakilas et al., *Piano Roles*, p. 349.

21. The ongoing question of the legitimacy of "authoritative" or "final" editions of Chopin's music is relevant here. As Jeffery Kallberg points out, such freezing of the score tends to erase the complexity of its publication history, Chopin's penchant for endless revision, and with it some of the improvisatory open-endedness of the compositions, especially of pieces like the Fantasy. Jeffrey Kallberg, *Chopin at the Boundaries: Sex, History, and Musical Genre* (Cambridge, MA: Harvard University Press, 1996).

22. For a discussion of metaphor and hermeneutics see Lawrence Kramer's "Music, Metaphor and Metaphysics," *Musical Times* 145.1888 (Autumn 2004), pp. 5–18.

23. On the paradox of mobility's "privatization" by capital, see Raymond Williams, *Television: Technology and Cultural Form* (New York: Schocken, 1975).

24. Scott Paulin cites this specifically in his take on the end of *Rope:* "By enunciating the norm in this way, *Rope* negates the oppositional force of fantasy which the music had offered—in other words, the (musical or sexual) other was never really there; and if it was, it is easily corrected and erased." Paulin, "Unheard Sexualities," p. 39.

25. For a sustained analysis of capital and the queer in relation to heterotopia, see Cesare Casarino, *Modernity at Sea: Melville, Marx, Conrad in Crisis* (Minneapolis: University of Minnesota Press, 2002).

Notes on Contributors

RICK ALTMAN is Professor of Cinema and Comparative Literature, University of Iowa. He has published extensively on Hollywood genres: *Genre: The Musical* (1981), *The American Film Musical* (1987), *Film/Genre* (1999), and on film sound: *Cinema/Sound* (1980), *Sound Theory / Sound Practice* (1992), *The State of Sound Studies* (1999), *Global Experiments in Early Synchronous Sound* (1999), *The Sounds of Early Cinema* (2001), and *Silent Film Sound* (2004), which has recently been awarded both the Limina Prize and the Theatre Library Association Prize. He is currently working on a general study of classical Hollywood sound and on a wide-ranging narrative theory.

PHILIP BROPHY is a filmmaker, musician, and writer. His latest book is *100 Anime*, for the BFI, London (2005). His other BFI book, *100 Modern Soundtracks* (2004), has been translated into Japanese by Film Art, Tokyo (2005). He was also director of the CINESONIC International Conference on Film Scores and Sound Design, held annually in Melbourne between 1998 and 2001, and has edited three books from the conference published by the Australian Film, Television, and Radio School. He recently completed the radio series *Traces of Soundtracks* (2005), commissioned by ABC Classical-FM, Australia. His current book projects include *Colour Me Dead* and *The Body Horrible*.

MICHEL CHION is Professor of Cinema, University of Paris (New Sorbonne), and the École supérieure d'Études cinématographiques (Paris). He is author of twenty-five books, of which several have been translated into English, including *Audio-Vision: Sound on Screen* (1994), *David Lynch* (1995), *The Films of Jacques Tati* (1997), *The Voice in Cinema* (1999), *Kubrick's Cinema Odyssey* (2001), and *Eyes Wide Shut* (2002), and he is also a composer of *musique concrète* and a director of film shorts and videos. He is currently writing an essay on Terrence Malick's film *The Thin Red Line*.

NICHOLAS COOK is Professorial Research Fellow in Music at Royal Holloway, University of London, where he directs the AHRC Research Centre for the History and Analysis of Recorded Music (CHARM). Among his books are *Music, Imagination,* *and Culture* (1990), *Beethoven: Symphony No. 9* (1993), *Analysing Musical Multimedia* (1998), and *Music: A Very Short Introduction* (1998). His latest book, *The Schenker Project: Culture, Race, and Music Theory in Fin-de-siècle Vienna*, is in production with Oxford University Press. Editor of *Journal of the Royal Musical Association* from 1999 to 2004, he was elected a Fellow of the British Academy in 2001.

RICHARD DYER is Professor of Film Studies, University of Warwick. He has written on the theoretical concept of movie stars and fandom, issues of racial and sexual representation in popular culture, and lesbian and gay culture. He is the author of numerous books, including *Stars* (1979), *Only Entertainment* (1992), *Matter of Images: Essays on Representations* (1993), *White* (1997), and *Now You See It: Studies in Lesbian and Gay Film* (2002).

PETER FRANKLIN is Professor of Music, Oxford University, where he is a Fellow of St. Catherine's College. His published work includes *Mahler Symphony No. 3* (1991) and *The Life of Mahler* (1997). He also writes on early twentieth-century opera and classical Hollywood film music; recent film-music essays explore Steiner's *King Kong*, in *Film Music: Critical Approaches* (2001), ed. Kevin J. Donnelly; and Korngold's score for *Deception*, in *Film Music II: History, Theory Practice*, ed. Claudia Gorbman and Warren M. Sherk (2004). He is coeditor, with Robynn Stilwell, of the forthcoming Cambridge University Press volume, *Companion to Film Music*.

KRIN GABBARD is Professor of Comparative Literature and English, State University of New York at Stony Brook. His work deals with the representation of jazz and race in cinema. He has edited *Jazz among the Discourses* (1995) and *Representing Jazz* (1995), and written *Jammin' at the Margins: Jazz and the American Cinema* (1996) and *Black Magic: White Hollywood and African American Culture* (2004). His current project is a cultural history of the trumpet with special attention to its role in constructions of masculinity.

DANIEL GOLDMARK is Assistant Professor of Musicology, Case Western Reserve University. He is the author of *Tunes For 'Toons: Music and the Hollywood Animated Cartoon* (2005), and coeditor, with Yuval Taylor, of *The Cartoon Music Book* (2002). Goldmark worked for five years as research editor and producer at Rhino Entertainment in Los Angeles, and also worked as archivist and music coordinator at Spümcø Animation.

CLAUDIA GORBMAN is Professor of Film Studies in the Interdisciplinary Arts and Sciences program and Director of the Global Honors Program at the University of Washington, Tacoma. She is the author of *Unheard Melodies: Narrative Film Music* (1987), and has translated several books from French, including three by composer-critic Michel Chion (*Audio-Vision: Sound on Screen*, *The Voice in Cinema*, and *Kubrick's Cinema Odyssey*). She is currently writing a book on the films of the director Agnès Varda, to be published by University of Illinois Press, and co-translating Chion's *Un Art sonore: Le cinéma*.

BERTHOLD HOECKNER is Associate Professor of Music and the Humanities, University of Chicago, and the author of *Programming the Absolute: Nineteenth-*

Century German Music and the Hermeneutics of the Moment (2002). He is currently working on a monograph on music, memory, and visual culture.

LAWRENCE KRAMER is Professor of English and Music, Fordham University, and the editor of *19ᵗʰ Century Music*. His most recent books are *Musical Meaning: Toward a Critical History* (2002), *Opera and Modern Culture: Wagner and Strauss* (2004), and *Why Classical Music Still Matters* (2007), all of which include material on visual and cinematic culture. Several of his recent essays do likewise, involving, for example, Jane Campion's use of Schubert in her *Portrait of a Lady* (*Critical Inquiry*, 2002) and Ingmar Bergman's use of Chopin in his *Autumn Sonata* (*The Musical Times*, 2004).

RICHARD LEPPERT is Professor of Comparative Studies in Discourse and Society, University of Minnesota. His books include *Arcadia at Versailles* (1978), *Music and Society: The Politics of Composition, Performance, and Reception* (co-edited with Susan McClary, 1987), *Music and Image* (1988), *The Sight of Sound: Music, Representation, and the History of the Body* (1993), *Art and the Committed Eye: The Cultural Functions of Imagery* (1996), and an edition with commentary of musical writings by Theodor W. Adorno, *Essays on Music* (2002). He is currently preparing *Musical Extremes: The Dialectics of Virtuosity*.

SUSAN McCLARY is Professor of Musicology, UCLA; she taught at the University of Minnesota from 1977 to 1991. Her books include *Music and Society: The Politics of Composition, Performance, and Reception* (co-edited with Richard Leppert, 1987), *Feminine Endings: Music, Gender, and Sexuality* (1991), *Georges Bizet: Carmen* (1992), *Conventional Wisdom: The Content of Musical Form* (2000), and *Modal Subjectivities: Self-Fashioning in the Italian Madrigal* (2004). She is now writing *Power and Desire in Seventeenth-Century Music*. McClary received a MacArthur Fellowship in 1995.

MITCHELL MORRIS is Associate Professor of Musicology, UCLA. He has published on topics including musical ethics, bio-regionalism and "green" composers, American popular music, opera, and musical representations of gender and sexuality. He is author of *The Persistence of Sentiment: Essays on Display and Feeling in '70s Pop Music* (2007).

ROBYNN J. STILWELL is Associate Professor of Musicology, Georgetown University. Her publications have engaged film and television music, Beethoven and masculinity, rock music and femininity, French/American musical and dance culture interactions, and figure skating. She is coeditor with Peter Franklin of *Film Music Companion* (forthcoming from Cambridge University Press), and with Phil Powrie of *Changing Tunes* (Ashgate, 2006) and *Composing for the Screen in the USSR and Germany* (forthcoming from Indiana University Press). She is currently writing *The Voice in the Underscore*, an exploration of gender, film theory, developmental psychology, and historical scoring practices.

GARY C. THOMAS is Associate Professor of Cultural Studies, University of Minnesota. His publications include essays on German song, a critical edition of seventeenth-century German poet-composer Constantin Christian Dedekind's *Ael-bianische Musen-Lust* (1990) and, co-edited with Philip Brett and Elizabeth Wood, *Queering the Pitch: The New Gay and Lesbian Musicology* (2nd ed., 2006). His research interests focus on voices from the social margins, dissident musics and noise, and the carnivalesque genres of comedy.

Works Cited

Abel, Richard. "That Most American of Attractions, the Illustrated Song." In *The Sounds of Early Cinema,* edited by Richard Abel and Rick Altman, 144–55. Bloomington: Indiana University Press, 2001.

Adams, Frank Stewart. "*Way Down East* and the Future." *American Organist* (January 1921): 23–27.

Adorno, Theodor W. *Aesthetic Theory.* Edited by Gretel Adorno and Rolf Tiedemann, translated by Robert Hullot-Kentor. Minneapolis: University of Minnesota Press, 1997.

———. "The Curves of the Needle." In *Essays on Music,* edited by Richard Leppert, translated by Thomas Y. Levin, 271–76. Berkeley and Los Angeles: University of California Press, 2002.

———. *Essays on Music.* Edited by Richard Leppert, translated by Susan H. Gillespie. Berkeley and Los Angeles: University of California Press, 2002.

———. *Gesammelte Schriften in zwanzig Bänden.* Edited by Rolf Tiedemann et al. Frankfurt am Main: Suhrkamp Verlag, 1970–86.

———. *In Search of Wagner.* Translated by Rodney Livingstone. London: NLB, 1981.

———. *Introduction to the Sociology of Music.* Translated by E. B. Ashton. New York: Seabury Press, 1976.

———. *Mahler: A Musical Physiognomy.* Translated by Edmund Jephcott. Chicago: University of Chicago Press, 1992.

———. "On the Contemporary Relationship of Philosophy and Music." In *Essays on Music,* edited by Richard Leppert, translated by Susan H. Gillespie, 135–61. Berkeley and Los Angeles: University of California Press, 2002.

———. "On the Fetish-Character in Music and the Regression of Listening." In *Essays on Music,* edited by Richard Leppert, translated by Susan Gillespie, 288–317. Berkeley and Los Angeles: University of California Press, 2002.

———. "Wagner's Relevance for Today." In *Essays on Music,* edited by Richard Leppert, translated by Susan Gillespie, 584–602. Berkeley and Los Angeles: University of California Press, 2002.

Agamben, Giorgio. *Remnants of Auschwitz: The Witness and the Archive,* translated by D. Heller-Roazen. New York: Zone, 1999.

Adorno, Theodor, and Hanns Eisler. *Composing for the Films*. London: Athlone Press, 1994.

Albrecht, Theodore, ed. *Letters to Beethoven and Other Correspondence*. Lincoln: University of Nebraska Press, 1996.

Allen, Woody, and Stig Björkman. *Woody Allen about Woody Allen*. New York: Grove Press, 1995.

Altman, Rick. *The American Film Musical*. Bloomington: Indiana University Press, 1987.

———. "The Silence of the Silents." *Musical Quarterly* 80.4 (1997): 648–718.

———. *Silent Film Sound*. New York: Columbia University Press, 2004.

Anderson, Emily, ed. *The Letters of Beethoven*. 3 vols. London: Macmillan, 1961.

Anderson, Tim. "Reforming 'Jackass Music': The Problematic Aesthetics of Early American Film Music Accompaniment." *Cinema Journal* 37.1 (Fall 1997): 3–22.

Arnheim, Rudolf. *Film as Art*. London: Faber and Faber, 1958.

Ashbery, John. *Houseboat Days*. New York: Viking, 1977.

Attali, Jacques. *Noise: The Political Economy of Music*. Translated by Brian Massumi. Minneapolis: University of Minnesota Press, 1985.

Bailey, Peter J. *The Reluctant Film Art of Woody Allen*. Lexington: University Press of Kentucky, 2001.

Barrier, Michael. *Hollywood Cartoons: American Animation in Its Golden Age*. New York: Oxford University Press, 1999.

Barrier, Michael, Milton Gray, and Bill Spicer. "An Interview with Carl Stalling." *Funnyworld* 13 (Spring 1971): 21–29.

BBC press release. "Ian Hart is Beethoven in unique dream of the first performance of the Eroica Symphony." http://www.bbc.co.uk/pressoffice/pressreleases/stories/2003/05_may/19/eroica.shtml (accessed 14 April 2004).

BBC press release. http://www.bbc.co.uk/pressoffice/pressreleases/stories/2003/08_august/26/bbc2_drama_eroica.pdf (accessed 14 April 2004).

Behlmer, Rudy. *Inside Warner Bros. (1935–1951)*. London: Weidenfeld and Nicolson, 1986.

Benjamin, Walter. *Illuminations,* edited by Hannah Arendt, translated by Harry Zohn. New York: Schocken, 1969.

Berg, S. M. "Music for the Picture." *Moving Picture World* (25 December 1915): 2367

———. "Music for the Picture." *Moving Picture World* (11 November 1916): 856.

Beynon, George W. "Music for the Picture." *Moving Picture World* (2 March 1918): 1242.

———. "Music for the Picture." *Moving Picture World* (9 March 1918): 1374.

———. *Musical Presentation of Motion Pictures*. New York: Schirmer, 1921.

———. "Proper Presentation of Pictures Musically. The Theme." *Moving Picture World* (23 February 1918): 1093.

Blanchot, Maurice. *The Writing of the Disaster,* translated by Ann Smock. Lincoln: University of Nebraska Press, 1996.

Blank, Les, and James Bogan, eds. *Burden of Dreams: Screenplay, Journals, Reviews, Photographs*. Berkeley: North Atlantic Books, 1984.

Bordman, Gerald. *American Musical Theatre: A Chronicle,* 2nd ed. New York: Oxford University Press, 1992.

Brackett, David. "Banjos, Biopics, and Compilation Scores: The Movies Go Country." *American Music* 19.3 (Autumn 2001): 247–90.

Brandon, Ruth. *Being Divine: A Biography of Sarah Bernhard.* London: Secker & Warburg, 1991.

Brophy, Philip. "Revolutionizing the Cinema: Or, How I Put Rock 'n' Roll in the Movies. Jack Nitzsche in conversation with Philip Brophy." In *Cinesonic: Experiencing the Soundtrack,* edited by Philip Brophy, 1–13. North Ryde, Australia: Australian Film Television and Radio School, 2001.

———. "Secret History of Film Music Part 3: Violent Silences." *The Wire* 161 (July 1997): 38–39.

———. "Secret History of Film Music Part 4: Once Upon a Time in the East." *The Wire* 162 (August 1997): 40–41.

Brown, Royal. *Overtones and Undertones: Reading Film Music.* Berkeley and Los Angeles: University of California Press, 1994.

Buck-Morss, Susan. *The Origin of Negative Dialectics: Theodor W. Adorno, Walter Benjamin, and the Frankfurt Institute.* New York: Free Press, 1977.

———. *Thinking Past Terror: Islamism and Critical Theory on the Left.* London and New York: Verso, 2003.

Buhler, James, Caryl Flynn, and David Neumeyer, eds. *Music and Cinema,* Hanover, NH: Wesleyan University Press, 2000.

Buhler, James, Anahid Kassabian, David Neumeyer, and Robynn Stilwell. "Roundtable on Film Music." *Velvet Light Trap* 51 (Spring 2003): 73–91.

Burnham, Scott. *Beethoven Hero.* Princeton, NJ: Princeton University Press, 1995.

Burr, Aaron. "Repeat Theme—." *American Organist* (February 1922): 67.

Bush, W. Stephen. "The Art of Exhibition II." *Moving Picture World* (31 October 1914): 627.

———. "Opening of the Strand." *Moving Picture World* (18 April 1914): 371.

———. "The Theatre of Realization." *Moving Picture World* (15 November 1913): 714.

Cabarga, Leslie. *The Fleischer Story,* 2nd ed. New York: Da Capo Press, 1988.

Caltvedt, Lester. "Herzog's *Fitzcarraldo* and the Rubber Era." *Film & History* 18.4 (December 1988): 74–84.

Cano, Cristina, and Giorgio Cremonini. *Cinema e musica. Il racconto per sovrapposizioni.* Florence: Vallecchi, 1990.

Carroll, Brendan. *The Last Prodigy: A Biography of Erich Wolfgang Korngold.* Portland, OR: Amadeus Press, 1997.

Carroll, John B., ed. *Language, Thought, and Reality: Selected Writings of Benjamin Lee Whorf.* Cambridge, MA: M.I.T. Press, 1956.

Carroll, Noël. "Prospects for Film Theory: A Personal Assessment." In *Post-Theory: Reconstructing Film Studies,* edited by David Bordwell and Noël Carroll, 37–70. Madison: University of Wisconsin Press, 1996.

Caruth, Cathy. *Unclaimed Experience: Trauma, Narrative, and History.* Baltimore, MD: Johns Hopkins University Press, 1996.

Casarino, Cesare. *Modernity at Sea: Melville, Marx, Conrad in Crisis.* Minneapolis: University of Minnesota Press, 2002.

Chion, Michel. *Un Art sonore, le cinema: histoire, esthétique, poétique.* Paris: Cahiers du cinéma/essais, 2003.

———. *Audio-Vision: Sound on Screen.* Edited and translated by Claudia Gorbman. New York: Columbia University Press, 1994.

———. *La Musique au cinéma.* Paris: Fayard, 1995.

———. *The Voice in Cinema.* Edited and translated by Claudia Gorbman. New York: Columbia University Press, 1999.

———. *Le Voix au Cinéma.* Paris: Cahiers du cinéma, 1982.

Cinema Pressbooks from the Original Studio Collections. Woodbridge, CT: Research Publications, 1988.

Citron, Marcia J. *Opera on Screen.* New Haven, CT: Yale University Press, 2000.

Collier, Richard. *The River That God Forgot: The Story of the Amazon River Rubber Boom.* New York: Dutton, 1968.

"Colonial Theater, West Hoboken, N.J." *Moving Picture World* (18 November 1911): 560.

Crafton, Donald. *Before Mickey: The Animated Film 1898–1928.* Chicago: University of Chicago Press, 1993.

Crawford, Tim. "The Use and Misuse of Themes." *Metronome* (1 May 1927): 24.

Cronin, Paul, ed. *Herzog on Herzog.* London: Faber and Faber, 2002.

Cunningham, Michael. Brochure notes for *The Hours.* Nonesuch 79693–2, 2002.

———. *The Hours.* New York: Picador, 1998.

Curtis, Scott. "The Sound of the Early Warner Bros. Cartoons." In *Sound Theory, Sound Practice,* edited by Rick Altman, 191–203. New York: Routledge, 1992.

Czerny, Carl. *Erinnerungen aus meinem Leben,* ed. Walter Kolneder. Strasburg: Heitz, 1968.

Dahlhaus, Carl. *Between Romanticism and Modernism: Four Studies in the Music of the Later Nineteenth Century.* Berkeley and Los Angeles: University of California Press, 1980.

———. *Ludwig van Beethoven: Approaches to His Music.* Translated by Mary Whittall. Oxford: Clarendon Press, 1991.

Darnell, Regna. *And Along Came Boas: Continuity and Revolution in Americanist Anthropology.* Amsterdam: John Benjamins, 1998.

———. *Invisible Genealogies: A History of Americanist Anthropology.* Lincoln: University of Nebraska Press, 2001.

Davidson, John E. "As Others Put Plays upon the Stage: *Aguirre,* Neocolonialism, and the New German Cinema." *New German Critique* 60 (Fall 1993): 101–30.

———. "Contacting the Other: Traces of Migrational Colonialism and the Imperial Agent in Werner Herzog's *Fitzcarraldo.*" *Film & History* 24, nos. 3–4 (1994): 66–83.

Davies, Stephen. *Musical Meaning and Expression.* Ithaca, NY: Cornell University Press, 1994.

Davies, Terence. *A Modest Pageant: Children, Madonna and Child, Death and*

Transfiguration, Distant Voices, Still Lives and The Long Day Closes: Six Screenplays with an Introduction. London: Faber and Faber, 1992.

"A De Luxe Presentation." *Motion Picture News* (6 December 1913): 16.

De Santi, Pier Marco. *Nino Rota. Le immagini e la musica.* Florence: Giunti, 1992.

DeNora, Tia. *Beethoven and the Construction of Genius: Musical Politics in Vienna, 1792–1803.* Berkeley and Los Angeles: University of California Press, 1996.

Derrida, Jacques. *The Gift of Death.* Chicago: University of Chicago Press, 1995.

Descartes, René. *Discourse on Method* (1637), translated by Laurence J. Lafleur. Indianapolis: Bobbs-Merrill, 1950.

Dickinson, Kay, ed. *Movie Music: The Film Reader.* London: Routledge, 2003.

Dolkart, Ronald H. "Civilization's Aria: Film as Lore and Opera as Metaphor in Werner Herzog's *Fitzcarraldo.*" *Journal of Latin American Lore* 11.2 (1985): 125–41.

———. "Elitelore at the Opera: The Teatro Colón of Buenos Aires." *Journal of Latin American Lore* 9.2 (1983): 231–50.

Donnelly, K. J., ed. *Film Music: Critical Approaches.* Edinburgh: Edinburgh University Press, 2001.

Dwork, Deborah, and Robert Jan van Pelt. *Holocaust: A History.* New York: Norton, 2002.

Edson, Frank A. "Samuel L. Rothapfel: The Belasco of the Moving Picture World." *Metronome* (August 1915): 18.

Engh, Barbara. "After His Master's Voice." *New Formations* 38 (Summer 1999): 54–63.

"*Eroica:* About the Film." http://www.bbc.co.uk/music/classicaltv/eroica/ (accessed 14 April 2004).

Everett, Wendy. *Terence Davies.* Manchester: Manchester University Press, 2004.

Fabris, Dinko, ed. *Nino Rota compositore del nostro tempo.* Bari: Orchestra Sinfonica di Bari, 1987.

Farassino, Alberto, ed. *Neorealismo. Cinema italiano 1945–1949..* Turin: E. D. T. P., 1989.

Fauset, Jessie Redmon. *Plum Bun.* Boston: Beacon, 1990 [1928].

Felman, Shoshana, and Dori Laub. *Testimony: Crises of Witnessing in Literature, Psychoanalysis, and History.* New York: Routledge, 1992.

Fenton, Maurice. "The Birth of the Theme Song." *Photoplay* (November 1929): 66–136.

"Fine Demonstration." *The Overture* 8.6 (October 1928): 22.

Fink, Robert. *Repeating Ourselves: American Minimal Music as Cultural Practice.* Berkeley and Los Angeles: University of California Press, 2005.

Flinn, Caryl. *The New German Cinema: Music, History, and the Matter of Style.* Berkeley and Los Angeles: University of California Press, 2004.

———. *Strains of Utopia: Gender, Nostalgia, and Hollywood Film Music.* Princeton, NJ: Princeton University Press, 1992.

Forster, E. M. *Howard's End.* London: G. P. Putnam's Sons, 1910.

Freestone, J., and H. J. Drummond. *Enrico Caruso: His Recorded Legacy.* London: Sidgwick and Jackson, 1960.

Frogley, Alain. "Beethoven's Music in Performance: Historical Perspectives." In *The Cambridge Companion to Beethoven,* edited by Glenn Stanley, 255–71. Cambridge: Cambridge University Press, 2000.

Frohlich, Louis D., and Charles Schwartz. *The Law of Motion Pictures, Including the Law of the Theatre, Treating of the Various Rights of the Author, Actor, Professional Scenario Writer, Director, Producer, Distributor, Exhibitor and the Public, with Chapters on Unfair Competition, and Copyright Protection in the United States, Great Britain and her Colonial Possessions.* New York: Baker, Voorhis and Company, 1918.

Fuld, H. S. "Music and the Picture." *Moving Picture News* (10 April 1915): 114.

———. "Using the Resources of an Orchestra to Interpret a Photoplay." *Motion Picture News* (12 December 1914): 114.

Gabbard, Krin. *Black Magic: White Hollywood and African American Culture.* New Brunswick, NJ: Rutgers University Press, 2004.

Gaffney, Terresa. "*Eroica* Movie Review." http://www.thezreview.co.uk/reviews/e/eroica.htm (accessed 1 November 2005).

Garner, Ken. "Would You Like to Hear Some Music? Music In-and-out-of Control in the Films of Quentin Tarantino." In *Film Music: Critical Approaches,* edited by K. J. Donnelly, 188–205. New York: Continuum, 2001.

Garrett, Charles. "*Chinatown,* Whose Chinatown? Defining America's Borders with Musical Orientalism." *Journal of the American Musicological Society* 57.1 (Spring 2004): 119–73.

Gerhardt, Charles, with the National Philharmonic Orchestra. *Max Steiner's Classic Film Score "Gone With the Wind."* RCA Victor GD80452, BMG Music, 1974; remastered 1989.

Glass, Philip. "Interview with Philip Glass." *The Hours.* DVD. Directed by Stephen Daldry. Miramax Films, 2002.

Goethe, Johann Wolfgang von. *The Sorrows of Young Werther, and Selected Writings.* Translated by Catherine Hutter. New York: New American Library, 1962.

Goldman, Albert, and Evert Sprinchorn, eds. *Wagner on Music and Drama: A Compendium of Richard Wagner's Prose Works.* New York: Da Capo, 1988.

Goldmark, Daniel. *Tunes for 'Toons: Music in Hollywood Cartoons.* Berkeley and Los Angeles: University of California Press, 2005.

Goldmark, Daniel, and Yuval Taylor, eds. *The Cartoon Music Book.* Chicago: A Cappella Books, 2001.

Goodson, Carol. "Song as Subtext: The Virtual Reality of Lyrics in the Films of Woody Allen." In *Woody Allen: A Casebook,* edited by Kimball King, 1–10. New York: Routledge, 2001.

Goodwin, Michael. "Up the River with Werner Herzog." In *Burden of Dreams: Screenplay, Journals, Reviews, Photographs,* edited by Les Blank and James Bogan, 212–34. Berkeley, CA: North Atlantic Books, 1984.

Gorbman, Claudia. "Ears Wide Open: Kubrick's Music." In *Changing Tunes: The Use of Pre-existing Music in Films,* edited by Phil Powrie and Robynn Stilwell. London: Ashgate Press, forthcoming.

———. "Music as Salvation: Notes on Fellini and Rota." *Film Quarterly* 28.2 (Winter 1974/1975): 17–25.

———. *Unheard Melodies: Narrative Film Music.* Bloomington: Indiana University Press, 1987.

Harris, Charles K. *After the Ball.* New York: Frank-Maurice, 1926.

Harwell, Richard, ed. *Gone with the Wind, as Book and Film.* Columbia: University of South Carolina Press, 1983.

Henkel, Guido. "Werner Herzog the Real Fitzcarraldo." *DVD Review,* 1 November 1999. http://www.dvdreview.com/html/dvd_review_-_werner_herzog.shtml (accessed 22 October 2005).

Herzog, Werner. *Fitzcarraldo: The Original Story.* Translated by Martje Herzog and Alan Greenberg. San Francisco: Fjord Press, 1982.

Highsmith, Patricia. *The Talented Mr. Ripley.* New York: Coward-McCann, 1955.

Hillman, Roger. *Unsettling Scores: German Film, Music, and Ideology.* Bloomington: Indiana University Press, 2005.

"Incidental Music for Edison Pictures." *Kinetogram* (15 September 1909): 13.

Jameson, Fredric. *The Political Unconscious: Narrative as a Socially Symbolic Act.* Ithaca, NY: Cornell University Press, 1981.

Joe, Jeongwon, and Rose Theresa, eds. *Between Opera and Cinema.* New York: Routledge, 2002.

Johnson, James Weldon. *The Autobiography of an Ex-Colored Man.* New York: Penguin, 1990 [1912].

Johnson, May. "Musical Comedy—Drama—Motion Pictures." *Musical Courier* (2 June 1921): 64.

Kahn, Ashley. *Kind of Blue: The Making of the Miles Davis Masterpiece.* New York: Da Capo Press, 2000.

Kalinak, Kathryn. *Settling the Score: Music and the Classical Hollywood Film.* Madison: University of Wisconsin Press, 1992.

Kallberg, Jeffrey. *Chopin at the Boundaries: Sex, History, and Musical Genre.* Cambridge, MA: Harvard University Press, 1996.

Kassabian, Anahid. *Hearing Film: Tracking Identifications in Contemporary Hollywood Film Music.* New York: Routledge, 2001.

Kermol, Enzo, and Mariselda Tessarolo, eds. *La music del cinema.* Rome: Bulzoni, 1996.

Kittler, Friedrich. *Gramophone, Film, Typewriter.* Translated by Geoffrey Winthrop-Young and Michael Wutz. Stanford, CA: Stanford University Press, 1999.

———. "World-Breath: On Wagner's Media Technology." In *Opera Through Other Eyes,* edited by David J. Levin, 215–38. Stanford, CA: Stanford University Press, 1993.

Kivy, Peter. *The Corded Shell: Reflections on Musical Expression.* Princeton, NJ: Princeton University Press, 1980.

———. "Music in the Movies: A Philosophical Enquiry." In *Film Theory and Phi-*

losophy, edited by Richard Allen and Murray Smith, 308–28. Oxford: Oxford University Press, 1997.

Kluge, Alexander. *Die Macht der Gefühle.* Frankfurt am Main: Zweitausendeins, 1984.

Koepnick, Lutz P. "Colonial Forestry: Sylvan Politics in Werner Herzog's *Aguirre* and *Fitzcarraldo.*" *New German Critique* 60 (Fall 1993): 133–59.

Kracauer, Siegfried. *Theory of Film: the Redemption of Physical Reality.* New York: Oxford University Press, 1960.

Kramer, Lawrence. *After the Lovedeath: Sexual Violence and the Making of Culture.* Berkeley and Los Angeles: University of California Press, 1997.

———. "Music, Metaphor and Metaphysics." *Musical Times* 145.1888 (Autumn 2004): 5–18.

———. *Musical Meaning: Toward a Critical History.* Berkeley and Los Angeles: University of California Press, 2001.

———. "Recognizing Schubert: Musical Subjectivity and Cultural Change in Jane Campion's *The Portrait of a Lady.*" *Critical Inquiry* 28 (2002): 25–52.

———. "Subjectivity Rampant! Music, Hermeneutics, and History." In *The Cultural Study of Music: A Critical Introduction,* edited by Martin Clayton, Trevor Herbert, and Richard Middleton, 124–35. New York: Routledge, 2003.

LaCapra, Dominick. *History and Memory After Auschwitz.* Ithaca, NY: Cornell University Press, 1998.

———. *Writing History, Writing Trauma.* Baltimore, MD: Johns Hopkins University Press, 2001.

Laing, Heather. "Emotion by the Numbers." In *The Musical: Hollywood and Beyond,* edited by Bill Marshall and Robynn Stilwell, 5–13. Exeter, UK: Intellect Press, 2000.

Lang, Edith, and George West. *Musical Accompaniment of Moving Pictures.* Boston: Boston Music Company, 1920.

Langer, Mark. "Max and Dave Fleischer." *Film Comment* 11.1 (January–February 1975): 48–56.

Langer, Suzanne K. *Feeling and Form.* New York: Scribner's, 1953.

Larsen, Nella. *Passing.* New York: Penguin, 1997 [1929].

Lee, Peggy. *The Whorf Theory Complex: A Critical Reconstruction.* Amsterdam: John Benjamins, 1996.

Leppert, Richard. "Cultural Contradiction, Idolatry, and the Piano Virtuoso: Franz Liszt." In James Parakilas et al., *Piano Roles: Three Hundred Years of Life with the Piano,* 252–81. New Haven, CT: Yale University Press, 1999.

———. *The Sight of Sound: Music, Representation, and the History of the Body.* Berkeley and Los Angeles: University of California Press, 1993.

Levi, Primo. *The Drowned and the Saved,* translated by R. Rosenthal. New York: Viking, 1989.

Luz, Ernst. "The Musician and the Picture." *Moving Picture News* (12 October 1912): 20.

———. "Theme Playing as Used and Abused." *Motion Picture World* (14 August 1915): 130.

Magee, Jeffrey. "Irving Berlin's 'Blue Skies': Ethnic Affiliations and Musical Transformations." *Musical Quarterly* 84.4 (Winter 2000): 537–80.

Mann, Thomas. *Doctor Faustus*. Stockholm: Bermann-Fischer, 1947.

Marks, Martin. "Music, Drama, Warner Brothers: The Cases of *Casablanca* and *The Maltese Falcon*." In *Music and Cinema*, edited by James Buhler, Caryl Flinn, and David Neumeyer, 161–86. Hanover, NH: University Press of New England, 2000.

Martin, George. "Verdi Onstage in the United States: *Ernani*." *Opera Quarterly* 20.2 (Spring 2004): 171–96.

Marvin, Roberta Montemorra. "Verdian Opera Burlesqued: A Glimpse into Mid-Victorian Theatrical Culture." *Cambridge Opera Journal* 15.1 (March 2003): 33–66.

McClary, Susan. *Conventional Wisdom: The Content of Musical Form*. Berkeley and Los Angeles: University of California Press, 2000.

———. "Rap, Minimalism, and Structures of Time in Late Twentieth-Century Music." *The Geske Lecture*. Lincoln: University of Nebraska Press, 1999.

McLuhan, Marshall. *Understanding Media: The Extensions of Man*. New York: McGraw-Hill, 1964.

McQuade, James S. "The Belasco of Motion Picture Presentations." *Moving Picture World* (9 December 1911): 796.

Medcalfe, Roy L. "Themes." *American Organist* (February 1922): 67–68.

Mendoza, David. "The Theme Song." *American Hebrew* (15 March 1929): 124.

Meyer, Leonard B. *Emotion and Meaning in Music*. Chicago: University of Chicago Press, 1956.

Miceli, Sergio. *Musica e cinema nella cultura del Novecento*. Florence: Sansoni, 2000.

Miller, D. A. "Anal Rope." In *Inside/Out: Lesbian Theories, Gay Theories*, edited by Diana Fuss, 119–41. New York and London: Routledge, 1991.

Modleski, Tania. "Film Theory's Detour." *Screen* 23.5 (1982): 72–79.

Moretti, Franco. *The Way of the World: The* Bildungsroman *in European Culture*. London: Verso, 1987.

Morrey, Douglas. "History of Resistance / Resistance of History: Godard's *Eloge de l'amour* (2001)." *Studies in French Cinema* 3.2 (2003): 123–24.

Morris, Mitchell. "Ecotopian Sounds: The Music of John Luther Adams and Strong Environmentalism." In *Crosscurrents and Counterpoints: Offering in Honor of Bengt Hambr{ae}us at 70*, edited by Per F. Broman, Nora A. Engebretsen, and Bo Alphonce, 129–41. Göteborg: University of Göteborg, 1998.

Morton, Donald. *The Material Queer: A LesBiGay Cultural Studies Reader*. Boulder, CO: Westview Press, 1996.

"Music Suggestions." *Vitagraph Bulletin of Life Portrayals* (October 1913): 14.

"Music to Fit the Picture." *Metronome* (June 1928): 32.

Musser, Charles. "Engaging with Reality: Documentary." In *The Oxford History of World Cinema*, edited by Geoffrey Nowell-Smith, 322–32. Oxford: Oxford University Press, 1996.

Neumeyer, David. "Source Music, Background Music, Fantasy and Reality in Early Sound Film." *College Music Symposium* 37 (1997): 13–20.

Neumeyer, David, and James Buhler. "Analytical and Interpretive Approaches to Film Music (I): Analyzing the Music." In *Film Music: Critical Approaches*, edited by Kevin J. Donnelly, 16–38. New York: Continuum, 2001.

Newcomb, Anthony. "Sound and Feeling." *Critical Inquiry* 10 (1980): 623–41.

Nietzsche, Friedrich. *The Birth of Tragedy*. New York: Vintage Books, 1967.

Nyman, Michael. "The Composer's Note." In *The Piano, Original Compositions for Solo Piano*. London: Chester Music, 1993.

O'Sullivan, Joseph. "Adaptation of Music to Motion Pictures." *Metronome* (July 1917): 58.

Parakilas, James, et al. *Piano Roles: Three Hundred Years of Life with the Piano*. New Haven, CT: Yale University Press, 1999.

Paulin, Scott D. "Unheard Sexualities?: Queer Theory and the Soundtrack." *Spectator* 17.2 (1997): 36–49.

Petts, Leonard. *The Story of "Nipper" and the "His Master's Voice" Picture Painted by Francis Barraud*. Bournemouth, UK: The Talking Machine Review International, 1973/1983.

Pollack, Howard. *Skyscraper Lullaby: The Life and Music of John Alden Carpenter*. Washington and London: Smithsonian Institution Press, 1995.

Powrie, Phil. "On the Threshold between Past and Present: 'Alternative Heritage'." In *British Cinema, Past and Present*, edited by Justine Ashby and Andrew Higson, 316–26. London: Routledge, 2000.

Poznansky, Alexander. *Tchaikovsky: The Quest for the Inner Man*. New York: Schirmer, 1991.

Prendergast, Roy M. *Film Music: A Neglected Art. A Critical Study of Music in Films*. New York: Norton, 1992.

Presser, Beat, ed. *Werner Herzog*. Berlin: Jovis Verlag and Arte Edition, 2002.

Rapée, Erno. *Encyclopedia of Music for Motion Pictures*. New York: Belwin, 1925.

Raykoff, Ivan. "Hollywood's Embattled Icon." In *Piano Roles: Three Hundred Years of Life with the Piano*, edited by James Parakilas et al., 329–58. New Haven, CT: Yale University Press, 2000.

Reggio, Godfrey. "Interview: The Essence of Life." *Koyaanisqatsi*. DVD. Directed by Godfrey Reggio. MGM, 2002.

Rizzardi, Veniero, ed. *L'undicesima musa. Nino Rota e i suoi media*. Rome: RAI–ERI, 2001.

Robinson, Jenefer. *Music and Meaning*. Ithaca, NY: Cornell University Press, 1997.

Robinson, Francis. *Caruso: His Life in Pictures*. New York: Studio Publications in association with Thomas Y. Crowell, 1957.

Rogers, Holly. "Fitzcarraldo's Search for Aguirre: Music and Text in the Amazonian Films of Werner Herzog." *Journal of the Royal Musical Association* 129 (2004): 77–99.

Rosen, Philip. "Adorno and Film Music: Theoretical Notes on *Composing for the Films*." *Yale French Studies* 60 (1980): 157–82.

Rousseau, Jean Jacques. *Dictionary of Music.* Translated by William Waring. New York: AMS Press, 1975.

Sabato, Ernesto. *On Heroes and Tombs.* Translated by Helen R. Lane. Boston: David R. Godine, 1981.

———. *Sobre Héroes y Tumbas.* Barcelona: Editorial Seix Barral, 2003.

Sacks, Howard L., and Judith Rose Sacks. *Way Up North in Dixie: A Black Family's Claim to the Confederate Anthem.* Urbana: University of Illinois Press, 2003.

Sanjek, Russell. *American Popular Music and Its Business: The First Four Hundred Years,* vol. 3. New York: Oxford University Press, 1988.

Sanyal, Debarati. "A Soccer Match in Auschwitz: Passing Culpability in Holocaust Criticism." *Representations* 79 (2002): 1–27.

Sartin, Hank. "From Vaudeville to Hollywood, From Silence to Sound." In *Reading the Rabbit,* edited by Kevin S. Sandler, 67–85. New Brunswick, NJ: Rutgers University Press, 1998.

Sauer, Rodney. "Photoplay Music: A Reusable Repertory for Silent Film Scoring, 1914–1929." *American Music Research Center Journal* 8/9 (1998–1999): 55–76.

Sheer, Miriam. "The Godard/Beethoven Connection: On the Use of Beethoven's Quartets in Godard's Films." *Journal of Musicology* 18.1 (Winter 2001): 170–88.

Sipe, Thomas. *Beethoven: Eroica Symphony.* Cambridge: Cambridge University Press, 1998.

Sk! "Interview with Filmmaker Godfrey Reggio." *Green Anarchy* 12 (Spring 2003). http://www.greenanarchy.org/zine/GA12/reggio.php (accessed 15 April 2004).

Small, Christopher. *Musicking: The Meanings of Performing and Listening.* Hanover, NH: University Press of New England, 1988.

Smith, Jeff. "Unheard Melodies? A Critique of Psychoanalytic Theories of Film Music." In *Post-Theory: Reconstructing Film Studies,* edited by David Bordwell and Noel Carroll, 230–47. Madison: University of Wisconsin Press, 1996.

Solomon, Maynard. *Beethoven.* London: Cassell, 1978.

———. *Beethoven Essays.* Cambridge, MA: Harvard University Press, 1988.

Sontag, Susan. "Notes on 'Camp.' " In *Against Interpretation and Other Essays,* 275–92. New York: Noonday Press / Farrar, Straus & Giroux, 1966.

Spaeth, Sigmund. *Read 'em and Weep: The Songs You Forgot to Remember.* New York: Halcyon House, 1939.

Starobinski, Jean. "The Idea of Nostalgia." *Diogenes* 54 (1966): 81–103.

Sullivan, John William Navin. *Beethoven: His Spiritual Development.* London: Jonathan Cape, 1927.

Szwed, John. *So What: The Life of Miles Davis.* New York: Simon and Schuster, 2002.

Tambling, Jeremy. *Opera, Ideology and Film.* New York: St. Martin's Press, 1987.

Tarantino, Quentin. "Interview with Quentin Tarantino." *Kill Bill: Volume 1.* DVD. Directed by Quentin Tarantino. Miramax Films, 2003.

Thayer, Alexander Wheelock. *Thayer's Life of Beethoven,* vol. 1. Revised and edited by Elliot Princeton, NJ: Princeton University Press, 1967.

"Theme Songs Help Good Pictures." *Exhibitors' Herald* (5 January 1929): 45–46.

Tomlinson, Gary. "Cultural Dialogics and Jazz: A White Historian Signifies." *Black Music Research Journal* 11.2 (1991): 229–64.

Tootell, George. *How to Play the Cinema Organ: A Practical Book By a Practical Player.* London: W. Paxton & Co., n.d.

Trinity. "*Eroica.*" www.iofilm.co.uk/fm/e/eroica_2003.shtml (accessed 1 November 2005).

Turner, Victor Witter. *From Ritual to Theatre: The Human Seriousness of Play.* New York: Performing Arts Journals, 1982.

Tyson, Alan. "Ferdinand Ries (1784–1838): The History of His Contribution to Beethoven Biography." *19th-Century Music* 7 (1984): 209–21.

Urmson, Jo. "Representation in Music." *Royal Institute of Philosophy Lectures* 6 (1973): 132–46.

"Variations, by the Editor-in-Chief." *Musical Courier* (14 June 1928): 33.

Vernon, Howard. "On Representational Music." *Noûs* 6 (1972): 41–54.

Volek, Tomislav, and Jaroslav Macek. "Beethoven's Rehearsals at the Lobkowitz's." *Musical Times* 127 (February 1986): 75–80.

Wackenroder, Wilhelm Heinrich. "The Remarkable Musical Life of the Musician Joseph Berglinger" (1797). In *Source Readings in Music History, Volume 6: The Nineteenth Century.* Edited by Ruth A. Solie, 19–30. New York: W. W. Norton, 1998.

Wagner, Cosima. *Cosima Wagner's Diaries.* Edited by Martin Gregor-Dellin and Dietrich Mack, translated by Geoffrey Skelton. 2 vols. New York: Harcourt Brace Jovanovich, 1978–80.

Watts, Jill. *Hattie McDaniel: Black Ambition, White Hollywood.* New York: Amistad, 2005.

Wegeler, Franz, and Ferdinand Ries. *Remembering Beethoven: The Biographical Notes of Franz Wegeler and Ferdinand Ries.* London: André Deutsch, 1988.

Weis, Elisabeth. *The Silent Scream: Alfred Hitchcock's Soundtrack.* Rutherford, NJ: Fairleigh Dickinson University Press, 1982.

Weis, Elisabeth, and John Belton. *Film Sound: Theory and Practice.* New York: Columbia University Press, 1985.

Weisel, J. Harold. "Cue Sheets: Two Dimensions." *American Organist* (July 1922): 290.

Wenders, Wim. "There are a few things I want to say about the music of Madredeus." *Lisbon Pages.* http://lisboa.kpnqwest.pt/i/ouvir/madredeus/madredeus.html#wimwenders (accessed 1 November 2005).

Whorf, Benjamin Lee. "The Punctual and Segmentative Aspects of Verbs in Hopi." *Language* 12 (1936): 127–31; reprinted in *Language, Thought, and Reality: Selected Writings of Benjamin Lee Whorf,* edited by John B. Carroll, 51–56. Cambridge, MA: M.I.T. Press, 1956.

———. "Science and Linguistics." *Technology Review* (M.I.T.) 42 (1940): 61–63, 80–83.

Williams, Raymond. *Television: Technology and Cultural Form.* New York: Schocken, 1975.

Williams, William H. A. *'Twas Only an Irishman's Dream: The Image of Ireland and the Irish in American Popular Song Lyrics, 1800–1920.* Urbana: University of Illinois Press, 1996.

Woolf, Virginia. *The Diary of Virginia Woolf, Vol. II (1920–1924).* Edited by Quentin Bell and Angelica Garnett. New York: Harcourt Brace & Company, 1978.

"Words & Music: Barry Ackroyd BSC Reflects on Two Very Different New Projects—*Eroica* for TV and *Ae Fond Kiss* for Cinema." *Exposure* 26 (Autumn 2003): 16–17.

Index of Films Cited

Abie's Irish Rose. (Victor Fleming, US, 1928), 221

Adrienne Lecouvreur. (Louis Mercanton and Henri Desfontaines, France, 1913), 114n7

Aguirre, der Zorn Gottes. (Werner Herzog, West Germany, 1972), 100, 117n24

Amadeus. (Milos Forman, US, 1984), 27

American Beauty. (Sam Mendes, US, 1999), 282, 288

Un americano in vacanza [An American on Holiday]. (Luigi Zampa, Italy, 1945), 252, 253

Anchors Aweigh. (George Sidney, US, 1945), 177

Angels and Insects. (Philip Haas, US/UK, 1995), 51–54

Apocalypse Now. (Francis Ford Coppola, US, 1979), 105

Ascenseur pour l'échafaud [Elevator to the Gallows]. (Louis Malle, France, 1957), 257n5, 262–67, 275

L'Atalante. (Jean Vigo, France, 1934), 157

Le Bal. (Ettore Scola, Italy, 1983), 139

Beethoven's Nephew. (Paul Morrissey, France, 1985), 27

The Birth of a Nation. (D. W. Griffith, US, 1915), 218, 220

Blue Collar. (Paul Schrader, US, 1978), 266

The Brand of Cowardice. (John W. Noble, US, 1916), 210–11

The Bridges of Madison County. (Clint Eastwood, US, 1995), 265

Brief Encounter. (David Lean, UK, 1945), 50, 246

Buena Vista Social Club. (Wim Wenders, US/Germany/France/Cuba, 1999), 152

Campane a martello [Alarm Bells]. (Luigi Zampa, Italy, 1948), 253

Index of Names

Text: 10/13 Aldus
Display: Franklin Gothic
Compositor: Binghamton Valley Composition
Printer and binder: Maple-Vail Manufacturing Group